Lecture Notes in Computer Science 6952

Commenced Publication in 1973
Founding and Former Series Ed[
Gerhard Goos, Juris Hartmanis,

T0074239

Editorial Board

Uwe Stilla   Franz Rottensteiner
Helmut Mayer   Boris Jutzi
Matthias Butenuth (Eds.)

Photogrammetric Image Analysis

ISPRS Conference, PIA 2011
Munich, Germany, October 5-7, 2011
Proceedings

 Springer

Volume Editors

Uwe Stilla
Technische Universität München, Germany
E-mail: stilla@tum.de

Franz Rottensteiner
Leibniz Universität Hannover, Germany
E-mail: rottensteiner@ipi.uni-hannover.de

Helmut Mayer
Universität der Bundeswehr München, Neubiberg, Germany
E-mail: helmut.mayer@unibw.de

Boris Jutzi
Karlsruhe Institute of Technology, Germany
E-mail: boris.jutzi@kit.edu

Matthias Butenuth
Technische Universität München, Germany
E-mail: matthias.butenuth@bv.tum.de

ISSN 0302-9743   e-ISSN 1611-3349
ISBN 978-3-642-24392-9   e-ISBN 978-3-642-24393-6
DOI 10.1007/978-3-642-24393-6
Springer Heidelberg Dordrecht London New York

Library of Congress Control Number: 2011937634

CR Subject Classification (1998): I.4, I.5, I.2, I.2.10, H.3, F.2.2

LNCS Sublibrary: SL 3 – Information Systems and Application, incl. Internet/Web
and HCI

Typesetting: Camera-ready by author, data conversion by Scientific Publishing Services, Chennai, India

Printed on acid-free paper

Springer is part of Springer Science+Business Media (www.springer.com)

Preface

Automated extraction of objects from remotely sensed data is an important topic of research in photogrammetry, computer vision, remote sensing, and geoinformation science. PIA11 addressed researchers and practitioners from universities, research institutes, industry, government organizations, and private companies. The range of topics covered by the conference is reflected by the terms of reference of the cooperating working groups (WGs) of the International Society for Photogrammetry and Remote Sensing (ISRPS):

- Lidar, SAR and Optical Sensors (WG I/2)
- Pose Estimation and Surface Reconstruction (WG III/1)
- Complex Scene Analysis and 3D Reconstruction (WG III/4)
- Image Sequence Analysis (WG III/5)

After the successful series of ISPRS conferences on Photogrammetric Image Analysis in Munich in 1999, 2003, and 2007, in 2011 the PIA11 event again discussed recent developments, the potential of various data sources, and future trends in automated object extraction with respect to both sensors and processing techniques, focusing on methodological research. It was held at the Technische Universitaet Muenchen (TUM) in Munich, Germany, during October 5-7, 2011.

Prospective authors were invited to submit full papers of a maximum length of six A4 pages . We received 54 full papers coming from 18 countries for review. The submitted papers were subject to a rigorous double-blind peer-review process. Forty-two papers were reviewed by three members of the Program Committee, whereas the rest (12 papers) were reviewed by two members of the committee. In total we received 150 reviews from 29 reviewers. Altogether 30 papers were accepted based on the reviews, which corresponds to a rejection rate of 44%. Finally, 25 of the 54 papers (46%) were published in this book.

Additionally, authors who intended to present application-oriented work particularly suitable for interactive presentation were invited to submit extended abstracts. Altogether, PIA11 featured seven oral sessions, two poster sessions, and two invited talks, namely, "Convex Optimization Methods for Computer Vision" (Daniel Cremers) and "Exploiting Redundancy for Reliable Aerial Computer Vision" (Horst Bischof).

Finally, the editors wish to thank all contributing authors and the members of the Program Committee. In addition, we would like to express our thanks to the Local Organizing Committee, without whom this event could not have taken place. Ludwig Hoegner did a great job managing the conference tool. The final editing of all incoming manuscripts and the preparation of the proceedings by Michael Schmitt are gratefully acknowledged. Konrad Eder and Dorota Iwaszczuk did a great job organizing the social events and accomodation, Florian

Burkert in caring for the technical equipment, and Sebastian Tuttas in supervising the Local Organizing Committee assistants. We would also like to thank Christine Elmauer, Carsten Goetz, and Gabriele Aumann for their support in making PIA11 a successful event.

Last but not least we would like to thank our sponsors MVTec Software GmbH and INPHO GmbH - A TRIMBLE COMPANY, and our supporting institutions ISPRS, ASPRS, DGPF, EuroSDR, EARSeL, and IAG for their assistance, as well as the Springer Verlag for giving us the opportunity to publish selected papers of PIA11 in the LNCS series.

October 2011   Uwe Stilla
                                                         Franz Rottensteiner
                                                             Helmut Mayer
                                                                 Boris Jutzi
                                                         Matthias Butenuth

Organization

PIA11 was organized by the Department of Photogrammetry and Remote Sensing, Technische Universitaet Muenchen (TUM), and sponsored by the International Society for Photogrammetry and Remote Sensing (ISPRS).

information from imagery

Cooperating ISPRS Working Groups:

- Lidar, SAR and Optical Sensors (WG I/2)
- Pose Estimation and Surface Reconstruction (WG III/1)
- Complex Scene Analysis and 3D Reconstruction (WG III/4)
- Image Sequence Analysis (WG III/5)

PIA11 Conference Chair and Co-chairs

Uwe Stilla	Technische Universitaet Muenchen (TUM), Germany
Franz Rottensteiner	Leibniz Universitaet Hannover, Germany
Helmut Mayer	Universitaet der Bundeswehr Muenchen, Germany
Boris Jutzi	Karlsruhe Institute of Technology (KIT), Germany
Matthias Butenuth	Technische Universitaet Muenchen (TUM), Germany

Program Committee

Michael Arens	Fraunhofer IOSB, Germany
Caroline Baillard	SIRADEL, France
Richard Bamler	German Aerospace Center (DLR), Germany
Matthias Butenuth	Technische Universitaet Muenchen (TUM), Germany
Ismael Colomina	Institut de Geomatica Castelldefels, Spain
Wolfgang Foerstner	University of Bonn, Germany
Jan-Michael Frahm	University of North Carolina, USA
Markus Gerke	University of Twente, The Netherlands
Norbert Haala	University of Stuttgart, Germany
Christian Heipke	Leibniz Universitaet Hannover, Germany
Olaf Hellwich	Technische Universitaet Berlin, Germany
Stefan Hinz	Karlsruhe Institute of Technology (KIT), Germany
Boris Jutzi	Karlsruhe Institute of Technology (KIT), Germany
Clement Mallet	Institut Geographique National (IGN), France
Helmut Mayer	Universitaet der Bundeswehr Muenchen, Germany
Chris McGlone	SAIC, USA
Jochen Meidow	Fraunhofer IOSB, Germany
Franz Josef Meyer	University of Alaska Fairbanks, USA
Stephan Nebiker	University of Applied Sciences Northwestern Switzerland, Switzerland
Nicolas Paparoditis	Institut Geographique National (IGN), France
Camillo Ressl	Vienne University of Technology, Austria
Franz Rottensteiner	Leibniz Universitaet Hannover, Germany
Konrad Schindler	ETH Zürich, Switzerland
Uwe Soergel	Leibniz Universitaet Hannover, Germany
Gunho Sohn	York University, USA
Uwe Stilla	Technische Universitaet Muenchen (TUM), Germany
Christoph Strecha	EPLF, Switzerland
Charles Toth	Ohio State University, USA
Yongjun Zhang	Wuhan Univiersity, China

Local Organizing Committee

Florian Burkert	Technische Universitaet Muenchen (TUM), Germany
Konrad Eder	Technische Universitaet Muenchen (TUM), Germany
Christine Elmauer	Technische Universitaet Muenchen (TUM), Germany
Carsten Goetz	Technische Universitaet Muenchen (TUM), Germany
Ludwig Hoegner	Technische Universitaet Muenchen (TUM), Germany
Dorota Iwaszczuk	Technische Universitaet Muenchen (TUM), Germany
Michael Schmitt	Technische Universitaet Muenchen (TUM), Germany
Sebastian Tuttas	Technische Universitaet Muenchen (TUM), Germany

Sponsors

 MVTec Software GmbH

 INPHO GmbH - A TRIMBLE COMPANY

Supporting Societies

  ISPRS – International Society for Photogrammetry and Remote Sensing

  ASPRS – American Society for Photogrammetry and Remote Sensing

  DGPF – German Society for Photogrammetry, Remote Sensing and Geoinformation

  EuroSDR – Spatial Data Research

  EARSeL – European Association of Remote Sensing Laboratories

  IAG – International Association of Geodesy

Table of Contents

3D-Reconstruction and DEM

Classification

People and Tracking

Image Processing

Efficient Video Mosaicking by Multiple Loop Closing

Jochen Meidow

Fraunhofer Institute of Optronics, System Technologies and Image Exploitation
IOSB, 76275 Ettlingen, Germany
`jochen.meidow@iosb.fraunhofer.de`

Abstract. The rapid generation of aerial mosaics is an important task for change detection, e.g. in the context of disaster management or surveillance. Unmanned aerial vehicles equipped with a single camera offer the possibility to solve this task with moderate efforts. Unfortunately, the accumulation of tracking errors leads to a drift in the alignment of images which has to be compensated by loop closing for instance. We propose a novel approach for constructing large, consistent and undistorted mosaics by aligning video images of planar scenes. The approach allows the simultaneous closing of multiple loops possibly resulting from the camera path in a batch process. The choice of the adjustment model leads to statistical rigorous solutions while the used minimal representations for the involved homographies and the exploitation of the natural image order enable very efficient computations. The approach will be empirically evaluated with the help of synthetic data and its feasibility will be demonstrated with real data sets.

Keywords: Image alignment, mosaic, loop closing, homography, exponential representation, parameter estimation.

1 Introduction

1.1 Motivation

Up-to-date aerial image mosaics reveal valuable information for various applications such as change detection for disaster management or surveillance. Small Unmanned Aerial Vehicles (UAV) are convenient platforms to accomplish this task with moderate efforts and costs. Because of their limited cargo bay and payload usually only a single camera can be used leading to monocular imagery. Furthermore, the accuracy of navigation solutions from deployable inertial measurement units is usually too low to rely on it. Then again assuming planar scenes and chaining consecutive image pairs of the video stream suffers from error accumulation due to systematic errors and the uncertainty of feature tracking or matching. This becomes evident when a loop is detected — the arising drift appears in discrepancies at the joints. Therefore, strategies are needed to update the mosaic by detecting loops and adjusting the involved mappings.

U. Stilla et al. (Eds.): PIA 2011, LNCS 6952, pp. 1–12, 2011.
© Springer-Verlag Berlin Heidelberg 2011

1.2 Related Work

In Szeliski (2006) a comprehensive survey of mapping models is given together with a discussion on pros and cons of direct and feature-based image alignment, including global registration via bundle adjustment. These stitching techniques do not address the special nature of dense video streams explicitly.

In Turkbeyler and Harris (2010) aerial mosaics are build and geo-located in order to indicate movements on the ground. Observations for the corresponding adjustment task are the image-to-image homographies of a video stream captured by a downward looking airborne camera. The homographies are fixed by Euclidean normalization, i.e. by setting $H_{33} = 1$. The stochastic model assumes additive noise for the algebraic transformation parameters. An adjustment for loop closing is performed with the parameters of the image-to-mosaic transformations for each image as unknowns.[1] For problems of moderate size this leads already to huge band diagonal normal equation matrices with sparse off-diagonal terms. This makes the task of mosaicking several thousands of images computationally intensive, cf. Unnikrishnan and Kelly (2002b).

The detection of loops in an image sequence and another scheme for loop closing is discussed in Caballero et al. (2007): Loops are being hypothesized and detected by considering the pairwise Mahalanobis distances of the estimated positions of the image centers on the mosaic in conjunction with their uncertainties. For the subsequent update of the loops' homographies an optimization procedure is launched by applying and extended Kalman filter. For the subtraction within the filter's update equations a normalization of the homographies is necessary within each update step to fix the scale of the homogeneous representation.

1.3   Contribution

We propose an efficient feature-based method to build large and globally consistent mosaics from video streams captured for instance by a downward looking airborne camera. The approach assumes planar scenes or a fixed projection center. Furthermore, we assume uncalibrated cameras but straight-line preserving optics, i.e. no presence of lens distortion. The approach allows multiple simultaneous loop closing in a batch process after a loop detection stage. Considering the image-to-image homographies as observations, we chose an adjustment model with constraints for theses homographies only, leading to small equation systems to be solved. The involved stochastic model rigorously incorporates the uncertainties of feature extraction, tracking, and matching respectively. By taking advantage of the utilized exponential representation of the homographies the computations become simple and efficient which paves the way for on-board computations.

---

[1] The authors use the term "bundle adjustment" while our notion on this concept implies the simultaneous estimation of motion parameters (homographies) and structure parameters (image feature positions).

2 Theoretical Background and Modeling

After defining a homography in general we introduce concepts and technical terms for certain homographies needed for the proposed loop closing technique. The discussed adjustment procedure including its model takes advantage of the used minimal parameterization and the resulting simplicity of the constraint equations for the loops to be closed.

2.1 Notation and Preliminaries

Homogeneous vectors are denoted with upright boldface letters, e.g. $\mathbf{x}$ or $\mathbf{H}$, Euclidean vectors and matrices with slanted boldface letters, e.g. $\boldsymbol{l}$ or $\boldsymbol{R}$. For homogeneous coordinates "=" means an assignment or an equivalence up to a common scale factor $\lambda \neq 0$.

For the minimal parameterization of a homography we exploit the power series

$$\exp\left(\boldsymbol{K}\right) = \sum_{k=0}^{\infty} \frac{1}{k!} \boldsymbol{K}^k = \boldsymbol{I}_3 + \boldsymbol{K} + \frac{1}{2!}\boldsymbol{K}^2 + \ldots \tag{1}$$

being the matrix exponential for square matrices analogous to the ordinary exponential function.

For the analytical computations of Jacobians we will use the rule

$$\mathrm{vec}(\boldsymbol{ABC}) = (\boldsymbol{C}^\mathsf{T} \otimes \boldsymbol{A})\mathrm{vec}(\boldsymbol{B}) \tag{2}$$

frequently where the vec operator stacks all columns of a matrix and $\otimes$ denotes the Kronecker product.

2.2 Homographies

Definition. A planar projective transformation is a linear transformation on homogeneous 3-vectors represented by a non-singular 3×3 matrix $\mathbf{H} = (H_{ij})$, cf. Hartley and Zisserman (2000):

$$\begin{bmatrix} u' \\ v' \\ w' \end{bmatrix} = \begin{bmatrix} H_{11} & H_{12} & H_{13} \\ H_{21} & H_{22} & H_{23} \\ H_{31} & H_{32} & H_{33} \end{bmatrix} \begin{bmatrix} u \\ v \\ w \end{bmatrix} \tag{3}$$

more briefly, $\mathbf{x}' = \mathbf{H}\mathbf{x}$. The transformation is unique up to scale and has therefore eight degrees of freedom. It can be written in inhomogeneous form as

$$x' = \frac{H_{11}x + H_{12}y + H_{13}}{H_{31}x + H_{32}y + H_{33}} \quad \text{and} \quad y' = \frac{H_{21}x + H_{22}y + H_{23}}{H_{31}x + H_{32}y + H_{33}} \tag{4}$$

with $\mathbf{x} = [x, y, 1]^\mathsf{T}$ and $\mathbf{x}' = [x', y', 1]^\mathsf{T}$.

Homographies form a group. Thus, one can "undo" a transformation by computing and applying the inverse transformation (matrix inversion). The concatenation or chaining of two or more transformations results from direct matrix multiplication. In the following we will use products of homography matrices extensively and will denoted them by an overbar representing sequential chaining of temporal adjacent images within the video stream. The homography matrix for the transformation from image i to image k reads

$$^{k}\overline{\mathbf{H}}_{i} = \prod_{j=i}^{k-1} {}^{j+1}\mathbf{H}_{j} \tag{5}$$

where the product symbol induces matrix multiplications from the left.

Sequential Links and Cross Links. During a flight essentially two kinds of links can occur. For the characterization of these links we adopt the terminology used in Turkbeyler and Harris (2010): Pairwise homographies of consecutive, temporal adjacent images are called *sequential links*. Other homographies are given by image pairs with overlap at crossings after completing a circuit. They constitute the *cross links* of non-temporally adjacent images used for loop closing. Figure 1 shows on the left side an example for a flight with numerous sequential links and a few cross links which can be used to adjust the corresponding loops.

   The chaining by homographies can be considered as a topological graph which is non-planar in general. Its cycles constitute the loops. Single connected components are part of no loop. Thus, they will not be affected by the adjustment. The set of cycles that may be used must form an independent and complete cover. Figure 2 shows such a fundamental cycle basis. Of course, choosing the smallest-size cycle basis would reduce the computational costs, cf. Unnikrishnan and Kelly (2002b). But for the sake of simplicity we establish loops along the camera path only.

Cumulative Homographies. In analogy to cumulative sums and cumulative products we define a cumulative homography as the concatenation of homographies starting with the very first sequential homography $^{2}\mathbf{H}_{1}$ between image 1 and 2:

$$^{i}\overline{\mathbf{H}}_{1} = \prod_{k=1}^{i-1} {}^{k+1}\mathbf{H}_{k} \tag{6}$$

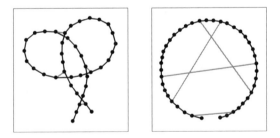

Fig. 1. Left: A hypothetical flight (sequential links in black) with four established cross links (gray) schematically. Right: The corresponding topological graph.

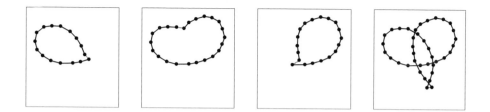

Fig. 2. The cycle basis for the graph depicted in Figure 1 resulting from four detected and established loops along the flight path

In the following we will extensively use these entities. The subsequence (5) from image i to image k for instance can easily represented by

$$^{k}\overline{\mathbf{H}}_{i} = {}^{k}\overline{\mathbf{H}}_{1}\,{}^{1}\overline{\mathbf{H}}_{i} = {}^{k}\overline{\mathbf{H}}_{1}\left({}^{i}\overline{\mathbf{H}}_{1}\right)^{-1} \tag{7}$$

using cumulative homographies only.

2.3 Parameterization

Fixing the scale of a homography in homogeneous representation can be accomplished in various ways: Popular approaches are the fixing of one matrix element or the matrix' Frobenius norm. Fixing one of the elements of $\mathbf{H} = (H_{mn})$, e.g. $H_{33} = 1$, is too restrictive since the case of zero or close to zero entries cannot be excluded in general, cf. (Hartley and Zisserman, 2000, p. 41). Fixing the scale by the Frobenius norm, i.e. $||\mathbf{H}|| = 1$, is frequently used to obtain closed form solutions as this constraint is quadratic in the elements of the matrix $\mathbf{H}$. Both approaches suffer from numerical problems when chaining many transformations as needed for cumulative homographies. Thus, usually a computational expensive re-normalization is necessary after each multiplication. More favorable is the constraint $\det(\mathbf{H}) = 1$ which opens up the vista of minimal representations, too.

Exponential Representation. Minimal representations have recently attract increased attention, cf. Förstner (2010). By avoidance of redundancy additional parameters constraints become superfluous and the resulting equation systems smaller.

A homography matrix can be decomposed in an approximate transformation $\mathbf{H}_0$ and a small, unknown correcting homography $\Delta\mathbf{H}$

$$\mathbf{H} = \Delta\mathbf{H} \cdot \mathbf{H}_0. \tag{8}$$

This multiplicative expansion facilitates linearization. If both matrices on the r.h.s. have determinant one, the resulting homography matrix has determinant one, too. This can be achieved by using the exponential representation $\Delta\mathbf{H} = \exp(\boldsymbol{K})$, cf. (1), for the homography update. For square matrices $\boldsymbol{A}$ the relation

$\det(\exp(A)) = \exp(\operatorname{tr}(A))$ holds. Thus, requiring $\det(\Delta H) = 1$ is equivalent to $\operatorname{tr}(K) = 0$. The matrix

$$K = \begin{bmatrix} k_1 & k_4 & k_7 \\ k_2 & k_5 & k_8 \\ k_3 & k_6 & -k_1 - k_5 \end{bmatrix} \tag{9}$$

is trace-less and depends linearly on the eight parameters $k = [k_1, \ldots, k_8]^\mathsf{T}$ constituting the correction parameters, cf. Begelfor and Werman (2005).

Error Propagation. In the following we will use the exponential representation only. Estimates $(\widehat{k}, \widehat{\Sigma}_{\widehat{k}\widehat{k}}, H_0)$ for the unknown homography parameters and their corresponding covariance matrix are obtained by given sets of point correspondencies with $\widehat{k} = 0$ since H_0 is updated during the estimation process. The estimated covariance matrix for the nine corresponding homography parameters $\widehat{h} = \operatorname{vec}(\widehat{H})$ is obtained by error propagation for the update transformation (8) with

$$G = \begin{bmatrix} I_8 \\ -1,0,0,0,-1,0,0,0 \end{bmatrix} \tag{10}$$

since $\operatorname{vec}(K) = Gk$ holds for (9). The Jacobian for the error propagation $\widehat{\Sigma}_{\widehat{h}\widehat{h}} = J\widehat{\Sigma}_{\widehat{k}\widehat{k}}J^\mathsf{T}$ is then simply $J = (H_0^\mathsf{T} \otimes I_3)G$ being a specialization of the rule (2). For synthetic data we validate this stochastic model in subsection 4.1.

3   Realization

This contribution focuses on the loop closing procedure explicated below in the subsections 3.2 and 3.3. Nevertheless, in the following subsection we present at least an idea how the search area for potential loop closure events can be narrowed down.

3.1   Loop Detection

For the generation of hypothetical loops we consider the Mahalanobis distances between the (error free) image center x_c and its transformation $^j x_c = {}^j H_i x_c$ for each image pair (i, j). The homographies can be obtained from the cumulative ones by (7). Applying the law of error propagation for the relation $^j \overline{H}_1 = {}^j \overline{H}_i {}^i \overline{H}_1$ we get the uncertainty of the homography $^j \overline{H}_i$. In terms of the covariance matrices $^i \overline{\Sigma}_1$ and $^j \overline{\Sigma}_1$ of the cumulative homographies it is

$$^j \overline{\Sigma}_i = A^{-1}({}^j \overline{\Sigma}_1 - B^i \overline{\Sigma}_1 B^\mathsf{T}) A^{-\mathsf{T}}, \tag{11}$$

with $A = {}^i \overline{H}_1 \otimes I_3$, $B = I_3 \otimes {}^j \overline{H}_i$, and the corresponding independence assumption.

Hence, the covariance matrix of the predicted image center $^{j}\mathbf{x}_c$ in homogeneous coordinates is $\boldsymbol{\Sigma}_{dd} = \boldsymbol{C}^{j}\overline{\boldsymbol{\Sigma}}_i\boldsymbol{C}^{\mathsf{T}}$ with $\boldsymbol{C} = \mathbf{x}_c^{\mathsf{T}} \otimes \boldsymbol{I}_3$ and the Mahalanobis distances read

$$d_{ij}^2 = \mathbf{d}^{\mathsf{T}}\boldsymbol{\Sigma}_{dd}^{+}\mathbf{d} \qquad \text{with} \quad \mathbf{d} = {}^{j}\mathbf{x}_c - \mathbf{x}_c \tag{12}$$

with spherical normalized entities.

Figure 5 visualizes the discretized reciprocal values of the computed Mahalanobis distances (12) for the example prepared in the introduction and carried out later in subsection 4.2. The image clearly reveals the four loop closing events sketched in Figure 1 by regions of local minima.

3.2   Adjustment Model and Adjustment Procedure

In practice, the number of video frames is large which prohibits approaches estimating all image-to-mosaic homographies. Therefore, we carry out an adjustment for the image-to-image homographies which constitute loops, only. For closing the loops' gaps we chose the adjustment model with constraints between observations only, cf. Koch (1999); McGlone et al. (2004). In the following we consider the estimated correction parameters $\widehat{\boldsymbol{k}} = \mathbf{0}$ for the homographies as observations accompanied by their estimated covariance matrices $\boldsymbol{\Sigma}_{\widehat{k}\widehat{k}}$. Since the number of loops is usually small we get small equation systems, too.

Adjustment Model. Among N observations $\boldsymbol{l}$ we have the G constraints $\boldsymbol{g}(\widehat{\boldsymbol{l}}) = \mathbf{0}$ which have to hold for the true values as well as for the estimated values $\widehat{\boldsymbol{l}}$, namely the fitted observations $\widehat{\boldsymbol{l}} = \boldsymbol{l} + \widehat{\boldsymbol{v}}$ with the estimated corrections $\widehat{\boldsymbol{v}}$. An initial covariance matrix $\boldsymbol{\Sigma}_{ll}^{(0)}$ of the observations is assumed to be known and related to the true covariance matrix $\boldsymbol{\Sigma}_{ll}$ by $\boldsymbol{\Sigma}_{ll} = \sigma_0^2\boldsymbol{\Sigma}_{ll}^{(0)}$ with the possibly unknown scale factor σ_0^2 which can be estimated from the residuals.

Linearization of the constraints by Taylor expansion yields

$$\boldsymbol{g}(\widehat{\boldsymbol{l}}) = \boldsymbol{g}(\boldsymbol{l}_0) + \boldsymbol{J}\widehat{\boldsymbol{\Delta l}} + \dots \tag{13}$$

with approximate values $\boldsymbol{l}_0$ and $\widehat{\boldsymbol{l}} = \boldsymbol{l} + \widehat{\boldsymbol{v}} = \boldsymbol{l}_0 + \widehat{\boldsymbol{\Delta l}}$. Thus the linear model is $\boldsymbol{g}_0 + \boldsymbol{J}\widehat{\boldsymbol{v}} = 0$ with the contradiction vector $\boldsymbol{g}_0 = \boldsymbol{g}(\boldsymbol{l}_0) + \boldsymbol{J}(\boldsymbol{l} - \boldsymbol{l}_0)$.

The Lagrangian incorporating the method of least squares reads

$$L = \frac{1}{2}\widehat{\boldsymbol{v}}^{\mathsf{T}}\boldsymbol{\Sigma}_{ll}^{-1}\widehat{\boldsymbol{v}} + \boldsymbol{\lambda}^{\mathsf{T}}(\boldsymbol{g}_0 + \boldsymbol{J}\widehat{\boldsymbol{v}}) \tag{14}$$

and its minimization w.r.t. the residuals and the Lagrangian multipliers $\boldsymbol{\lambda}$ yields the estimates

$$\widehat{\boldsymbol{v}} = -\boldsymbol{\Sigma}_{ll}\boldsymbol{J}^{\mathsf{T}}\left(\boldsymbol{J}\boldsymbol{\Sigma}_{ll}\boldsymbol{J}^{\mathsf{T}}\right)^{-1}\boldsymbol{g}_0 \tag{15}$$

for the estimated corrections being the negative residuals.

Adjustment Procedure. The covariance matrix for observations $l = [k_1, k_2, \ldots]^{\mathsf{T}}$ is block-diagonal

$$\Sigma_{ll} = \mathrm{Diag}\left(\Sigma_{k_1 k_1}, \Sigma_{k_2 k_2}, \ldots\right) \tag{16}$$

with 8×8 blocks and has full rank. The size of the matrix to be inverted for the estimation (15) is small for problems of moderate size and complexity. Its size is $8L \times 8L$ with the number of loops L.

During the iterative estimation procedure we do not update the adjusted observations but the approximate homography matrices $\mathbf{H}_0$ by applying $\mathbf{H}_0^{(\nu+1)} = \exp(\widehat{\boldsymbol{K}})\mathbf{H}_0^{(\nu)}$ where ν is the iteration number. The adjusted "observations" $\boldsymbol{k}$ remain zeros.

3.3 Loop Constraints and Jacobians

Loop Constraints. With the observed cross links $^k\mathbf{H}_i$ and the observed cumulative homographies $^k\overline{\mathbf{H}}_i$ the constraints $\boldsymbol{g}(\boldsymbol{l}_0)$ for each loop are simply

$$^k\overline{\mathbf{H}}_i - {}^k\mathbf{H}_i = \boldsymbol{O}_{3\times 3} \tag{17}$$

with $\det(^{\bullet}\mathbf{H}_{\bullet}) = 1$ for all homography matrices. One has to select eight independent equations. An alternative formulation of the loop constraints is $^k\overline{\mathbf{H}}_i{}^i\mathbf{H}_k = \boldsymbol{I}_3$ cf. Unnikrishnan and Kelly (2002a), whereby the Jacobian w.r.t. the cross links depends on the sequential links, too.

Jacobians. For the cross links the exponential representation is $^k\mathbf{H}_i = \Delta\mathbf{H} \cdot \mathbf{H}_0 \approx \Delta\mathbf{H}(\boldsymbol{I}_3 + \boldsymbol{K})\mathbf{H}_0$ and therefore the Jacobian w.r.t. the parameters $\boldsymbol{k}_i$ is

$$\boldsymbol{J}_c^{(i)} = -(\mathbf{H}_0^{\mathsf{T}} \otimes \boldsymbol{I}_3)\boldsymbol{G} \tag{18}$$

with (10) and the rule (2). For sequential links we consider the update $^k\overline{\mathbf{H}}_i = {}^k\overline{\mathbf{H}}_j \cdot \Delta\mathbf{H}_j{}^j\overline{\mathbf{H}}_i$ for a homography as part of a sequence from frame i to k. Expressed in terms of cumulative homographies this reads

$$^k\overline{\mathbf{H}}_i = {}^k\overline{\mathbf{H}}_1{}^1\overline{\mathbf{H}}_j \cdot \Delta\mathbf{H}_j \cdot {}^j\overline{\mathbf{H}}_1{}^1\overline{\mathbf{H}}_i = {}^k\overline{\mathbf{H}}_1\left(^j\overline{\mathbf{H}}_1\right)^{-1} \cdot \Delta\mathbf{H}_j \cdot {}^j\overline{\mathbf{H}}_1\left(^i\overline{\mathbf{H}}_1\right)^{-1} \tag{19}$$

with the cumulative homographies for the start frames $^i\overline{\mathbf{H}}_1$ and the end frames $^k\overline{\mathbf{H}}_1$ of each loop. The Jacobians of the cross links w.r.t. the correction parameters $\boldsymbol{k}_j$ are now

$$\boldsymbol{J}_s^{(j)} = \left[\left(^j\overline{\mathbf{H}}_1{}^i\overline{\mathbf{H}}_1^{-1}\right)^{\mathsf{T}} \otimes \left(^k\overline{\mathbf{H}}_1{}^j\overline{\mathbf{H}}_1^{-1}\right)\right]\boldsymbol{G}. \tag{20}$$

The joint Jacobian is a full matrix for the sequential links augmented by a usually much smaller block-diagonal matrix for the L cross links

$$\boldsymbol{J} = \begin{bmatrix} \boldsymbol{J}_s^{(1)} & \boldsymbol{J}_c^{(1)} & \boldsymbol{O} & \cdots & \boldsymbol{O} \\ \boldsymbol{J}_s^{(2)} & \boldsymbol{O} & \boldsymbol{J}_c^{(2)} & \cdots & \boldsymbol{O} \\ \vdots & \vdots & \vdots & \ddots & \vdots \\ \boldsymbol{J}_s^{(L)} & \boldsymbol{O} & \boldsymbol{O} & \cdots & \boldsymbol{J}_c^{(L)} \end{bmatrix}. \tag{21}$$

Its entries depend on cumulative homographies between the start and end image of each loop only.

Note that no special treatment of the homographies not being part of any loop is necessary. The corresponding estimates for the corrections (15) will simply be zeros. No case-by-case analysis is necessary.

4   Experiments

In the following the proposed approach will be empirically evaluated with the help of synthetic data sets and its feasibility will be demonstrated with real data sets.

4.1   Numerical Simulation

To validate the stochastic model of the homography parameterization and to evaluate the performance of the proposed loop closing approach we used simulated data. For each homography we generated a random transformation next to the identity with the eight parameters $k = (k_i)$ being Gaussian distributed according to $k_i \sim N(0, 0.02)$. Then 50 points x_i with coordinates uniformly distributed in $[-1, +1]$ have been transformed according to $x'_i = Hx_i$ and $H = \exp(K)$. Gaussian noise with $\sigma = 0.001$ has finally been added to all coordinates.

Figure 3 shows the empirical distribution of the Mahalanobis distance

$$d = \left(\widehat{h} - \widetilde{h}\right)^{\mathsf{T}} \widehat{\Sigma}_{\widehat{h}\widehat{h}}^{+} \left(\widehat{h} - \widetilde{h}\right) \tag{22}$$

for the estimated parameters $\widehat{h} = \mathrm{vec}(\widehat{H})$ w.r.t. the true homography parameters $\widetilde{h}$ obtained for 1,000 samples. As to be expected, the distribution follows the χ^2_8-distribution.

To specify the performance of the loop closing procedure, we generated various sets of sequential and cross links with loops consisting of 100 sequential links in each case. Figure 4 summarizes the computational times needed for these configurations using non-optimized MATLAB code. The number of iterations has been three for the adjustment procedure. The results show that the computational time needed is proportional to the number of homographies to be considered and to the number of loops to be closed.

4.2   Real Data

For the provision of imagery we abused a virtual globe as camera simulator. This guarantees the model assumptions to be valid; all uncertainties stems from tracking and matching respectively. The camera path corresponds to the topology depicted in Figure 1 with varying height above ground and changing roll, pitch, and yaw angles. During the flight the camera fulfilled a 180-degree-turn around its optical axis. Figure 6 shows one of the 1,024 captured images exemplary.

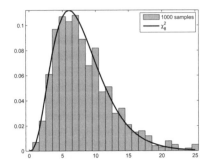

	sequential links		
	1,000	2,000	4,000
2	0.47 sec	0.88 sec	1.71 sec
cross 4	0.56 sec	1.04 sec	1.97 sec
links 8	0.78 sec	1.37 sec	2.50 sec
16	1.32 sec	2.20 sec	4.00 sec

Fig. 3. Empirical distribution of the Mahalanobis distance (22) following the χ_8^2-distribution

Fig. 4. Computational times in seconds for various numbers of homographies and loops to be closed. Performed on a standard CPU @ 1.59 GHz with non-optimized MATLAB code.

Fig. 5. The visualization of the $I(I-1)/2$ Mahalanobis distances (12) reveals four potential areas of cross links (white spots) for the sequence of I images.

Fig. 6. Exemplary video image of size 320×480 (©GeoContent provided by Google)

For each image, salient points have been extracted by the Förstner operator (Förstner and Gülch (1987)) and tracked in the corresponding subsequent image by the Lucas-Kanade tracker, cf. Lucas and Kanade (1981). The respective positional uncertainties – represented by covariance matrices – have been determined for incorporation into the adjustment, too. Four loop closing events have been identified by visual inspection. The correspondencies of the cross links have then been established by applying the scale invariant feature transform (Lowe (2004)) in combination with the random sample consensus, cf. Fischler and Bolles (1981).

Fig. 7. Left: aerial mosaic built using the estimated 1023 sequential links only. Right: mosaic adjusted by closing the four loops depicted in Figure 2

The mosaic obtained by applying the consecutive homographies only (linear mosaic) is shown in Figure 7 and reveals numerous discrepancies due to the inevitable drift. Figure 7 shows the result of the loop closing procedure proposed in Section 2, too. The computing time was 1.4 seconds on a standard CPU @ 1.59 GHz with non-optimized MATLAB Code in four iterations.

5   Conclusions and Outlook

The proposed loop closing technique offers an easy and efficient way to build large and consistent mosaics quickly in a batch process. It is especially well suited for the processing of video streams since the approach exploits the natural order of these images. The chosen adjustment model, the formulation of the loop constraints, and the exponential parameterization of the homographies lead to efficient computations which can be performed already on board during the flight. The consideration of uncertainties of feature extraction, tracking, and matching makes the approach statistics rigorous.

The capability of instantaneous loop closing compensates for unavoidable drift errors and eases the task of hypotheses testing for potentially occurring loops in the following. Therefore, this technique paves the way for navigation tasks, too, cf. Unnikrishnan and Kelly (2002b) for instance. Another potential application is given in the context of image stabilization or panorama stitching.

For a fully automatic build-up of mosaics an automatic loop detection is necessary. Based on the approach sketched in subsection 3.1 this will be the subject of future investigations. Last but not least the robustness of the approach w.r.t. violated model assumptions — especially non-planarity — should be tested.

Acknowledgments. The author would like to thank Wolfgang Förstner for his inspiration on minimal representations and Eckart Michaelsen for his unweary readiness for discussions.

References

Begelfor, E., Werman, M.: How to put Probabilities on Homographies. IEEE Trans. on Pattern Recognition and Machine Intelligence 27, 1666–1670 (2005)

Caballero, F., Merino, L., Ferruz, J., Ollero, A.: Homography Based Kalman Filter for Mosaic Building. Applications to UAV Position Estimation. In: IEEE International Conf. on Robotics and Automation, pp. 2004–2009 (2007)

Fischler, M.A., Bolles, R.C.: Random Sample Consensus: A Paradigm for Model Fitting with Applications to Image Analysis and Automated Cartography. Communications of the ACM 24(6), 381–395 (1981)

Förstner, W.: Minimal Representations for Uncertainty and Estimation in Projective Spaces. In: Proc. of Asian Conf. on Computer Vision (2010)

Förstner, W., Gülch, E.: A Fast Operator for Detection and Precise Location of Distinct Points, Corners and Centres of Circular Features. In: ISPRS Intercommission Workshop, Interlaken (1987)

Hartley, R., Zisserman, A.: Multiple View Geometry in Computer Vision. Cambridge University Press, Cambridge (2000)

Koch, K.R.: Parameter Estimation and Hypothesis Testing in Linear Models, 2nd edn. Springer, Berlin (1999)

Lowe, D.: Distinctive Image Features from Scale-Invariant Keypoints. International Journal of Computer Vision 60(2), 91–110 (2004)

Lucas, B.T., Kanade, T.: An Iterative Image Registration Technique with an Application to Stereo Vision. In: Proc. of Image Understanding Workshop, pp. 130–212 (1981)

McGlone, J.C., Mikhail, E.M., Bethel, J. (eds.): Manual of Photogrammetry, 5th edn. American Society of Photogrammetry and Remote Sensing (2004)

Szeliski, R.: Image alignment and stitching: A tutorial. Foundations and Trends in Computer Graphics and Computer Vision 2(1), 1–104 (2006)

Turkbeyler, E., Harris, C.: Mapping of Movement to Aerial Mosaic with Geo-Location Information. In: Optro 2010 (2010)

Unnikrishnan, R., Kelly, A.: A Constrained Optimization Approach to Globally Consistent Mapping. In: 2002 IEEE/RSJ Int'l Conf. on Intelligent Robots and Systems (IROS 2002), vol. 1, pp. 564–569 (2002a)

Unnikrishnan, R., Kelly, A.: Mosaicing Large Cyclic Environments for Visual Navigation in Autonomous Vehicles. In: IEEE International Conf. on Robotics and Automation (ICRA 2002), vol. 4, pp. 4299–4306 (2002b)

Estimating the Mutual Orientation in a Multi-camera System with a Non Overlapping Field of View

Daniel Muhle[1], Steffen Abraham[2],
Christian Heipke[1], and Manfred Wiggenhagen[1]

[1] Institut für Photogrammetrie und GeoInformation, Nienburgerstr. 1
D-30167 Hannover
[2] Robert Bosch GmbH, Robert-Bosch-Str. 200, D-31139 Hildesheim

Abstract. Multi-camera systems offer some advantages over classical systems like stereo or monocular camera systems. A multi-camera system with a non-overlapping field of view, able to cover a wide area, might prove superior e. g. in a mapping scenario where less time is needed to cover the entire area. Approaches to determine the parameters of the mutual orientation from common motions exist for more than 30 years. Most work presented in the past neglected or ignored the influence different motion characteristics have on the parameter estimation process. However, for critical motions a subset of the parameters of the mutual orientation can not be determined or only very inaccurate. In this paper we present a strategy and assessment scheme to allow a successful estimation of as many parameters as possible even for critical motions. Furthermore, the proposed approach is validated by experiments.

Keywords: Mutual orientation, non-overlapping field of view, bundle adjustment, motion, image sequence.

1   Introduction

The evaluation of image sequences to obtain geometric information about the environment is relevant in a wide range of applications like autonomous navigations of vehicles or robots, the automated survey of indoor-space or in the area of virtual and augmented reality.

An image sequence can be captured with very different camera configurations like single cameras, stereo cameras or multi-camera systems. To obtain geometric information it is usually necessary to know the parameters of the camera's exterior orientation between at least two captured images. If two images share some overlapping areas the orientation can be determined easily e.g. through identifying identical points in both images followed by a computation of the relative orientation.

In most cases the precondition of an overlapping field of view is given for single cameras moving in space or for stereo systems. For a multi-camera system an overlapping field of view might not be given for all combinations of image

U. Stilla et al. (Eds.): PIA 2011, LNCS 6952, pp. 13–24, 2011.

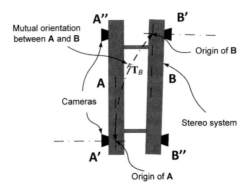

Fig. 1. A multi-camera system investigated in this work: Two stereo systems are fixed on a common plattform in a way that the respective fields of view do not overlap

pairs. For such a situation the results obtained by the different cameras can only be related to each other if the mutual orientation between the camera systems having no overlapping field of view is known. An example for a multi-camera system with non-overlapping fields of view which is used in the experiments of this paper is shown in Fig. 1.

For such a camera system the mutual orientation cannot be determined easily using corresponding image features. An alternative approach to estimate the mutual orientation in a multi-camera system is to use the common motion of all cameras while the system is moving. If it can be guaranteed that the configuration of the cameras remains stable over time, the motions of the different cameras are related to each other by the same mutual orientation. An overview of existing approaches to estimate the orientation from motions is given in Sect. 2.1.

In the existing literature not very much attention is paid to the influence of different motion characterics on the parameter estimation. For a given motion it is important to know: Is it possible to determine all parameters of the mutual orientation reliably? Which accuracy can be expected for the parameters?

In most cases, the existing literature is restricted to analytical investigations of extreme examples, where a subset of the parameters of the mutual orientation cannot be determined because of linear dependencies in the system of equations that must be solved. An overview of the existing literature related to critical motions is given in Sect. 2.2. A strategy to avoid the linear dependencies is given in Sect. 2.3.

Critical motions leading to linear dependencies include purely translational motions without any rotation or motions that are restricted to a given plane where rotation is only possible around the normal of the plane and translation is not possible along the direction of that normal. These specific motion characteristics often appear in multi-camera systems used in cars or robots.

The key contribution of this paper is a detailed analysis of the influence of different motion characteristics on the achievable accuracy of the parameters of the mutual orientation and on the set of parameters that can be determined reliably from the given motions. Special attention is paid to the extreme cases leading to linear dependencies between the parameters. This work is an advancement of the approach presented in Muhle et al. (2008). Section 3 introduces the observational model used in an bundle adjustment to estimate the parameters of the mutual orientation. Results from experiments to validate the proposed approach are shown in Sect. 4. Finally, a conclusion and an outlook is given in Sect. 5.

2   Related Work

2.1   Estimating the Mutual Orientation

Probably the first work proposing a solution to the *robot hand-eye calibration,* i. e. to determine the mutual orientiation between the coordinate frame of a camera attached to the gripper of a robot and the coordinate frame of the robot using common motions is given in Shiu and Ahmad (1987). The key observation Shiu and Ahmad used to determine the mutual orientation $^{B}\boldsymbol{T}_{A}$ between the coordinate systems $\mathbf{A}$ of the camera and $\mathbf{B}$ of the robot is that a point $^{B_j}\boldsymbol{x}$ observed at time $t = j$ can be transformed into a point $^{A_i}\boldsymbol{x}$ observed at time $t = i$ along two different *paths* using (1) and (2),

$$^{A_i}\boldsymbol{x} = {}^{B}\boldsymbol{T}_{A} \circ {}^{B_i}\boldsymbol{T}_{B_j} \circ {}^{B_j}\boldsymbol{x} \tag{1}$$

$$^{A_i}\boldsymbol{x} = {}^{A_i}\boldsymbol{T}_{A_j} \circ {}^{B}\boldsymbol{T}_{A} \circ {}^{B_j}\boldsymbol{x} \tag{2}$$

where $^{B}\boldsymbol{T}_{A} = \begin{bmatrix} {}^{B}\boldsymbol{R}_{A} & {}^{B}\boldsymbol{t}_{A} \\ \mathbf{0}_{[1\times3]} & 1 \end{bmatrix}$ represents a transformation matrix containing the rotation matrix $^{B}\boldsymbol{R}_{A}$ and the translation vector $^{B}\boldsymbol{t}_{A}$ that transforms the homogenous point $^{A}\boldsymbol{x} = [x,\ y,\ z,\ 1]^{T}$ defined in the coordinate system of $\mathbf{A}$ into the coordinate system $\mathbf{B}$. The symbol $\circ$ denotes the multiplication of transformation matrices or of an transformation matrix and an homogenous point.

Equations (1) and (2) reveal the relationship existing between the motions observed in the coordinate frames of $\mathbf{A}$ and $\mathbf{B}$. It can be seen that the orientation between two points in time, observed in the different coordinate systems $\mathbf{A}$ and $\mathbf{B}$ are related by the mutual orientation $^{B}\boldsymbol{T}_{A}$. This observation leads to (3) and is used as a model to determine the mutual orientation $^{B}\boldsymbol{T}_{A}$.

$$^{B}\boldsymbol{T}_{A} \circ {}^{B_i}\boldsymbol{T}_{B_j} = {}^{A_i}\boldsymbol{T}_{A_j} \circ {}^{B}\boldsymbol{T}_{A} \tag{3}$$

Further approaches related to robot hand-eye calibration based on the relationships given in (3) are presented in Chou and Kamel (1988), Tsai and Lenz (1989) and Chen (1991). The key ideas outlined above to solve the robot hand-eye calibration were later transferred to multi-camera systems. Approaches determining the parameters of the mutual orientation for camera systems with a non-overlapping field of view can be found e. g. in Caspi and Irani (2002), Kim et al. (2007), Esquivel et al. (2007) and Oskiper et al. (2007).

2.2   Influence of Different Motion Characteristics

Already in Shiu and Ahmad (1987) the authors show analytically that a single motion between two epochs, described by the difference of the parameters of the exterior orientation, is not sufficient to determine all parameters of the mutual orientation $^{B}\boldsymbol{T}_{A}$. It is necessary to use a third epoch where the orientation has a different rotation axis and a non-zero translation to estimate all parameters. A more detailed analysis on the influence of different motion characterics on the parameters of the mutual orientation is given e. g. in Tsai and Lenz (1989) and Chen (1991).

To summarize the insights of the mentioned investigations related to the determinability of the parameters of the mutual orientations with respect to different motion characteristics, there exist limitations for a) **purely translational motion**, where the multi-camera system moves straight on without any rotation. For this type of motion only the two parameters of the rotation of the mutual orientation can be determined – the rotation around the direction of translation and the translation can not be determined and b) **motion restricted to a plane**, where the motion of the multi-camera system is restricted to a given plane (e. g. the ground plane) where rotation is only possible around the normal of the plane and translation is not possible along the direction of that normal. In such a situation the translation parallel to the normal of the plane can not be determined. There exist further critical types of motion, but the two motion characteristics described above represent the cases that are the most relevant in practical applications.

Nearly all literature quoted above investigate the effect of critical motions using analytical techniques. No suggestions are made for a strategy to estimate only a subset of the parameters of the mutual orientation when the executed motions are close to critical motions. To the knowledge of the authors the only exception is the work of Esquivel et al. (2007). Here the authors propose to use a simpler model only capable of determining the three parameters of the mutual rotation for motions that are close to pure translations. The decision to switch between the complete and the reduced model is based on a heuristic derived from simulations.

This work proposes a strategy that allows to estimate as many parameters of $^{B}\boldsymbol{T}_{A}$ as possible even for critical motions. To avoid the linear dependencies associated with the critical motions a-priori knowledge for the parameters of the mutual orientation is integrated into the bundle-adjustment. Such a strategy was also chosen e. g. in Abraham (2000) to avoid linear dependencies between the intrinisic parameters of a camera that are estimated from monocular image sequences captured by a moving car.

2.3   Avoiding Singularities by Using a-Priori Knowledge

As noted in Sect. 2.2 there exist some critical types of motion leading to linear dependencies between the parameters of $^{B}\boldsymbol{T}_{A}$. The resulting system of normal equations has a rank defect and becomes singular. A solution to avoid the rank defect is to integrate a-priori knowledge for the parameters of the mutual orientation. The a-priori knowledge is modeled as having random noise and added to the bundle adjustment as additional observations. The necessary initial values can be taken e. g. from construction drawings of the multi-camera system, from recent adjustment processes or from the approaches presented in Sect. 2.1.

The integration of a-priori knowledge together with an associated, possibly fictious, accuracy leads to biased results of the adjustment. For the evaluation of the experiments given in Sect. 4 this bias must be considered. For every adjustment the question must be answered if the integration of a-priori knowledge was necessary for the executed motions or if the adjustment of the parameters would have been successful without it.

An answer to that question can be given using the method presented in Förstner (1980). Förstner presented a) a statistical test that allows to check for every parameter if it can be determined reliably from the given motion and b) a computational scheme to transform the estimated parameters and their standard deviations from an adjustment employing a-priori knowledge to the case of an adjustment without such knowledge.

The transformation of the results is based on the tests for gross errors in observations using standardized residuals which are shown e.g. in Förstner (1987). The computation of the standardized residuals together with their associated redundancy numbers r_i is shown in (4),

$$\bar{v}_i = \frac{-v_i}{\sigma_i \sqrt{r_i}} \qquad\qquad r_i = 1 - \frac{\hat{q}_i}{q_i} \qquad\qquad (4)$$

where $v_i = \beta_i^{(0)} - \hat{\beta}_i$, $\beta_i^{(0)}$ is the a-priori knowledge of a parameter with assigned variance q_i ($\sigma_i = \sqrt{q_i}$) and $\hat{\beta}_i$ is the value of a parameter after an adjustment with a-priori knowledge with its respective variance $\hat{q}_i$.

Equation (4) shows that for a parameter whose variance after the adjustment has only improved slightly with respect to the given accuracy q_i of the a-priori knowledge $r_i \approx 0$. That implies that for the corresponding parameter of ${}^B T_A$ the a-priori knowledge can not be controlled from the given motion characteristic and therefore the result is almost fully determined by the introduced a-priori knowledge.

Using the redundancies r_i of (4) the variances $\hat{q}_i$ and the adjusted parameters $\hat{\beta}_i$ can be transformed subsequently to variances $\hat{q}_i'$ and parameters $\hat{\beta}_i'$ of an adjustment without a-priori knowledge using (5).

$$\hat{q}_i' = \frac{\hat{q}_i}{r_i} \qquad\qquad \hat{\beta}_i' = \beta_i^{(0)} + \frac{v_i}{r_i}. \qquad\qquad (5)$$

In general, the relationships shown in the equations above are only valid for a single parameter β_i, if the values are not correlated. Nevertheless, they can be used as approximate values for practical purposes. The final transformation of the results to a case of an adjustment without a-priori knowledge makes the results independent of any assumptions about the accuracy of the a-priori knowledge and allows for an unbiased comparison of the results.

To check the introduced assumptions about the mutual orientation the statistical test shown in (6) is proposed in Förstner (1980).

$$w_i = \frac{v_i}{\sigma_i \sqrt{r_i} \sqrt{1 - r_i}} \tag{6}$$

This test checks if the additional observations introduced as a-priori knowledge for ^BT_A are consistent with respect to the mean and variance of the results from the transformation onto the case of an adjustment without such knowledge. The test statistic w_i is compared with a threshold $k(\alpha)$, where α is the probability of the test. For a probability of e.g. $\alpha = 99\ \%$ the threshold is $k = 2.33$.

3   Using Bundle Adjustment to Estimate the Mutual Orientation

3.1   Definition of Coordinate Systems and Datum

The definition of the observational and statistical model for the bundle adjustment needs a definition of the coordinate systems and the datum, which is also called *gauge* in the computer vision literature e.g. in McLauchlan (2000). The definition of the coordinate systems is part of the observational model and has no influence on the statistical model. The definition of the datum is part of the statistical model and defines an error free reference system. The estimated covariance matrix and the standard deviations of the parameters are defined with respect to that reference system. Additionally, the definition of the datum can help to fix the rank deficiency inherent to reconstruction approaches employing freely moving cameras without an external reference (McLauchlan, 2000).

The observational model uses three different coordinate systems:

Coordinate system of the stereo systems: The origin and orientation of the coordinate system of the stereo system is chosen without loss of generality to be identical with the origin and orientation of the cameras $\mathbf{A}'$ and $\mathbf{B}'$.

Coordinate system of the multi-camera system: The origin and orientation of the coordinate system of the multi-camera system is chosen without loss of generality to be identical with the origin and orientation of the stereo system $\mathbf{A}$.

World coordinate system: The origin and orientation of the world coordinate system is chosen without loss of generality to be identical with the origin and orientation of the multi-camera system at an arbitrary point in time t_{ref}.

As a consequence of the chosen definitions, the world and multi-camera coordinate system are identical for t_{ref}. This makes it possible to define the gauge and fix the rank deficiency by setting the parameters of the orientation of the world coordinate system with respect to t_{ref} to $\mathbf{T} = \begin{bmatrix} \mathbf{I} & \mathbf{0} \\ \mathbf{0}^{\mathrm{T}} & 1 \end{bmatrix}$ and use them as constant parameters in the bundle adjustment.

Another effect of the chosen gauge definition is that the gauge is independent of the executed motions and identical for all the experiments and thus assures the comparability of the results.

3.2   Definition of the Observation Model

Used as observations in the model are projections of 3D-points that are seen by the multi-camera system. Points seen from the stereo system **A** are never seen by **B**.

The projection of a 3D-point $\boldsymbol{x}$ defined in the world coordinate system onto the sensor of a camera is performed by chaining three transformations followed by a perspective projection onto the sensor. The following steps show how the projection of a 3D-point $\boldsymbol{x}$ onto the sensor of a camera is done. Here the equations are given for the cameras $\mathbf{A}''$ and $\mathbf{B}''$ of the stereo systems $\mathbf{A}$ and $\mathbf{B}$. They are analogous for the cameras $\mathbf{A}'$ and $\mathbf{B}'$.

1. Transform $\boldsymbol{x}$ defined in the world coordinate system into the coordinate system of a single camera through the chaining of three (two) different transformations according to (7).

$$^{A''}\boldsymbol{x} = {}^{A''}\boldsymbol{T}_A \circ {}^{t_i}\boldsymbol{T} \circ \boldsymbol{x} \qquad\qquad ^{B''}\boldsymbol{x} = {}^{B''}\boldsymbol{T}_B \circ {}^{B}\boldsymbol{T}_A \circ {}^{t_i}\boldsymbol{T} \circ \boldsymbol{x} \qquad (7)$$

2. Project $^{A''}\boldsymbol{x}$ or $^{B''}\boldsymbol{x}$ onto the sensor resulting in a 2D image point $^{A''}\boldsymbol{y}$ or $^{B''}\boldsymbol{y}$ using a perspective projection.

With the chaining of transformations followed by the projection onto the cameras sensor given by the equations above, we obtain (8) and (9) which are used as the observational model in a least-squares bundle adjustment based on the Gauss-Markov model.

$$^{A''}\boldsymbol{y} = f(\boldsymbol{\beta}_{A''}) = f_A(\boldsymbol{IOR}_{A''}, {}^{A''}\boldsymbol{T}_A, {}^{i}\underline{\boldsymbol{T}}, \underline{\boldsymbol{x}}) \qquad (8)$$

$$^{B''}\boldsymbol{y} = f(\boldsymbol{\beta}_{B''}) = f_B(\boldsymbol{IOR}_{B''}, {}^{B''}\boldsymbol{T}_B, {}^{B}\underline{\boldsymbol{T}}_A, {}^{i}\underline{\boldsymbol{T}}, \underline{\boldsymbol{x}}) \qquad (9)$$

The vector $\boldsymbol{\beta}_{A''}$ includes all parameters of the observational model. Parameters that are estimated during the adjustment process are underlined. All remaining parameters are considered as constant. The symbol $\boldsymbol{IOR}_{A''}$ or $\boldsymbol{IOR}_{B''}$ in (8) and (9) represents the interior parameter of the cameras $\mathbf{A}''$ and $\mathbf{B}''$. The transformation $^{t_i}\boldsymbol{T}$ represents the exterior orientation between the epoch at $t = i$ and t_{ref} and is defined with respect to the world coordinate system, $^{B}\boldsymbol{T}_A$ represents the investigated mutual orientation and $^{A''}\boldsymbol{T}_A$ and $^{B''}\boldsymbol{T}_B$ are the relative orientations of the stereo systems.

4   Experiments and Results

4.1   Structure of the Experiments

The focus of the experiments is on motion characteristics that are critical for the parameter estimation of the mutual orientation like planar or purely translational motions. To evaluate the presented approach employing a-priori knowledge to avoid linear dependencies, a first experiment is performed that is based on synthetically generated data. Finally the results of the simulations are compared to results achieved with real data. For different motion characteristics it should be investigated:

– Which parameters of $^B\boldsymbol{T}_A$ can be determined from the given motion?
– Which accuracy can be achieved for the parameters of $^B\boldsymbol{T}_A$ in dependency of the performed motions?
– Is it possible to check the introduced a-priori knowledge with the given motion?

For the experiments a passage of the multi-camera system shown in Fig. 1 through a hallway is chosen. This scenario presents a common task e. g. for a robot platform.

4.2 Results with Simulated Data

The simulated motion is mainly in the direction of the x-axis. The z-axis in the simulations is aligned with the optical axis of the stereo system $\mathbf{A}$ at $t = 0$. The changes of the exterior orientation at different epochs are generated with a sine-function that is parametrized with different values for the amplitude and the frequency.

For the experiment five motions with different characteristics were generated. The first two experiments simulate two of the extreme cases (pure translation and motion restricted to a plane) identified in Chen (1991) where some of the parameters of $^B\boldsymbol{T}_A$ can not be estimated. These extreme cases will possibly never be reached in practical situations due to very small motions and measurement noise. This situation is covered by the remaining experiments where the amplitude is reduced stepwis until the motion reaches almost a pure translation.

For the simulation the stereo system is chosen to have a baseline of 500 mm and the optical axes are parallel to each other. No lens-distortion is modeled. The dimension of a camera's sensor is 640×480 pixel and it has a focal length of $c = 465$ [pel]. The coordinates of the principal point are $x_h = 320$ [pel] and $y_h = 240$ [pel]. The same values are used for all cameras.

For the adjustment of the simulations the following statistical assumptions were made:

Variance of the image coordinates: The same standard deviation is assumed for all image measurements leading to the following covariance matrix: $\boldsymbol{\Sigma}_u = 0.25^2 \cdot \boldsymbol{I}$ [pel^2].

Standard deviation of the a-priori knowledge: For the parameters of $^B\boldsymbol{T}_A$ and their assigned accuracy, the following values are assumed:

	t_x [mm]	t_y [mm]	t_z [mm]	ω [°]	ϕ [°]	κ [°]
$^B\boldsymbol{T}_A$	500	0	−500	0	180	0
$\sigma_{^B\boldsymbol{T}_A}$	1	1	1	0.05	0.05	0.05

The first two columns of Tab. 1 documents the results from the first two experiments where the executed critical motions make the adjustment impossible without the usage of a-priori knowledge. The results prove the expectation that some of the parameters are fully controlled by the introduced a-priori knowledge as $u_i = 1 - r_i = 1$. For a pure translational motion the parameters of the translation and the rotation around the direction of the translation (ω) can not

Table 1. Results of the experiments 1–5: Standard deviation transformed to the case of adjustment not employing a-priori knowledge. The influence $u_i = 1 - r_i$ of the prior knowledge onto the adjusted Parameter is shown in brackets.

	σ_i (u_i) **1**	σ_i (u_i) **2**	σ_i (u_i) **3**	σ_i (u_i) **4**	σ_i (u_i) **5**
t_x [mm]	∞ (1.00)	0.72 (0.34)	1.56 (0.71)	4.60 (0.96)	51.60 (1.00)
t_y [mm]	∞ (1.00)	∞ (1.00)	1.20 (0.59)	3.84 (0.94)	36.68 (1.00)
t_z [mm]	∞ (1.00)	0.84 (0.42)	1.92 (0.79)	15.96 (1.00)	165.56 (1.00)
ω [°]	∞ (1.00)	0.014 (0.06)	0.032 (0.24)	0.107 (0.78)	0.879 (1.00)
ϕ [°]	0.009 (0.02)	0.010 (0.03)	0.015 (0.06)	0.009 (0.02)	0.009 (0.02)
κ [°]	0.04 (0.33)	0.011 (0.04)	0.021 (0.12)	0.038 (0.30)	0.040 (0.33)

be determined. For a motion restricted to a plane only the part of the translation parallel to the normal of the plane (i. e. t_y) can not be determined. As was expected for both experiments the rotation parameter ϕ can be determined reliably ($u_i \ll 1$). The same was expected for κ from the analytical investigations found in the literature. The results for the first experiment show that the influence of the a-priori can not be neglected ($u_i = 0.33$) though. The same can be observed for the parameters t_x and t_z in the second experiment as the influence of the prior knowledge is clearly visible with 30 % and 43 %. Furthermore show the results for the the transformed standard deviations of these parameters that no clear improvement w. r. t. the introduced assumptions can be established using the assumed accuracy of the image measurements, the rather low sensor resolution and the given motions.

The remaining columns in Tab. 1 document the results of the experiments 3–5 where the executed motion is reduced stepwise. It shows the strong influence of the a-priori knowledge on the adjustment results for the translation with respect to the executed motions and accuracy of the a-priori knowledge. The influence reaches about 60 % already in the third experiment. The standard deviation transformed to the case of an adjustment without a-priori knowledge is worse than the assumed accuracy in all the experiments. For the parameter ϕ it can be seen again that the prior knowledge has almost no influence. For the parameter ω which can not be determined when approaching a purely translational motion, it becomes clear that already in the fourth experiment the influence of the a-priori knowledge is about 80 %. The same behaviour as in the first two experiments becomes visible for κ. The effect that in Tab. 1 some values for the transformed standard deviation are given although the corresponding $u_i = 1$ can be explained with small rounding errors. The large values for the transformed accuracies illustrate that the parameters can not be determined reliably from the given motions.

A conclusion of the conducted experiments, supported by the strong influence of the a-priori knowledge, is that even for an unconstrained motion, as performed in experiment three, the initially given standard deviation of the parameters of the translation can not be improved with the assumed accuracy of the image measurement, the rather low sensor resolution and the performed motions. Nevertheless, the proposed methodology was successful in handling singular and close-to singular motions in unified way and produced the expected results.

4.3   Results with Real Data

For the image sequences that have been acquired to verify the results from the simulation, motions were chosen similar to those from the simulations. For the first and second experiment the system was placed on a small wagon and moved in a way that led to motions restricted to a plane and pure translations. In the third experiment the multi-camera system shown in Fig. 1 was held by hand and moved freely.

The free motions of the third experiment allows to run an adjustment without using any prior knowledge. Thus, the variances from that adjustment can be used as accuracy information for the prior knowledge instead of using fictious accuracies as was done in the simulations. For the experiments a covariance-matrix of the image measurements identical to the one used in the simulation was chosen.

The values of the mutual orientation and their standard deviations estimated in an adjustment of the first experiment without the use of a-priori knowledge are shown in the following table:

	t_x [mm]	t_y [mm]	t_z [mm]	ω [°]	ϕ [°]	κ [°]
$^B T_A$	598.68	−1.58	−465.79	−179.4700	0.1643	−179.7863
$\sigma_{B T_A}$	0.30	0.28	0.97	0.0057	0.0057	0.0115

It should be noted that the results for the computed standard-deviations for κ and t_z are larger than the values for the remaining parameters as it has been predicted by the simulations.

The results of the transformation onto the case of an adustment without any prior knowledge is given in Tab. 2(a). To check the introduced a-priori knowledge and its accuracy the Tab. 2(b) shows the test-values computed according to (6).

The inspection of the results in Tab. 2(a) and 2(b) reveals two interesting details:

1. The expectation that the parameters t_x and ω can not be determined from a close to planar motion is not completely met by the results. These parameters can be determined with a standard deviation that might be acceptable for some scenarios although the influence of the a-priori knowledge is at about 99 %.

Table 2. Results from experiments 1–3 for recorded sequences

(a) Standard deviation transformed to the case of adjustment not emplyoing a-priori knowledge. Influence u_i of prior knowledge is given in brackets.

(b) Test statistics to check introduced prior knowledge.

	σ_i (u_i) 1	σ_i (u_i) 2	σ_i (u_i) 3
t_x [mm]	**2.95** (0.99)	0.64 (0.82)	0.29 (0.49)
t_y [mm]	∞ (1.00)	∞ (1.00)	0.27 (0.47)
t_z [mm]	∞ (1.00)	1.64 (0.74)	0.97 (0.50)
ω [°]	**0.0817** (0.99)	0.0181 (0.91)	0.0059 (0.52)
ϕ [°]	0.0068 (0.59)	0.0080 (0.66)	0.0038 (0.31)
κ [°]	0.0292 (0.87)	0.0152 (0.64)	0.0098 (0.42)

	w_i 1	w_i 2	w_i 3
t_x	-0.62	**-3.23**	0.00
t_y	−	−	0.00
t_z	−	1.34	0.00
ω	-1.46	**-2.69**	0.00
ϕ	5.31	20.47	0.00
κ	-23.70	-15.91	0.00

2. The test-values given in Tab. 2(b) suggest that at least a subset of the mutual orientation $^B T_A$ has changed during the experiments. Even for a very high probability of $\alpha = 99$ % and a corresponding value of $k = 2.33$ the test statistics indicate that the used a-priori knowledge is not consistent with the estimated and transformed values.

A closer look into the motion characteristics of the first experiment revealed that at the beginning of the image seqence a small rotation around the ground normal combined with a small lateral translation is executed. A repetition of the first experiment without the small motion at the beginning produced the expected results: only the two parameters of the rotation can be determined.

Another repetion was done for the second experiment where a-priori knowledge was only introduced for the parameter t_y that can not be determined from planar motion. For the remaining parameters no prior knowledge was used. The difference (Δ) between the estimated parameters of the repetition and the values of $^B T_A$ that were initially used as a-priori knowledge are given in the following table:

	t_x [mm]	t_y [mm]	t_z [mm]	ω [°]	ϕ [°]	κ [°]
Δ	2.30	–	−1.73	−0.013	−0.076	−0.101

It becomes obvious that the indications for a change of $^B T_A$, stressed by the large values of the w_i in Tab. 2(b), are correct. The mutual orientation has changed during the experiments possibly due to mechanical instabilities of the used platform.

5   Conclusions and Future Work

The evaluation of simulated and recorded image sequences has shown that the integration of a-priori knowledge into the bundle adjustment assures optimal results even for critical motions. For practical applications the motion characterics to be expected are usually not known in advance. Therefore, it ist proposed to use existing prior knowledge about the mutual orientation in every situation. After an adjustment with these additional observations, the transformation and testing scheme developed in Förstner (1980) can be applied to check which parameters can be determined reliably from the given motion and if there are errors in the assumptions about the available a-priori knowledge.

The predictions about the accuracy of the parameters of $^B T_A$ made in the simulations mostly correspond to the results achieved in the evaluation of the real image sequences. The simulation has proven to be a valuable tool that can be used in advance to assess the accuracy that can be accomplished for different motion characteristics. The only parameter of $^B T_A$ that differs from the theoretical predictions is the translation in direction of the optical axis (z-axis). Here further experiments are necessary investigating the influence of the structure of the observed point cloud or the overlap between images.

References

Abraham, S.: Kamera-Kalibrierung und metrische Auswertung monokularer Bildfolgen. Shaker, Aachen (2000)

Caspi, Y., Irani, M.: Aligning non-overlapping sequences. International Journal of Computer Vision 48(1), 39–51 (2002)

Chen, H.: A screw motion approach to uniqueness analysis of head-eye geometry. In: CVPR, pp. 145–151 (1991)

Chou, J., Kamel, M.: Quaternions approach to solve the kinematic equation of rotation, A A x= A x A b, of a sensor-mounted robotic manipulator. In: ICRA, pp. 656–662 (1988)

Esquivel, S., Woelk, F., Koch, R.: Calibration of a multi-camera rig from non-overlapping views. In: Hamprecht, F.A., Schnörr, C., Jähne, B. (eds.) DAGM 2007. LNCS, vol. 4713, pp. 82–91. Springer, Heidelberg (2007)

Förstner, W.: Zur Prüfung zusätzlicher Parameter in der Ausgleichung. Zeitschrift für Vermessungswesen, 510–519 (1980)

Förstner, W.: Reliability analysis of parameter estimation in linear models with applications to mensuration problems in computer vision. Computer Vision, Graphics, and Image Processing 40(3), 273–310 (1987)

Kim, J.H., Hartley, R., Frahm, J.M., Pollefeys, M.: Visual odometry for non-overlapping views using second-order cone programming. In: Yagi, Y., Kang, S.B., Kweon, I.S., Zha, H. (eds.) ACCV 2007, Part II. LNCS, vol. 4844, p. 353. Springer, Heidelberg (2007)

McLauchlan, P.F.: Gauge Independence in Optimization Algorithms for 3D Vision. In: Triggs, B., Zisserman, A., Szeliski, R. (eds.) ICCV-WS 1999. LNCS, vol. 1883, pp. 183–199. Springer, Heidelberg (2000)

Muhle, D., Abraham, S., Heipke, C., Wiggenhagen, M.: Automatische Orientierung von zwei gemeinsam bewegten Stereosystemen ohne gegenseitige Korrespondenzen. In: Luhmann, T., Müller, C. (eds.) Photogrammetrie, Laserscanning, Optische 3D-Messtechnik, pp. 186–193. Wichmann Verlag, Heidelberg (2008)

Oskiper, T., Zhu, Z., Samarasekera, S., Kumar, R.: Visual Odometry System Using Multiple Stereo Cameras and Inertial Measurement Unit. In: ICRA, pp. 1–8 (2007)

Shiu, Y., Ahmad, S.: Finding the mounting position of a sensor by solving a homogeneous transform equation of the form AX= XB. In: ICRA, vol. 4, pp. 1666–1671 (1987)

Tsai, R., Lenz, R.: A new technique for fully autonomous and efficient 3D robotics hand/eye calibration. IEEE Transactions on Robotics and Automation 5(3), 345–358 (1989)

Absolute Orientation of Stereoscopic Cameras by Aligning Contours in Pairs of Images and Reference Images

Boris Peter Selby[1], Georgios Sakas[1], Wolfgang-Dieter Groch[2], and Uwe Stilla[3]

[1] Medcom GmbH, Image Guided RT, Darmstadt, Germany
[2] Dept. of Computer Sciences, University of Applied Sciences, Darmstadt, Germany
[3] Dept. of Photogrammetry and Remote Sensing, Technische Universitaet Muenchen, Muenchen, Germany

Abstract. Most approaches use corresponding points to determining an object's orientation from stereo-images, but this is not always possible. Imaging modalities that do not produce correspondences for different viewing angles, as in X-ray imaging, require other procedures. Our method works on contours in images that do not need to be equivalent in length or contain corresponding points. It is able to determine corresponding contours and resamples those, creating new sets of corresponding points for registration. Two sets of in-plane transformations from a stereo-system are used to determine spatial orientation. The approach was tested with three ground truth datasets and sub-pixel accuracy was achieved. The approach is originally designed for X-ray based patient alignment, but it is versatile and can also be employed in other close range photogrammetry applications.

Keywords: Camera orientation, Contour registration, Automatic Alignment.

1 Introduction

Determination of the orientation of a multiple-view camera system has numerous applications in different fields of science and engineering. In satellite and aerial imaging a stereoscopic system can be used to determine the current position of the object carrying the cameras. In case that the camera system's orientation is already known, this is equivalent to estimating the alignment of a 3-D object in space. In close range photogrammetry, this can enable determining the position and orientation of an object of interest, like a car in a street scene or some object on an assembly line, etc. The natural approaches to this task are to find corresponding pairs of image locations that are projections of the same feature in space as it is done in the PMF algorithm (Pollard et al., 1985). Alternatively in-depth locations can be determined by use of a disparity map (Kim et al., 2006) or the object alignment can be computed by comparing corresponding edge information from stereo-images (Demuynck et al., 2009). In calibrated optical stereo camera systems the search for corresponding positions in the opposite image can be narrowed to positions on the respective epipolar line, or to positions close to it, if small uncertainties of the relative orientation between the cameras are expected.

U. Stilla et al. (Eds.): PIA 2011, LNCS 6952, pp. 25–36, 2011.

Anyway, it is not always possible to find any correspondences at all. This applies to images from optical cameras were the image content does not allow sufficient segmentation or, in particular to images were the image formation process is not mapping single object features to the projection plane. Typical examples are X-ray images, where pixels do not represent a certain location, but are formed by integrals over rays through a photon absorbing object. We target to determine the absolute orientation of "cameras" relative to an imaged object from radiographic or fluoroscopic images. The application is to align a human patient relative to a fixed and calibrated X-ray camera system, as for image guided radio-oncological treatment (Selby et al., 2007b; Engelsman et al., 2008). Therefore, in most cases, correspondences do only exist if artificial objects with high absorption, like special metallic beads, are attached to the object (Selby et al., 2007a). Nevertheless, determining external camera orientation is still possible if a model of the projected image is given, that can be compared to the real projection image. In this case, the model can be considered the reference image I and the real images can be considered floating images I', for which a transformation to the modelled image can be determined. This transformation, mapping I' onto I, can be computed either by using landmarks, detected in the images, or directly based on intensities of the image pixels (Maes et al., 1997; Selby et al., 2010). As neither determination of exact landmark positions nor the intensity based method can be used for all kind of image data, we propose another method, using contour lines that have been detected or manually defined in the images. Note that definition of contour lines at approximately the same positions in I and I' is often much easier than to define a particular image location and to find its correspondence.

Yet, to accomplish the contour based alignment computation, the problem of finding correspondences of possibly error prone and incomplete contour lines must be solved. Arkin et al. (1991) proposed a method for computing a translational, rotational, and scale invariant measure for the similarity of polygons. The polygons are transformed in a representation by their turning angles and a distance metric is computed as the L_2 norm of the turning function distances. We will call the metric Turning Function Distance TF-Distance. Tanase et al. (2005) extended the TF-Distance to be able to find the correspondence of single parts of a polygonal shape, i.e. a polyline to a full polygonal shape, in order to find template shapes in images with occluded or badly segmented contours.

We adopt their measure for our novel alignment estimation approach to initially compute the correspondence of contour parts defined in a pair of images. A by-product of the shape similarity computation - a translational parameter describing where one contour is located on the path of the other contour - is used to create point-wise correspondences. These allow computing the rigid 2-D transformation between an arbitrary number of polylines. To deal with outliers, we deploy the Random Sample Consensus (RANSAC) method as shown by Fischler et al. (1981).

Finally, the rigid in-plane transformations of a set of stereo images are used to determine the camera system's orientation with respect to the contours in 5 degrees of freedom (DOF) – note that full 6 DOF reconstruction from two projection images is not possible this way.

2 Methods

We first want to give an overview over the complete camera orientation reconstruction algorithm as visualized in Fig. 1.

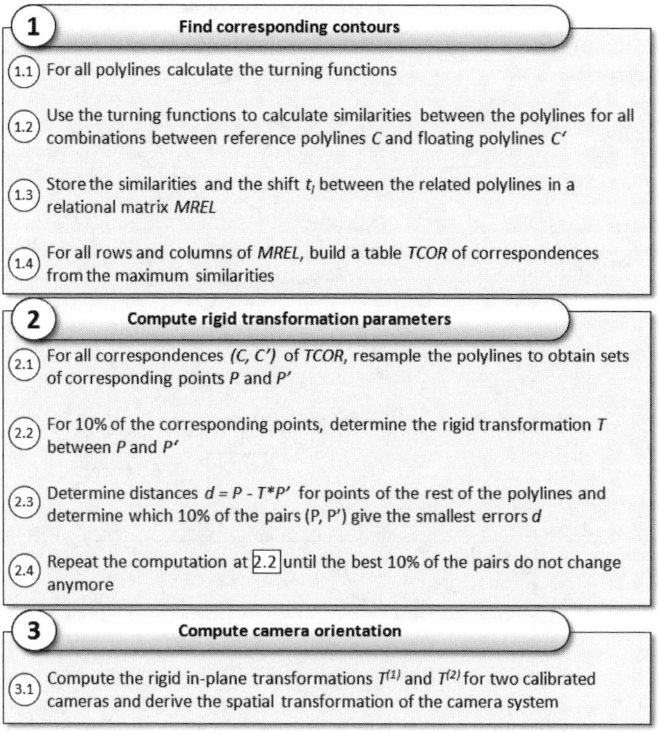

1 Find corresponding contours

(1.1) For all polylines calculate the turning functions

(1.2) Use the turning functions to calculate similarities between the polylines for all combinations between reference polylines C and floating polylines C'

(1.3) Store the similarities and the shift t_l between the related polylines in a relational matrix $MREL$

(1.4) For all rows and columns of $MREL$, build a table $TCOR$ of correspondences from the maximum similarities

2 Compute rigid transformation parameters

(2.1) For all correspondences (C, C') of $TCOR$, resample the polylines to obtain sets of corresponding points P and P'

(2.2) For 10% of the corresponding points, determine the rigid transformation T between P and P'

(2.3) Determine distances $d = P - T*P'$ for points of the rest of the polylines and determine which 10% of the pairs (P, P') give the smallest errors d

(2.4) Repeat the computation at 2.2 until the best 10% of the pairs do not change anymore

3 Compute camera orientation

(3.1) Compute the rigid in-plane transformations $T^{(1)}$ and $T^{(2)}$ for two calibrated cameras and derive the spatial transformation of the camera system

Fig. 1. The three major parts of the alignment detection algorithm

The procedure can be divided into three major parts. The first part (Fig. 1 - 1), which is the most difficult, is to find corresponding points P and P' between reference polylines C and floating lines C'. It must be considered, that one contour might be only a part of the other and that points are not defined at the same position on the route. Therefore points (P, P') might not exist and must be created by sampling from corresponding pairs (C, C'). When sets P and P' are known for all polylines, corresponding points can be selected and are used to compute rigid transformation T, mapping P' onto P (Fig. 1 - 2). An algorithm similar to the RANSAC approach is used to find the best data points for defining T. Finally, the in-plane transformations are used to determine the spatial alignment in 5 DOF.

2.1 Finding Corresponding Contours

Our initial situation is that we have two pairs of images, each pair representing a different view, consisting of a projection image and a modelled projection image.

Both images of each pair contain some contours defined as polylines, i.e. interconnected sets of points. Some of the polylines in one might be sub-parts of the contours in the other image or vice versa or even have no correspondences at all. To assess, which of the polylines correspond to each other, we first compute a turning angle representation and then the TF-Distance similar as proposed by Arkin et al. (1991). In Fig. 2a, two polylines are shown: a reference line C defined through 7 points and a floating line C' defined through 6 points. C' is a subset of C and contains some minor errors.

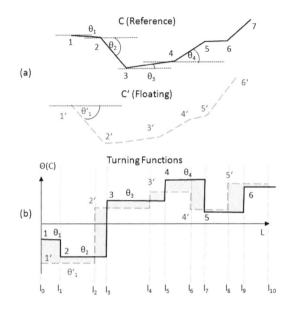

Fig. 2. Schematic visualization of two polylines represented a) as planar contours and b) as turning functions Θ over path length L. Points are numbered consecutively. The shaded areas between the turning functions represent a distance measure. l_0 to l_{10} are ordered, discrete sample locations where either the value of $\Theta(C)$ or $\Theta(C')$ changes.

In Fig. 2b, the turning function representations Θ of C and C' are displayed. While Arkin et al. (1991) use the cumulative angle between two line segments, we simply compute θ as the slope for the line between two points of C by

$$\theta_i(C) = \text{atan2}\left(\frac{y_{i+1} - y_i}{|P_{i+1} - P_i|}, \frac{x_{i+1} - x_i}{|P_{i+1} - P_i|}\right) \qquad (1)$$

where x, y are coordinates of consecutive points P_i and P_{i+1}. The difference of areas dA under the turning functions is a distance measure between the polylines:

$$dA(C, C') = \int_0^L |\theta(l) - \theta'(l)| dl \qquad (2)$$

with dA being the difference of the areas under C and C' and L being the length of the path for the computation. Let L be a path length on a polyline, starting from an arbitrary position L_0 and reaching until the last point of one of the contours, namely the shorter one, if no shift between the contours is considered. Then, $dA(C, C')$ can be computed very efficiently using samples at discrete positions l_i where either the value of $\Theta(C)$ or $\Theta(C')$ changes (see Fig. 2b). dA becomes a sum of rectangular areas:

$$dA(C,C') = \sum_i (l_{i+1} - l_i)\left|(\theta(l) - \theta'(l))\right| \tag{3}$$

Note that the measure is still sensitive to the overall rotation of the contour, as well as to the shift and scale between contours. While Tanase et al. (2005) removed the scale dependency of dA by normalizing the contour path lengths to 1.0, we will keep it, because we only expect rigid transformations between the images. By minimizing dA with starting position L_0, path length L and relative shift t_l of the floating contour as free parameters, we obtain the metric

$$d(C,C') = \min_{L_0, t_l \in R, L \in R^+} \int_{L_0}^{L_0 + L} \left(\theta(l) - \theta'(l - t_l) - \Delta\theta_0\right)^2 dl \tag{4}$$

where $\Delta\theta_0$ is the initial angle difference for C and C' at L_0 and t_l is the shift of the floating contour C' against C. Optimisation of L_0 is done to cope with contours that start at different points, while length L is optimised to cope with contours that do not correspond after a certain path distance. This includes being able to handle contours that are different in length. Let's say for example that contour C is shorter than contour C'. We can initialise L_0 and t_l with 0 and L to the length of the shorter contour C. When L_0 is growing or a shift t_l is introduced, L becomes shorter in the optimisation of (Equation 4).

Minimization is done with the Nelder-Mead Downhill simplex in three dimensions (Nelder et al., 1965). To deal with possible local minima, we repeat minimization at different starting positions until no improvements in minimizing d can be achieved anymore. Length L is restricted to half of the length of the smaller contour, to avoid that a contour degenerates to a very short section, in order to satisfy Equation 4. Restricting the minimization is done by multiplying a constant factor that makes the target function artificially larger, causing the optimiser to avoid these situations. $\Delta\theta_0$ makes the measure insensitive against the relative orientation between the contours.

After computing the distance between each contour pair, we store the relations rel

$$rel(C,C') = (d_{Max} - d(C,C'))d_{Max}^{-1} \in [0,1] \tag{5}$$

between the contours together with the parameters L_0, L and t_l in a matrix of $MREL_{n \times m}$ with n contours occurring in the reference and m contours in the floating image respectively. Fig. 3a shows an example for reference and floating contours. Some of the contours are not defined completely as a single polyline (C_2, C_3 and C'_3, C'_4), e.g. because they are occluded by some other object in the image data. The 4 + 4 contours are used to build the matrix $MREL_{4 \times 4}$ as can be seen in Fig. 3b.

Next, the particular relations in $MREL$ that represent corresponding contours have to be found. Therefore the pairs with the highest similarity (i.e. the lowest distance d) are stored in a table of correspondences $TCOR$. Pairs are selected by row and column maxima from the relation matrix. Duplicate and contradicting entries are removed from the table, so that in the best case, all existing correspondences are represented in the table. Note that there might be cases where some correct correspondences are deleted. This should not matter as long as enough contours have been defined initially, i.e. if redundancy is high enough. False positives, the events that wrong correspondences remain in the table, are unlikely. They require that each member of the wrong contour pair (C, C') is given higher similarity than in all other comparisons of either C or C' with the other contours.

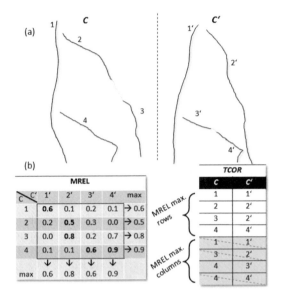

Fig. 3. Finding corresponding contours: a) Four examples for possible reference and floating contours C and C'; b) A relational matrix *MREL* is built from the contour relations. Each row- and column maximum is considered a possibly corresponding pair and entered in a table of correspondences *TCOR*. Duplicate and contradicting correspondences are removed from *TCOR* (as the struck out entries in the picture).

2.2 Floating to Reference Contour Registration

When the corresponding contours are finally known, they can still not be used directly for registration. To be able to find a transformation T that maps a contour C' onto corresponding contour C

$$C = T * C' \tag{6}$$

we have to sample points from the contours that can directly be compared via their coordinates. Knowing the sections of the contours that correspond and the shift t_l between the contour parts from the distance minimization of Equation 4, we can sample two polylines from *TCOR* in the range $[L_0, L_0+L]$ at all positions where the turning functions $\Theta(C)$ or $\Theta(C'-t_l)$ change, i.e. wherever a point of C or C' is defined (similar as depicted for l_0 to l_{10} in Fig. 2b). If for example at a position l_i a point is defined in C, but not in C', then a new Point P_i' is created for C' at the corresponding position. Note that P_i' is created at a position that is linear interpolated from P_{i-1}' and P_{i+1}', which means, that the contour lines should follow an object's shape. If this is not the case, the interpolation might create erroneous points. We finally obtain corresponding point sets P and P'. From now on, the point sets are not related to their contours anymore and are directly used for registration.

To cope with outliers we do not use all points P and P', but follow a RANSAC approach. Let set S be 10% of the points that are initially selected by random out from all points P. The rigid 2-D transformation T (with translations t_x, t_y and in-plane rotation r_z) is now computed via

$$T = \operatorname*{argmin}_{T \in R^3} \sum_i \left(S_i - T * S_i'\right)^2, \quad S \subset P, \; S' \subset P' \tag{7}$$

where T represents the in-plane transformations and S_i, S_i' are selected reference and floating points. After T is computed the residual errors for all P_i are determined by

$$r_i = P_i - T * P_i' \tag{8}$$

with residual errors r_i for points P_i and P_i'. The 10% of corresponding pairs (P_i, P_i') with the smallest r_i are repetitively used as S and S' until the sets of points do not change anymore, i.e., in the end $r_i(S_i, S_i')$ become the smallest 10% of $r_i(P_i, P_i')$.

2.3 External Orientation

With two transformations $T^{(1)}$ and $T^{(2)}$ for two cameras with different viewing angles, external orientation of the system can be computed strait forward, albeit only in 5 DOF. As shown in Fig. 4a, one rotational degree of freedom is lost through projection, if only in-plane transformations can be considered.

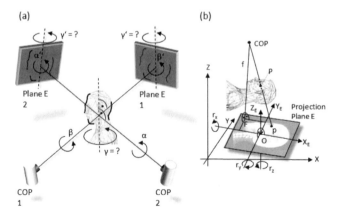

Fig. 4. a) Schematic view of a stereo X-ray system; The X-ray generating tubes are the centres of projection (COP). Spatial rotations α and β have an in-plane component on the projection planes, but rotation γ cannot be detected from two in-plane transformations. Hence, spatial orientation of the system can be determined in 6-1 = 5 DOF; b) Camera model, showing COP C, projection plane E and focal point F. An object is projected from a World coordinate system onto the projection plane.

With the camera model from Fig. 4b and the Equations of Collinearity one can define the inverse projection by:

$$P^{(i)}\left(Z^{(i)}\right)=\begin{pmatrix} X_C^{(i)} \\ Y_C^{(i)} \end{pmatrix}+\left(Z^{(i)}-Z_C^{(i)}\right)\frac{\begin{pmatrix} r_{11}^{(i)}\bar{x}_{pF}^{(i)}+r_{12}^{(i)}\bar{y}_{pF}^{(i)}+r_{13}^{(i)}Z_F^{(i)} \\ r_{21}^{(i)}\bar{x}_{pF}^{(i)}+r_{22}^{(i)}\bar{y}_{pF}^{(i)}+r_{23}^{(i)}Z_F^{(i)} \end{pmatrix}}{r_{31}^{(i)}\bar{x}_{pF}^{(i)}+r_{32}^{(i)}\bar{y}_{pF}^{(i)}+r_{33}^{(i)}Z_F^{(i)}} \tag{9}$$

$$\bar{x}_{pF}^{(i)}=\left(x-X_F^{(i)}\right); \quad \bar{y}_{pF}^{(i)}=\left(y-Y_F^{(i)}\right)$$

Where

i	=	index of the camera (here 1 or 2)
$P^{(i)}$	=	spatial point determined from camera i
x, y	=	coordinates of the projected point on the plane E
X_C, Y_C, Z_C	=	Coordinates of the COP
Z	=	z-coordinate of the back-projected point
F	=	focal point on the projection plane E
r	=	rotation matrix component for E

Three basis vectors b' are defined in each camera's projection plane for the floating images. The transformed vector components b for the resulting reference images are computed through:

$$b'^{(1)}=b'^{(2)}=I_{3x3}; \quad b^{(1)}=T^{(1)}*b'^{(1)}; \quad b^{(2)}=T^{(2)}*b'^{(2)} \tag{10}$$

The basis vectors $b^{(1,2)}$ and $b'^{(1,2)}$ are considered corresponding points with origins $O^{(1,2)}$ (= origins of the respective projection planes, see Fig. 4b). Together with Equation 9, they are used to perform the inverse projection with spatial points

$$P = \min\left|P^{(1)}-P^{(2)}\right| \tag{11}$$

resulting in reference vectors B and floating vectors B' in world coordinates. Finally the spatial transformation T is obtained:

$$B = TB'; \quad T = B'B^{-1} \tag{12}$$

3 Experiments and Results

The algorithm was tested on medical X-ray images for patient alignment before radiation treatment. High accuracy and reliability are crucial in this scope. The X-ray images serve as floating images I', while models for the X-ray images, so-called DRRs (Digitally Reconstructed Radiographies) that are automatically created by ray-tracing from a computed X-ray tomography (CT) for an assumed camera geometry, serve as reference data I. Figure 5a shows the set-up for acquisition of the data for a human head phantom. In Figure 5b a floating X-ray image and the reference DRR of a human pelvis (here the femoral bone) are displayed for a single camera. Some contours have been defined manually and are overlaid to the images. Note that they do not fit initially, but after registration, corresponding contours are correctly overlaid to each other.

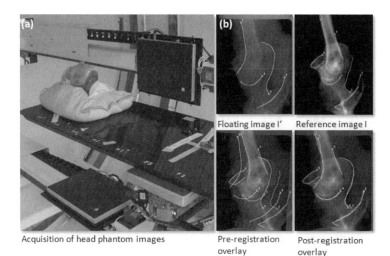

Floating image I'   Reference image I

Acquisition of head phantom images   Pre-registration   Post-registration
overlay   overlay

Fig. 5. a) Set-up for acquisition of images of a head phantom with orthogonal X-ray cameras; b) Floating X-ray image of a human pelvis I' and the respective model (DRR) as reference I; some contours are overlaid to the images. Before registration, the overlaid view of the images shows that the contours do not match. After registration, most parts of the contours C and C' fit together.

Three different datasets were used for evaluation of the algorithm. For each dataset, a rigid gold standard transformation in 3-D space was established, using 4-5 metallic beads that were attached to the X-rayed bodies and could easily be located in the projection images. The pixel-size of the DRRs is 1.3 mm/pixel, the X-ray images have a pixel-size of less than 0.13 mm/pixel. Each dataset consists of two X-ray images and two simulated X-ray images (DRRs) for a stereoscopic X-ray camera set-up with orthogonal viewing angles and distances of 1.5 m COP (= X-ray tube) to object and 1.0 m object to projection plane (= X-ray detector).

Gold standard dataset 1 (GS1) was created from an anatomical head phantom for dose measurement. The registration error between the 5 attached metallic markers after landmark based alignment computation in 6 DOF was FRE = 0.35 mm. FRE means Fiducial Registration Error, which is the root mean square of the remaining errors between the markers. Gold standard dataset 2 (GS2) was from a human patient for brain tumour treatment with initial FRE = 0.2 mm and Gold standard dataset 3 (GS3) was created from a patient for prostate treatment with data from the pelvis region (see Fig. 5 b). The FRE is 0.1 mm respectively. For GS3, there is an out-of-plane rotation of 2° present in the images. For the other datasets it is below 0.1°.

The evaluation was done by creating initial misalignments in the projection planes, with random components of in-plane shifts and rotations, ranging from 0.0 cm up to 4.0 cm FRE. From this initial offsets, the algorithm had to determine the orientation of the camera system for each dataset. The results are compared to the gold standard that was established with the attached markers. The final FRE was computed to assess the algorithm's performance.

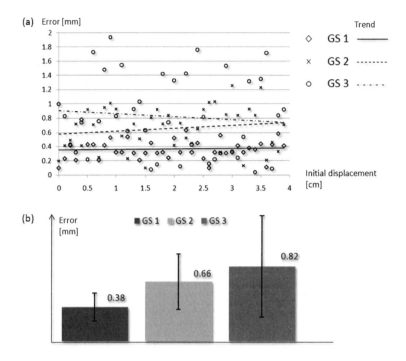

Fig. 6. Results for three gold standard datasets: a) scatter plot with linear trend lines for final error (as FRE) over initial displacements (also as FRE) for 40 tests, and b) mean errors and standard deviations of the 40 results of each dataset.

Summarizing the resulting errors for all 40 test runs of each dataset, the measured FRE values are given as mean FRE ± 1 standard deviation as follows: 0.38 ± 0.15 mm, 0.66 ± 0.30 mm, and 0.82 ± 0.56 mm for GS1, GS2, and GS3 respectively. All registrations and computations of 5 DOF alignments could be performed within less than a second for $|C| = 4$ and $|C'| = 6$ contours. Note that the errors for the GS3 data are largest, which is not surprising, because of the out-of-plane rotation inherent to the data, that could not be determined by the contour based approach. In Figure 6 the results are visualized as scatter plot over the initial mis-alignments (a) as well as mean errors with standard deviations (b). The linear trend lines in Figure 6a show no clear tendency to increasing alignment errors with larger initial mis-alignment. This means that one can expect good performance, also for data with large initial mis-alignment between reference and floating data.

4   Discussion

The registration method proposed in this contribution is well suited for all applications that perform model based registration and rely on projected contours. Comparison with ground truth registrations show, that it achieves sub-pixel accuracy, as required by image guided medical procedures, and that it provides good performance regarding low computation time. When spatial orientation has to be determined, the approach can, basing on computation of two in-plane transformations, not establish full 6 degrees of freedom. On the other hand, 6 DOF might not be required for all applications, as e.g. for patient alignment at treatment sites that do not allow mechanical alignment for all degrees of freedom of the patient orientation (Allgower et al., 2007). Anyway, the algorithm is accurate, fast and stable, but requires pre-defined image contour information.

5 Conclusions

Our approach is well suited for the use with X-ray or fluoroscopy as imaging modality, where no corresponding points can be found in images from different viewing angles. However, the method is not limited to this scope of application, and could be used in other applications that perform model based alignment estimation, e.g. with simulated Radar images (Domik et al., 1984) etc. It is fast and accurate and can be an alternative for those cases, were point correspondence based or intensity based alignment is not feasible. Further work to improve the usability could be automatic contour detection as well as automatic adaptation of the contours to projection model changes, which would allow alignment computation in full 6 degrees of freedom.

Acknowledgements. We like to thank the team from Brandis GmbH, Germany for technical support with X-ray equipment and radiation control issues and SelbyTec, Germany for technical support with the implementation.

References

Allgower, C.E., Schreuder, A.N., Farr, J.B., Mascia, A.E.: Experiences with an Application of industrial Robotics for accurate Patient Positioning in Proton Radiotherapy. International Journal of Medical Robotics and Computer Assisted Surgery 3, 72–81 (2007)

Arkin, E.M., Chew, L.P., Huttenlocher, D.P., Kedem, K., Mitchell, J.S.B.: An efficiently computable Metric for comparing Polygonal Shapes. IEEE Transactions on Pattern Analysis and Machine Intelligence 13, 209–216 (1991)

Demuynck, O., Cedeño, C.P., Moore, A.L.: Edge based 3D Object localization for fast and precise industrial Machine Vision Applications. International Journal of Systems Applications, Engineering & Development 3, 45–52 (2009)

Domik, G., Leberl, F., Kobrick, M.: Radar Image Simulation and its Application in Image Analysis. In: Archives of the International Society of Photogrammetry and Remote Sensing, vol. 25(A3a), pp. 99–105 (1984)

Engelsman, M., Mazal, A., Jaffray, D.A.: Patient Positioning and Set-up Verification for Planning and Treatment. In: de Laney, T.F., Kooy, H.M. (eds.) Proton and Charged Particle Radiotherapy, 1st edn., pp. 57–69. Lippincott Williams & Wilkins, Philadelphia (2008)

Fischler, M.A., Bolles, R.C.: Random Sample Consensus: a Paradigm for Model Fitting with Applications to Image Analysis and automated Cartography. Communications of the ACM 24, 381–395 (1981)

Kim, H., Choi, J., Chang, H., Yu, K.: Generation of a Disparity Map using piecewise linear Transformation. In: Mastorakis, N., Cecchi, A. (eds.) Proceedings of 5th International Conference on Computational Intelligence, Man-Machine Systems and Cybernetics, Venice, Italy, pp. 40–45 (2006)

Maes, F., Collignon, A., Vandermeulen, D., Marchal, G., Suetens, P.: Multimodality Image Registration by Maximization of Mutual Information. IEEE Transactions on Medical Imaging 16, 187–198 (1997)

Nelder, J.A., Mead, R.: A Simplex Method for Function Minimization. The Computer Journal 7, 308–313 (1965)

Pollard, S.B., Mayhew, J.E., Frisby, J.P.: PMF: A Stereo Correspondance Algorithm using a Disparity Gradient Limit. Perception 14, 449–470 (1985)

Selby, B.P., Sakas, G., Walter, S., Groch, W.-D., Stilla, U.: Detection of Pose Changes for Spatial Objects from projective Images. In: Stilla, U., Meyer, H., Rottensteiner, F., Heipke, C., Hinz, S. (eds.) Proceedings of Photogrammetric Image Analysis Conference (PIA), Munich, Germany, vol. 36, pp. 105–110 (2007)

Selby, B.P., Sakas, G., Walter, S.: 3D Alignment Correction for Proton Beam Treatment. In: Proceedings of Conference of the German Society for Biomedical Engineering (DGBMT), Aachen, Germany (2007)

Selby, B.P., Sakas, G., Walter, S., Groch, W.-D., Stilla, U.: A Radiometry tolerant Method for direct 3D/2D Registration of Computed Tomography Data to X-ray Images: Transfer Function independent Registration. In: Deserno, T.M., Handels, H., Meinzer, H.-P., Tolxdorff, T. (eds.) Conference on Medical Imaging (BVM), Informatik Aktuell, pp. 117–121. Springer, Heidelberg (2010)

Tanase, M., Veltkamp, R.C., Haverkort, H.J.: Multiple Polyline to Polygon Matching. In: Deng, X., Du, D.-Z. (eds.) ISAAC 2005. LNCS, vol. 3827, pp. 60–70. Springer, Heidelberg (2005)

Matching between Different Image Domains

Charles Toth, Hui Ju, and Dorota Grejner-Brzezinska

The Center for Mapping, The Ohio State University,
470 Hitchcock Hall, 2070 Neil Avenue, Columbus, OH 43210
toth@cfm.ohio-state.edu

Abstract. Most of the image registration/matching methods are applicable to images acquired by either identical or similar sensors from various positions. Simpler techniques assume some object space relationship between sensor reference points, such as near parallel image planes, certain overlap and comparable radiometric characteristics. More robust methods allow for larger variations in image orientation and texture, such as the Scale-Invariant Feature Transformation (SIFT), a highly robust technique widely used in computer vision. The use of SIFT, however, is quite limited in mapping so far, mainly, because most of the imagery are acquired from airborne/spaceborne platforms, and, consequently, the image orientation is better known, presenting a less general case for matching. The motivation for this study is to look at the feasibility of a particular case of matching between different image domains. In this investigation, the co-registration of satellite imagery and LiDAR intensity data is addressed.

Keywords: Image registration/matching, LiDAR, satellite imagery.

1 Introduction

Image registration is a core technique for various applications in digital photogrammetry, computer vision, remote sensing, and vision-aided navigation. The basic idea is to find the correspondences between images and image pairs acquired at different times, perspectives or even from different sensors. With rapid developments in sensor technologies, increasing data volume are acquired from spaceborne, airborne and mobile platforms in various data domains. While the georeferencing of images is improving, which is essential to constrain the search space, the need for methods that can provide robust co-registration between various image domains is sharply growing.

The majority of the image registration/matching methods are applicable to images acquired by either identical or similar sensors from various positions. Simpler techniques assume some object space relationship between sensor reference points, such as near parallel image planes, certain overlap and comparable radiometric characteristics; all are typical in airborne surveying. More robust methods allow for larger variations in image orientation and texture. One of these techniques is the Scale-Invariant Feature Transformation (SIFT), proposed by Lowe in 1999, a highly robust technique that has been widely used in the computer vision community. Though, SIFT is known in mapping circles, its use is quite limited so far, mainly,

U. Stilla et al. (Eds.): PIA 2011, LNCS 6952, pp. 37–47, 2011.

because most of the imagery are acquired either from airborne or spaceborne platforms, and, consequently, the image orientation is better known, presenting a less general case for matching. In addition, the accuracy of SIFT is modest to digital photogrammetric practice. As an increasing number of various image sensors provide multiple image coverage worldwide, the need for co-registering imagery acquired in different domains is growing. Several satellite systems deliver high-resolution imagery in short repeat time, large-format aerial digital cameras provide multispectral imagery, LiDAR systems collect both range and intensity images at local scale, IfSAR data are acquired from spaceborne and airborne platform at global scale, etc., all these data should be accurately co-registered for data fusion to support better geospatial data and information extraction.

The motivation for this study is coming from two applications: terrain-based navigation and improving the georeferencing of satellite imagery by using ground control. Commercial satellite systems have shown remarkable improvements recently; the image resolution of several systems has increased to the maximum allowable 0.5 m GSD, and the georeferencing accuracy is around the few meter level. Given the worldwide availability of satellite imagery and its short repeat time, satellite images represent valuable data for terrain-based navigation.

Identifying conjugate feature points from LiDAR data is practically impossible, as the LiDAR point cloud is sparse and furthermore the intensity associated with the points has different characteristics compared to optical imagery. Therefore, other image primitives such as 3D straight lines and surface patches are generally considered (Habib, Bang, Aldelgawy, Shin, & Kim, 2007; Habib, Ghanma, & Tait, 2004; Habib, M.S.Ghanma, Morgan, & Mitishita, 2004; Kim & Habib, 2009). With increasing laser point density, better LiDAR intensity images are formed, which could be potentially registered to optical imagery. Due to its robust scale- and rotation-invariant properties, SIFT (Lowe, 1999; Brown, Lowe, 2002; Lowe, 2004) is a widely used matching technique in optical image domain (Abedini, Hahn, & Samadzadegan, 2008). Based on earlier experiences, SIFT was successfully applied to satellite and aerial image registration (Toth, Ju, & Grejner-Brzezinska, 2010). However, in our tests, SIFT failed to provide robust registration between optical and LiDAR intensity images. Therefore, an alternative method has been developed in this study.

2   SIFT Matching

The Scale Invariant Feature Transform (SIFT) matching is a technique to extract highly invariant features from images and to perform reliable matching; a thorough description on SIFT can be found in (Lowe, 2004). To achieve robust performance, the features for image matching should be generally invariant to scale, rotation, affine distortion and intensity changes to handle varying imaging conditions. The SIFT algorithm consists of several stages and the computation requirements are quite substantial; in particular, the matching of the extracted features could be a challenge for larger number of features, as it is based on k-D tree structure. There are also some modifications to SIFT to make it more effective: PCA-SIFT (Ke and Sukthankar, 2004), GLOH (Gradient Location-Orientation Histogram) (Mikolajczyk and Schmid,

2005), CSIFT (Abdel-Hakim and Farag, 2006), SR-SIFT (Yi et al., 2008), SURF (Speeded-Up Robust Features) (Bay et al., 2008) and Robust SIFT (Li et al., 2009). In our study, the baseline SIFT implementation was used. Since generally there are many mismatched SIFT features, blunder detection, based on RANSAC, (RANdom SAmple Consensus) (Fischler and Bolles, 1981), is applied. Figures 1a-b show two aerial images captured over an intersection, where the radius of the circles is proportional to the strength of the feature and the hand in the circle represents the orientation of the feature. In Figures 1c-d, red and green mark the removed and kept matched SIFT features, respectively.

(a)   (b)

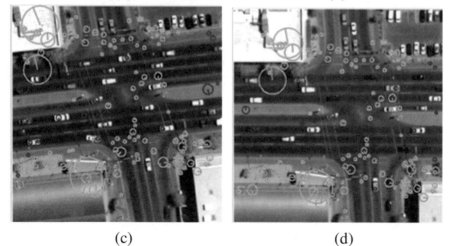

(c)   (d)

Fig. 1. Aerial image pair with SIFT features, extracted (yellow) and matched (red) in (a) and (b), and removed (red) and kept (green) in (c) and (d)

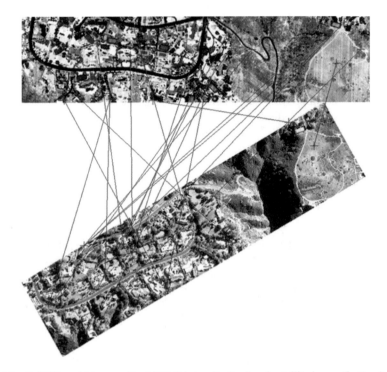

Fig. 2. SIFT matching results; LiDAR intensity (top) and satellite image (bottom)

Fig. 2 shows typical SIFT matching results between LiDAR intensity and satellite images. Compared to the intersection example, the number of matched features is rather small, and, more importantly, none of the matches is correct for this image pair, though there are keypoints extracted at similar locations. The main reason for the failed SIFT registration is that it is very difficult to find similar keypoints in both images due to the substantial difference in radiometric characteristics between the intensity and satellite images.

3   Multiple-Domain Matching

In this study, a method based on LPFFT (Log-Polar FFT or Log-Polar Fast Fourier Transform)(Reddy and Chatterji, 1996; Wolberg and Zokai, 2000; Zokai and Wolberg, 2005), Harris Corner points and PDF descriptor matching, is introduced for the multiple-domain image matching between the intensity and satellite images. The hybrid registration scheme uses a from-coarse-to-fine strategy. In the first step, a similarity transformation relationship is assumed between the image pair, and, subsequently, estimated in two steps by employing the LPFFT registration. Generally, the scale and rotation parameter estimation is rather stable. But in case the translation parameter estimation fails, these parameters could be still approximated by using FFT-accelerated normalized cross correlation (FFT phase correlation). At this point, the estimated similarity transformation provides the coarse geometric model for the image pair. Based on this information, the region features in one image, defined as circular regions centred at strong Harris Corner points, are transformed to the other image, and, subsequently, used for matching. In other words, each image has its own region features and imported region features from the other image. Next, the scale- and rotation-invariant kernel-based probability density function descriptor (PDF descriptor) is used to describe the circular region features. The intensity PDF of a region can be approximated by the normalized histogram (Comaniciu et al., 2003). The transformed feature location indicates the search area in the other image, and then, the best correspondence is obtained in the search area when the local maximum similarity between the two PDF descriptors is found by employing a mean-shift approach (Comaniciu et al., 2003). Obtaining sufficient correspondence between the image pair, an affine transform, or a more sophisticated model, is estimated to describe the geometrical relationship between the image pair. Finally, the outliers are removed by using RANSAC.

The reason using LPFFT over mutual information similarity measure, generally considered for global matching, was that LPFFT is a rotation- and scale-invariant approach, and consequently it can provide the rotation and scale estimates at once. LPFFT can handle image pair with different scale and rotation, while mutual information similarity measure can be applied to finding the translation only after the rotation and scale are roughly recovered.

3.1 Similarity Transformation Estimation

Using the LPFFT transformation, two parameters (scale and rotation) of the similarity model are estimated in the first step. Then the second image is transformed based on the scale and rotation values, so the images have comparable orientation and scale. Finally, the translation parameters are estimated by NCC (Normalized Cross-Correlation). For efficient processing, FFT-accelerated NCC is used (FFT NCC).

3.2 Validation of the Similarity Model

Since the correctness of the similarity transformation is essential for the subsequent processing steps, it is important to validate it; in particular, the rotation and scale estimation could be wrong and, subsequently, the NCC surface may have no clear maximum. Therefore, a Monte Carlo test is performed for a set of rotation and scale values:

$$S := \{s | s_i = s_0 \pm i \cdot \delta s\}$$
$$\Phi := \{\phi | \phi_i = \phi_0 \pm i \cdot \delta\phi\}$$

where, the two originally estimated parameters, (s_0, ϕ_0), are perturbed by a combination of the $(\delta s, \delta\phi)$ values. The whole process, including FFT NCC, is executed for each parameter set, and the maximum and mean parameters are computed for NCC surfaces (between the original and transformed images). In addition, the absolute maximum value is determined. Based on these three values the following evaluation is done:

- If all the three parameters point to one unique solution, then this similarity model is accepted.

- If only two of them agree, then the rotation and scale are likely to be correct, and the translation must be better determined. Based on our experiences, the 3rd parameter, the translation, is most likely the difficult one, in which case, an FFT-accelerated sum of square difference (FFT SSD) template matching is used to estimate the translation parameters. This solution is also accepted but with a flag indicating a lower confidence level.
- If all the three parameters point to different solutions, then this image pair cannot be handled, so matching is unavailable.

Note that the greedy algorithm could be also considered instead of the MC method, as it potentially offers faster processing, though it may fail in some cases.

Fig. 3 shows typical similarity surfaces based on wrong (left) and good estimates (right). Note the differences between the two surface in terms of smoothness and score values.

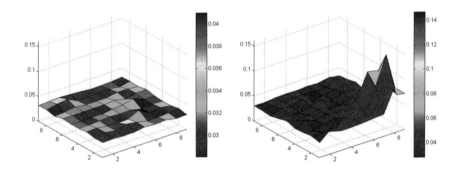

Fig. 3. NCC-based similarity surfaces; failed (left), and correct estimation (right)

3.3 Feature Matching

The Harris Corner detector (HC) is used to extract feature points, and circular regions centred on strong HC features are created in both images, including the imported locations from the other image. Next the scale- and rotation-invariant PDF (probability density function) descriptor is used to describe the feature region. The PDF function is represented in a 256-dimensional feature descriptor. The similarity between two feature descriptors is computed via the Bhattacharyya Coefficient, which is the cosine of angle correlation between the two feature descriptors, defined as:

$$\rho = \rho(p, q) = \sum_{u=1}^{m} \sqrt{p_u \cdot q_u} = cos\theta \geq 0$$

where

$$\sum_{u=1}^{m} p_u = 1 \text{ and } \sum_{u=1}^{m} q_u = 1$$

ρ is always non-negative, as the two normalized unit vectors p and q are both non-negative. The maximal similarity score is 1, which means the two feature descriptors are exactly the same. The minimal similarity score is 0 which means the two feature descriptors are orthogonal to each other; in other words, they don't have any relation.

3.4 Model Formation

Depending on object space characteristics, either affine or collinearity models can be formed based on the matched feature locations. In both cases, blunder detection is necessary, which is based on RANSAC.

4 Experimental Results

Satellite imagery acquired GeoEye in January 2010 and LiDAR data by Fugro-EarthData in 2009, shown in Fig. 2, were used in our tests. The San Diego, CA area represents a typical mix of terrain topography and landscape, including residential areas, roads and vegetated areas. The rasterized LiDAR intensity image was used as reference and the satellite image was transformed based on the similarity model estimation as shown in Fig. 4.

Fig. 4. LiDAR intensity image (top) and the transformed satellite image (bottom)

Based on strength and spatial distribution, 97 HC features were kept and, subsequently, used for matching. Using the PDF descriptors, 33 feature locations were successfully matched. Since the terrain undulation is moderate, an affine model was satisfactory and chosen in our test. Specifying a 0.5 pixel threshold for residual errors, the RANSAC process removed 15 points; obviously, the 18 kept points were more than enough to determine the 6 parameters of the affine transformation. Fig. 5 shows the matching results in original image orientation.

Another example from the same area, shown in Fig. 6, produced similar results; for the same error threshold, 14 out of 25 matched locations were kept by RANSAC.

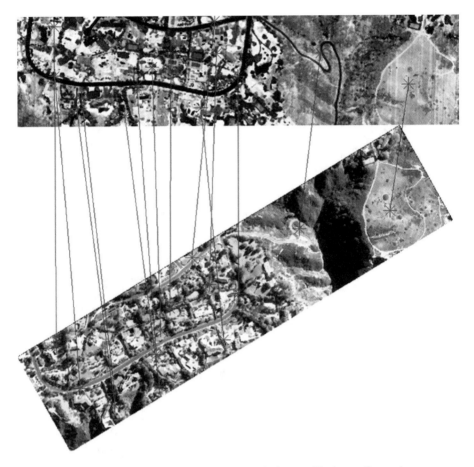

Fig. 5. LiDAR intensity image (top) matched to satellite image (bottom)

5   Conclusion

The feasibility of matching between airborne LiDAR intensity and satellite imagery was investigated. First the applicability of the SIFT feature-based matching was studied in this paper. Due to the very different characteristics of the keypoints of the different image domains, SIFT was unable to deliver acceptable results, based on our somewhat limited dataset. Next, a method was proposed to achieve better matching performance, and, ultimately, realize robust matching. The suggested process starts with the initial estimation of rotation and scale between the two images. Once these parameters have determined, one image is transformed to bring the images to near identical orientation and scale. In the next step, the translations are approximated to form a similarity model between the two images. To check the validity of the estimated parameters of the similarity transformation, a brute force Monte Carlo test is carried out, and the results are analysed to either accept or reject the solution. If the similarity transformation has been successfully formed, Harris Corner detector was

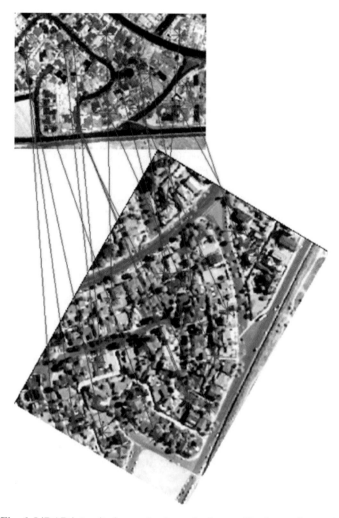

Fig. 6. LiDAR intensity image (top) matched to satellite image (bottom)

used to extract feature points in both images. The strongest feature points were projected to the other image and PDF-based matching was performed was performed for regions around the feature locations. In the final step, blunder detection is implemented based on RANSAC; note that an affine model was used in our testing. The results on a few image pairs showed good performance as pixel/sub-pixel matching accuracy was obtained. Since the method has many independent processes, further improvements are possible if more advanced techniques are incorporated. For example, other interest point operators could be considered or different area matching techniques can be applied, etc.

Acknowledgements. The authors thank the GeoEye Foundation and Fugro-EarthData for the data provided for this research.

References

1. Abdel-Hakim, A.E., Farag, A.A.: CSIFT: A SIFT Descriptor with Color Invariant Characteristics. In: Proceedings of the 2006 IEEE Computer Society Conference on Computer Vision and Pattern Recognition, vol. 2, pp. 1978–1983 (2006)
2. Abedini, A., Hahn, M., Samadzadegan, F.: An Investigation into the Registration of LiDAR Intensity Data and Aerial Images using the SIFT Approach. International Archives of Photogrammetry, Remote Sensing and Spatial Information Sciences, XXXVII Part B1 WG I/2, 169 (2008)
3. Bay, H., Ess, A., Tuytelaars, T., Gool, L.V.: SURF: Speeded Up Robust Features. Computer Vision and Image Understanding (CVIU) 110(3), 346–359 (2008)
4. Brown, M., Lowe, D.G.: Invariant feature from interest point groups. In: British Machine Vision Conference, Cardiff, Wales, pp. 656–665 (2002)
5. Comaniciu, D., Ramesh, V., Meer, P.: Kernel-Based Object Tracking. IEEE Transcations on Pattern Analysis and Matchine Intelligence 25(5), 564–577
6. Fischler, M.A., Bolles, R.C.: Random Sample Consensus: A Paradigm for Model Fitting with Applications to Image Analysis and Automated Cartography. Communications of the ACM 24, 381–395 (1981)
7. Habib, A.F., Bang, K.I., Aldelgawy, M., Shin, S.W., Kim, K.O.: Integration of Photogrammetric and LiDAR Data in a Multi-Primitive Triangulation Procedure. In: Proceedings of ASPRS 2007 Annual Conference - Identifying Geospatial Solutions, Tampa, FL, May 7-11, CD-ROM (2007)
8. Habib, A.F., Ghanma, M.S., Tait, M.: Integration of LiDAR and Photogrammetry for Close Range Applications. International Archives of Photogrammetry, Remote Sensing and Spatial Information Sciences XXXV, Part B5 (2004)
9. Habib, A.F., Ghanma, M.S., Morgan, M.F., Mitishita, E.: Integration of Laser and Photogrammetric Data for Calibration Purpose. International Archives of Photogrammetry, Remote Sensing and Spatial Information Sciences XXXV, part B2, 170 (2004)
10. Ke, Y., Sukthankar, R.: PCA-SIFT: A more distinctive representation for local image descriptors. In: Proceedings International Conferences on Computer Vision, Washington DC, pp. 506–513 (2004)
11. Kim, C., Habib, A.: Object-Based Integration of Photogrammetric and LiDAR Data for Automated Generation of Complex Polyhedral Building Models. Sensors 9(7), 5679–5701 (2009)
12. Li, Q.L., Wang, G.Y., Liu, J.G., Chen, S.B.: Robust Scale-Invariant Feature Matching for Remote Sensing Image Registration. IEEE Geoscience And Remote Sensing Letters 6(2), 287–291 (2009)
13. Lowe, D.G.: Object recognition from local scale-invariant features. In: Proceedings International Conferences on Computer Vision, Corfu, Greece, pp. 1150–1157 (1999)
14. Lowe, D.G.: Distinctive Image Features from Scale-Invariant Keypoints. International Journal of Computer Vision 60(2), 91–110 (2004)
15. Mikolajczyk, K., Schmid, C.: A performance evaluation of local descriptors. IEEE Trans. Pattern Anal. Mach. Intell. 27(10), 1615–1630 (2005)
16. Reddy, B.S., Chatterji, B.N.: An FFT-Based Technique for Translation, Rotation, and Scale-Invariant Image Registration. IEEE Transactions On Image Processing 5(8), 1266–1271 (1996)

17. Toth, C.K., Ju, H., Grejner-Brzezinska, D.A.: Experiences with using SIFT for Mulitple Image Domain Matching. In: Proceedings of ASPRS Annual Conference, San Diego, CA, April 26-30, CD-ROM (2010)
18. Wolberg, G., Zokai, S.: Robust Image Registration using Log-Polar Transform. In: Proceedings 2000 International Conference on Image Processing, vol. 1, pp. 493–496 (2000)
19. Yi, Z., Cao, Z.G., Yang, X.: Multi-spectral remote image registration based on SIFT. Electronic Letter 44(2), 107–108 (2008)
20. Zokai, S., Wolberg, G.: Image Registration using Log-Polar Mappings for Recovery of Large-Scale Similarity and Projective Transformations. IEEE Transactions On Image Processing 14(10), 1422–1434 (2005)

Reliable Image Matching with Recursive Tiling

David Novák, Emmanuel Baltsavias, and Konrad Schindler

Institute of Geodesy and Photogrammetry, ETH Zürich, 8093 Zürich, Switzerland

Abstract. This paper presents a method to improve the robustness of automated correspondences while also increasing the total amount of measured points and improving the point distribution. This is achieved by incorporating a tiling technique into existing automated interest point extraction and matching algorithms. The technique allows memory intensive interest point extractors like SIFT to use large images beyond 10 megapixels while also making it possible to approximately compensate for perspective differences and thus get matches in places where normal techniques usually do not get any, few, or false ones. The experiments in this paper show an increased amount as well as a more homogeneous distribution of matches compared to standard procedures.

Keywords: Matching, Processing, Orientation, Reconstruction.

1 Introduction

In the past decade several techniques have been introduced for automatic interest point detection and matching over wide baselines (i.e. large changes in viewing direction and/or scale). Blob detectors such as SIFT (Lowe [2004]) and SURF (Bay et al. [2008]) or multi-scale corner detectors like Harris-Affine (Mikolajczyk et al. [2002]) are used to extract feature points, and descriptors of their local neighbourhoods are attached to these points. The descriptors are then used to establish correspondence across views, usually with variants of (approximate) nearest neighbour matching (Lowe [2004]).

Detectors and descriptors are designed to be invariant to moderate changes in scale, rotation, and even affinity. This strategy has been very successful for low-resolution tasks like image retrieval (Csurka et al. [2004]) and low-accuracy image orientation (Snavely et al. [2006]). However in high-accuracy applications such as photogrammetric surveying and industrial metrology it still has important limitations. In such applications one is interested in matching thousands of points in very high resolution images – typically 10-50 megapixels – and in convergent network geometry. However, under serious distortions (especially large scale difference) standard methods at best find a handful of correct matches. A further classic problem of wide-baseline methods is that repetitive textures are easily mismatched. This tendency is amplified by invariant descriptors, which suppress subtle differences between repetitive elements.

To the best of our knowledge few attempts have been made to remedy the problem of inaccurate automated orientation of images. (Barazzetti et al. [2010])

U. Stilla et al. (Eds.): PIA 2011, LNCS 6952, pp. 49–60, 2011.

have shown that it is possible to improve the accuracy of current computer vision implementations by introducing robustness via photogrammetric methods, yielding satisfying results.

An obvious strategy to overcome the mentioned difficulties is to match iteratively, i.e. find a few correct correspondences with a highly robust estimator such as RANSAC, estimate the relative orientation, then match again under a loosely enforced epipolar constraint, update the orientation, and so forth. However this strategy is computationally costly because of the large amount of samples required to reliably and repeatedly estimate and refine the relative orientation in the presence of many outliers. In addition many incorrect matches are generated, only to be discarded again. Furthermore, it is possible that the relative orientation does not yield a correct solution thus creating false epipolar lines. Finally, epipolar rectification does not help to remove foreshortening along the epipolar lines, which can still impair matching.

Therefore, a hierarchical matching strategy is proposed in order to overcome limitations of wide-baseline matching and make it more usable for practical photogrammetry with high resolution images. This discussion is limited to the two-view case, and the two images are called the *source* and *target* image. Instead of directly estimating the relative orientation, the target image is recursively split into tiles. For each tile only a small number of very reliable matches are found with a restrictive nearest neighbour threshold. Then the tiles are warped with individually estimated projective transformation matrices (homographies) to better match the source image. After warping, each tile is split into four tiles again. As the tiles get smaller, the observed 3D structure on average deviates less and less from a planar patch, such that the homography becomes an ever better local approximation of the perspective distortion.

The tiling is more global than affine-invariant interest-point detection, since it operates in a top-down fashion and estimates the image distortion for larger neighbourhoods, while at the same time being more local than global geometric verification, which uses the matches from the entire image. As a side effect, the split into local tiles also circumvents the problem of matching the many thousands of points found in a high-resolution image in one step, which requires more memory than is typically available even on modern workstations.

The number of reliable matches increases as the tiles become smaller, because of the diminishing perspective distortion, and also because of the reduction of similar points from repetitive texture, which are then not found in the same tile any more. This yields a larger set of correspondences as well as a reduced amount of outliers. The algorithm has been implemented in a C++ program called "Gummireifen" (German for "rubber tyre"). Experimental results on several datasets show a consistent improvement in matching performance compared to conventional wide-baseline matching, with an average increase of $2 - 3 \times$ more matches. In addition a correctness of 95% or better can be achieved on average before any relative orientation is applied. With additional crude relative orientation the correctness of the matches rises above 98%, while the number of matches diminishes by less than 10%.

2   Tiling

2.1   In a Nutshell

The method can be explained intuitively by considering the observed 3D surface. If a digital surface model and the camera orientations were available, one could project the target image onto the surface and render it from the viewpoint of the source image, then the resulting synthetic image should perfectly match the source image pixel by pixel up to radiometric differences.

In the absence of the surface model, one can replace it with a projective transformation which is estimated from four point correspondences. Since the planar approximation of the surface induces distortions, it is integrated into a multi-level partition of local tiles, which each have their own projective transformation matrix. In this way, each tile of the target image at the lowest level is almost in correspondence with the source image and thus matching is more reliable. The tiling and approximate local projective transformation per tile limit the search space for matching, which avoids many false matches. It improves matching robustness by reducing the perspective distortion of objects and reduces memory usage since each tile can be processed separately. Furthermore, it yields approximate camera positions for 3D point triangulation and iterative relative orientation, from the projectivity estimated at the highest level.

2.2   Details

The images for the tiling approach are automatically preprocessed with a Wallis filter (Wallis [1976]) for contrast enhancement. The next steps do not differ from standard wide-baseline matching: SIFT interest points are extracted independently in the two images, and matched with nearest-neighbour search and a nearest-neighbour threshold of 0.5. With the detected correspondences, a homography from the target to the source image is estimated with RANSAC [Fischler and Bolles, 1981]. Note that homography fitting is more efficient and also considerably more reliable than directly estimating the relative orientation. Not only does it require 4 correspondences instead of 5 (the minimal set exponentially influences the required number of samples), but more importantly the constraint has dimension 1 instead of 2 (i.e. the residuals are point-to-point distances, not point-to-line distances), such that incorrect fits are a lot less likely.

Next, the target image is warped with the homography thus obtained. Then the images are divided into four equal tiles. While for strongly non-planar surfaces the homography is only a rough approximation, it will nevertheless align the target image sufficiently well with the source image to ensure that the overwhelming majority of possible matches are between points in the same tile (e.g. the upper-left tiles of the source and target images contain approximately the same part of the 3D scene) as can be seen in Figure 1. In the next step, one can therefore repeat the procedure (interest point extraction / matching / homography estimation) for each tile independently, and then split each tile again into four sub-tiles, thereby generating a recursive grid of local projective

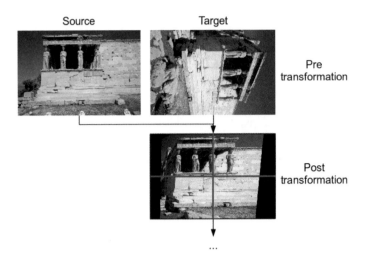

Fig. 1. The first tiling step of the procedure

alignments. The nearest-neighbour threshold is reduced to 0.4 to improve the overall correctness of the matches.

As the recursive tiling progresses, the projective alignment becomes a better approximation in most tiles, simply because the true object surface deviates less from a plane in a smaller neighbourhood (except at discontinuities). The natural stopping point would be when the 3D scene in one tile is perfectly planar, or tiles become so small that they no longer contain enough texture to find four good matches. This is obviously scene-dependent: scenes with large planes and/or large homogeneous areas will reach that point with bigger tiles. Empirically a final tile size of about 500 pixels has been determined to be sufficient for close-range photogrammetry applications, corresponding to 2 – 4 recursive splits. Note that at the lowest level it is not necessary to estimate homographies. For the last step a nearest neighbour threshold of 0.33 is chosen.

It turns out that after projective alignment the remaining distortions are so small that the matches can be verified with more discriminative, less invariant similarity measures, in order to further reduce the number of matching errors. First, all correspondences are tested with normalized cross-correlation and those with a correlation coefficient smaller than 0.5 are discarded. Finally, the image coordinates of the remaining correspondences are refined with least-squares matching (Grün [1985]) for further computations, and in the process those are discarded for which the matching does not converge, indicating that there is no reasonable affine transformation which optimally aligns the patches. Before this step is finished, duplicate matches as well as ambiguous ones (i.e. two points share the same coordinate in the source image but have a different coordinate in the target image) are being eliminated.

Only after the described image measurement stage we proceed to calculating the relative orientation. To start the orientation we exploit the projective transformation fitted in the previous step. The projectivity of the first tiling step indicates the rough position of the target image relative to the source image. The base vector between the source and target image can be found with

$$B_x = -x_0 - \frac{C_{11} \cdot x_0 + C_{12} \cdot y_0 + C_{13}}{C_{31} \cdot x_0 + C_{32} \cdot y_0 + C_{33}} , \tag{1}$$

$$B_y = 1 - \frac{A_{before}}{A_{after}} , \tag{2}$$

$$B_z = y_0 - \frac{C_{21} \cdot x_0 + C_{22} \cdot y_0 + C_{23}}{C_{31} \cdot x_0 + C_{32} \cdot y_0 + C_{33}} . \tag{3}$$

C_{nn} denotes the elements of the projective transformation matrix, x_0, y_0 denote the centre of the target image. A_{before}, A_{after} are the area of the target image before and after the transformation.

B_x, B_y and B_z correspond to the $[X, Y, Z]$ baseline of the target image relative to the source image (i.e. the camera centres are $[X, Y, Z]$ for the target and $[0, 0, 0]$ for the source). The angular values ω, ϕ and κ for the source and target image are initialized to $[\frac{\pi}{2}, 0, 0]$, such that they look into the same direction. With these starting values, iterative relative orientation based on the coplanarity condition (Mikhail et al. [2001]) is performed. To avoid problems with outliers, five matches are randomly chosen and a relative orientation is calculated as part of a RANSAC procedure. All image measurements that have a residual that is larger than five pixel are excluded. It is possible that the approximations for the base vector are not correct (wrong sign), which causes the model to be flipped along the X-axis. This can be avoided by checking the Y values of the model coordinates and correcting the sign accordingly.

3   Experiments

3.1   Experimental Set-Up

In all experiments the same SIFT and nearest neighbour library (Hess [2010]) has been used (as included in the Gummireifen package). The exception is the comparison to Bundler (Snavely et al. [2006]), where the nearest neighbour matching is done within the Bundler package.

Each dataset has been processed several times: The *standard* version is simple SIFT & nearest-neighbour matching with full resolution images. The nearest-neighbour threshold has been set to 0.33 and the image has been doubled in size (Lowe [2004]). The *standard-Wallis* version is the same as the *standard* version, except that it uses Wallis-filtered images as input. The *tiling-meas* version only applies the tiling algorithm without geometric verification by relative orientation, and without refinement by cross-correlation and least-squares matching. The *tiling-full* version applies all of the mentioned techniques above including a relative orientation for further outlier reduction. All tests have been performed on a 64-bit operating system thus allowing the normal SIFT procedure to use full resolution images. Each test shows the amount of matched points as well as the percentage of correct matches which have been investigated visually. Furthermore, a point distribution map shows the distribution of the points in one of the images for the *standard* and the *tiling-full* version. The point distribution map shows dark areas with less matched points and bright areas with more matched points. Furthermore a comparison has been done between Bundler, standard SIFT & nearest-neighbour matching and Gummireifen. All three versions generate image measurements which are imported into Bingo (Kruck [1984]) where relative orientation is computed with the RELAX (Kruck and Trippler [1995]) module and then bundle adjustment is performed in order to yield error statistics. The row with the number of points shows the amount of points going into the bundle adjustment (in) and the amount of points that were accepted (out). For Bundler, the matched points before its internal bundle adjustment procedure have been used as number of input points. The amount of output points is obtained after the internal bundle adjustment and processing with Bingo.

If a dataset is marked as *(calibrated)* it means that additional camera parameters have been used in the Gummireifen package to correct the lens distortion. In Bundler the additional parameters were omitted, since they cannot be introduced manually. The results are given in Tables 1 and 2, and discussed below in Section 4.

3.2   Relative Orientation Experiments

The relative orientation approximations, coming from the projectivity, are very helpful to ensure converging bundle adjustment. Experiments showed that more measurements do not necessarily mean that the possibility of multiple solutions in relative orientation is reduced. The approximations do help in this case to create a robust and correct relative orientation which can be later used in the bundle adjustment. One example of a two-image case is shown in figure 2. Standard relative orientation without approximations fails in RELAX. When the approximations for the orientation parameters and model coordinates are introduced from the Gummireifen package, the relative orientation is successful.

4   Discussion

The most obvious observation of the experiments is that except for the bread-basket dataset, the tiling approach achieves more matches than a standard procedure commonly used. Furthermore, the point distribution in the tiling approach is more homogeneous. If enough texture information is available in the images the tiling approach generates up to five times more matches in the overlap area than a standard procedure. The standard procedure delivers generally a lower number of correct matches and lower correctness than Gummireifen, even with a restrictive nearest-neighbour threshold.

Two datasets are particularly interesting: the *Sternwarte* dataset and the *bread basket* dataset. In case of the *Sternwarte* the standard procedure delivers a rather poor performance which comes from the high amount of repeated texture

Table 1. Matching and orientation results (part 1)

Sternwarte Zürich (calibrated)			# matched points	% correct
		standard	308	53.8
		standard-wallis	709	61.7
		tiling-meas	2199	95
		tiling-full	2049	99.8

standard	tiling-full	Bundle Adjustment Results		
			# of points (in/out)	RMSE x/y (μm/px)
		Standard	RO failed	RO failed
		Bundler	209 / 118	2.93 / 0.53
		Gummireifen	2049 / 1970	1.02 / 0.19

Octocopter over HXD (not calibrated)			# matched points	% correct
		standard	286	94.8
		standard-wallis	205	91.7
		tiling-meas	708	98.4
		tiling-full	688	100

standard	tiling-full	Bundle Adjustment Results		
			# of points (in/out)	RMSE x/y (μm/px)
		Standard	RO failed	RO failed
		Bundler	267 / 253	0.61 / 0.30
		Gummireifen	688 / 659	1.14 / 0.57

Bocca (calibrated)			# matched points	% correct
		standard	220	78.2
		standard-wallis	88	87.5
		tiling-meas	284	98.6
		tiling-full	279	100

standard	tiling-full	Bundle Adjustment Results		
			# of points (in/out)	RMSE x/y (μm/px)
		Standard	220 / 169	4.64 / 0.76
		Bundler	192 / 170	3.01 / 0.49
		Gummireifen	279 / 278	1.00 / 0.16

Table 2. Matching and orientation results (part 2)

Erechtheion (not calibrated)			# matched points	% correct
		standard	703	91.9
		standard-wallis	662	92.1
		tiling-meas	3100	98.5
		tiling-full	3028	100

standard	tiling-full	Bundle Adjustment Results		
			# of points (in/out)	RMSE x/y (μm/px)
		Standard	703 / 635	8.98 / 1.10
		Bundler	669 / 593	5.38 / 0.66
		Gummireifen	3028 / 3006	9.26 / 1.13

Pontresina bread basket (not calibrated)			# matched points	% correct
		standard	134	82.1
		standard-wallis	130	82.3
		tiling-meas	123	83.7
		tiling-full	107	96.3

standard	tiling-full	Bundle Adjustment Results		
			# of points (in/out)	RMSE x/y (μm/px)
		Standard	134 / 97	0.8 / 0.24
		Bundler	110 / 90	1.20 / 0.35
		Gummireifen	107 / 106	2.21 / 0.65

and a convergence angle of roughly 30°. A lot of interest points have been placed on similar looking object features which are matched incorrectly. The tiling keeps this under control.

The bread basket dataset is shown as a failure case and in which the projective transformation is estimated inaccurately. In this case, a lot of points have been found in two small areas. The transformation only fits well to these areas but does not extrapolate well, such that the remainder of the image is warped incorrectly. This in turn means that the tiles no longer represent the same area of the object and that few matches with poor distribution are found. Furthermore, the dataset itself has the problem that the depth-to-distance ratio of the scene is very large.

The use of the Wallis filter seems to be generally beneficial as recommended in (Baltsavias [1991]) but it is not fully consistent as can be seen in the *Octocopter* dataset where there is a higher amount of correct matches without the Wallis

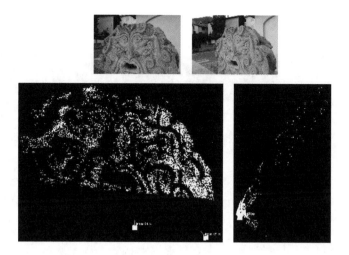

Fig. 2. *(left)* successful relative orientation; *right)* failed relative orientation

filter. This is most likely caused by the noise and the vegetation, found in the dark areas of this dataset. The Wallis filter enhances contrast especially in dark areas and the repetitive texture of trees and grass cause matching errors. Generally though it seems to be at least similar to the non-Wallis-filtered case with some cases clearly indicating an improvement.

The bundle adjustment results of Gummireifen might seem to contradict the claims of the paper because the *Octocopter, bread basket* and *Erechtheion* datasets deliver higher RMSE than Bundler even though there is a very high correctness of the matches. This is caused by the fact that Bundler discards a lot of points near the border of the images, either because the feature extraction did not extract anything or because Bundler did discard them during its built-in outlier rejection. The accuracy in these areas is naturally lower due to an increased influence of the radial distortion and poor ray intersection – all three datasets were adjusted without calibration parameters. Figure 3 illustrates this problem for the Erechtheion dataset. The confidence ellipsoids for the porch of the Caryatids in the foreground are roughly the same in both procedures. However the error ellipsoids on the back wall are rather large and only show up in the Gummireifen case – since these points are situated near the border of the image, they get influenced more by the radial distortion, leading to a higher RMSE value. The same happens in the *Octocopter* dataset where points far away from the house are obtained with Gummireifen and used in the adjustment while Bundler only keeps points near the centre of the image, resulting in lower RMSE in spite of a solution, which is less accurate near the image borders.

The fact that the standard case in the Erechtheion dataset delivers slightly better results than Gummireifen stems from the fact that fewer points have been found on the back wall, again thus reducing the influence of the radial distortion and the RMSE. The standard version fails to perform relative orientation in two cases. For the Sternwarte it is easily explainable since there is no pre-processing

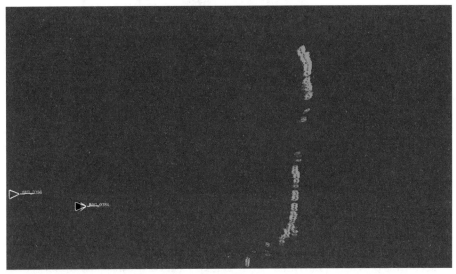

Bundler

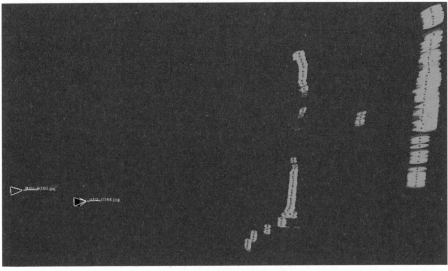

Gummireifen

Fig. 3. Reconstructed 3D points for Bundler and Gummireifen (cameras are on the left). Note the aditional points only recovered by Gummireifen (on the right, with larger confidence ellipsoids).

done thus the outlier rate of over 40% causes RELAX to fail. In the Octocopter case the small baseline causes a flip of the camera positions and the relative orientation fails as well.

The main drawback of the tiling technique is speed. Usually it takes about three times longer to measure points than the standard case. If cross-correlation and least-squares matching as well as relative orientation are included, the processing takes up to five times longer than that of the standard procedure.

5   Conclusion and Outlook

The experiments show that the tiling approach creates more matches with higher correctness than a standard procedure. However, a price has to be paid for the increased density and correctness, hence it is less suitable for time-critical applications.

Further improvements can be made to increase robustness. One of them would be to adjust the tile size/shape adaptively, depending on the point distribution and image content. Furthermore, a non-linear warping function instead of the projective transformation might in certain situations work even better.

As has been shown in (Barazzetti et al. [2010]) it is possible to improve the image measurements to produce results that do not have an error of loop closure as seen in Bundler. Error of loop closure is a common problem in structure from motion software when walking around a building or recording the walls of a plaza. Further investigations will be done to see, if the technique proposed in this paper can achieve similar results. Once the software can handle multiple images it will be interesting to compare the accuracy to existing packages. It is expected that the overall more homogeneous point distribution and the approximations for the relative orientation will allow for a robust and accurate orientation.

Acknowledgements. I'd like to thank Luigi Barazzetti from the Politecnico Milano for allowing me to use the Bocca dataset. I'd also like to thank everyone else.

References

Baltsavias, E.P.: Multiphoto geometrically constrained matching, Ph.D. Dissertation, Institute of Geodesy and Photogrammetry, ETH Zrich, Mitteilungen No. 49 (1991)

Barazzetti, L., Scaioni, M., Remondino, F.: Orientation And 3D Modelling From Markerless Terrestrial Images: Combining Accuracy With Automation. The Photogrammetric Record 24(132), 356–381 (2010)

Bay, H., Ess, A., Tuytelaars, T., Van Gool, L.: SURF: Speeded Up Robust Features. Computer Vision and Image Understanding 110(3), 346–359 (2008)

Csurka, G., Dance, C.R., Fan, L., Willamowski, J., Bray, C.: Visual categorization with bags of keypoints. In: Proceedings in Workshop on Statistical Learning in Computer Vision, ECCV, pp. 1–22 (2004)

Fischler, M.A., Bolles, C.R.: Random Sample Consensus: A Paradigm for Model Fitting with Applications to Image Analysis and Automated Cartography. Comm. of the ACM 24, 381–395 (1981)

Grün, A.W.: Adaptive Least Squares Correlation: A Powerful Image Matching Technique. South African Journal of Photogrammetry, Remote Sensing and Cartography 14, 175–187 (1985)

Hess, R.: An Open Source SIFT Library. In: Proceedings ACM Multimedia, MM (2010)

Kruck, E.: BINGO: A Program for Bundle Adjustment for Engineering Applications – Possibilities, Facilities and Practical Results. International Archives of Photogrammetry and Remote Sensing, Comm. V XXV(A5), 471–480 (1984)

Kruck, E., Trippler, S.: Automatic Computation of Initial Approximations for Bundle Block Adjustment with Program RELAX. In: Optical 3-D Measurement Techniques III, Vienna, October 2-4 (1995)

Lowe, D.G.: Distinctive image features from scale-invariant keypoints. International Journal of Computer Vision 60(2), 91–110 (2004)

Mikhail, E.M., Bethel, J.S., McGlone, J.C.: Introduction to Modern Photogrammetry. John Wiley & Sons, New York (2001)

Mikolajczyk, K., Schmid, C.: An affine invariant interest point detector. In: Heyden, A., Sparr, G., Nielsen, M., Johansen, P. (eds.) ECCV 2002. LNCS, vol. 2350, pp. 128–142. Springer, Heidelberg (2002)

Schaffalitzky, F., Zisserman, A.: Automated Location matching in movies. Computer Vision and Image Understanding 92(2), 236–264 (2003)

Snavely, N., Seitz, S.M., Szeliski, R.: Photo Tourism: Exploring image collections in 3D. ACM Transactions on Graphics (Proceedings of SIGGRAPH 2006)

Wallis, R.: An approach to the space variant restoration and enhancement of images. In: Proceedings of Symposium on Current Mathematical Problems in Image Science, pp. 329–340 (1976)

In-Strip Matching and Reconstruction of Line Segments from UHR Aerial Image Triplets

Ali Özgün Ok[1], Jan Dirk Wegner[2], Christian Heipke[2],
Franz Rottensteiner[2], Uwe Soergel[2], and Vedat Toprak[1]

[1] Dept. of Geodetic and Geographic Information Tech.,
Middle East Technical University, 06531 Ankara, Turkey
{oozgun,toprak}@metu.edu.tr
[2] Institute of Photogrammetry and Geoinformation,
University of Hannover, 30167 Hannover, Germany
{wegner,heipke,rottensteiner,soergel}@ipi.uni-hannover.de

Abstract. In this study, we propose a new line matching and reconstruction methodology for aerial image triplets that are acquired within a single strip. The newly developed stereo reconstruction approach gives us better line predictions in the third image which in turn helps to improve the performance of the matching. The redundancy information generated in each stereo match gives us ability to reduce the number of false matches while preserving high levels of matching completeness. The approach is tested over four test patches and produced highly promising line matching and reconstruction results.

Keywords: Three-View Matching, In-strip Line Matching, Reconstruction, Aerial Images, Pair-wise Matching.

1 Introduction and Motivation

The matching and reconstruction of the line segments in ultra-high-resolution (UHR) stereo aerial images is a very challenging task for various reasons, e.g. a substantial change in viewpoints, inconsistency of line endpoint locations, lack of rich textures in line local neighbourhood, repetitive patterns, etc. A significant number of research papers have been published (Schmid and Zisserman, 1997; Baillard and Dissard, 2000; Scholze et al., 2000; Zhang and Baltsavias, 2000; Suveg and Vosselman, 2004; Wang et al., 2009; Ok et al., 2010a, b); however, in a stereo environment, the ambiguity problem of line matching is an issue that remains unsolved. The general attempt to reduce the ambiguity problem is to strengthen the geometrical constraint by integrating additional view(s) to the matching stage (Roux and McKeown, 1994; Bignone et al., 1996; Schmid and Zisserman, 1997; Collins et al., 1998; Henricsson, 1998; Moons et al., 1998; Baillard et al., 1999; Scholze, 2000; Heuel and Förstner, 2001; Noronha and Nevatia, 2001; Jung et al., 2002; Elaksher et al., 2003; Jung and Paparoditis, 2003; Kim and Nevatia, 2004; Taillandier and Deriche, 2004; Zhang, 2005; Xiao et al., 2010). Although most of these multi-view approaches are capable of integrating any number of images, the common trend followed by many of the researchers is to utilize at least 4 images, of which at least one is from another strip

U. Stilla et al. (Eds.): PIA 2011, LNCS 6952, pp. 61–72, 2011.
© Springer-Verlag Berlin Heidelberg 2011

than the rest; thus, the problem of nearly collinear image perspective centers is solved and better intersection angles of the projection planes are guaranteed. On the other hand, utilizing additional images in the cross-strip direction leads to new problems in matching. Since those images are acquired in adjacent strips, there is a time delay between those images, which causes a difference in the illumination; thus, the moving shadow phenomenon occurs. As a result, the overall geometric quality of the final reconstruction is negatively affected (Haala, 2009). Moreover, from an economical point of view, any increase of side-overlap during image acquisition results in longer flight times and increases costs. Therefore, from an operational perspective, the number of strips must be minimized. For those reasons, the matching and reconstruction of line segments from aerial images acquired in a single strip has a major importance. This paper focuses on this vivid field of research.

To our knowledge, four research studies investigated line matching in terms of three-view aerial imagery. Noronha and Nevatia (2001) developed a line matching approach to guide the detection and modeling of the buildings. However, the images utilized include nadir as well as oblique views, acquired at different times of a day or on different days in a year. Zhang (2005) developed a line matching approach for UHR linear array images for the automated generation of DSMs. In his work, a-priori matched point features are integrated into the line matching stage to reduce the matching ambiguities. As the pushbroom geometry is characterized by nearly parallel projection in flight direction, the relief distortion of the line segments observed is greatly reduced during matching. Schmid and Zisserman (1997) proposed a line matching algorithm which utilized direct and warped correlation measures computed around the line neighbourhoods. Later, their algorithm is extended to multiple views by Baillard et al. (1999). First, they collect line matches in image triples from a single strip. Next, the matches are verified in images from adjacent strip(s). Both methods described in Schmid and Zisserman (1997) and Baillard et al. (1999) revealed good performance (around 98%) for matching lines in three views, but the performance of the approaches is only given for the cases in which the line segments are not (nearly) aligned with the epipolar line.

To summarize, matching lines over images acquired in a single strip presents a fundamental advantage in terms of image photometric characteristics, but the geometry of the images suffers from the collinearity of the perspective center coordinates (epipolar alignment problem). In this context, almost all the previous work related with line matching relies on various descriptors specialized for one to one line matching in which the relations between the line features are not handled effectively. However, for the images acquired in a single strip, the integration of those line relations during matching exposes new constraints and further possibilities to improve the quality and the performance of the matching. In a recent work, we presented a novel approach for the pair-wise matching of line features for stereo aerial images (Ok et al., 2010a), which was further improved in order to deal with repetitive linear patterns in (Ok et al., 2010b). In this paper, we propose a new in-strip multi-stereo approach in which the third image is fully integrated to the matching. Thanks to a new height estimation method which also relies on line to line relations developed in the pair-wise approach, we can reconstruct and predict the position of a stereo line match in the third image even if the matched lines are nearly parallel ($< 10°$) to the epipolar line.

2 Matching and Reconstruction of Line Segments

2.1 Line Extraction and Pair-Wise Stereo Line Matching

For the matching of line features, we have proposed a new relational approach in which the line correspondences between stereo aerial images are established by considering line pairs in both images. In this paper, we only briefly summarize the pair-wise matching algorithm. The interested reader is referred to (Ok et al., 2010a, b) for further details. The algorithm consists of three fundamental steps: (i) 2D line extraction, (ii) stereo matching of the extracted lines with a pair-wise relation approach, and (iii) final iterative pair-based post-processing.

In the first step, in order to maximize the performance of the line detection, existing multispectral information in aerial images is fully utilized throughout the steps of pre-processing and edge detection. To accurately describe the straight edge segments, a principal component analysis technique is adapted and the extracted segments are converted to their line counterparts using orthogonal regression. In addition, during the raster to vector conversion, we also allowed the curved structures to be approximated by their piecewise linear representations. In the second step, to establish the pair-wise line correspondences between the stereo images, a new pair-wise stereo line matching approach is utilized. The developed approach initially generates reference line pairs in the base image and collects all potential matching candidate pairs from the search image with the aid of a-priori known image to image geometry. Next, the number of matching candidate pairs of each line pair in the base image is significantly reduced after imposing a weighted pair-wise matching similarity score computed over a total of eight pair-wise constraints (an epipolar, three geometric, two photometric, a correlation and a spatiogram constraint). In the last step, an iterative pair-based post-processing algorithm is applied. For each line in the base image, the best corresponding line in the search image is assigned after an iterative final disambiguation process in which the matching inconsistencies are further eliminated using nearest/next distance ratios and a final similarity voting scheme. At this step, the line to line relations are fully taken into account by imposing new measures, such as line local matching support.

2.2 Stereo Line Reconstruction

It is well-known that the reconstruction of straight lines which are nearly parallel to the epipolar line is almost impossible within a stereo image pair or a single image strip (Zhang, 2005). For that reason, Zhang (2005) proposed an alternative way which relies on free-form line structures generated from multiple line segments. However, the difficulty with the free-form structures is that the problematic line(s) must have an edge connection with the other neighbouring lines, which is rarely the case for most of the line segments. Therefore, we presented a stereo reconstruction approach relying on the line-to-line relations used in the pair-wise approach. Using this method, we can reconstruct those problematic line segments without using such an edge connectivity assumption. Here we briefly review the approach; more details can be found in (Ok et al., 2011).

The reconstruction process starts with a test which determines the angle difference ($0 - 90°$) between the line segments and the related epipolar line. Based on our experience, line segments having angle differences of less than $10°$ are highly susceptible to produce inaccurate reconstruction results. The reconstruction of line segments having angle differences larger than $10°$ is performed by intersecting the projection planes (Fig. 1a), $\mathbf{A}^1(l_1)$ and $\mathbf{A}^2(l_2)$, with the method of direct construction as introduced in Heuel and Förstner (2001) and Heuel (2001).

The approach for the reconstruction of line segments that are nearly aligned ($\leq 10°$) with the epipolar line is to manipulate the redundancy (Ok et al., 2010b) inherent in pair-relations to generate artificial 3D point entities ($\mathbf{X}_i$) and utilize those points during the estimation process. In this way, the neighbouring line segments that have a pair-connection with the problematic segment contribute to the height estimation (Fig. 1b). As can be seen in Fig. 1b, since the two projection planes are nearly-parallel, the intersecting 3D line in object space is not reliable. However, with the aid of artificial point entities ($\mathbf{X}_1$, $\mathbf{X}_2$ and $\mathbf{X}_3$), the 3D line can be accurately reconstructed. It is important to state that the reconstruction cannot be performed in a single framework, since all 2D intersection points generated in image space lie exactly on the problematic line segments; thus they also belong to the projection plane. Therefore, each artificial 3D point entity ($\mathbf{X}_i$) must be generated beforehand, and the final estimation should be jointly performed along with the related projection planes ($\mathbf{A}_i$).

For the estimation procedure, we parameterize the 3D lines in Plücker representation $\boldsymbol{L}^T = (\boldsymbol{L}_h^T, \boldsymbol{L}_0^T) = (L_1, L_2, L_3; L_4, L_5, L_6)$ and utilize an iterative linear Gauss-Markoff model with constraints. The algebraic expressions of the form $\mathbf{g}_i(\beta; \gamma_i) = \mathbf{0}$ with respect to all possible observation and unknown entities are developed and explicitly given in Förstner et al. (2000) and Heuel and Förstner (2001). In our case, we search for an unknown line $\mathbf{M}$ which must lie in two planes; thus, $\mathbf{g}_1(\mathbf{M}; \mathbf{A}_i) = \Pi^T(\mathbf{A}_i)\mathbf{M} = \mathbf{0}$, where Π is the homogeneous matrix representation of planes $\mathbf{A}_i$ (Heuel, 2001). In addition to the projection planes, the unknown line should also contain artificial 3D point entities ($\mathbf{X}_i$) generated from the neighbouring line segments and thus must satisfy $\mathbf{g}_2(\mathbf{M}; \mathbf{X}_i) = \overline{\Pi}^T(\mathbf{X}_i)\mathbf{M} = \mathbf{0}$, where $\overline{\Pi}$ is the

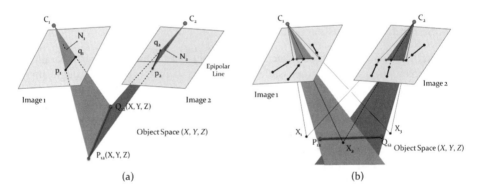

Fig. 1. The reconstruction of the line segments (a) that are not aligned with the epipolar line, and (b) that are nearly-aligned with the epipolar line

homogeneous matrix form of points X_i (Heuel, 2001). However, at this stage we do not exactly know whether the two lines in a pair really intersect on the Earth surface or not. Therefore, before the estimation process, we compute weights for each 3D point entity generated. These weights depend on three measures computed in a pair-wise manner: minimum 2D Euclidean distance (d_{ij}) between two lines $(l_i$ and $l_j)$, the minimum angle (θ_{ij}) enclosed by line segments l_i and l_j, and the minimum orthogonal distance (d_{ij}^e) between the intersection points and related epipolar lines (l_{epi}). In principle, reliability of a point increases if both the distances d_{ij} and d_{ij}^e are relatively short, and it decreases if the intersection angle is quite narrow (e.g. $< 10°$). Therefore, we designed the new cumulative weight function (W_{ij}) as:

$$W_{ij} = t_{ij} \cdot e^{-\left(\frac{\sigma_2 d_{ij} + \sigma_1 d_{ij}^e}{2\sigma_1\sigma_2}\right)}$$

$$t_{ij} = \begin{cases} 0 & \text{if } \theta_{ij} \leq 10° \\ 1 & \text{if } \theta_{ij} > 10° \end{cases}$$

(1)

where the parameters σ_1 and σ_2 control the weighting for metrics d_{ij} and d_{ij}^e, respectively.

For each nearly-aligned matching case ($\leq 10°$), the existing 3D point entities (X_i) are collected and their weights (W_{ij}) are automatically determined using Eq. (1). However, it is not logical to integrate all observed point entities directly to the estimation process, since some of those points may be generated from wrong matches. Therefore, among the available point entities, only the points that have the highest weights are integrated to the estimation process along with the observed projection planes. For the estimation, we form the plane-line (g_1) and point-line (g_2) incidence relations in 3D space and perform an iterative linear Gauss-Markoff model with constraints. For each 3D line (L_i), we have 6 unknowns and 2 constraints (the Plücker constraint and length). The required initial values can be taken from the SVD solution and the covariance matrices of the estimated 3D line entities can be computed from the inverted normal equation matrix of the Gauss-Markoff model.

2.3 Three-View In-Strip Matching

In this paper, we propose a new in-strip multi-stereo approach in which the third image is fully integrated to the line matching. The proposed approach is summarized in Fig. 2. The matching starts with multi-stereo processing in which we only use pairs of adjacent images (images #1-2 & #2-3). For those image pairs, we independently perform the pair-wise line matching (cf. section 2.1). Since the selected image pairs have the shortest baselines among all possible image pairs, the computed pair-based relations (geometric, photometric etc.) reveal the highest possible similarities during pair-wise line matching. In the next step, we automatically infer triple matching combinations from the stereo matches #1-2 and #2-3 based on the fact that the lines extracted in image #2 are common for both stereo matches. The triple combinations are tested based on their re-projection errors (Baillard et al., 1999) computed over three images. As a result, the verified triple combinations are directly added to the final matching list. On the other hand, triple combinations that could not be verified are split and restored into their stereo matching sets for further verification. The matches that are only visible in two images are verified in a way similar to Schmid and Zisserman (1997) and Baillard et al. (1999). First, the 3D lines are hypothesized using stereo reconstruction (as described in section 2.2) and the expected locations of those lines are found in the third image. The verification starts with a geometric test in which we search for line segments at the predicted location. If such segments are found, we further check the photometric similarity of the line local neighbourhoods using the (un-corrected) correlation scores. If the photometric test is also passed, the stereo match is accepted as a triple match along with the lines found in the predicted location. On the other hand, if the geometric test is not passed, the stereo match can also be verified using the photometric similarity computed at the predicted location with the same neighbourhood correlation strategy.

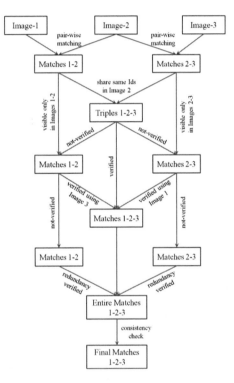

Fig. 2. Proposed three-view in-strip matching

In general, this "predict and verify" strategy has two major limitations. The first limitation occurs due to the epipolar geometry of in-strip acquisition: the success of the verification stage depends on the prediction step, which relies on the precision of the reconstructed line in stereo geometry. Thus, it is almost impossible to verify line segments that are nearly parallel to the epipolar line. However, the estimation method proposed in section 2.2 allows us to reconstruct and predict the location of a stereo line match in the third image even if the matched lines are nearly parallel ($< 10°$) to the epipolar line (Fig. 3). The second limitation is also critical: some of the correct stereo matches could be lost during the verification stage due to the (self-) occlusion problem (Fig. 4). As can be seen in Fig. 4, although the stereo matches found on images (b) and (c) are correct, the predicted locations on image (a) are occluded by the building itself. Thus, the correlation scores computed for those matches have no reason to exceed the pre-defined threshold. To overcome this limitation, we propose to utilize the new redundancy measure proposed in (Ok et al., 2010b). The redundancy measure provides a possibility to integrate local matching support for those lines. Thus, only the stereo matches that have sufficient matching support are regarded as correct matches and the ones that have weak correlation and redundancy values are eliminated from the matching list. The final matches are formed after a consistency check between the triple and stereo matches, in which we remove the matching inconsistencies from the stereo matches based on the fact that most of our triple matches are directly generated after combining the results of the two independent pair-wise matches. The final end-points of a 3D line segment in object space are determined by the longest line segment available for each match in the final matching list. Thus, if a short line segment in one image is matched to a longer line segment in the other image, the final end-points are based on the longest line segment observed.

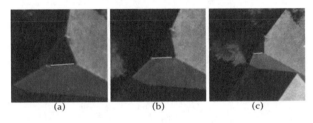

(a)   (b)   (c)

Fig. 3. A (nearly) aligned (< 1°) stereo line match on images (a - b), and its accurately predicted line position on image (c)

(a)   (b)   (c)

Fig. 4. One of the limitations of "predict and verify" strategy. The line matches are found on images (b - c), and their predicted positions are occluded on image (a).

3 Test Sites and Results

Our test patches are chosen from two different test fields selected over Germany (Fig. 5). The first test field belongs to the city of Vaihingen (Cramer, 2010) and the second test field is located in Aalen. For those test fields, image triplets were acquired by the

DMC digital camera with 70% forward overlaps. The focal length of the camera was 120 mm and the flying heights for the test fields were approximately 800 m above ground, which corresponds to ground sampling distances (GSD) of approximately 8 cm. During the experiments, for all test patches, we applied a 50 m ($\approx$ 162 pixels) search range difference along the epipolar lines. We also compared the results of our approach with the results of the three-view approach presented in Baillard et al. (1999). The approach was originally developed by Schmid and Zisserman (1997) and the related MatLab toolbox can be found in Werner and Zisserman (2002). In this study, we further adapted the original toolbox to deal with the photometric verification as described in Baillard et al. (1999). We also investigated the approach with and without epipolar ordering constraint (Werner, 2002) in order to fully expose the matching limits of their approach. To perform a meaningful comparison, for both

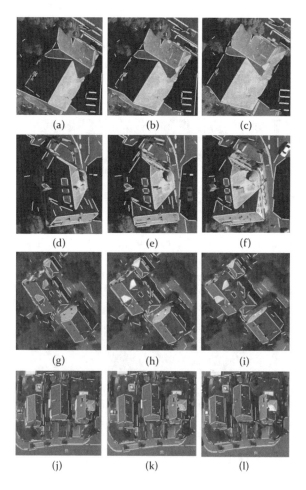

Fig. 5. The selected test patches from Vaihingen (a-f) and Aalen (g-l). The line matches found are illustrated in white color.

approaches, we utilized the same straight lines extracted by the method proposed in (Ok et al., 2010a). During the tests, the number of correct and false line matches was determined manually. In order to assess and compare the quality of the approaches, we further manually analyzed the number of matches missed by the approaches; thus, the comparative results in terms of the correctness and the completeness levels (Rutzinger et al., 2009) for each test patch are also provided (Table 1).

Based on the results given in Table 1, for all test patches, ours and Baillard's approach achieved very similar correctness levels (97% - 99%). However, the improvement observed after imposing the constraint of epipolar ordering is very clear; all test patches revealed consistently 99% correctness levels, which means only a few (1-2) wrong line matches are left after matching. However, it is also noteworthy that the ordering constraint has a critical drawback that some lines belonging to thin objects (mostly details of buildings) will be lost. Therefore, although it is rarely seen in the selected test patches in this study, the constraint also tends to eliminate some of the correct matches while eliminating the wrong ones. If we take into account the completeness values computed for the approaches, once again, our approach revealed a very high rate of completeness values ranging between 90% and 98%. However, Baillard's approach reached a maximum completeness value of 69% with a minimum of 59%. Obviously, our approach can provide an improvement of more than 30% in terms of the matching completeness while preserving the same level of correctness. This is due to limitations of "predict and verify" strategy mentioned in section 2.3; our approach can better preserve the matches by taking into account the redundancy measure both in the reconstruction and matching stages. It is also clear from those results that the epipolar ordering constraint had no negative effect on the matching completeness; thus, as an additional improvement, the ordering constraint can also be applied to our approach to further reduce the number of false matches.

For the Vaihingen data set, the accuracy of the reconstructed lines could be evaluated by comparing them to LIDAR data. The LIDAR data of the test site were captured with a Leica ALS50 system with an accuracy of 3.3 cm (Haala et al., 2010). In order to compare the reconstructed lines, we automatically extracted 3D planes from the point cloud in the vicinity of each line. Depending on the type of the line, this plane reconstruction process resulted in one plane if the line

Table 1. Comparison of the Correctness (Corr.) and Completeness (Comp.) levels computed

Patch Id	Baillard et al. (1999)		Baillard et al. (1999) + Epi. Ordering		Proposed	
	Corr.	Comp.	Corr.	Comp.	Corr.	Comp.
1	99%	64%	99%	64%	99%	98%
2	97%	62%	99%	63%	97%	90%
3	98%	69%	99%	69%	99%	94%
4	98%	59%	99%	59%	98%	95%

Table 2. Comparison of the RMS distances. The numbers in brackets show the total number of planes observed.

Patch Id	RMS Average Distance (m)	
	Proposed	Baillard et al. (1999) + Epi. Ordering
1	0.174 (195)	0.184 (142)
2	0.156 (158)	0.163 (118)

corresponded to a step edge and in two planes if the line corresponded to the intersection of two planes. Thereafter, we determined the line's average orthogonal distance from its neighbouring planes and used these distances to compute the RMS average distance between the reconstructed lines and the LIDAR planes. The results for the first two patches are given in Table 2. During the reconstruction, for our approach, the reconstruction of the matching triples that are nearly aligned with the epipolar line is performed with the method proposed in section 2.2, but in this case, the best artificial point entities are selected from both stereo matches and integrated along with three projection planes. The results in Table 2 demonstrate that our approach provides slight RMS improvements compared to the approach of Baillard et al. (1999). However, a crucial point of those results is that we can reach the same levels of reconstruction performances despite the fact that some of stereo and/or triples matches in our approach are nearly aligned with the epipolar line.

4 Conclusions

In this paper, we have proposed a new line matching and reconstruction methodology for aerial image triplets that are acquired within a single strip. Our three-view matching approach fully utilizes the line-to-line relations developed in the pair-wise approach to improve the quality of the matching and reconstruction of the image triplets. The newly developed stereo reconstruction approach gives us better line predictions in the third image which in turn helps to improve the performance of the verification step. The redundancy information generated in each stereo match gives us ability to reduce the number of false matches while preserving high matching completeness levels. We tested our approach over four test patches from two German sites, and based on the results, the proposed approach produced highly promising line matching and reconstruction results. The approach is flexible and can also be utilized during the in-strip line matching of aerial images (N > 3) that are acquired with 80% or more forward overlaps.

Acknowledgments. The Vaihingen data set was provided by the German Society for Photogrammetry, Remote Sensing and Geoinformation (DGPF) (Cramer, 2010): http://www.ifp.uni-stuttgart.de/dgpf/DKEP-Allg.html (in German). The Aalen dataset was provided by the Intergraph Deutschland GmbH, and the authors would like to thank Ömer KAYA for providing the Aalen aerial images.

References

Baillard, C., Schmid, C., Zisserman, A., Fitzgibbon, A.: Automatic line matching and 3D reconstruction of buildings from multiple views. In: ISPRS Conference on Automatic Extraction of GIS Objects from Digital Imagery, IAPRS, vol. 32, pp. 69–80 (1999)

Bailard, C., Dissard, O.: A Stereo Matching Algorithm for Urban Digital Elevation Models. Photogrammetric Engineering and Remote Sensing 66(9), 1119–1128 (2000)

Bignone, F., Henricsson, O., Fua, P., Stricker, M.: Automatic Extraction of Generic House Roofs from High Resolution Aerial Imagery. In: Buxton, B.F., Cipolla, R. (eds.) ECCV 1996. LNCS, vol. 1065, pp. 85–96. Springer, Heidelberg (1996)

Collins, R.T., Jaynes, C.O., Cheng, Y.Q., Wang, X., Stolle, F., Riseman, E.M., Hanson, A.R.: The Ascender System: Automated Site Modeling from Multiple Aerial Images. Computer Vision and Image Understanding 72(2), 143–162 (1998)

Cramer, M.: The DGPF Test on Digital Aerial Camera Evaluation – Overview and Test Design. Photogrammetrie – Fernerkundung – Geoinformation 2, 73–82 (2010)

Elaksher, A.F., Bethel, J.S., Mikhail, E.M.: Roof Boundary Extraction using Multiple Images. Photogrammetric Record 18(101), 27–40 (2003)

Förstner, W., Brunn, A., Heuel, S.: Statistically Testing Uncertain Geometric Relations. In: Sommer, G., Krüger, N., Perwass, C. (eds.) Mustererkennung, DAGM, pp. 17–26. Springer, Heidelberg (2000)

Haala, N.: Come Back of Digital Image Matching. Photogrammetric Week, 289–301 (2009); Wichmann Verlag, Heidelberg

Haala, N., Hastedt, H., Wolff, K., Ressl, C., Baltrusch, S.: Digital Photogrammetric Camera Evaluation – Generation of Digital Elevation Models. Photogrammetrie – Fernerkundung – Geoinformation 2, 99–115 (2010)

Henricsson, O.: The Role of Color Attributes and Similarity Grouping in 3-D Building Reconstruction. Computer Vision and Image Understanding 72(2), 163–184 (1998)

Heuel, S., Förstner, W.: Matching, Reconstructing and Grouping 3d Lines from Multiple Views using Uncertain Projective Geometry. In: CVPR 2001. IEEE, Los Alamitos (2001)

Heuel, S.: Points, Lines and Planes and their Optimal Estimation. In: Radig, B., Florczyk, S. (eds.) DAGM 2001. LNCS, vol. 2191, pp. 92–99. Springer, Heidelberg (2001)

Jung, F., Tollu, V., Paparoditis, N.: Extracting 3d Edgel Hypotheses from Multiple Calibrated Images: A Step Towards The Reconstruction of Curved and Straight Object Boundary Lines. In: Proceedings of PCV 2002, Graz, vol. B, pp. 100–104 (2002)

Jung, F., Paparoditis, N.: Extracting 3D Free-Form Surface Boundaries of Man-Made Objects from Multiple Calibrated Images: A Robust, Accurate and High Resolving Power Edgel Matching and Chaining Approach. In: IAPRS, 34, Part 3/W8 (2003)

Kim, Z., Nevatia, R.: Automatic Description of Complex Buildings from Multiple Images. Computer Vision and Image Understanding 96(1), 60–95 (2004)

Moons, T., Fr'ere, D., Vandekerckhove, J., Van Gool, L.: Automatic Modelling and 3D Reconstruction of Urban House Roofs from High Resolution Aerial Imagery. In: Proc. 5th European Conference on Computer Vision, Freiburg, Germany, pp. 410–425 (1998)

Noronha, S., Nevatia, R.: Detection and Modeling of Buildings from Multiple Aerial Images. IEEE Transactions on Pattern Analysis and Machine Intelligence 23(5), 501–518 (2001)

Ok, A.O., Wegner, J.D., Heipke, C., Rottensteiner, F., Soergel, U., Toprak, V.: A New Straight Line Reconstruction Methodology from Multi-Spectral Stereo Aerial Images. IntArchPhRS 38(3A), 25–30 (2010a)

Ok, A.O., Wegner, J.D., Heipke, C., Rottensteiner, F., Soergel, U., Toprak, V.: A Stereo Line Matching Technique For Aerial Images Based on A Pair-Wise Relation Approach. IntArchPhRS XXXVIII-1/W17 (2010b); Istanbul (on CD-ROM)

Ok, A.O., Wegner, J.D., Heipke, C., Rottensteiner, F., Soergel, U., Toprak, V.: Accurate Matching And Reconstruction of Line Features From Ultra High Resolution Stereo Aerial Images. In: Proceedings of ISPRS Hannover Workshop, High Resolution Earth Imaging for Geospatial Information, Hannover, Germany (2011)

Roux, M., McKeown, D.M.: Feature Matching for Building Extraction from Multiple Views. In: Proc. IEEE Conference on Computer Vision and Pattern Recognition (1994)

Rutzinger, M., Rottensteiner, F., Pfeifer, N.: A Comparison of Evaluation Techniques for Building Extraction from Airborne Laser Scanning. IEEE Journal of Selected Topics in Applied Earth Observations and Remote Sensing 2(1), 11–20 (2009)

Schmid, C., Zisserman, A.: Automatic Line Matching Across Views. In: Proceedings of CVPR, pp. 666–671 (1997)

Scholze, S.: Exploiting Color for Edge Extraction and Line Segment Multiview Matching. Technical Report BIWI–TR–257, Communication Technology Laboratory, Computer Vision Group, ETH, Zurich, Switzerland (2000)

Scholze, S., Moons, T., Ade, F., Van Gool, L.: Exploiting Color for Edge Extraction and Line Segment Stereo Matching. In: IAPRS, pp. 815–822 (2000)

Suveg, I., Vosselman, G.: Reconstruction of 3D Building Models from Aerial Images and Maps. ISPRS Journal of Photogrammetry and Remote Sensing 58, 202–224 (2004)

Taillandier, F., Deriche, R.: Automatic Buildings Reconstruction from Aerial Images: a Generic Bayesian Framework. In: IAPRS, 35, Part 3A (2004)

Wang, Z., Wu, F., Hu, Z.: MSLD: A Robust Descriptor for Line Matching. Pattern Recognition 42, 941–953 (2009)

Werner, T.: Matching of Line Segments across Multiple Views: Implementation Description. Visual Geometry Group, UK (2002)

Werner, T., Zisserman, A.: New Techniques for Automated Architectural Reconstruction from Photographs. In: Heyden, A., Sparr, G., Nielsen, M., Johansen, P. (eds.) ECCV 2002. LNCS, vol. 2351, pp. 541–555. Springer, Heidelberg (2002), http://cmp.felk.cvut.cz/cmp/software/lmatch/

Xiao, J., Gerke, M., Vosselman, G.: Automatic Detection of Buildings with Rectangular Flat Roofs from Multi-View Oblique Imagery. IntArchPhRS 38(3A), 251–256 (2010)

Zhang, C., Baltsavias, E.P.: Edge Matching and 3D Road Reconstruction using Knowledge-Based Methods. Schriftenreihe der Fachrichtung Geodaesie 10, 251–265 (2000)

Zhang, L.: Automatic Digital Surface Model (DSM) Generation from Linear Array Images, PhD Thesis, Swiss Institute of Technology Zurich (2005)

Refined Non-rigid Registration of a Panoramic Image Sequence to a LiDAR Point Cloud

Arjen Swart[1,2], Jonathan Broere[1], Remco Veltkamp[2], and Robby Tan[2]

[1] Cyclomedia Technology BV, Waardenburg, The Netherlands
{aswart,jbroere}@cyclomedia.com
[2] Utrecht University, Utrecht, The Netherlands
{Remco.Veltkamp,robby}@cs.uu.nl

Abstract. The combination of LiDAR data with panoramic images could be of great benefit to many geo-related applications and processes such as measuring and map making. Although it is possible to record both LiDAR points and panoramic images at the same time, there are economic and practical advantages to separating the acquisition of both types of data. However, when LiDAR and image data is recorded separately, poor GPS reception in many urban areas will make registration between the data sets necessary. In this paper, we describe a method to register a sequence of panoramic images to a LiDAR point cloud using a non-rigid version of ICP that incorporates a bundle adjustment framework. The registration is then refined by integrating image-to-reflectance data SIFT correspondences into the bundle adjustment. We demonstrate the validity of this registration method by a comparison against ground truth data.

Keywords: Mobile Mapping, LiDAR, Multi sensor, Registration, Point Cloud, Panorama.

1 Introduction

Panoramic images have become widely used by both governments and businesses for a variety of geo-related processes. Among the many applications are the assessment of permits and inspection of security risks, real estate valuation, and the tracking and managing of objects in the public space, such as traffic signs, lampposts, park benches and greenery. Panoramas are also being used for measuring and map-making. Many of these processes could be greatly simplified or enhanced by the addition of 3D information from a mobile LiDAR system.

There are several mobile mapping systems currently in use that record LiDAR points and color imagery at the same time. However, there are some advantages to separating image and LiDAR acquisition. In many countries, mornings and evenings in winter are too dark to produce high-quality panoramas. And of course large-scale photography at night is simply not feasible at all. LiDAR sensors on the other hand do not require an external light source to operate. Because LiDAR devices suitable for mobile mapping applications are very expensive,

U. Stilla et al. (Eds.): PIA 2011, LNCS 6952, pp. 73–84, 2011.

they should be idle as little as possible. This is especially true if the goal is to cost-effectively acquire point clouds for very large areas of the country, rather than for several relatively small projects. But even for smaller projects, separate acquisition can be economically advantageous. In the Netherlands for example, annually renewed parallax-free panoramic images are already available for the entire country. Combining these with separately recorded LiDAR data could save the potentially costly integration of the LiDAR sensors with a parallax-free panoramic camera system.

Separate acquisition of panoramas and point clouds does mean that the positioning information from GPS/INS is acquired separately as well. Especially in environments with poor GPS reception, like areas with many trees, or urban canyons, there could be a significant shift between the two data sets. The direction and size of this shift can change over the course of the trajectory. It is therefore necessary to register the sequence of panoramic images to a LiDAR point cloud of the same environment in a non-rigid manner.

Algorithms for the registration of color images to a 3D model or point cloud can generally be statistics based or feature based. Statistics based algorithms attempt to use a statistical dependence between the image and the point cloud. Mastin et al. (2009) register aerial images to LiDAR data by maximizing the mutual information between the image and the grayscale encoded height. When present, they use LiDAR reflectance values as well. If multiple images are available, a 3D model can also be registered using the photo-consistency principle (Clarkson et al., 2001). When the model is correctly registered, 3D points are likely to have the same color in multiple images. This principle can be used to optimize a cost function.

Feature based algorithms find matching features between images and a point cloud. For urban environments, Liu and Stamos (2005) find corresponding rectangular parallelepipeds between range scans and images. They also make use of line parallelism and orthogonality to estimate camera parameters. Böhm and Becker (2007) have used the SIFT feature detector (Lowe, 2004) to find corresponding interest points between the reflection image from a laser range scan and a photograph in order to register the two. Zhao et al. (2005) applied a dense 3D

Fig. 1. Part of a panorama projected onto the triangle mesh generated from a LiDAR point cloud, before and after registration

reconstruction technique to change the problem of image-to-point cloud registration into a 3D-to-3D registration. ICP (Chen and Medioni, 1991; Besl and McKay, 1992) is used to register a dense point cloud generated from a pair of key frames in an aerial video sequence to a 3D model or point cloud. The transformation computed by ICP for each pair of key-frames is then added as an observation in a bundle adjustment framework. The bundle adjustment interpolates the registration of the non-key frames and can partially correct large errors in the ICP registration. Li and Low (2009) use a semi-automatic method to find an initial registration of indoor photographs and laser range data. After the initial registration, they match 3D points from a sparse 3D reconstruction with the closest plane detected in the LiDAR cloud. These correspondences are added to a bundle adjustment framework, which is used to refine the registration in order to handle non-uniform spatial distortion.

Our main contribution in this paper is the application of non-rigid ICP to the problem of registering image and LiDAR trajectories by means of a bundle adjustment framework. A similar approach was taken by Lothe et al. (2009). However, we also integrate the use of feature point correspondences between images and LiDAR reflectance data into this framework. Results obtained by our method are verified by comparison to a ground truth data set.

High quality line or point correspondences between image and LiDAR data can be difficult to find in many real-world environments. This is especially so with mobile LiDAR systems, which don't reach the same spatial resolution possible with stationary scanners. Therefore, our system uses 3D-to-3D registration of a reconstructed sparse point cloud and the LiDAR data as its core. We build on the idea of Li and Low that the observations of reconstructed 3D points in the images can be used in bundle adjustment to constrain a non-rigid deformation of the sparse cloud itself. This applies especially to the type of data found in outdoor sequences. In a sparse 3D reconstruction from a long trajectory, the majority of the reconstructed points will only have been detected in several neighboring images. This causes the resulting network to be fairly weak and incapable of correcting errors that slowly build up over time. However, the connections are sufficiently strong to function as regularization. Due to IMU drift under sub-optimal GPS conditions, the non-rigid deformation of the trajectories can easily be too severe to handle with a single application of bundle adjustment. Therefore, we propose to wrap the bundle adjustment in a non-rigid ICP procedure. Each iteration, a rigid ICP step is performed first on successive segments of the trajectory in order to find the required correspondences. This is followed by the bundle adjustment stage, which updates the camera parameters and the sparse point cloud for the next iteration. The process is described in section 3.1.

After this registration, the now greatly improved initialization makes it easier to find more direct correspondences between the images and the LiDAR cloud. It is not necessary that these feature correspondences can solve the entire registration problem by themselves. By adding the information to the bundle adjustment stage, they can contribute wherever possible. We believe this is the key to building a robust system for registration that can handle a wide variety of environments. In section 3.2, we describe our method for adding SIFT interest point matches to the procedure. The results of our experiments are presented in section 4. We provide a comparison of the output of the registration procedure to a ground truth data set constructed using manually selected correspondences for each panorama.

2   Data

Our main test site is an approximately 750m long trajectory in the Dutch city of Enschede. At this site, LiDAR data was recorded in December 2008 and panoramic images in September 2009. This means that roughly nine months passed between the dates that both systems recorded their data. During this time, many things changed in the scene, making the registration task more challenging. These changes included, but were not limited to, the relocation of small street furniture, temporary road/traffic signs, and the absence or presence of parked vehicles at various locations. Both data sets contain several moving objects such as cars and pedestrians. A Lynx mobile mapping system from Optech (Optech, 2007) was used to obtain LiDAR data of the area. The mapping system was equipped with two LiDAR scanners that can each produce up to one hundred thousand points per second.

Parallax free spherical panoramic images were obtained by a CycloMedia DCR7 recording system (van den Heuvel et al., 2008). Location and orientation data are available for each panorama from the integrated GPS/INS system.

The CycloMedia recording vehicle did not drive along the exact same trajectory as the Lynx system. Rather, a panorama trajectory of 147 recordings at 5 m intervals that approximately follows the LiDAR point cloud was pieced together from several tracks recorded at different times during the day.

3   Algorithms

3.1   Initial Registration

The goal of the initial registration is to compute a non-rigid deformation of the panorama trajectory so that, at least in the local area, each panorama fits well to the LiDAR point cloud. This is accomplished by a non-rigid Iterative Closest Point (ICP) process that includes both rigid ICP and bundle adjustment (BA). We use a Structure from Motion (SfM) technique based on SIFT interest point matching between consecutive panoramas to obtain a sparse reconstruction of the environment. It is this reconstructed point cloud that is initially registered to the LiDAR cloud. The positions and orientations of the panoramas in the trajectory are adjusted along with the sparse reconstruction. Each iteration of the non-rigid registration procedure first uses rigid ICP on segments of the trajectory to find correspondences between the sparse cloud and the LiDAR data, and then a bundle adjustment stage to estimate the transformation. The process is initialized with the GPS/INS positions and continues until convergence is reached.

Rigid Iterative Closest Point. We use rigid ICP to solve for rigid registrations of the two point clouds. Because the non-rigid changes along the trajectory can be large, the LiDAR cloud is split into several segments containing a fixed number of points. The sparse point cloud is then registered to each sequential segment. This makes it possible to find a better local fit with only a rigid transformation. Remaining errors will be handled in the next stage.

In every rigid ICP iteration, we find the closest corresponding LiDAR point for each 3D point in the sparse reconstruction using a Kd-Tree. To make ICP more robust against outliers, the only points that are used are those within a Relative Motion Threshold e_t (Pomerleau et al., 2010) that scales based on how well the solution is converging. A minimum threshold ϵ is added to e_t, in order to handle noise in the data, and to allow for residual errors due to the assumption of rigidity.

Approximately planar structures like building facades, pavement, traffic signs and bus stops are common in urban environments. This makes our problem suitable for minimizing the point-to-plane distance, which leads to improved convergence compared to the point-to-point distance. The required normal vectors of the LiDAR points are calculated beforehand based on their local neighborhood. Each LiDAR point can now be considered as a locally valid plane.

No closed form solution for point-to-plane based registration exists, so after having matched the points within the current threshold, the 6 rigid transformation parameters are computed with the Levenberg-Marquardt algorithm. For increased robustness, errors are re-weighted according to the Huber cost function (Huber, 1973). With this adjusted error function, outliers will have less influence on the solution.

When the sparse point cloud has been registered to all LiDAR segments, the computed rigid transformations are no longer necessary. Only the final point-to-plane matches are required for the next stage.

Bundle Adjustment. Bundle adjustment is executed to solve for non-rigid deformations of the trajectory and to smooth transitions between the different ICP sections. It optimizes both the camera parameters and the SfM points by minimizing the cost function

$$K = K_{rpe} + K_{ptpe} + K_{ce}, \tag{1}$$

where K_{rpe} represents the summed re-projection errors, K_{ptpe} the point-to-plane correspondences as observations, and K_{ce} cameras as observations.

The re-projection error component is defined as

$$K_{rpe} = \sum_i \sum_j a \left\| f(\hat{\mathbf{C}}_i, \hat{\mathbf{X}}_j) - \mathbf{u}_{ij} \right\|^2, \tag{2}$$

where $\mathbf{u}_{ij}$ is the observation of 3D scene point j in camera i, and $f(\hat{\mathbf{C}}_i, \hat{\mathbf{X}}_j)$ defines the projection of the scene point estimate $\hat{\mathbf{X}}_j$ in camera i using the estimated camera parameters $\hat{\mathbf{C}}_i$. The squared error is weighted by a. The re-projection error term preserves the relative motion between the panoramas as determined by SfM. Due to the sequential structure of the network, these links are strongest between panoramas that are close to each other in the sequence. This term will propagate information from the point-to-plane matches to the nearby area. It also serves as a smoothness constraint by allowing some defor-mation of the panorama trajectory in order to follow deformations in the LiDAR trajectory, but resisting large changes. The amount of deformation allowed de-pends on the weight a.

The point-to-plane correspondence term K_{ptpe} is added to the bundle adjust-ment as

$$K_{ptpe} = \sum_i b \left\| (\hat{\mathbf{X}}_i - \mathbf{P}_i) \cdot \mathbf{N}_i \right\|^2 , \qquad (3)$$

where $\hat{\mathbf{X}}_i$ is an estimated 3D scene point from the sparse reconstruction, $\mathbf{P}_i$ a LiDAR point matched with scene point i during the rigid ICP stage, $\mathbf{N}_i$ is the surface normal at point $\mathbf{P}_i$, and b the weight used for point-to-plane corre-spondences. This term ties the LiDAR and panorama trajectories together. If a mistake was made in creating a certain match by the rigid ICP stage, this will not necessarily lead to a large error in the cost function. As long as the LiDAR point was on the correct, or a similar plane, the scene point can slide along this plane with little or no extra cost. In the next iteration, ICP can then select a better match using the output of the bundle adjustment stage as the initialization.

The different camera positions and orientations from the GPS/INS based trajectory data have also been added as observations:

$$K_{ce} = \sum_i \sum_j c_{ij} b \left\| (\hat{C}_{ij} - C_{ij}) \right\|^2 \qquad (4)$$

Here we sum over each camera $\mathbf{C}_i$, where c_{ij} is the weight for observed camera parameter C_{ij}, and $\hat{C}_{ij}$ is the estimate for parameter C_{ij}. This term prevents the cameras from drifting too far from their original absolute positions. However, since the deformations in both the panorama and the LiDAR trajectories must be compensated for, the weights are set to a very low value.

It is likely that there will be outliers in the data, especially because of the significant changes in the environment in the time between the recording of both sets. The Huber cost function has been used to re-weight the residuals of the re-projection and point-to-plane correspondence components. After performing the bundle adjustment once, the potential outliers exceeding a threshold are removed, and the procedure is repeated.

The bundle adjustment was implemented using a heavily modified version of the SBA sparse bundle adjustment software package (Lourakis and Argyros, 2009).

3.2   Refinement

Having improved the panorama positions using the initial registration algorithm, there is often still room for improvement by exploiting the reflectance information from the LiDAR data (see section 4 for quantitative examples). Our method for improved registration is based on the idea that after the initial registration, color and reflectance images as observed from the same position should be very similar.

However, while a vehicle mounted LiDAR system can produce reflectance data per point, it cannot directly produce a reflectance image that can be used to find matching feature points with a panorama image. It would of course be possible to project the points into an image, but simple Z-buffering would not be sufficient to handle occlusions, unless very large pixels were used. Since the density of the point cloud is not uniform, this would needlessly waste resolution in some parts of the image. Therefore, we generate a triangle mesh from the LiDAR point cloud using the method described by Carlberg et al. (2008). Intensity images can then be produced by rendering the mesh from the point of view of a virtual camera.

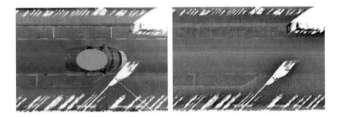

Fig. 2. Color and reflectance images created with the initial registration

The SIFT feature detector is robust enough to handle some of the differences between the panorama images and LiDAR reflectance data. However, it works best when perspective deformation is minimal. For that reason, the positions from the initial registration are used to render both color and reflectance images from the same virtual camera position. If there were no mis-registration at all, the feature points derived from LiDAR reflectance and panorama data would have the same location. So if we assume the remaining registration error is small, like shown in Fig. 2, the search area for matching feature points can be limited. We orient the virtual camera towards the ground, because the point density is highest near the trajectory of the recording vehicle. This is important for good localization of the features.

For each panorama, the matched points from the corresponding color and LiDAR reflectance images are transformed back into panorama-coordinates. Since the 3D positions of the LiDAR reflectance SIFT points are known, the result of each matching pair is a 2D point in the panorama matched to a 3D point from the LiDAR. With enough point correspondences, it would be possible to filter out erroneous matches and use a spatial resection algorithm. However, this would force us to throw away points when a panorama has less than three intensity matches, or if the points are in a configuration unsuitable for resection.

Since many of the reflectance intensity SIFT points are found on road markings, it is certainly possible to only have matches on a single line. These points would not be enough to solve for the registration of the panorama by themselves, but combined with other information, they can still contribute to the solution. For this reason, the matches are only filtered by a simple distance threshold, and we rely on the next stage of the algorithm to remove outliers.

In order to combine all of this information in a single framework, we include the reflectance matches in the process described in section 3.1 as an extra term to Equation 1, as

$$K_{ipe} = \sum_i \sum_j d \left\| f(\hat{\mathbf{C}}_i, \hat{\mathbf{Y}}_j) - \mathbf{v}_{ij} \right\|^2 + \sum_i e \left\| \hat{\mathbf{Y}}_i - \mathbf{Y}_i \right\|^2, \qquad (5)$$

where $\mathbf{v}_{ij}$ is the SIFT point observed in the color image of camera i, corresponding to 3D point $\mathbf{Y}_j$ as obtained from the reflectance image. This term adds the reflectance points to the bundle adjustment as control points. Like the points created by SfM, they are subject to filtering by the error detection procedures. The entire non-rigid ICP process is repeated from the start with the new matches.

4   Results

To validate our approach, we have compared the results of our algorithm with a ground truth data set. Because the panorama and LiDAR data sets were recorded at different times under moderately difficult GPS conditions, no actual ground truth was available. Therefore, we have generated a ground truth by manually selecting point correspondences between the LiDAR reflectance data and the panoramas. The registration was solved by using bundle adjustment with these correspondences as control points. Naturally, point-to-plane and reflectance matches were not included in this. To check the validity of the ground truth, the manual selection was performed twice, each time by a different person. The RMS error between the resulting camera position sequences was approximately 1.9 cm. Although the algorithm was run on the full trajectory, only the first part (about 250m) of the full trajectory contained enough clear LiDAR reflectance features to consistently find correspondences for manual registration. Therefore, we can only visually confirm the results on the second part, and just the first part is shown in comparisons with the ground truth data. This causes a bias in the results favoring the refinement stage, since good LiDAR reflectance features can be used by SIFT as well. Nevertheless, a comparison of the results with ground truth data generated in this manner can reveal patterns that might be less obvious with only visual validation.

It should be noted that the LiDAR cloud itself is not deformed in the manual registration. Just like the automated registration algorithms, its goal is to find a good local fit. Registration errors for LiDAR points far from the position of a panorama are less visible and not as important.

In Fig. 3, we show the distance of successive panoramas in the trajectory to the ground truth. The initial registration with ICP and BA is already a large

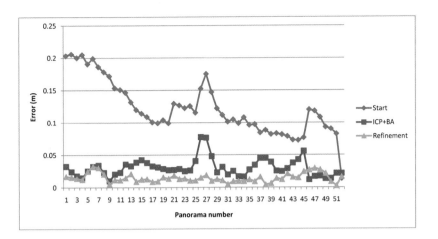

Fig. 3. Distance (m) to the ground truth of each panorama in the sequence

improvement over the starting positions from GPS/INS. Refinement brings the error down to about 2 cm. This is approximately the precision level of the ground truth, so a further reduction would not be meaningful.

Some of the peaks visible in the graphs are explained as follows. Between panoramas 26 and 27, and also 45 and 46, there is a gap in the data set. The reason is that the full panorama trajectory that follows the LiDAR trajectory is actually pieced together from different panorama sequences. Because panoramas closer than 5 m to another panorama are not stored by the recording system, there are often gaps at crossroads. When the recording vehicle comes in from an area with different GPS conditions, the error relative to the LiDAR will be different as well. The gaps cause a decrease in the number of SIFT matches between the panoramas, thereby weakening the connection just where it is needed most. With enough direct matches between the panoramas and the LiDAR reflectance in the area near the gaps, the inter-panorama links become less important.

A displacement of just 15 cm can already have a significant impact on the usability of the data. But in practice, it is quite possible to have much larger differences. We have simulated bad GPS conditions by adding an artificial additional error to the initial positions in the panorama trajectory. The added error gradually increases (and later decreases) with time in order to simulate IMU drift. All processing, including the structure from motion estimation was repeated on the new data. The results of registration with an artificial initial error are shown in Fig. 4. We can see that the registration procedures are capable of correcting quite large non-rigid deformations in the panorama-trajectory. Fig. 5 illustrates the results of the registration process on one part of the scene. Our method has also been tested on several other data sets, but due to the difficulty of obtaining manual correspondences, only visual confirmation of the registrations could be made. Fig. 1 shows a small part of the results on a triangulated

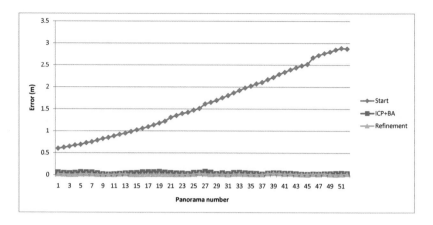

Fig. 4. Distance (m) to the ground truth of each panorama in the sequence. The starting positions have been given an additional, increasing offset (following a gaussian curve) in order to simulate drift in adverse GPS conditions..

Fig. 5. A panorama onto the triangle mesh, before and after registration

point cloud in Ghent (Belgium). The results on the Ghent data set appeared to be slightly worse than on the Enschede set, possibly due to the fact that many LiDAR points on the ground were missing.

5   Conclusions and Future Work

The results presented in this paper show that the automated registration of separately acquired panorama and LiDAR trajectories is feasible. This was achieved using a novel combination of non-rigid ICP and panorama-to-reflectance data interest point matching. The bundle adjustment framework used can be expanded to include other types of correspondences.

As noted in section 3.1, only the panorama-trajectory is currently updated by our algorithm. It can be expected that the quality of the LiDAR trajectory will often be higher than that of the panorama trajectory. Environments with challenging GPS reception conditions, such as city centers can be scheduled at night, when there is less traffic. The LiDAR recording vehicle will then be able to move faster through these areas with poor GPS reception, thus minimizing IMU drift. Still, the LiDAR trajectory will occasionally be worse, and if we are interested in absolute positioning rather than just registration of the data sets, then the independent GPS measurements from both trajectories should be taken into account with the appropriate weighting. To prevent unreasonable deformations of the LiDAR cloud, it would be necessary to constrain the LiDAR trajectory. Besides any GPS information, the INS data could be used to enforce smoothness. In fact, integrating raw GPS/IMU/DMI measurements into the adjustment procedure may be advantageous for the panorama trajectory as well.

As mobile LiDAR scanners capable of producing higher densities at reasonable driving speeds become available, direct interest point or line matching between images and LiDAR reflection data or geometry is likely to contribute more to the solution. Higher level features such as lampposts and windows can help as well. For the registration to work well in a wide range of environments, a combination of several different types of features should be integrated into the bundle adjustment.

Acknowledgements. Part of this research has been supported by the GATE project, funded by the Netherlands Organization for Scientific Research (NWO) the Netherlands ICT Research and Innovation Authority (ICT Regie). The authors thank TopScan GmbH and Teccon bvba for the use of their data sets.

References

Besl, P., McKay, N.: A Method for Registration of 3-D Shapes. IEEE T. Pattern Anal. 14(2), 239–256 (1992)

Böhm, J., Becker, S.: Automatic Marker-Free Registration of Terrestrial Laser Scans using Reflectance Features. In: 8th Conference on Optical 3D Measurement Techniques, pp. 338–344 (2007)

Carlberg, M., Andrews, J., Gao, P., Zakhor, A.: Fast Surface Reconstruction and Segmentation with Ground-Based and Airborne Lidar Range Data. In: 4th International Symposium on 3D Data Processing, Visualization and Transmission, pp. 97–104 (2008)

Chen, Y., Medioni, G.: Object Modeling by Registration of Multiple Range Images. In: 1991 IEEE International Conference on Robotics and Automation, pp. 2724–2729 (1991)

Clarkson, M., Rueckert, D., Hill, D., Hawkes, D.: Using Photo-Consistency to Register 2D Optical Images of the Human Face to a 3D Surface Model. IEEE T. Pattern Anal. 23(11), 1266–1280 (2001)

van den Heuvel, F., Beers, B., Verwaal, R.: Method and system for producing a panoramic image from a vehicle. European Patent EP1903534 (2008)

Huber, P.: Robust Regression: Asymptotics, Conjectures and Monte Carlo. Ann. Stat. 1(5), 799–821 (1973)

Li, Y., Low, K.: Automatic Registration of Color Images to 3D Geometry. In: Proceedings of the 2009 Computer Graphics International Conference, pp. 21–28. ACM, New York (2009)

Liu, L., Stamos, I.: Automatic 3D to 2D Registration for the Photorealistic Rendering of Urban Scenes. In: 2005 IEEE Computer Society Conference on Computer Vision and Pattern Recognition, vol. 2, pp. 137–143 (2005)

Lothe, P., Bourgeois, S., Dekeyser, F., Royer, E., Dhome, M.: Towards Geographical Referencing of Monocular SLAM Reconstruction using 3D City Models: Application to Real-Time Accurate Vision-Based Localization. In: 2009 IEEE Computer Society Conference on Computer Vision and Pattern Recognition, pp. 2882–2889 (2009)

Lourakis, M., Argyros, A.: SBA: A Software Package for Generic Sparse Bundle Adjustment. ACM. T. Math. Software 36(1), 1–30 (2009)

Lowe, D.: Distinctive Image Features from Scale-Invariant Keypoints. Int. J. Comput. Vision 60(2), 91–110 (2004)

Mastin, A., Kepner, J., Fisher, J.: Automatic Registration of LIDAR and Optical Images of Urban Scenes. In: 2009 IEEE Computer Society Conference on Computer Vision and Pattern Recognition, pp. 2639–2646 (2009)

Optech: Lynx mobile mapper data sheet (2007),
http://www.optech.ca/pdf/LynxDataSheet.pdf

Pomerleau, F., Colas, F., Ferland, F., Michaud, F.: Relative Motion Threshold for Rejection in ICP Registration. In: Howard, A., Iagnemma, K., Kelly, A. (eds.) Field and Service Robotics: Results of the 7th International Conference, pp. 229–238. Springer, Heidelberg (2010)

Zhao, W., Nister, D., Hsu, S.: Alignment of Continuous Video onto 3D Point Clouds. IEEE T. Pattern Anal. 27(8), 1305–1318 (2005)

Image Sequence Processing in Stereovision Mobile Mapping – Steps towards Robust and Accurate Monoscopic 3D Measurements and Image-Based Georeferencing

Fabian Huber[1,*], Stephan Nebiker[1], and Hannes Eugster[1,2]

[1] FHNW, University of Applied Sciences Northwestern Switzerland,
School of Architecture, Civil Engineering and Geomatics,
Inst. of Geomatics Engineering, CH-4132 Muttenz, Switzerland
{fabian.huber,stephan.nebiker,hannes.eugster}@fhnw.ch
[2] iNovitas AG, Mobile Mapping Solutions
Gründenstrasse 40, CH-4132 Muttenz, Switzerland
hannes.eugster@inovitas.ch

Abstract. Stereo vision based mobile mapping systems enable the efficient capturing of directly georeferenced stereo pairs. With today's camera and storage technologies imagery can be captured at high data rates resulting in dense stereo sequences. The overlap within stereo pairs and stereo sequences can be exploited to improve the accuracy and reliability of point measurements. This paper aims at robust and accurate monoscopic 3d measurements in future vision-based mobile mapping services. Key element is an adapted Least Squares Matching approach yielding point matching accuracies at the subpixel level. Initial positions for the matching process along the stereo sequence, are obtained by projecting the matched point position within the reference stereo pair to object space and by reprojecting it to the adjacent pairs. Once homologue image positions have been derived, final 3D point coordinates are estimated. Investigations with real-world data show, that points can successfully and reliably be matched over extended stereo sequences.

Keywords: Stereoscopic, Vision, Mobile Mapping, Image Matching, Sequence Processing.

1 Introduction

First experimental Mobile Mapping Systems (MMS) date back some 20 years and have since undergone a continuous development until reaching a certain level of maturity, i.e. a productive stage between 2005 and 2010. While early systems were primarily camera-based, laser scanners started to become the dominant MMS sensors both in industry and in research. In many systems imagery was degraded to documentary data or a special kind of metadata associated with the laser scanning data.

---

* Corresponding author.

U. Stilla et al. (Eds.): PIA 2011, LNCS 6952, pp. 85–95, 2011.

However, recent progress in the domains of *dense* or *multiray image matching* algorithms and computing power in general has led to a revival of image-based mobile mapping and 3d reconstruction approaches. Vision-based mobile mapping has been a primary research focus at the Institute of Geomatics Engineering of the University of Applied Science Northwestern Switzerland (FHNW) over the last few years and has led to the establishment of a stereo-vision based mobile mapping system (Fig. 1) which serves as a general purpose research platform. The system permits the acquisition of accurately synchronized stereo image sequences in the order of 10 frames per second. An accurate inertial navigation system (INS) with GNSS support permits the direct georeferencing of the acquired stereo sequences yielding 3D point measurements accuracies in the order of 2-5 cm in X, Y and Z under optimal GNSS conditions (Cavegn, 2010).

By applying recent dense matching algorithms such as semi-global matching (SGM) (Hirschmüller, 2005) dense and accurate disparity and depth maps can be obtained for each stereo pair. This depth information of the stereo sequences can successfully be exploited, for example, in the automatic extraction of road signs (Cavegn, 2011) or for generating dense 3d point clouds with perfectly co-registered RGB color information.

The goal of this work was the design and development of an algorithm permitting the automated matching of control points, tie points or other arbitrary features through a mobile mapping stereo image sequence. By exploiting the high degree of redundancy provided by the imagery overlapping both cross-track and along-track, robust and highly accurate monoscopic 3d measurement functionality is to be achieved. The stereo sequence point matching functionality is later to be used in the automated tie point generation for a bundle adjustment supporting highly accurate integrated georeferencing or even image-based georeferencing of vehicle trajectories and measured points in adverse GNSS conditions.

2   Related Work

2.1 Multi-image Matching

In aerial photogrammetry various image matching techniques have been developed over the last 30 years. Their main focus was the extraction of digital terrain and surface models from overlapping aerial or satellite imagery. In these air- or space-borne scenarios, in contrast to the close-range scenarios prevailing in mobile mapping, the relative depth variability is generally small and initial height values are relatively accurate. Both facts facilitate the image matching process.

Of particular interest are the approaches developed by Grün and Baltsavias (1988), Baltsavias (1991) and Heipke (1992) where a least squares matching (LSM) using geometric constraints (optimal intersection of homologue image rays) is carried out across multiple homologue image positions. In these approaches the equation system of the original LSM by Grün (1985) is extended by observation equations for the geometric constraints. This allows the simultaneous estimation of shifts in the image locations as well as the XYZ object coordinates.

Maas (1992) exploits the known relative orientations between multiple images. This permits a significant reduction of the search space for corresponding features. First, point features are extracted using an interest operator. These features are then matched by exploiting the epipolar geometry. This approach can be extended to an arbitrary number of images. However, it requires that interest operator extracts roughly identical features in all images, which requires similar acquisition geometries (distance and direction to object points).

An abundance of research on point matching in stereo images, particularly on pixel-based matching (dense matching) has also been carried out in Computer Vision. An important example, which closely relates to photogrammetric tasks, is the semi-global matching algorithm by Hirschmüller (2005).

2.2 Semi-automatic Point Matching in Mobile Mapping

Early research in the domain of semi-automated point matching in stereo imagery from mobile mapping was carried out at Ohio State University and at Calgary University. He and Novak (1992) developed a three stage approach, which first defines a search (epipolar lines) based on the known system geometry. Subsequently a cross correlation based search for the optimal position in this search space is determined. From there optimal position is determined at subpixel level using a LSM estimation. The approach by He and Novak (1992) is limited to point matching in stereo pairs.

Tao (1997) presented a similar approach to that of Maas (1992). But instead of using extracted features, a point is measured in a reference image which is subsequently matched in the stereo partner based on a weighted cross correlation along epipolar lines as originally introduced by (Mori et al., 1973). The search area along the epipolar line is restricted based on a predefined measurement range. The search may yield more than one candidate homologue point. A set of candidates can be filtered for consistency using a multiocular epipolar condition. During this process the corresponding epipolar line for each candidate is projected to the subsequent stereo pair.

This method was later adapted and further researched by Tao (2000). It was shown that the reliability of point matching in stereo sequences is significantly better than in stereo pairs only. However, it was also shown that the weighted cross correlation based matching is not suitable in cases with great differences in image to object distance.

3 Data Source and Preprocessing

The following investigations were carried out using data from the stereo vision based mobile mapping system shown in Fig. 1.

Fig. 1. Stereo vision based mobile mapping system of the University of Applied Sciences Northwestern Switzerland (FHNW)

The system features a forward looking stereo configuration with two full HD sensors and a stereo base of approx. 1 m. For further specifications see Tab. 1.

Table 1. Specifications of the FHNW MMS

navigation system	Applanix Pos LV 210
sensor resolution	1926x1082 pixels (2x)
radiometric resolution	max. 12 bit
pixel size (sensor)	7.4µm
pixel size (object space)	9mm @ 10m distance
image capturing rate	approx. 8 frames/s
stereo base	92cm
acquisition speed	30-50 km/h (max. 100 km/h)

Exterior orientation parameters for every image are determined by direct georeferencing using INS/GNSS integration and a number of transformation steps. The interior orientation and the relative orientation of the stereo cameras as well as the boresight misalignment (lever arm and misalignment) are determined in a field calibration prior to the mapping mission. The interior and relative orientations from the field calibration are used to generate distortion and y-parallax free normal images (Fig. 2) which facilitate the creation of 3D videos, the interactive display in the stereo viewer as well as the subsequent matching and object extraction processes. Furthermore, depth or disparity maps for each stereo pair are extracted using a dense matching algorithm (Willow Garage, 2011).

Fig. 2. Left and right distortion free normalized images, captured with the FHNW MMS

It should be noted that the inertial navigation system not only provides direct georeferencing information but also accurate relative orientations between subsequent stereo pairs – even in cases of degraded GNSS coverage such as in urban or forested areas.

4 Concept

The proposed approach for matching homologue image features in stereo sequences consists of two parts:

1. *Matching within the stereo pair* – For this task two different approaches were considered and investigated. The first one extends the approach of He and Novak (1992). The second approach exploits the depth maps for restricting the search space.
2. *Matching within the image sequence* – For the task of matching image features in previous and subsequent stereo pairs a method was applied which uses approximated object space coordinates in the restriction of the search space.

4.1 Stereo Matching

Within a stereo pair homologue image positions are matched using cross correlation and LSM. Since normal images are used in this process, corresponding features are located in the same image row. By using a distance criterion (min. and max.) or by directly using the information from the depth map, the search space can be further limited. The correlation coefficients of each pixel within the restricted search space are subsequently analyzed for significant locations with high correlation values. These are later on used as initial positions for the subsequent LSM process (Fig. 3). There is a possibility that this approach yields more than one candidate for the LSM step.

By exploiting the depth information, which was derived from the stereo imagery using dense matching, initial positions for the LSM process can directly be determined.

Image matching at the subpixel level is achieved using the LSM method. In our case 6 parameters for an affine geometric transformation and 2 parameters for a radiometric transformation between the reference template and the target image are estimated.

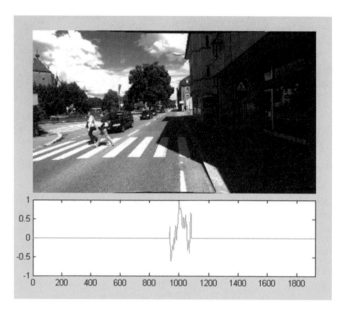

Fig. 3. Correlation function within the search space and detected maximum (Point No. 11)

This mathematical model assumes planar object surface patches and a planar image sensor (Bethmann and Luhmann, 2011). In order to force the convergence, the Gauss-Newton optimization by means of the Levenberg-Marquardt algorithm (LMA) is employed (Levenberg, 1944; Marquardt, 1963). The LMA approach enables adapting the step-width of the gradient descent between individual iterations. Fig. 4 illustrates the improved robustness of the LMA over the standard Gauss-Newton optimization in a typical mobile mapping stereo scene.

In cases where the cross-correlation search yields multiple candidates, an LSM search is performed for each candidate. The image location with a converging LSM and the lowest standard deviation of unit weight is considered as the best match.

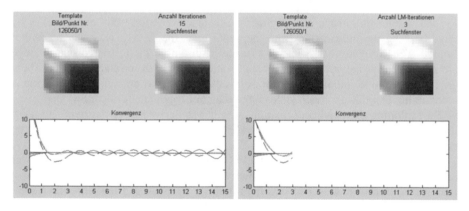

Fig. 4. Comparison of optimisation approaches. Left: no convergence with the Gauss-Newton approach; right: rapid convergence with the Levenberg-Marquardt algorithm.

4.2 Matching within the Image Sequence

Once the homologue image position has been located within the reference stereo pair, 3d object coordinates of the point can be determined by space intersection. This point in object space can now be re-projected to the neighboring images within the sequence. These image locations serve as initial positions for the subsequent LSM at the subpixel level. Two different approaches for propagating the reference image location through the image sequence were investigated (Fig. 5):

a) The template of the left reference image is directly transferred to and matched with all images of the sequence containing the point location.
b) The template of the left reference image is matched with the images of the preceding and successive stereo frames and thus propagated through the entire sequence.

The potential drawback of option b) in comparison with a) is that small errors in the (original) image location can propagate along the sequence. However, this effect can be minimized with suitable LSM convergence criteria. The major advantage of option b) is the reduction of projective distortion between the matched image locations resulting in an improved matching performance over longer image sequences.

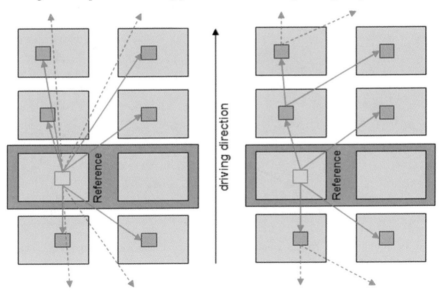

Fig. 5. Options for the matching process within the image sequence,left: Option a), right: Option b)

5   Investigations

5.1 Matching Accuracy in Image Space

The automatically matched image positions were introduced into an unconstrained network adjustment in order to determine the matching accuracy of image locations with the given setup (see section). The observations consisted of approx. 10-12 natural targets per stereo frame with equal weights for all image observations. The bundle adjustment resulted in a mean standard deviation of 0.2-0.3 pixels in image space. This matching accuracy meets the a priori estimates for LSM based image matching (Grün, 1985).

5.2   Accuracy Potential in Object Space

For each stereo pair within the sequence with successfully matched points, 3d object coordinates were calculated based on the image positions and the GNSS/INS-based exterior orientation parameters of the images. The final object coordinates were determined using a robust mean with distance-based weights. Coordinates from stereo pairs which are located closer to the object point and which were determined with a better image geometry are introduced with larger weights. Investigations included the assessment of the interior or relative accuracy of the averaged coordinates as well as the assessment of the absolute accuracy within the geodetic reference system.

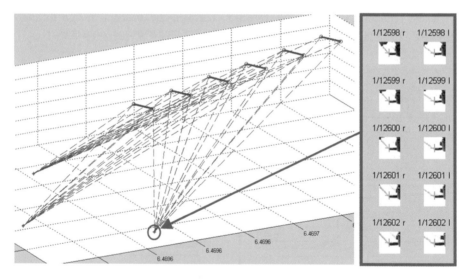

Fig. 6. Point observation geometry and image matching results within stereo sequence; left: geometry of image rays, right: matched image locations

Interior Accuracy of Point Coordinates
The INS of the utilized mobile mapping system provides highly accurate 'relative' or 'frame-to-frame' orientations over short stereo sequences. This results in very good interior accuracies of the averaged 3d point coordinates which are typically better than 1 cm. One of the key factors affecting the accuracy of averaged point coordinates is the definition of measured points. Well-defined natural points – and artificial targets – which are visible in multiple stereo pairs (>3) can be determined with the mentioned interior accuracy at the sub-centimeter level. For poorly defined points and for points located at the lateral edges of the stereo scene the standard deviation of the object coordinates can degrade to several cm.

Thus, for well-defined natural points which can be tracked over multiple stereo frames, highly accurate distances and / or coordinate differences can be determined. Due to the medium- to high-quality INS used, this good relative accuracy can also be maintained in cases with poor GNSS signal reception.

Absolute Georeferencing Accuracy

In order to determine the absolute georeferencing accuracy of the proposed approach 150 well-defined natural points, e.g. corners of road markings, along the main street of Laufenburg were determined in 3d in the distortion-free LV95 geodetic reference frame with an accuracy of approx. 2 cm in position and in height using tachymetric observations. These points served as check points for the evaluation of the absolute georeferencing accuracy.

Investigations showed that the absolute 3d point determination accuracy using a stereo image sequence is not significantly better than the point determination using a single stereo frame. This is mainly due to the absolute accuracy of the trajectory which is typically lower than the image-based relative position accuracy shown above. However, by moving from single stereo frames to stereo sequences, the reliability of 3d point determination can be significantly improved.

With the stereo system configuration used, absolute 3d point measurement accuracies of better than 5 cm at driving speeds of 30-50 km/h can be achieved under optimal GNSS conditions (Cavegn, 2010). This accuracy level and the findings of Cavegn (2010) were confirmed by a first evaluation using the stereo sequence processing approach.

6 Conclusion and Outlook

The proposed approach enables a robust and accurate semi-automatic 3d point determination over sequences of stereo image pairs acquired with a stereovision mobile mapping system. The sequence-based approach has a number of advantages over 3d point determination in single frame stereo imagery:

- It supports *accurate and reliable monoscopic 3d measurements* in normalized stereo image sequences and does not require stereoscopic measurements. This is particularly important if image-based mobile mapping services are to be exploited not only by experienced photogrammetrists but by the actual domain experts themselves, e.g. by urban planners or by road planning specialists.
- The presented approach provides a dramatic *improvement in reliability* of 3d point determination over interactive stereoscopic (or monoscopic) measurements in a single stereo pair.

The possibility of monoscopic point measurements in a single image with the subsequent automatic matching in all images of a stereo sequence makes the presented approach particularly suitable for control point measurements. These control point measurements are a key element in transforming mobile mapping imagery data with an accuracy potential at the centimeter level into local reference frameworks. Up until now these measurements had to be repeated in multiple stereo pairs.

Tests and comparisons with accurate reference data demonstrated the robustness of the approach and showed an excellent interior accuracy at the (sub-) centimeter level, which permits accurate measurements of spatial distances across multiple stereo frames. The proposed stereo sequence matching approach with monoscopic 3d measurements yields a slightly better absolute 3d point accuracy than interactive stereoscopic measurements in a single stereo frame. While the GNSS/INS direct georeferencing accuracy remains a limiting factor, the redundancy and improved geometry of the multiray point estimation outweigh the higher depth measurement accuracy of single stereoscopic measurements.

The presented stereo sequence based point determination approach represents an important first step towards an integrated georeferencing solution for highly accurate and reliable absolute 3d point measurements even under adverse GNSS conditions, most particular in urban areas. The goal of our ongoing and future work is a highly automated 'INS-aided image-based georeferencing' solution. As part of this effort we are extending the current framework towards a fully automatic tie point extraction and integration into a robust bundle block adjustment. In combination with sparsely placed control points, this approach should provide absolute georeferencing accuracies for vision-based mobile mapping systems equal to or better than what can today be achieved with GNSS/INS-based positioning under ideal conditions.

References

Baltsavias, E.P.: Multiphoto Geometrically Constrained Matching. Dissertation. ETH Zürich, Switzerland (1991)

Bethmann, F., Luhmann, T.: Kleinste-Quadrate-Zuordnung mit erweiterten geometrischen Transformationen. Photogrammetrie Fernerkundung Geoinformation (2), 57–69 (2011)

Cavegn, S.: Automatisierte Verkehrszeichenkartierung aus mobil erfassten Stereobilddaten. Master-Thesis. FHNW Muttenz, Switzerland (2011)

Cavegn, S.: Fahrzeuggestützte stereobildbasierte Geodatenkartierung. MSE Projektarbeit. FHNW Muttenz, Switzerland (2010)

Grün, A.: Adaptive Least Squares Correlation - a powerful image matching technique. South African Journal of Photogrammetry, Remote Sensing and Cartography 14(3), 175–187 (1985)

Grün, A., Baltsavias, E.P.: Geometrically Constrained Multiphoto Matching. Photogrammetric Engineering & Remote Sensing 54(5), 633–641 (1988)

He, G., Novak, K.: On line Data Capture by Image Matching on the Mobile Mapping System. In: Proceedings on SPIE, Boston, USA, vol. 1820, pp. 50–56 (1992)

Heipke, C.: A Global Approach for Least-Squares Image Matching and Surface Reconstructionin Object Space. Photogrammetric Engineering & Remote Sensing 58(3), 317–323 (1992)

Hirschmüller, H.: Accurate and Efficient Stereo Processing by Semi-Global Matching and Mutual Information. In: IEEE Conference on Computer Vision and Pattern Recognition, San Diego, USA (2005)

Levenberg, K.: A method for the solution for certain nonlinear problems in least-squares. The Quarterly Journal of Mechanics and Applied Mathematics 2, 164–168 (1944)

Maas, H.-G.: Digitale Photogrammetrie in der dreidimensionalen Strömungsmesstechnik. Dissertation. ETH Zürich, Switzerland (1992)

Marquardt, D.W.: An Algorithm for Least-Squares Estimation of Nonlinear Parameters. Journal of the Society for Industrial and Applied Mathematics 11(2), 431–444 (1963)

Mori, K., Kidodi, M., Asada, H.: An Iterative Prediction and Correction Method for Automatic Stereo Comparison. Computer Graphics and Image Processing 2, 393–401 (1973)

Tao, C.V.: Automated Approaches to Object Measurement and Feature Extraction from Georeferenced Mobile Mapping Image Sequences. Dissertation. University of Calgary, Canada (1997)

Tao, C.V.: Semi-Automated Object Measurement Using Multiple-Image Matching from Mobile Mapping Image Sequences. Photogrammetric Engineering & Remote Sensing 66(12), 1477–1485 (2000)

Garage, W.: OpenCV. Open Source Computer Vision Library (2011), http://opencv.willowgarage.com

Gable Roof Detection in Terrestrial Images

Vincent. Brandou and Caroline. Baillard

SIRADEL, 3 allée Adolphe Bobierre,
CS 14343, 35043 Rennes, France
{vbrandou,cbaillard}@siradel.com

Abstract. This paper presents an automatic method for gable roof detection in terrestrial images. The purpose of this study is to refine the roofs of a 3D city model automatically derived from aerial images. The input images consist of geo-referenced terrestrial images acquired by a mobile mapping system (MMS). The raw images have been rectified and merged into seamless façade texture images (one texture per façade). Firstly, each image is pre-processed in order to remove small structures and to smooth homogeneous areas. Secondly, line segments are extracted and analysed to define the lateral edges of the roof. Finally, the analysis of the lowest part of the roof leads to the classification of the roof as gable or non-gable. The method was tested on more than 150 images and shows promising results.

Keywords: Terrestrial, building, detection, classification, cartography, modelling.

1 Introduction

The SIRADEL Company has produced a large number of 3D city models around the world using stereo aerial imagery. The building roofs can be automatically estimated from the 2D building outlines and a Digital Elevation Models (DEM) using a method based on [1]. The input DEM is derived from aerial imagery using a multi-resolution correlation algorithm. The quality of the result is however very dependent on the input imagery. When the image resolution decreases, the resulting DEM can be very smooth. As a result, the gable roofs are frequently misinterpreted as hip roofs in the 3D model (see Fig. 1).

a   b   c

Fig. 1. Common error on automatic roof modelling (a) aerial image with reference roof edges, (b) DEM with building outline; (c) roof edges automatically derived from the DEM and the building outline

U. Stilla et al. (Eds.): PIA 2011, LNCS 6952, pp. 97–108, 2011.

The purpose of this study is to check and to refine the roof models automatically derived from the DEM. More precisely, this paper focuses on the automatic detection of gables in terrestrial images. It is particularly important to detect gables before texturing the building models: whereas standard roof planes are textured using aerial imagery, gables should be merged with their supporting wall and textured using terrestrial imagery. Importantly, the detection method should be quick enough to be applied on every visible façade of the city model.

The roofs can generally be classified as one of the roof types illustrated in Fig. 2. A gable is the traditionally triangular portion of a wall between the edges of a sloping roof. As an extension, all the roofs listed in the top row of Fig. 2 could be associated to a gable. In this paper, we only focus on the detection of gables in gable roofs, saltbox roofs and gambrel roofs. The gables are therefore characterized by a vertical plane and at least two oblique roof edges. Besides, it is assumed that the gable is covered with the same material as the corresponding wall; in particular, a vertical roof plane covered by tiles or slates will not be classified as a gable.

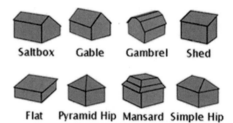

Fig. 2. The different types of roofs; First row: roofs with a gable; Second row: roofs without gable

The paper is organized as follows. First, a brief state-of-the-art is given in Section 2. The main input data are presented in Section 3. Our method for gable detection is detailed in Section 4. Experimental results are presented and discussed in Section 5. Finally, concluding remarks and future research directions are given in Section 6.

2 Related Work

To our knowledge there is no study specifically dedicated to gable detection in terrestrial images. Several methods based on image segmentation or classification have been proposed for the analysis of collective building facades [2-7]. They take advantage of the repetition of architectural elements and cannot deal with individual houses. [8] presents a general method for the semantic segmentation of street-side images: the regions are classified as building facade, sky, cloud, roof, ground, vegetation or grass. First, within a learning process, a color histogram is created for each category; then, within a classification process, the region color is compared to the class histogram. However, at a city level, the facade and roof colors vary too much to detect gables with this type of method.

[9] presents another kind of method to refine building models generated from terrestrial laser points. It is based on feature extraction rather than pixel segmentation,

and it uses strong line features extracted from the images to locate the façade edges. Since a gable is characterized by a very specific shape but a texture dependent on the covering material, it seems appropriate to rely on a contour-based approach involving mainly geometric criteria.

3 Input Data

The input data consist of geo-referenced terrestrial images and a laser point cloud. They are registered against available building 3D models using the method described in [10]. The terrestrial images are used to compute a texture map of the facades. A façade texture generally consists of a mixture of 10 to 20 overlapping input views which are geometrically rectified and merged [11]. Only the facades directly visible from the vehicle are associated to a photorealistic texture image. These images often show only a part of the roof, and they contain more occlusions than aerial images, mostly due to vegetation.

The purpose of this study is to detect the gable roofs, which are not easily recognizable in a low-resolution DEM. The input data are the ortho-rectified façade images automatically generated using [11]. The input 3D model and the laser point cloud are currently not used.

4 Gable Detection Process

Every façade is processed independently, which enables the management of complex roofs. Although the method is applicable to any type of building, some initial assumptions are made. As mentioned earlier, it is assumed that the gable is covered with the same material as the corresponding wall. The facade must correspond to the greatest part of the image. It must be approximately centered, with no large occluding objects in front of the roof. Only building facades with one single gable are currently considered, which corresponds to most European buildings.

The method consists of two main stages: lateral roof edge detection and bottom edge detection. In this section, an overview of the method is given, and each step is then detailed.

4.1 Method Overview

The input data consist of a single rectified façade image derived from a terrestrial acquisition system. The gable detection process is illustrated in Fig. 3. It consists of two main stages: the extraction of the lateral roof edges, and the research of a horizontal edge at the bottom of the roof. If two lateral roof edges are detected in the image without a horizontal bottom edge, then the building façade is classified as a gable. For instance, the facade illustrated in Fig. 3 will not be classified as a gable.

4.2 Lateral Roof Edge Detection

First two filtering steps are applied on the source image: morphological closing and bilateral filter. Then the lateral roof edges are detected and extended if necessary.

Morphological closing. The purpose of this step is to cull out possible sources of errors like antennas, electric cables, wall patterns or streetlights, whilst preserving relevant building edges. A morphological closing operation (image dilation followed by erosion) is applied with a 3×3 square structuring element, which determines the maximal size of the structures we want to filter out. The middle column of Fig. 4 shows an example of results after morphological closing: the roof edges are preserved, but the wall texture is smoothed.

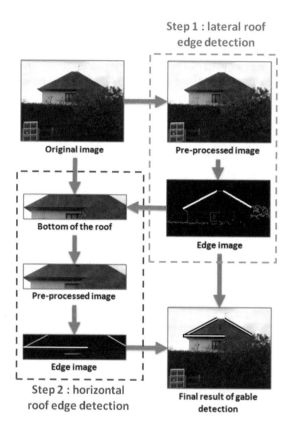

Fig. 3. General process for gable detection

Bilateral filter. A bilateral filter [12-14] is an edge-preserving and noise reducing smoothing filter. It allows the regularization of the image by averaging close pixels with similar gray levels. A weight is assigned to each neighbouring pixel. It decreases with both the distance in the image and the distance on the intensity axis, using a Gaussian as a decreasing function. Each resulting pixel is a weighted average of its neighbours. This filter smoothes the facade radiometry but preserves the roof edges (see Fig. 4, right column).

Fig. 4. Original image with errors on image mosaicking (left column), result after morphological closing (middle column), and result after bilateral filtering (right column)

Fig. 5 shows another example of an image after morphological closing and bilateral filtering. The small structures like antennas, streetlights, electric cables or branches are much less constrasted or even removed from the image after the morphological closing operation. The bilateral filter smoothes the facade radiometry and the vegetation outlines, whilst preserving the roof edges.

Fig. 5. Original images (top), and the corresponding images after morphological closing and bilateral filtering (bottom)

Extraction of lateral roof edges. First, image edges are extracted applying the Canny edge detector on the preprocessed image [15]. The filter parameters are chosen in order to only extract edges with a strong gradient. The lateral roof edges are often well contrasted and are easily detected, along with most vegetation contours. However, the bottom roof edges are usually not extracted during this stage (see Fig. 6(b)). Then all line segments of a minimum size are extracted in the edge image using the progressive probabilistic Hough transform (PPHT) [16]. The result of this step is illustrated in Fig. 6(c).

The lines are further filtered out using a threshold on the direction, in order to only keep oblique segments. Then every segment hypothesis is weighted according to its position in the image. The purpose of this step is to take advantage of the knowledge that the source image is centered on the façade: the apex of the gable is often located near the top center of image. More precisely, a first weight w_1 is computed with respect to the distance between the highest vertex of the segment and the center of the image. A second weight w_2 is computed with respect to the distance between this vertex and the top of the image. The weight values vary according to a normal distribution (see Fig. 7). Each line is finally associated to a score S given by:

$$S = L \cdot w_1 \cdot w_2 \tag{1}$$

where L is the segment length, and w_1 and w_2 are the segment weights. The result of the scoring process is illustrated in Fig. 6(d).

Finally, the line segment with the positive slope (resp. negative slope) and the highest score is selected as the left (resp. right) lateral roof edge (see Fig. 6(e)). They are said valid if two conditions are met:

- they have a minimal size in relation to the image size (chosen as 5%);
- the bottom vertex of the "negative" segment is located at the left of the top vertex of the "positive" segment, and reciprocally.

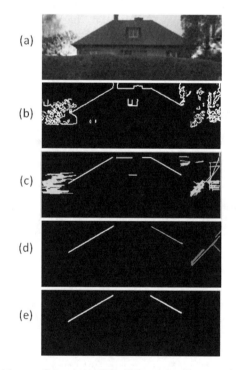

(a)

(b)

(c)

(d)

(e)

Fig. 6. (a) pre-processed image; (b) output of the Canny edge detector; (c) line extraction with the PPHT; (d) weights assigned to each line segment (light is for the highest score and dark is for the lowest score); (e) the two selected lateral roof edges

Fig. 7. Weight variation in the image ($w_1 . w_2$)

Roof edge extension. A lateral roof edge can sometimes be fragmented into several segments because of small occlusions or outline irregularities due to complex architectures or errors in image mosaicking (see Fig. 4).

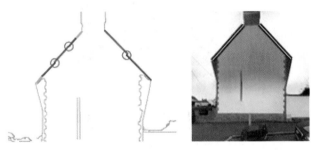

Fig. 8. (a): all segment extension hypotheses; (b): final lateral roof edges

In order to solve this problem, the lateral roof edges detected at the previous step can be extended.

First, all the neighbouring segments aligned with the current segment are extracted using collinearity tests. The algorithm is iteratively applied on the new segments until there is no further possible extension (see Fig. 8(a)). In order to solve the discontinuity problems, circular areas with fixed size are then defined around the reference segment end points. If they contain a vertex belonging to a neighbouring segment with a similar direction (with more tolerance than on the collinearity tests), it is merged with the reference segment (see Fig. 8(a)). This operation is repeated as long as new segments are added.

Fig. 9. Edges of a barn roof: the detected segments are in white

The final roof edges are valid if they intersect above the highest vertex (with a slight tolerance). Moreover, the extracted roof width must have a minimum size in relation to the width of the image.

This method allows the management of gambrel roofs or more complicate roofs like the one shown in Fig. 9.

4.3 Horizontal Roof Edge Detection

At this stage of the process, the lateral roof edges have been extracted from the images. In order to determine the presence of a gable, the presence of a horizontal roof edge must be investigated. If no horizontal edge is detected at the bottom of the roof, then the façade will be classified as a gable.

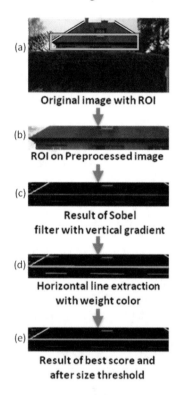

Fig. 10. Detection of horizontal roof edges

A region of interest (ROI) is first defined: it is centered in height on the lowest point of the roof lateral edges (a part of the roof may be hidden by vegetation as in Fig. 5 with the tree). The height of the area represents 20 percent of the image height; the width of the area is bounded by the bottom of the two lateral roof edges (see Fig. 10(a) and 10(b)).

A morphological closing is applied with a rectangular element of 6 pixels in width and 2 pixels in height, in order to highlight the horizontal elements within the ROI. Next a Sobel filter is applied to compute the gradient in the vertical direction (see Fig. 10(c)).

Line segments are then extracted using the Hough transform. Note that the parameters for straight line extraction are looser than previously because the bottom edge of a roof is often less contrasted than the lateral roof edges and the search area is smaller. Among all the extracted straight lines, the horizontal segments are selected and scored (see Fig. 10(d)). The score is defined according to its size and its distance to the ROI mid-height using a Gaussian as decreasing function.

Finally, the segment with the highest score is selected and said valid if it has a width larger than 50% of ROI width (see Fig. 10(e)).

If no valid horizontal roof edge has been found, then the façade is classified as a gable.

5   Experimentation

The method was tested using 158 façade images from the city of St. Grégoire in France, including 38 facades with a gable. Geo-referenced terrestrial images were taken using Siradel mobile mapping vehicle, then rectified and merged into ortho-rectified façade images.

5.1   Qualitative Results

Fig. 11 shows some results on different types of facades. The algorithm is robust with respect to the vegetation and various types of architecture.

The gables were correctly detected on the five examples of the first row. In Fig. 11(e), the adjacent facade appears in the image, and the roof ridge was extracted instead of the left lateral roof edge. However, the lateral roof edge is correct on the right side, and it is used to determine the possible location of the horizontal roof edge.

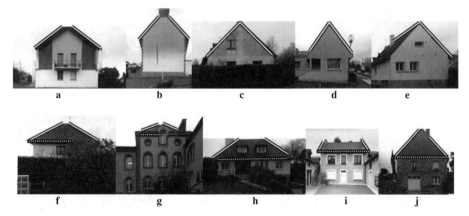

Fig. 11. Results of the gable detection. The first row shows roofs classified as gable roofs, whereas the second shows roofs classified as non-gable roofs. The lateral roof edges are shown with a white line, and the detected horizontal edges are shown with a dotted line. A gable is characterized by the absence of horizontal edge.

The second row in Fig. 11 shows examples where the roofs were classified as non-gable roofs. Fig. 11(j) is a gable covered with slate. The difference in materials is interpreted as a horizontal roof edge by the algorithm. Without depth information it is not possible to interpret it as a gable.

5.2 Quantitative Results

Table 1 shows the confusion matrix computed on the reference data set. Among the 38 gables present in the 158 images, 9 were not recognized (23.68%). However, there is no false detection of gable. Among the 9 gables that were not detected, 5 of them were missed because of a failure in the lateral roof edge detection, 3 others because a horizontal edge was found. In the last case, both errors were combined. These detection errors are discussed in the next section.

Table 1. Confusion matrix

		Predicted	
		Gable	Other
Reference	Gable	76.32%	23.68%
	Other	0%	100%

5.3 Limits of the Approach

The experimentation shows that gables can be missed for two main reasons: either the lateral roof edges are not well detected in the image, or a misleading horizontal edge is extracted at the roof bottom.

Fig. 12. Examples of false-negative cases, where no gable has been found. The first row shows examples of incomplete lateral edge detection. The second row shows examples of misleading horizontal edges.

Fig. 12 shows various cases of errors. Errors on lateral roof edge detection are mainly due to vegetation or other buildings in the background (Fig. 12(a) and (b)). If the background behind the gable has a radiometry similar to the facade, the lateral roof edges might not be extracted, because the threshold is set for strong gradients (corresponding to the boundary between roof and sky). Another source of failure is the presence of several gables in the image (Fig. 12(c)).

Erroneous detections of horizontal boundaries are often due to the façade architecture. For example, an edge is systematically detected on timbered houses (Fig. 12(d)). The stone houses can also lead to misdetections (Fig. 12(e)). Finally garage doors represent the most common risk of errors (Fig. 12(f)).

6   Conclusion and Future Work

The method for gable detection provides good results considering the diversity of buildings and the frequent occlusions. The algorithm is very robust to false detections, but still too many gables are missed. The main sources of errors are the occlusions and the structured facades.

The vegetation could be previously removed via colour-based image segmentation (Recky, 2009). It is also possible to use a segmentation algorithm based on entropy, as already used for aerial images [17]. The gradient entropy is generally larger on vegetation than on facades (see Fig. 13). The identification of the vegetation areas would enable to relax the parameters and to improve the lateral roof edge detection.

Fig. 13. Entropy computed on a facade image with vegetation after thresholding

The sky could also be previously identified using a color-based segmentation method. In [18], an algorithm is proposed to detect the sky under all weather conditions. This would reduce the number of errors due to low contrasted lateral roof edges.

In addition to the image, terrestrial laser data acquired by a MMS could also be used to identify roof gables. In particular, the depth information could help detecting gables covered with slates. Finally, the method should be extended to multiple gables and to shed roofs, which are also very difficult to recognize in the DEM.

References

1. Durupt, M., Taillandier, F.: Automatic building reconstruction from a digital elevation model and cadastral data: an operational approach. In: Photogrammetric Computer Vision, IAPRS & SIS, Bonn, Germany, vol. XXXVI Part 3 (2006)
2. Wang, X., Totaro, S., Taillandier, F., Hanson, A., Teller, S.: Recovering façade texture and microstructure from real-world images. In: ECCV Texture 2002 Workshop, Copenhagen, Denmark (2002)
3. Van Gool, L., Zeng, G., Van den Borre, F., Müller, P.: Towards Mass-produced Building Models. In: Photogrammetric Image Analysis, Munich, Germany (2007)
4. Korah, T., Rasmussen, C.: Analysis of Building Textures for Reconstructing Partially Occluded Facades. In: Forsyth, D., Torr, P., Zisserman, A. (eds.) ECCV 2008, Part I. LNCS, vol. 5302, pp. 359–372. Springer, Heidelberg (2008)
5. Hernández, J., Marcotegui, B.: Morphological Segmentation of Building Facade Images. In: IEEE International Conference on Image Processing, Cairo, Egypt (2009)
6. Wendel, A., Donoser, M., Bischof, H.: Unsupervised Facade Segmentation Using Repetitive Patterns. In: Goesele, M., Roth, S., Kuijper, A., Schiele, B., Schindler, K. (eds.) Pattern Recognition. LNCS, vol. 6376, pp. 51–60. Springer, Heidelberg (2010)
7. Teboul, O., Simon, L., Koutsourakis, P., Paragios, N.: Segmentation of building facades using procedural shape priors. In: Proceedings of CVPR 2010, pp. 3105–3112 (2010)
8. Recky, M., Leberl, F.: Semantic Segmentation of Street-Side Images. In: Proceedings of the Annual OAGM Workshop, pp. 271–282. Austrian Computer Society in OCG (2009)
9. Pu, S., Vosselman, G.: Refining building facade models with images. In: CMRT 2009: Object Extraction for 3D City Models, Road Databases and Traffic Monitoring: Concepts, Algorithms and Evaluation, ISPRS, Paris, vol. 38, pp. 217–222 (2009)
10. Denis, E., Baillard, C.: Refining Existing 3d Building Models With Terrestrial Laser Points Acquired From A Mobile Mapping Vehicle. In: IAPRS & SIS, Newcastle, UK, vol. XXXIX, Part 5 (2010)
11. Benitez, B., Denis, E., Baillard, C.: Automatic Production of Occlusion-Free Rectified Façade Textures using Vehicle-Based Imagery. In: Photogrammetric Computer Vision and Image Analysis, Paris, France, vol. (A), p. 275 (2010)
12. Aurich, V., Weule, J.: Non-linear gaussian filters performing edge preserving diffusion. In: Proceedings of the DAGM Symposium (1995)
13. Smith, S.M., Brady, J.M.: Susan - a new approach to low level image processing. International Journal of Computer Vision (23), 45–78 (1997)
14. Tomasi, C., Manduchi, R.: Bilateral filtering for gray and color images. In: Sixth International Conference on Computer Vision, New Delhi, pp. 839–846 (1998)
15. Canny, J.: A computational approach to edge detection. IEEE Transactions on Pattern Analysis and Machine Intelligence (8), 679–714 (1986)
16. Matas, J., Galambos, C., Kittler, J.: Robust detection of lines using the progressive probabilistic Hough transform. Computer Vision Image Understanding (78), 119–137 (2000)
17. Shorter, N., Kasparis, T.: Automatic Vegetation Identification and Building Detection from a Single Nadir Aerial Image. Remote Sensing 1(4), 731–757 (2009)
18. Schmitt, F., Priese, L.: Sky Detection in CSC-segmented Color Images. VISAPP (2), 101–106 (2009)

Multi-spectral False Color Shadow Detection

Mustafa Teke[1], Emre Başeski[1], Ali Özgün Ok[2],
Barış Yüksel[1], and Çağlar Şenaras[1]

[1] HAVELSAN A.Ş., Eskişehir Yolu 7.km 06520, Ankara, Turkey
{mteke,ebaseski,byuksel,csenaras}@havelsan.com.tr
[2] Middle East Technical University, Department of Geodetic and Geographic
Information Technologies, 06531, Ankara, Turkey
oozgun@metu.edu.tr

Abstract. With the availability of high-resolution commercial satellite
images, automated analysis and object extraction became even a more
important topic in remote sensing. As shadows cover a significant portion
of an image, they play an important role on automated analysis. While
they degrade performance of applications such as image registration,
shadow is an important cue for information such as man-made structures.
In this article, a shadow detection algorithm that makes use of near-
infrared information in combination with RGB bands is introduced. The
algorithm is applied on an application for automated building detection.

Keywords: Shadow detection, building detection, near-infrared, false
color.

1 Introduction

Aerial and satellite images contain varying amount of shadows depending on the
acquisition time, surface properties and number of objects on the surface that
cast shadow. Shading is considered as an important visual cue as it can be used
to reveal the shape of an object from a single image (see e.g., Zhang et al. (1999)
for a review). Therefore, detecting shaded areas on a remotely sensed image can
give valuable information for automated detection of man-made objects.

As the sun radiates light, photons collide with particles in the air and scatter.
The scattering of light is inversely proportional to the wavelength of photons
and this phenomenon is explained by Rayleigh scattering (Rees (1993)). In visible spectrum, blue component of light scatters most. Therefore, blue band has
higher values than green and red bands in shaded areas. Additionally, shaded
areas appear darker than their neighbors. Shadow detection algorithms usually exploit color values in different color spaces to make use of these facts. In
Polidorio et al. (2003), shadow detection on satellite and aerial images is performed by applying different threshold values to Saturation and Intensity differences. Sarabandi et al. (2004) exploits properties of c1c2c3 and suggests that
c1c2c3 color space produces better results than RGB and HSV. Both works use
manual thresholds and the results vary significantly depending on these thresholds. Tsai (2006) uses different color spaces (HSV, HSI, HCV, YIQ, YCbCr)

U. Stilla et al. (Eds.): PIA 2011, LNCS 6952, pp. 109–119, 2011.
© Springer-Verlag Berlin Heidelberg 2011

for shadow detection from aerial images where different Ratio Maps for each of these color spaces are compared. The method argues that the best performance is obtained using Hue and Intensity ratio in HSI color space and an automated thresholding is applied to the Ratio Map by using Otsu's method (Otsu (1979)). In Chung et al. (2009), an improvement to Tsai's method is proposed which uses a new ratio map and an automated successive thresholding scheme. Note that, these methods work on the RGB interval of the spectrum and do not exploit the potential of Near-Infrared (NIR) band.

In NIR band, shaded areas appear dark and this fact can be used to design algorithms that can discriminate shadow and other dark regions with a better performance. For example, Fredembach and Süsstrunk (2010) proposes an automatic shadow detection method which uses NIR band as an additional cue to create a darkness map that is based on both NIR and intensity.

Although the color of a shadow region is supposed to be dark, this darkness varies extensively (even in the same image) depending on the surface characteristics and material properties. The fundamental idea behind the work in this article is to darken the shaded areas on an image by removing the blue band as it scatters most and treating green, red, NIR bands as RGB. This new false-color space is then converted into HSI and an automated thresholding is applied on the Ratio Map histogram. The algorithm has been tested on IKONOS images with 1 meter and GeoEye images with 0.5 meter resolution. Also in Sect. 4, the potential of the proposed method is demonstrated on an application which makes use of shadow information for automated building detection.

2   Proposed Method

In this article, an automated shadow detection method that is based on visible and NIR part of the spectrum is proposed. In shadow areas, Blue band scatters most. As a result, pixel values in shadow areas have higher values in Blue band than the other bands such as Red or NIR. Also, Blue channel carries less information than Red and NIR bands as it spans a narrower portion of the spectrum. By removing the Blue band and shifting RGB color space to NIR band, one can obtain a false-color space (NIR-R-G) where the shadow areas become darker. We use the reflectance properties of shadows in this false-color space in order to detect shadows. The work-flow of the algorithm is illustrated in Fig. 1 and output of different steps of the algorithm is shown in Fig. 2.

Once the NIR-R-G image is obtained, it is converted into HSI color space (see Fig. 2-(b) for an example). Based on Polidorio et al. (2003), a difference map is calculated by using Equation 1.

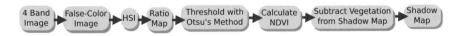

Fig. 1. Algorithm Steps

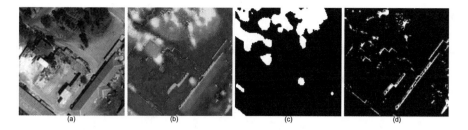

Fig. 2. Different steps of the algorithm. **(a)** Original image, **(b)** False color in HSI space, **(c)** Vegetation map, **(d)** Shadow detection result.

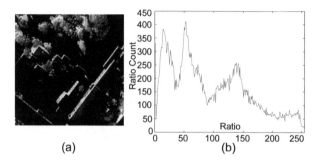

Fig. 3. **(a)** Ratio Map of the image that is shown in Fig. 2 **(b)** Histogram of the Ratio Map

$$S - I, \tag{1}$$

where S is normalized saturation and I is normalized intensity. Vegetation and dark objects have similar S-I values. In order to distinguish these areas, a Ratio Map is calculated by dividing the difference map into $S+I$ (Equation 2) since vegetated areas have higher S and I values compared to shaded areas. A sample Ratio Map and its histogram is shown Fig. 3.

$$\frac{S - I}{S + I}, \tag{2}$$

After the calculation of the Ratio Map, an automated threshold is applied to its histogram by using Otsu's method. As an example, Otsu's method finds the threshold as 100 for the histogram that is shown in Fig. 3-(b).

The automated thresholding scheme detects shadows and vegetation at the same time. Therefore, the vegetated areas are supposed to be eliminated to obtain only the shadow areas. By using Red and NIR bands, vegetation can be detected based on Normalized Difference Vegetation Index (NDVI) (see e.g., Tucker (1979) for details). A sample Vegetation Map is shown in Fig. 2-(c). To obtain the final Shadow Map, the Vegetation Map is used to eliminate the vegetated areas (see Fig. 2-(d) for an illustration).

3   Experimental Results

In this section, the evaluation of the proposed algorithm is presented. The experiments have been performed on a series of images whose shaded areas were labeled manually. Three IKONOS images with 1 meter (first three columns of Fig. 4) and one GeoEye image (fourth column of Fig. 4) with 0.5 meter resolution have been used. The labeled ground-truth images for the IKONOS images are presented on the second row of Fig. 4. Note that, the GeoEye image was evaluated only visually. The numerical evaluation of IKONOS images for different shadow detection algorithms is presented in Table 1, 2 and 3. The performance of the algorithms has been evaluated based on precision (Equation 3) and recall (Equation 4) measurements.

$$\text{Precision} = \frac{\text{True Positive}}{\text{True Positive} + \text{False Positive}}, \tag{3}$$

$$\text{Recall} = \frac{\text{True Positive}}{\text{True Positive} + \text{False Negative}}, \tag{4}$$

where True Positive regions are labeled as shadow and detected as shadow, False Positive regions are labeled as non-shadow and detected as shadow, True Negative regions are labeled as non-shadow and detected as non-shadow, and False Negative regions are labeled as shadow and detected as non-shadow.

Table 1. Evaluation of different algorithms on the image that is at the first column of Fig. 4

	True Positive	True Negative	False Positive	False Negative	Precision	Recall
Proposed	6587	189067	27361	12092	19.40%	35.26%
Polidorio	10893	187210	29218	7786	27.15%	58.31%
Tsai	15888	144080	72348	2791	18.00%	85.05%
Chung	8716	191325	25103	9963	25.77%	46.66%
Fredembach	4996	184299	32129	13683	13.45%	26.74%

Before discussing the numerical results, we would like to stress some important points about the visual results of the algorithms. As water appears dark both in visible and NIR spectrum, all algorithms detect water as shadow. Therefore, the number of False Positives increases drastically which reduces the Precision for the first and second images for all algorithms. Also, except the proposed method, the shadows of man-made objects are either missing or there are too many False Positives that make these shadows difficult to use for automated object extraction.

The results on the third column of Fig. 4 can be used as a fair evaluation criteria for precision as there is no water on the image. As the Table 3 suggests,

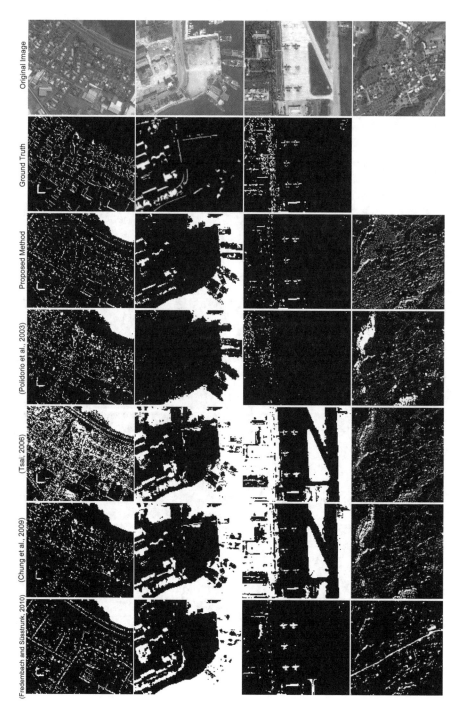

Fig. 4. Evaluation of different algorithms on IKONOS and GeoEye images

Fig. 5. Shadow detection results on various IKONOS and GeoEye images

Table 2. Evaluation of different algorithms on the image that is at the second column of Fig. 4

	True Positive	True Negative	False Positive	False Negative	Precision	Recall
Proposed	1726	56515	22924	4165	7.00%	29.29%
Polidorio	190	60379	19060	5701	0.98%	3.22%
Tsai	4868	46200	33239	1023	12.77%	82.63%
Chung	4664	47215	32224	1227	12.64%	79.17%
Fredembach	3904	48604	30835	198	11.23%	95.17%

Table 3. Evaluation of different algorithms on the image that is at the third column of Fig. 4

	True Positive	True Negative	False Positive	False Negative	Precision	Recall
Proposed	1561	220586	588	11919	72.63%	11.58%
Polidorio	3297	219904	1270	10183	72.19%	24.45%
Tsai	13214	101268	119906	266	9.92%	98.02%
Chung	12108	124210	96964	1372	11.10%	89.82%
Fredembach	3471	217204	3970	10009	46.64%	25.74%

the proposed method and Polidorio et al. (2003) give the best results for precision. On the other hand, Polidorio et al. (2003) is quite threshold dependent, and both the precision and the recall values can decrease drastically (see Table 2) depending on the threshold. While the algorithm in Tsai (2006) produces relatively high results for recall, the precision value in Table 3 and the visual results in Fig. 4 suggest that the algorithm produces too many False Positives. The algorithm in Chung et al. (2009) introduces an improvement on the algorithm in Tsai (2006) for both precision and recall but still the number of False Positives is higher than the rest of the algorithms. As mentioned in Sect. 1, the algorithm in Fredembach and Süsstrunk (2010) uses NIR band and the effect of illumination is less compared to the algorithms that use only visible spectrum.

When the visual and the numerical results are compared, one can observe that the main difference between the proposed method and the method in Fredembach and Süsstrunk (2010) is the number of False Positives. The proposed method finds more certain shadows than the method in Fredembach and Süsstrunk (2010). This leads to slightly more sparse shadows with a better precision for the proposed method.

More visual results of the proposed method is presented in Fig. 5. The first three rows are GeoEye images with 0.5 meter resolution and the last two rows are IKONOS images with 1 meter resolution. Visual inspection suggests that the proposed method can detect both artificial and natural shadows.

4 Building Detection as an Application

In this section, the potential of the proposed shadow detection algorithm is illustrated on a building detection scenario. Building detection is one of the challenging problems of automated target detection in remote sensing applications. A wide range of algorithms and models have been developed for automatic building extraction from monocular images. An exceptional survey can be found in Mayer (1999). Later, an extended version of this survey bounded in Mayers format was conducted by Unsalan and Boyer (2005). The trends followed within the state-of-the-art of building extraction can be found in Gruen et al. (1995, 1998); Baltsavias et al. (2001).

The main difficulty of building detection comes from the fact that the shape, color and textural properties of buildings change drastically from one image to another. The only property that is common about buildings is that their elevation is higher than the terrain surface. As mentioned in Sect. 1, shadows can be used as a fundamental cue to acquire the related height information from monocular images. Therefore, so far, manipulation of various shadow maps to estimate the position and height of the buildings is a widely accepted approach (see e.g., Huertas and Nevatia (1988); Irvin and McKeown (1989); Sirmacek and Unsalan (2008); Akcay and Aksoy (2010)).

In our building detection application, we exploit the shadow map produced by the proposed method. Buildings are extracted by using their neighboring shadows. In general, this type of extraction requires the knowledge of the exact sun direction and the sun angular elevation on a per image basis. With the knowledge of (i) the latitude, longitude, and height information of the image part being investigated, and (ii) the date/time the image was acquired, it is possible to compute the angles of sun azimuth and zenith (Reda and Andreas (2007)) during the image acquisition. Thereafter, the computed azimuth information can be utilized to infer buildings from the related shadow map.

In this study, we extracted the buildings using an approach similar to the one presented in Akcay and Aksoy (2010). The spatial relationships between the shadows and the buildings can be defined relative to each other. For sure, this relationship must be modeled with respect to a direction which is defined by the computed azimuth information. Given a shadow object (B) and the opposite direction of the computed azimuth angle (α), potential building landscape $\beta_{\alpha,\lambda,\tau}(B)$ around the shadow object along the given direction can be defined as a fuzzy function in image space (Cinbis and Aksoy (2007)):

$$\beta_{\alpha,\lambda,\tau}(B)(x) = (B \oplus \upsilon_{\alpha,\lambda,\tau})(x) \cap B^c \qquad (5)$$

$$\upsilon_{\alpha,\lambda,\tau}(x) = g_\lambda(\frac{2}{\pi}\Theta_\alpha(x,o)max\{0, 1 - \frac{\|\vec{ox}\|}{\tau}\}$$

where, υ is a fuzzy structuring element, g is a one-dimensional Bezier curve function with an inflection point λ, $\|\vec{ox}\|$ is the Euclidean distance of an image point x to the center (o) of the structuring element, $\Theta_\alpha(x,o)$ is the angle between the vector $\vec{ox}$ and the unit vector along the direction α, τ is a threshold corresponding to the distance where a point is no longer attracted from the shadow object, B^c represents complement of the shadow object, and $\oplus$ defines the morphological dilation. Once the potential building landscapes are generated, the

Fig. 6. Results of our building detection algorithm which uses the proposed shadow detection algorithm

buildings are detected by combining the similar segments along the defined building landscape. In Fig. 6 a sample building detection result is presented. Note that, the shadow map given in the last column of Fig. 4 has been used for this example.

5   Conclusion

We presented an automatic multi-spectral shadow detection algorithm which takes advantage of Near Infrared Band. It obtains a darkness image based on a false color spectrum where green, red, NIR bands are used as RGB. The final shadow mask is obtained by removing vegetation from a thresholded shadow map. The proposed method has been compared with the state-of-the-art shadow detection methods and the results have been evaluated both numerically and visually. Also, the potential of the algorithm has been illustrated on an application that is based on building detection.

The proposed method detects shadows with high precision but the detection results are relatively sparse compared to the other algorithms. Although this reduces the recall values, the algorithm detects shadows for most of the objects that cast shadow on the image. Therefore, it does not detect all shadows but detects shadows for most of the objects. Another advantage of the algorithm is its independence from manual thresholds. As it has been presented in Sect. 3, finding a universal threshold is not possible and finding the image specific thresholds is crucial.

As water appears dark both in visible and NIR spectrum, the proposed algorithm detects water as shadow. On the other hand, this is a common issue for all shadow detection algorithm and a shape based post processing is required to distinguish between water and shadow. A similar problem occurs in case of dark objects such as very dark roads. Contrast stretching and image adjusting for dark images which have narrow histogram are suggested to improve detection performance. However, histogram equalization is observed to produce too many false positives since distribution of pixel values is transformed in a non-linear way.

References

Akcay, H., Aksoy, S.: Building detection using directional spatial constraints. In: IGARSS, pp. 1932–1935 (2010)

Baltsavias, E.P., Gruen, A., Van Gool, L.: Automatic Extraction of Man-Made Objects from Aerial and Space Images (III). Balkema (2001)

Chung, K.L., Lin, Y.R., Huang, Y.H.: Efficient shadow detection of color aerial images based on successive thresholding scheme. IEEE Transactions on Geoscience and Remote Sensing 47(2), 671–682 (2009)

Cinbis, R.G., Aksoy, S.: Modeling spatial relationships in images. Tech. Rep. BU-CE-0702, Department of Computer Engineering, Bilkent University, Ankara, Turkey (2007)

Fredembach, C., Süsstrunk, S.: Automatic and accurate shadow detection from (potentially) a single image using near-infrared information. IEEE Transactions on Pattern Analysis and Machine Intelligence (2010)

Gruen, A., Baltsavias, E.P., Henricsson, O.: Automatic Extraction of Man-Made Objects from Aerial and Space Images (II). Birkhauser, Boston (1998)

Gruen, A., Kubler, O., Agouris, P.: Automatic Extraction of Man-Made Objects from Aerial and Space Images. Birkhauser, Boston (1995)

Huertas, A., Nevatia, R.: Detecting buildings in aerial images. Comput. Vision Graph. Image Process. 41(2), 131–152 (1988)

Irvin, R., McKeown, D.M.: Methods for exploiting the relationship between buildings and their shadows in aerial imagery. IEEE Transactions on Systems, Man and Cybernetics 19(6), 1564–1575 (1989)

Mayer, H.: Automatic object extraction from aerial imagery–a survey focusing on buildings. Computer Vision and Image Understanding 74(2), 138–149 (1999)

Otsu, N.: A threshold selection method from gray-level histograms. IEEE Transactions on Systems, Man and Cybernetics 9(1), 62–66 (1979)

Polidorio, A.M., Flores, F.C., Imai, N.N., Tommaselli, A.M.G., Franco, C.: Automatic shadow segmentation in aerial color images. In: Proc. XVI Brazilian Symp. Computer Graphics and Image Processing, pp. 270–277 (2003)

Reda, I., Andreas, A.: Solar position algorithm for solar radiation application. Tech. Rep. NREL/TP-560-34302, National Renewable Energy Laboratory, NREL (2007)

Rees, W.G.: Physical Principles of Remote Sensing (1993)

Sarabandi, P., Yamazaki, F., Matsuoka, M., Kiremidjian, A.: Shadow detection and radiometric restoration in satellite high resoluiton images. In: Proceedings of IEEE International on IGARES 2004, Anchorage, AK, vol. 6, pp. 3744–3747 (2004)

Sirmacek, B., Unsalan, C.: Building detection from aerial images using invariant color features and shadow information. In: Proceedings of the 23rd International Symposium on Computer and Information Sciences, ISCIS 2008, pp. 1–5. IEEE, Los Alamitos (2008)

Tsai, V.: A comparative study on shadow compensation of color aerial images in invariant color models. IEEE Transactions on Geoscience and Remote Sensing 44(6), 1661–1671 (2006)

Tucker, C.J.: Red and photographic infrared linear combinations for monitoring vegetation. Remote Sensing of Environment 8(2), 127–150 (1979)

Unsalan, C., Boyer, K.: A system to detect houses and residential street networks in multispectral satellite images. Computer Vision and Image Understanding 98(3), 423–461 (2005)

Zhang, R., Tsai, P., Cryer, J., Shah, M.: Shape from shading: A survey, vol. 21(8), pp. 690–706 (August 1999)

Extraction of Non-forest Trees for Biomass Assessment Based on Airborne and Terrestrial LiDAR Data

Matthias Rentsch[1], Alfons Krismann[2], and Peter Krzystek[1]

[1] Munich University of Applied Sciences, Department of Geoinformatics, Karlstraße 6,
80333 Munich, Germany
{rentsch,krzystek}@hm.edu
[2] University of Hohenheim, Institute for Landscape- and Plant-Ecology, August-v.-
Hartmann-Straße 3, 70593 Stuttgart, Germany
a_krismann@uni-hohenheim.de

Abstract. The main goal of the federal funded project 'LiDAR based biomass assessment' is the nationwide investigation of the biomass potential coming from wood cuttings of non-forest trees. In this context, first and last pulse airborne laserscanning (F+L) data serve as preferred database. First of all, mandatory field calibrations are performed for pre-defined grove types. For this purpose, selected reference groves are captured by full-waveform airborne laserscanning (FWF) and terrestrial laserscanning (TLS) data in different foliage conditions. The paper is reporting about two methods for the biomass assessment of non-forest trees. The first method covers the determination of volume-to-biomass conversion factors which relate the reference above-ground biomass (AGB) estimated from allometric functions with the laserscanning derived vegetation volume. The second method is focused on a 3D Normalized Cut segmentation adopted for non-forest trees and the follow-on biomass calculation based on segmentation-derived tree features.

Keywords: LiDAR, Vegetation, Correlation, Point Cloud, Segmentation, Three-dimensional.

1 Introduction

One of the main intensions of the Germany's climate initiative is the distinct enhancement of renewable energy resources (e.g. sun, wind, water, biomass) for the electric power supply until 2020. Beside biomass coming from short-rotation wood and forest fuel, the incorporation of wood cuttings from landscaping of non-forest trees is getting more and more attractive.

A comprehensive estimation of above-ground biomass based on first and last pulse data (density 0.7-1.2 pts/m^2) was carried out in Norway's boreal forests, leading to R^2=0.88 for AGB (Næsset and Gobakken, 2008). An ongoing nationwide project, 'LASER-WOOD' (Hollaus et al., 2010) aims to assess the growing stock and AGB potential for the Austrian forests using LiDAR (Light Detection and Ranging) and forest inventory data. The study of van Aardt et al. (2008) is dedicated to evaluate the potential of an object-oriented approach for forest type classification as well as

U. Stilla et al. (Eds.): PIA 2011, LNCS 6952, pp. 121–132, 2011.

volume and biomass estimation in the Virginia Piedmont, U.S.A. based on small-footprint multiple return LiDAR data. The classifications yield an overall accuracy up to 89%, and the estimates considering the volume and biomass estimations exhibit differences of no more than 5.5% with respect to field surveys.

However, many methods described in the literature were more or less applied to closed forest stands. In contrast, non-forest stands (e.g. open-grown trees, urban trees) are characterized by heterogeneous structures containing various species within a small area, complex shapes, and high fractions of bushy material which suppress the penetration of laser pulses. Up to now only a few studies are focused on the estimation of AGB of non-forest trees (Zhou et al., 2011). Straub (2010) is reporting about some studies in Germany, which are characterized by high uncertainties in terms of the amount of biomass. One reason is that the validation is performed only with a small number of random tests coming from destructive sampling. In Velázques-Martí et al. (2010), a prediction model was developed which allows the biomass estimation of a bushy Mediterranean forest area near Valencia/Spain consisting of 5 species using a LiDAR derived canopy height model (CHM). If this model can be transferred to the conditions in Germany was not yet examined. An investigation with emphasis on the estimation of urban green volume is presented by Hecht et al. (2008). Kato et al. (2009) have derived the crown volume of several species of a mixed urban forest by a wrapped surface reconstruction method. In most cases, the AGB of non-forest trees is deduced using an ordinary volume-to-biomass conversion. Herein, the vegetation volume is often approximated by simple geometric elements like cuboids, leading to high uncertainties in the volume determination, e.g. 32% (Cremer, 2007).

The main objective of our field calibrations is to determine the correlation of LiDAR derived vegetation volume and above-ground biomass to the reference biomass of selected grove types of non-forest trees. For this purpose, two different methods are introduced and described in Section 2. A brief overview concerning the LiDAR and field data can be found in Section 3. Section 4 presents the first results, followed by a discussion in Section 5 and a closing summary in Section 6.

2   Methods

The methods covered by our paper are focused on initial calibration efforts for several sample reference groves of pre-defined types. In the first method (Sections 2.2 and 2.3), the vegetation volume [m^3] is derived using a normalized digital surface model (nDSM) which is interpolated from the LiDAR point clouds. For two selected reference groves types a volume-to-biomass conversion factor is deduced which allows the transformation of the vegetation volume into the unit of totally dry AGB in form of wood chips, the bulk cubic meter [BCM]. Herein, the variation of the conversion factor for each grove type should be within fixed limits. In the second method (Sections 2.4 to 2.7), a 3D Normalized Cut segmentation of the LiDAR point clouds is performed. In doing so, the AGB of segmented trees can be derived from calculated tree segment features in a regression analysis using the estimated reference AGB (Section 2.1).

2.1 Allometric Estimation of Reference AGB

For the precise volume-to-biomass conversion in a region of interest (ROI), the determination of the exact above-ground biomass is mandatory. For this purpose, the destructive sampling of the trees within the reference groves is considered as the appropriate method. However, in most cases this procedure is not feasible and consequently, the biomass is estimated using allometric functions. In our study, we applied selected stem volume equations valid for forest-grown tree species in Europe (Zianis et al., 2005). For these equations, the DBH and the tree height serve as input variables. The DBH of reference trees can be measured directly by caliper or tape. In addition, the DBH and the tree locations can be derived from horizontal cross-sections for trees whose stems were captured by TLS without occlusions with an accuracy of 2-3 cm. The reference tree height h_i^{ref} is measured directly using a laser rangefinder TruePulse-Laser 360[®]. Unless the tree canopy is not detectable (e.g. the inner trees of forest islands), the tree heights are deduced by means of the TLS point clouds. For this purpose, the local maximum within a defined horizontal distance (e.g. 1 m) with respect to the stem position is determined and the elevation derived from a reference terrain model is subtracted.

The timber volume is estimated as the sum of the stem volume and the approximated branch volume (20% of the stem volume). Finally, the timber volume is transformed to the AGB by multiplying with the constant factor $fc_{m3,BCM}$ (=2.43) which relates the unit of the timber volume (=m^3) to the unit of the AGB (=BCM) (FNR, 2010). Thus, the AGB for a ROI is computed by

$$AGB_{ROI}^{ref} = 1.2 \times fc_{m3,BCM} \times \sum_{i=nRef} f_j(spec_j, DBH_i^{ref}, h_i^{ref}) \tag{1}$$

with $f_j(spec_j, DBH_i^{ref}, h_i^{ref})$ as the allometric equation of the tree species j and $spec_j$ as the parameters of tree species j.

It has to be mentioned that the applied allometric equations are actually valid for forest-grown trees. At the time of writing no relevant publications were known to the authors dealing with the allometric biomass estimation of central-European open-grown tree species, except some studies which mention the divergent relation of trunk and tree crown of non-forest trees (Hasenauer, 1997; Zhou et al., 2011) with respect to forest trees.

2.2 Vegetation Volume with Normalized DSM

In our first method we estimate the vegetation volume by using a nDSM which is simply calculated by subtracting a digital terrain model (DTM) from the digital surface model (DSM) of a reference grove. For the DTM generation, ground points are first of all extracted from merged TLS, FWF and F+L data by applying TerraScan® software package. Due to the high density of the filtered ground points the reference DTM is interpolated with 0.5 m grid spacing. The DSM is interpolated according to Reitberger et al. (2007) in the ROI from the LiDAR data with a grid width of 0.5 m for TLS and FWF, and 1.0 m for F+L and first pulse (FPL) data.

If we assume a grid width gw for the nDSM, the number of m quadratic cells in the ROI and H_{cell} as the relative height in a cell, the vegetation volume can be approximated with

$$Vol_{ROI}^{nDSM} = gw^2 \sum_{i=m} H_{cell_i}$$ (2)

2.3 Volume-to-Biomass Conversion

The objective of the first method is the derivation of meaningful volume-to-biomass conversion factors $V2BCF$ for each reference grove type k, for which the standard deviations $std(V2BCF_k)$ should be within distinct limits.

$$V2BCF_k = mean \sum_{k=nGrove} AGB_{ROI_k}^{ref} / Vol_{ROI_k}^{nDSM}$$ (3)

For this purpose, an appropriate number of reference groves (e.g. $nGrove$ = 30-50) have to be considered for each grove type. Accordingly, various test sites are selected in several federal states in Germany, like Bavaria, Baden-Württemberg, North Rhine-Westphalia, Lower Saxony and Brandenburg.

2.4 3D Normalized Cut Segmentation

Single trees are found by a 3D segmentation technique which is based on Normalized Cut segmentation known from image analysis (Reitberger et al., 2009). The key idea of this method is to feature the vegetation area in a voxel representation (Fig. 1a). The Normalized Cut segmentation applied in the voxel structure of a ROI is based on a graph G. The two disjoint segments A and B of the graph are found by maximizing the similarity of the segment members and minimizing the similarity between the segments A and B (Fig. 1b) solving the cost function

$$NCut(A,B) = \frac{Cut(A,B)}{Assoc(A,V)} + \frac{Cut(A,B)}{Assoc(B,V)}$$ (4)

with $Cut(A,B) = \sum_{i \varepsilon A, j \varepsilon B} w_{ij}$ as the total sum of weights between the segments A and B

and $Assoc(A,V) = \sum_{i \varepsilon A, j \varepsilon V} w_{ij}$ as the sum of the weights of all edges ending in the

segment A. The weights w_{ij} specify the similarity between the voxels and are a function of the laser point distribution and additional features calculated from the pulse width and the intensity of the single decomposed reflections in case of full-waveform LiDAR data. A minimum solution for (4) is found by means of a corresponding generalized eigenvalue problem.

The proposed 3D segmentation technique is able to improve the detection rate in lower vegetation areas significantly. Furthermore, the method can split single trees which do not appear in the canopy height model as isolated local maxima. Note that the method is not dependent on full waveform LiDAR data. It can also successfully be applied to conventional LiDAR data (e.g. F+L) just providing 3D point coordinates.

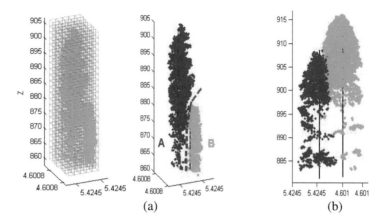

(a)   (b)

Fig. 1. Single tree segmentation using Normalized Cut: (a) Subdivision of ROI into a voxel structure and division of voxels into two tree segments and (b) segmentation results with the stems of the reference trees displayed as black lines

2.5   Feature Calculation

The Normalized Cut segmentation provides for each segmented tree corresponding laser points. According to Reitberger et al. (2007) crown points are separated from possible existing stem reflections by finding the crown base height. All the laser hits above the crown base height are forming the crown points. Triangulating this point cloud of each segmented tree i by 3D alpha shapes (Edelsbrunner and Mücke, 1994; Vauhkonen, 2010) leads to an approximation of the crown volume V_{crown}. Additionally, we estimate for each segmented tree i the tree area A_{stem} by calculating the maximum 2D convex hull of the crown points. Finally, we determine the tree height H_{tree} from the vertical distance of the highest laser points within the tree segment to the reference DTM and the crown height H_{crown} from the height difference between the highest and lowest crown point. The parameters V_{crown}, A_{stem}, H_{tree} and H_{crown} constitute tree features which are used in the subsequent linear regression to estimate the stem volume and above-ground biomass, respectively.

2.6   Segmentation-Derived Stem Volume and AGB

The $AGB_{stem,i}$ for a 3D segment is derived from the stem volume $V_{stem,i}$ (Reitberger et al., 2010) in a simplified manner. First, the volume of the branches is approximated with 20% of the stem volume and added. Then, the resulting timber volume which is represented by the unit cubic meter (m^3) is transformed to bulk cubic meter (BCM), the unit of the above-ground biomass (in form of absolute dry weight wood chips).

$$AGB_{stem_i} = 1.2 \times fc_{m3,BCM} \times V_{stem_i} \tag{5}$$

The transformation factor $fc_{m3,BCM}$ we apply in our investigations is 2.43 (FNR, 2010) and is unique for all tree species.

Since the AGB cannot be directly measured from ALS data, an indirect calculation is conducted according to equation (6) using the tree features $H_{tree,i}$, $A_{crown,i}$, $V_{crown,i}$ and $H_{crown,i}$.

$$AGB_{stem_i} = b_0 + b_1 H_{tree_i} + b_2 A_{crown_i} + b_3 V_{crown_i} + b_4 H_{crown_i} + b_5 H^2_{tree_i}$$

$$+ b_6 A^2_{crown_i} + b_7 V^2_{crown_i} + b_8 H^2_{crown_i} \qquad (6)$$

$$= f(b_j, H_{tree_i}, A_{crown_i}, V_{crown_i}, H_{crown_i})$$

2.7 Cross-Validation

The coefficients b_j $(j=1...8)$ in (6) are estimated in a least squares adjustment whereby $AGB_{stem,i}$ is the known AGB of reference tree i. The quality of the least squares approach is represented by the root mean squared error $RMSE$ with n as the number of reference trees used in the regression. The quality of the linear regression (6) is tested in a k-fold cross-validation (with $k=n/8$). The average error $RMSE(CV)$ across all k trials is calculated to evaluate the model. Finally, the estimated AGB of the ROI is obtained by summing up all biomass portions of the segmented trees with

$$AGB^{NCut}_{ROI} = \sum_{i=n} f(b_j, H_{tree_i}, A_{crown_i}, V_{crown_i}, H_{crown_i}) \qquad (7)$$

3 LiDAR and Field Data

The two calibration areas are located in South-eastern Germany, near Arnbruck (49°07.8'N, 12°59.8'E) and Regen (48°58.2'N, 13°07.7'E). For these two areas, a sum of 13 reference groves were chosen by visual inspection comprising the grove types 'Hedge with Trees '(HT) (4), 'Forest Island'(FI) (2) and 'Single Tree'(ST) (7). All of these groves were captured by FWF data (10 pts/m^2) in August 2009 by the Riegl LMS-Q560 scanner in leaf-on conditions. Furthermore, the areas were covered by routine F+L surveys on behalf of the Bavarian Survey Administration in April 2008 and October 2009. The acquisitions were performed in leaf-off conditions with a mean point density of 1-2 pts/m^2. In addition, all groves were measured by a precise and full 3D TLS registration in April and November 2010 using the Riegl LMS-Z390

Table 1. Specifications of the selected reference groves

Grove type	Reference grove	Test site	Number of trees	Tree biomass fractions (approx.)
Hedge with Trees (HT)	02_Reg_HT	Regen	89	aspen 92%, birch 6%
	13_Reg_HT	Regen	170	spruce 54%, aspen 25%, willow 14%
	21_Arn_HT	Arnbruck	21	willow 44%, aspen 38%, birch 18%
	25_Arn_HT	Arnbruck	37	oak 60%, birch 36%
Forest Island (FI)	08_Reg_FI	Regen	177	oak 75%, birch 17%, aspen 5%

in leaf-off conditions. The reference groves which have been prepared so far and are incorporated in the processing of our paper are listed in Table 1 (four of type 'Hedge with Trees', one of type 'Forest Island').

4 Results

4.1 Vegetation Volume-to-Biomass Conversion with nDSM

nDSMs are calculated for the selected reference groves based on TLS (case 1), FWF (case 2), F+L (case 3) and FPL data (case 4). The results for the vegetation volume,

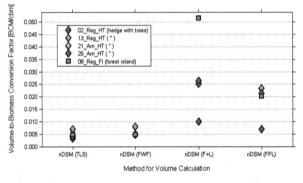

Fig. 2. Volume-to-biomass conversion factors

Table 2. Results for vegetation volume, AGB and volume-to-biomass conversion factors

Reference grove	LiDAR type	Volume [m^3]	AGB [BCM]	V2BCF [BCM/m^3]
02_Reg_HT	TLS	14263.3	61.6	0.0043
	FWF	13086.7		0.0047
	F+L	6229.6		0.0099
	FPL	8817.5		0.0070
13_Reg_HT	TLS	13572.1	95.1	0.0070
	FWF	12067.4		0.0079
	F+L	3766.6		0.0252
	FPL	4056.5		0.0234
21_Arn_HT	TLS	2449.5	8.0	0.0032
	FWF	1661.6		0.0048
	F+L	67.1		0.1186
	FPL	105.1		0.0757
25_Arn_HT	TLS	7541.5	30.7	0.0041
	FWF	6271.1		0.0049
	F+L	1164.4		0.0264
	FPL	1441.9		0.0213
08_Reg_FI	TLS	63758.2	301.6	0.0047
	FWF	62580.6		0.0048
	F+L	5858.6		0.0515
	FPL	14949.8		0.0202

AGB and volume-to-biomass conversion factors are listed in Table 2. Fig. 2 displays the results and variations of the derived volume-to-biomass conversion factors.

Fig. 2 shows that the conversion factors of grove type 'Hedge with Trees' for case 1 and 2 vary very little $(std(V2BCF) = 0.0016/0.0014)$. In contrast, the cases 3 and 4 (F+L and FPL data) show significant variations $(std(V2BCF) = 0.0431/0.0266)$. Thus, it can be assumed that the TLS and FWF data represent the grove type 'Hedge with Trees' at best due to the low variations of the conversion factors with respect to the corresponding reference groves.

4.2 3D Normalized Cut Segmentation

The 3D segmentation is applied to the F+L and FWF data using a voxel size of 1.0 m (F+L) and 0.5 m (FWF). Fig. 3 displays the polygon outlines of the resulting 3D segments as solid lines and the locations of the reference trees as colored dots.

Apparently, the 3D segmentation reveals a comparable number of segments for the F+L and the FWF situation. However, the segments based on F+L data display several gaps which are not visible if using the FWF data. Moreover, it can be seen that the segments of the outer zone are considerably larger than these of the inner region. This can be explained by the ability of the outer trees to form larger tree crowns than the inner trees which are more affected by adjacent trees.

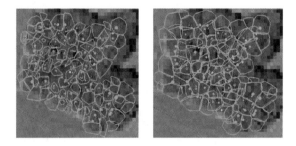

Fig. 3. Outline polygons (solid green lines) of 3D segments and locations of reference trees (colored dots) for grove '08_Reg_FI' (type 'Forest Island'); left: F+L, right: FWF

4.3 AGB Regression and Cross-Validation

The regression analysis with (6) is applied to all segments of each reference grove. Fig. 4 gives an overview for the performance of two representative groves of the types 'Hedge with Trees' and 'Forest Island'.

After the regression analysis a k-fold cross-validation (with $k=n/8$) is applied to the AGB estimations of the selected reference groves based on FWF, F+L and FPL data. The results of the regression analysis and the cross-validation are listed in Table 3, showing the coefficient of determination R^2, the root mean square error after the regression $RMSE$ and the average error of the cross-validation $RMSE(CV)$. The mean relative error per segment is given in brackets.

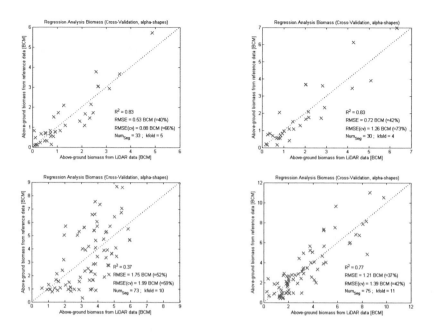

Fig. 4. AGB regression and cross-validation results of 3D segments for (top) grove '02_Reg_HT' and (bottom) '08_Reg_FI'; left: F+L; right: FWF

Table 3. Results of AGB regression analysis and cross-validation

Reference grove	LiDAR type	R^2	RMSE [BCM]	RMSE(CV) [BCM]
02_Reg_HT	FWF	0.83	0.72 (42%)	1.26 (73%)
	F+L	0.83	0.53 (40%)	0.88 (66%)
	FPL	0.83	0.42 (38%)	1.04 (93%)
13_Reg_HT	FWF	0.80	1.12 (36%)	1.86 (60%)
	F+L	0.96	0.66 (15%)	1.67 (37%)
	FPL	0.85	0.84(19%)	5.41 (123%)
21_Arn_HT	FWF	1.00	0.04 (4%)	0.26 (29%)
	F+L	n/a	n/a	n/a
	FPL	n/a	n/a	n/a
25_Arn_HT	FWF	0.97	0.50 (22%)	4.88 (208%)
	F+L	n/a	n/a	n/a
	FPL	1.00	0.09 (5%)	7.05 (390%)
08_Reg_FI	FWF	0.77	1.21 (37%)	1.39 (42%)
	F+L	0.37	1.75 (52%)	1.99 (59%)
	FPL	0.35	1.97 (55%)	2.25 (62%)

4.4   3D Segmentation Derived Biomass

Using the regression coefficients, the AGB of the ROI is calculated according to equation (7). Fig. 5 reveals the ratios of AGB_{ROI}^{NCut} derived after the 3D segmentation against the AGB_{ROI}^{ref} derived from the reference trees within the selected test groves. Again, the cases 3 and 4 representing F+L and FPL data reveal the largest variations whereas the case 2 (=FWF data) exhibits almost no changes over the selected groves.

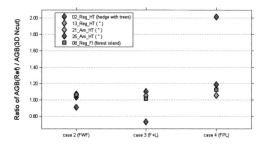

Fig. 5. AGB ratios: Reference vs. segmentation-derived

5   Discussion

Concerning the nDSM derived vegetation volume and the follow-on derivation of the volume-to-biomass conversion factors, apparently different results are deduced between the TLS/FWF, and the F+L/FPL data. The variations of *V2BCF* are small for TLS and FWF, but very high for F+L and FPL. As shown in Table 2, these high variations are caused by a significant underestimation of the vegetation volume for the F+L and FPL cases. This can be attributed mostly to the lower point density (1-2 pts/m^2) of F+L and FPL data, and to the data acquisition in leaf-off conditions.

The advantage of the second approach based on the 3D Normalized Cut segmentation is that the AGB can be directly calculated from segmentation-derived tree features. Herein, the calculated AGB shows a good coherence with the reference AGB for the FWF case (Fig. 5). For F+L and FPL, the results are rather worse showing high variations comparable to the outcomes from the nDSM approach.

The regression analysis and the cross-validation were applied to all selected reference groves, however, the results for the tree hedges '21_Arn_HT' and '25_Arn_HT' deliver unreliable numbers due to the insufficient number of segments (2 and 7, resp.) (see Table 3). The coefficient of determination R^2 is best for the remaining tree hedges (always ≥ 0.80). For the reference grove '08_Reg_FI' (type 'Forest Island') the R^2 is a little weaker and best for FWF data (R^2=0.77), but rather worse for F+L and FPL data. These values for '08_Reg_FI' reveal a higher discrepancy between the AGB estimations derived from LiDAR data and the reference trees in comparison to the tree hedges. Probably, due to several inclined trees within this grove type ('Forest Island'), the tree crowns are often not included in the segments with the corresponding stem positions. The results for the *RMSE* are ambivalent. For grove '02_Reg_HT' the *RMSE* is best for FPL (0.42 = 38%), and the *RMSE(CV)* = 1.26 is worst for the FWF case. The best results for grove '13_Reg_HT' are obtained in the F+L situation (*RSME* = 0.66; *RSME(CV)* = 1.67). In contrast, the FWF case offers the best results for the forest island '08_Reg_FI' with *RSME* = 1.21 (=37%) and *RSME(CV)* = 1.39 (=42%) . There is no clear explanation for the non-consistent results for the tree hedges (R^2 larger than 0.83) w.r.t. the forest island

(R^2 smaller than 0.37). All in all, the results for the FWF data are superior to the F+L and FPL data. This is mainly caused by the higher point density and – probably – the acquisition in leaf-on conditions.

6 Conclusions and Outlook

It can be resumed, that our methods show promising results in terms of accuracy and additional structural information. This is a significant improvement with respect to the common approaches used so far in which the vegetation volume is simply approximated by the product of mean tree height and base area, i.e. the green volume. The first directive for the next future will be the refinement of the 3D segmentation algorithm to fully exploit the capabilities of airborne LiDAR data. In this context, we have to account for the special conditions of non-forest trees with respect to forest trees, e.g. more complex structures, higher vegetation density and divergent tree shapes. It will be also necessary to classify deciduous and coniferous trees to account for their different influences on biomass estimation. Finally, the approach has to be validated including much more sample reference groves to derive significant outcomes. Finally, there is a strong need for destructive sampling of selected reference groves to calibrate the AGB estimations.

Acknowledgement. This research has been funded by the German Federal Ministry for the Environment, Nature Conservation and Nuclear Safety (BMU) under the reference 03KB037A.

References

1. Cremer, T.: Mobilisierung und wirtschaftliche Nutzung von Rohholz aus Wald und Landschaft zur Energieerzeugung. Final report, Deutsche Bundesstiftung Umwelt (DBU), Osnabrück, Germany (2007) (in German)
2. Edelsbrunner, H., Mücke, E.P.: Three-dimensional alpha shapes. ACM Transactions on Graphics 13, 43–72 (1994)
3. Fachagentur Nachwachsende Rohstoffe (FNR): Bioenergie - Basisdaten Deutschland (Stand: Juni 2010). Information broschure, Gülzow, Germany (2010) (in German)
4. Hasenauer, H.: Dimensional relationships of open-grown trees in Austria. Forest Ecol. Manag. 96, 197–206 (1997)
5. Hecht, R., Meinel, G., Buchroithner, M.F.: Estimation of urban green volume based on single-pulse LiDAR data. IEEE T. Geosci. Remote 46, 3832–3840 (2008)
6. Hollaus, M., Eysn, L., Schadauer, K., Jochem, A., Petrini, F., Maier, B.: LASER-WOOD: Estimation of the above ground biomass based on laser scanning and forest inventory data. In: 11. Österreichischer Klimatag, Vienna, Austria, p. 2 (2010)
7. Kato, A., Moskal, L.M., Schiess, P., Swanson, M.E., Calhoun, D., Stuetzle, W.: Capturing tree crown formation through implicit surface reconstruction using airborne lidar data. Remote Sens. Environ. 113, 1148–1162 (2009)
8. Næsset, E., Gobakken, T.: Estimation of above- and below-ground biomass across regions of the boreal forest zone using airborne laser. Remote Sens. Environ. 112, 3079–3090 (2008)

9. Reitberger, J., Krzystek, P., Stilla, U.: Combined tree segmentation and stem detection using full waveform LiDAR data. Int. Arch. Photogramm. Remote Sens. Spat. Inf. Sci. 36(3/W52), 332–337 (2007)

10. Reitberger, J., Schnörr, C., Krzystek, P., Stilla, U.: 3D segmentation of single trees exploiting full waveform LiDAR data. ISPRS J. Photogramm. 64, 561–574 (2009)

11. Reitberger, J., Heurich, M., Krzystek, P.: Estimation of stem volume by using 3D segments derived from full-waveform LiDAR data. In: Proceedings 10th Int. Conference on LiDAR Applications for Assessing Forest Ecosystems (Silvilaser 2010), Freiburg, p. 12 (2010)

12. Straub, C.: Acquisition of the bioenergy potential and the availability in the forest and non-forest land using new remote sensing techniques. PhD thesis, University of Freiburg, Germany (2010) (in German)

13. van Aardt, J.A.N., Wynne, R.H., Scrivani, J.A.: Lidar-based mapping of forest volume and biomass by taxonomic group using structurally homogeneous segments. Photogramm. Eng. Rem. Sens. 74, 1033–1044 (2008)

14. Vauhkonen, J.: Estimating crown base height for Scots pine by means of the 3D geometry of airborne laser scanning data. Int. J. Remote Sens. 31, 1213–1226 (2010)

15. Velázques-Martí, B., Fernández-González, E., Estornell, J., Ruiz, L.A.: Dendrometric and dasometric analysis of the bushy biomass in Mediterranean forests. Forest Ecol. Manag. 259, 875–882 (2010)

16. Zhou, X., Brandle, J.R., Awada, T.N., Schoeneberger, M.M., Martin, D.L., Xin, Y., Tang, Z.: The use of forest-derived specific gravity for the conversion of volume to biomass for open-grown trees on agricultural land. Biomass Bioenerg. 35, 1721–1731 (2011)

17. Zianis, D., Muukkonen, P., Mäkipää, R., Mencuccini, M.: Biomass and stem volume equations for tree species in Europe. Silva Fennica Monographs 4 (2005)

Detection of Windows in IR Building Textures Using Masked Correlation

Dorota Iwaszczuk, Ludwig Hoegner, and Uwe Stilla

Photogrammetry & Remote Sensing, Technische Universitaet Muenchen (TUM),
Arcisstr. 21, 80333 Munich, Germany
{iwaszczuk,hoegner,stilla}@bv.tum.de

Abstract. Infrared (IR) images depict thermal radiation of physical objects. Imaging the building hull with an IR camera allows thermal inspections. Mapping these images as textures on 3D building models, 3D geo-referencing of each pixel can be carried out. This is helpful for large area inspections. In IR images glass reflects the surrounding and shows false results for the temperature measurements. Consequently, the windows should be detected in IR images and excluded for the inspection. In this paper, an algorithm for window detection in textures extracted from terrestrial IR images is proposed. First, a local dynamic threshold is used to extract candidates for windows in the textures. Assuming a regular grid of windows masked correlation is used to find the position of windows. Finally, gaps in the window grid are replaced by hypothetical windows. Applying the method for a test dataset, 79% completeness and 80% correctness was achieved.

Keywords: Infrared, Image Sequences, Texture Mapping, Structure Detection.

1 Introduction

1.1 Motivation

In recent years, due to environmental problems and increasing energy cost, many measures to save energy have been taken. Research showed that in the European countries buildings consume 40% (Baden et al., 2006) of the energy. 47% of the energy consumed in buildings is used for heating (Hennigan, 2011). Therefore, reduction of the heat loss through the building hull became a very important topic. On one hand better standards for new buildings have been introduced, on the other hand it is attempted to inspect and improve old buildings. The heat emission of the building hull in the infrared (IR) domain can be depicted on thermal images captured with an IR camera. IR photographs can help to detect the weak spots and damages to the building hull.

In such inspections a spatial correspondence between IR-images and existing 3D building models can be helpful. Usage of the 3D building models enables processing of image sequences taken by a mobile platform capturing urban quarters (Hoegner et al., 2007) or entire cities (Chandler, 2011). The correspondence can be created by geo-referencing of the images. This can be done directly using GPS/INS data from the

U. Stilla et al. (Eds.): PIA 2011, LNCS 6952, pp. 133–146, 2011.
© Springer-Verlag Berlin Heidelberg 2011

devise mounted with the camera on the mobile platform. After system calibration, the 3D model can be projected on the image and for each surface of the model a region of the image can be selected for texture. Using terrestrial image sequences from a camera mounted on a vehicle, only frontal faces visible from the street level can be captured, while airborne image sequences can be capture faces from roofs and inner yards. Due to the fact, IR cameras have a detector matrix, which is much smaller compared to cameras working in visible domain, to achieve an adequate geometric resolution of an observed object, a smaller viewing angle than for normal video or photo cameras has to be chosen. Therefore, in terrestrial images it is not possible to record a complete building in dense urban areas with narrow streets in one image. Because of this, textures have to be combined from multiple images. On the other hand, in airborne images the resolution is low and not all the details can be seen.

In these 3D spatial referenced textures, certain structures (e.g. heat leakages, windows and other objects in walls and roofs) can be detected. These automatically get associated with the building. Glass in IR images reflects the temperature of surrounding. Hence paned windows depict not the real temperature of the façade, but rather the temperature of the neighboring buildings or sky. Accordingly, windows cannot be taken into consideration for building inspection and should be detected in textures.

Infrared images are usually blurred, so that the windows edges cannot be easily detected. Furthermore, due to the reflections, windows can appear differently. For window detection in IR textures an algorithm is needed which can match different appearances of the window and can deal with reflections inside the window frame.

1.2 Related Work

Algorithms for optical visual textures are introduced by Dick et al. (2004) using a texture previously generated from training data to identify image areas as supposable façade elements. A group of histograms is generated for every texture using horizontal and vertical wavelet transforms at different scale levels. A likelihood function evaluates possible structures with their priors. Ripperda (2008) and Mayer and Reznik (2006) propose reversible jump Markov chain Monte Carlo (rjMCMC) (Green 1995) for the estimation of optimal parameters for the windows. Ripperda (2008) uses a formal grammar to describe the behavior of the windows. Reznik and Mayer (2007) use implicit shape models (Leibe and Schiele 2004) to define a set of the windows to check with the given image. Werner and Zisserman (2002) use regular structure primitives like vanishing points or symmetry. Becker (2009) uses cell decomposition to extract geometry from images as well as from LiDAR point clouds. Textures from infrared images have been analyzed by Hoegner and Stilla (2009) using morphological operators to mask window areas focusing on their different temperature and thermal behavior over time compared to the façade. Edge points are hard to determine exactly. Window frames can appear lighter or darker than the façade. In Sirmacek et al. (2011) an approach using L-shape is used searching generalized geometric primitives in textures and combining them in a bottom up approach to identify windows. In this paper, the detection of windows is a combination of morphological operators as used by Hoegner and Stilla (2009) to detect areas which differ from the façade background as possible window candidates and a detection of corners by correlation. This method allows the detection of windows of different size by combining detected corner primitives (Sirmacek et al. 2011). Additional geometric constraints are inserted to search in a second step for non-detected windows in rows or columns.

1.3 Overview

In this paper we present an algorithm for window detection in textures extracted from IR images. Our method, described in Section 2, consists of four steps. First step: the region detection in the building textures using local dynamic threshold is carried out and morphological operations are used to improve the results of the segmentation (Section 2.1). Second step: adjustment into rows using a height histogram is applied, which is described in Section 2.3. Third step: masked correlation is carried out to detect the position and the size of the windows (Section 2.3). Last step: the grid of windows is completed (Section 2.4). The presented method was applied for a test dataset which was acquired in a densely built urban area of Munich (Section 3). Results of the first experiment are presented in Section 4 and finally they are discussed in Section 5.

2 Methodology

In optical images recorded in visible domain the appearance of objects depends on material properties, illumination and viewing angle. In IR images the appearance depends on material and viewing angle as well. However the viewing angle influences it less than in the visible domain apart from materials with specular (mirror-like) reflectivity. Instead of the illumination in visible domain, in IR images the radiation of objects depends on temperature distribution. Accordingly, the appearance of the windows in IR images depends on temperature and material of the object, imaging diffuse surfaces (e.g. wood, plastic), or on viewing angle and temperature of the surrounding, imaging specular surfaces (e.g. glass, aluminum).

In the Fig. 1 some examples of window appearance are presented. It can be observed, that in IR images the edges are blurred. Accordingly it is difficult to define appearance of the window basing on edges. Furthermore, in densely built urban areas usually the images taken from a vehicle are captured from small distance and looking from the bottom (street). Therefore, the window opening, which is orthogonal to the wall plane, can be seen on one side of the window. This is related to the fact that the windows do not lie in the plane of the façade, but they are shifted inside. For example in Fig. 1b the image was taken from left, so the opening can be seen on left. Moreover, the resolution for windows in upper rows (Fig. 1d) is lower than that of windows in lower rows Fig. 1a, 1b, 1c).

In our method, we assume that the windows are rectangular and build a grid on the façade. Moreover, we can observe, that usually at the corner of the window there is a blurred edge and a change of the intensity. However in every corner the change can be different. For example in Fig.1 b the lower left corner is darker inside than outside, while the top right corner is darker outside.

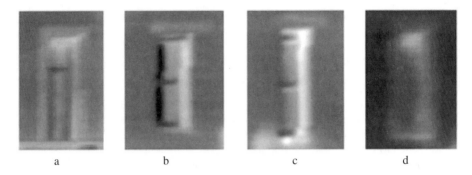

a   b   c   d

Fig. 1. Examples of windows imaged with a terrestrial IR camera. In examples a, b and c windows from the second floor (first floor = ground floor) are depicted. In example d we see a window from the third floor. Since the camera was mounted on a vehicle driving on the street, upper windows were far away from the camera than the lower windows, consequently the upper windows are depicted with lower resolution.

2.1 Region Detection

In first step of the presented technique for window detection we try to find regions in the image which are candidates for windows. First we smooth and scale down the image to remove small objects. Next, we use local dynamic threshold to segment the image. To compute the local dynamic threshold a second image is used as a reference. In the reference image local threshold values are stored. The reference image is determined using a smoothing filter. The filter mask size has to be adapted to the window size, so that the windows are removed in the reference image.

The local dynamic threshold is used because the windows, according to different reflections, appear differently even in the same texture and no global threshold can be found. After segmentation some windows are fused into one object. It occurs due to the heat leakages, which are classified similar to windows and often connect windows together. In such cases two or more windows together with the leakage build one object. To separate such combined windows, morphological operations (opening and closing) are used. These operations also help to remove false detections (small objects). Then, for every extracted region, which is a candidate for a window, a rectangular bounding box and its center of gravity is calculated.

2.2 Adjusting Rows

In most buildings the windows build a regular grid. The gaps between the columns and the rows are often of the same size. However the gravity centers extracted from IR textures in the previous step usually don't build a regular grid of the windows. It is related to the fact that the IR images depict a distribution of thermal radiation which does not have sharp borders, as well as to thermal leakages which are still included and could not be removed through the morphological operations. Hence, in the next step extracted gravity points should be adjusted to a regular grid.

However, in areas with buildings up to three floors it is difficult to adjust row and columns simultaneously. Thus, we propose first an adjustment in rows. For this purpose we group the candidates for windows into rows according to their height on the façade. The range of height within one group is approximately equal to half of the expected window height. In every group the points are counted and histogram of point height is created. Then the peaks in the histogram are searched. The number of peaks is the expected number of floors. The points are grouped again according to the detected number of floors and adjusted such that all points within a group have the same height. Points which are close to each other are merged.

2.3 Standardized Masked Correlation

In the next step we design the window model (Fig. 2a). We assume that a window is rectangular and appears on a homogeneous background. The window frame is usually different from the material of the wall, having mostly a different emissivity factor. Thus the window frame appears differently compared to the background, concerning the intensity. Inside the frame, reflecting panes and the other elements (e.g. sashes) are placed. These elements, according to the reflections, cannot be modeled in detail.

Basing on this model we build a binary mask which corresponds to the expected shape of the windows. Accordingly, the mask, which should search for edges separating the background from the window frame, is based on the rectangular shape and has a pre-defined size (Fig. 2b). This binary mask consists of "on" and "off" fields and of "don't care" areas. Since we search for intensity change between background and the window frame, the "on/off" fields are placed around expected corners. However, the corners can be moved independently during the correlation process, as long as they build a rectangle.   So the window size can also be adapted.   The rest of the mask is labeled as "don't-care-area" and is not used for calculations. Consequently, the edges between the background and window frame and reflections inside the frame are masked out for the correlation process.

Then, using equation (1) (Stilla 1993), the mask is correlated within a region of interest (ROI) given by the points detected in the previous step. According to correlation results the position and the size of the windows is adjusted using correlation coefficient as a weight.

$$c = sgn(\rho_\oplus - \rho_\ominus) \cdot sgn(\overline{g_\oplus} - \overline{g_\ominus}) \cdot \frac{1}{\sqrt{\frac{m}{m_\ominus}\left(\frac{\sigma_\oplus}{\overline{g_\oplus}-\overline{g_\ominus}}\right)^2 + \frac{m}{m_\oplus}\left(\frac{\sigma_\ominus}{\overline{g_\oplus}-\overline{g_\ominus}}\right)^2 + 1}} \qquad (1)$$

c – correlation coefficient

$\rho_\oplus$ – value of "on" mask

$\rho_\ominus$ – value of "off" mask

$\overline{g_\oplus}$ – mean value of intensity values in the image covered by "on" mask

$\overline{g_\ominus}$ – mean value of intensity values in the image covered by "off" mask

$m_\oplus$ – number of "on" pixels in the mask

$m_\ominus$ – number of "*off*" pixels in the mask

m – number of "*on*" and "*off*" pixels in the mask

$\sigma_\oplus$ – standard deviation of intensity values covered by "*on*" mask

$\sigma_\ominus$ – standard deviation of intensity values covered by "*off*" mask

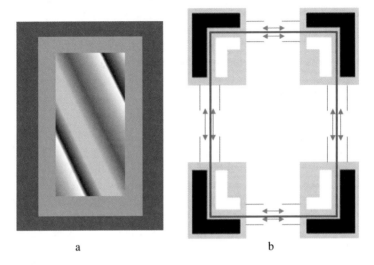

a   b

Fig. 2. Window modeling. a) The window model: dark grey - homogenous background, light grey - window frame and inside - glass; b) mask used for correlation: red – expected shape of the window; black & white – binary mask; blue – don't-care-areas.

2.4 Completing the Grid of Windows

The results of the correlation are again grouped and adjusted into rows (all windows in one row lie on the same height). Next, for every row it is checked whether in other rows at the same position a window was also detected. If not, this gap is a candidate for a window, and using masked correlation with estimated window size for this row this hypothesis is accepted or rejected. Finally, the gaps between windows in rows are examined. If a window fits in the gap it is again candidate for window, which will be verified using the correlation mask.

3 Experiments

The method presented in Section 2 was tested with an exemplary dataset consisting of terrestrial image sequences of a test area located in a densely built city area with buildings up to a few floors.

3.1 Terrestrial Image Sequences

Nowadays, IR cameras cannot achieve the geometric resolution closer to the resolution of the video cameras or digital cameras. The camera used for the acquisition of the test sequences has a focal plane array of 320x240 pixels with a field of view (FOV) of only 20°. The FLIR SC3000 camera records in the thermal infrared band (8 - 12 µm). The camera was mounted on a platform on the top of a van which can be rotated and shifted. The influence of the sun in infrared images is different from images in visible spectrum. In the thermal IR spectrum of 8-12 µm, the sun reflection is insignificant. But, the heating effect of the sun influences the temperature of structures. Depending on the sun influence or the temperature inside the building or outside, different elements of the façade may have a different contrast. For instance, heating pipes appear in the winter or at night, but show only a low contrast during a sunny day, when the whole façade is heated by the sunlight.

Caused by the small FOV and the low optical resolution it was necessary to record the scene in oblique view to be able to record the complete façades of the building from the floor to the roof with an acceptable texture resolution. The image sequences were recorded with a frequency of 50 frames per second. To minimize occluded parts of the façade in the textures caused by the oblique view, every façade was recorded with a forward looking view and a backward looking view. The viewing angle related to the along track axis of the van was kept constant. An example of a recorded sequence is shown in Fig.3. The position of the camera was recorded with GPS.

Fig. 3. Example images from one sequence taken on the path along one building complex

3.2 Textures

The terrestrial textures used for the experiment were extracted from terrestrial image sequences applying the method described in Hoegner et al. (2007). In the first step the image sequences were relatively oriented using the 5 point algorithm, resulting in a relative path. Further, the relative path was matched with the GPS path registered during the measurement, and with the 3D building model. Finally, the sequences were projected onto the 3D building model. The final texture for every façade was then generated combining all projected textures from all images with respect to the geometric resolution (Fig.4).

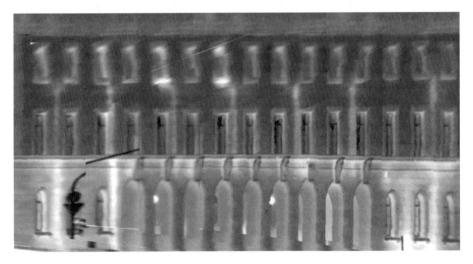

Fig. 4. An IR texture extracted from terrestrial data

3.3 Region Detection

Region detection was carried out using commercial software. The texture (Fig. 4) was smoothed and scaled down. The image was segmented using local dynamic threshold (Fig. 5a), then closing and opening operations were applied (Fig. 5b). Next from the segmented area the separate regions were extracted and for every region a rectangular bounding box was created (Fig. 6a). Finally gravity centers for every bounding box where calculated and taken for further processing (Fig.6b).

3.4 Grid and Correlation

For determination of the number of floors we applied method based on the height histogram, as described in Section 2.2. As shown in Fig. 6a, besides windows, heat leakages are also often detected as separate regions. This can cause detection of too many floors. To avoid this, prior knowledge about approximate window size can be used. We introduced a constraint that windows from two rows cannot overlap.

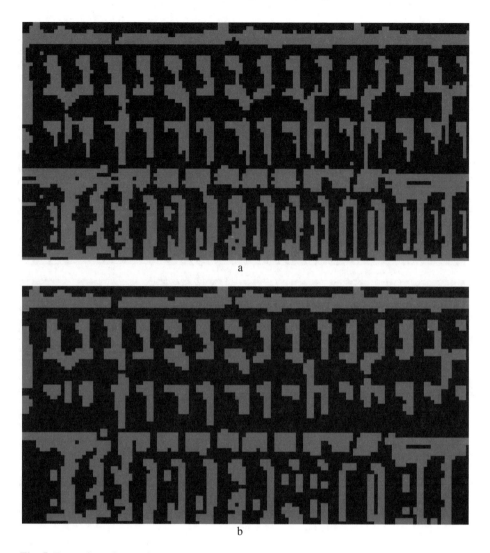

Fig. 5. Extraction of candidates for windows. a) Extraction from IR texture using local dynamic threshold (input: scaled down image from Fig. 4); b) separation of the regions and removing false detections using morphological operations.

Further, we applied the masked correlation as described in Section 2.3 and updated the expected window size for every row separately. Finally, we completed the grid with windows using method from Section 2.4.

The results of window detection are shown in Fig. 7.The method presented in Section 2 was tested with an exemplary dataset consisting of terrestrial image sequences of a test area located in a densely built city area with buildings up to a few floors.

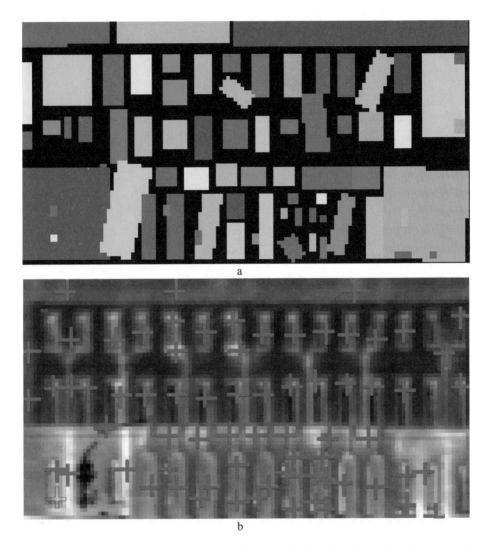

Fig. 6. Detected candidates for windows. a) Rectangular bounding boxes for the extracted regions (input: image from Fig. 5b); b) gravity centers

4 Results

Our first results on segmentation, regions and gravity centers extraction, presented in the Fig. 5 and in Fig. 6, show that many extracted gravity centers correspond to the approximated position of windows. However, sometimes two windows are connected with heat leakage. Then the gravity centre is placed between windows. In some other cases, for one window, two points are extracted, e.g. reflection in the bottom and reflection at the top of the window. These results show that further processing of the extracted points was necessary.

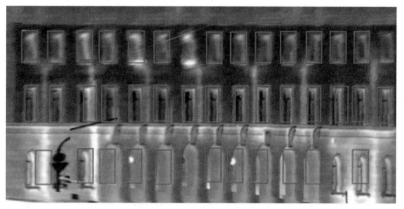

a

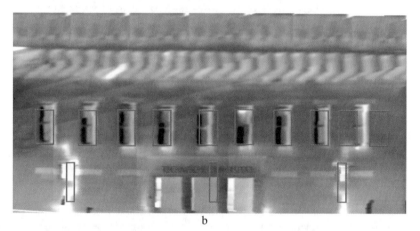

b

c

Fig. 7. Extracted windows in textures of three façades

Good results on window detection could be achieved applying masked correlation, adjustment in rows and complementing the gaps with windows. Most windows could be detected in correct position. Also the window size was adapted for every row separately. Even the lowest row was partially detected, although the shape of its windows was not exactly matched by assumed model. Accordingly, the detected size in the lowest row does not correspond to the real size.

The influence of heat leakages could be in most cases eliminated. However in few cases (e.g. Fig. 7a, 2nd row 3rd window) detected window is shifted because of closely neighboring heat leakage. Similarly, other window could not be detected because of strong reflections and heat leakage close to it (Fig. 7a, 1st row 7th window). There are also some problems with detection of windows which where deformed during texture extraction (e.g. Fig. 7c, 1st row 6th and 9th window).

To evaluate presented results completeness and correctness were calculated for our dataset. Completeness, defined as correctly detected windows divided by all windows in reality, is 79%. Correctness, defined as correctly detected windows divided by all detections, is 80%. The number of windows for ground truth was determined by a human operator. Hence, windows which are occluded (e.g. Fig. 7a, 3rd row 2nd window) were not taken into consideration.

5 Discussion and Future Work

Our first results on region extraction show that usage of the local dynamic threshold allows extracting appropriate candidates for windows. This segmentation technique helps to bridge the different appearance caused by various objects which are reflected in panes of windows. Masked correlation and geometric constrains allow refining the position of each window. Usage of the mask, which switches off irrelevant parts of the window and search for intensity change in the image around the window corners, delivers promising results. However, the mask applied in this research does not match all possible window shapes (the lower rows in Fig. 7a and 7c). Hence, the window model should be extended, so that more shapes are allowed, for example arcs in the upper part of the window.

Further problem in window detection are occlusions by trees, traffic signs and lights as well as by other buildings (e.g. Fig.7a 3rd row 2nd window). Thus, more effort is needed on occlusion free texture extraction (Benitez et al., 2010).

The achieved results with completeness and correctness around 80% are satisfying for first results, but still can be improved. We expect an enhancement of completeness and correctness by extending the method with searching for window candidates using multiple levels of the image pyramid. Candidates, which are detected in many scales, can be weighted higher while adjusting. Another possibility to improve the results is to combine textures extracted from terrestrial and airborne IR image sequences. Also here, windows detected in both textures could get a higher weight. Moreover, also laser point clouds can be used to determined candidates for windows (Tuttas and Stilla, 2011).

In further studies the presented method for window detection should be integrated into a stochastic process to determine possibilities of window positions. Then the presented geometric constrains could be described by probabilities, which would allow also exceptions from a typical case, which is most likely. Applying this solution also rows with different window size could be modeled.

References

Avbelj, J., Iwaszczuk, D., Stilla, U.: Matching of 3D wire-frame building models with image features from infrared video sequences taken by helicopters. In: Proceedings of PCV 2010 - Photogrammetric Computer Vision and Image Analysis. International Archives of Photogrammetry, Remote Sensing and Spatial Geoinformation Sciences, vol. 38(3B), pp. 149–154 (2010)

Baden, S., Fairey, P., Waide, P., Laustsen, J.: Hurdling Financial Barriers to Lower Energy Buildings: Experiences from the USA and Europe on Financial Incentives and Monetizing Building Energy Savings in Private Investment Decisions. In: Proceedings of 2006 ACEEE Summer Study on Energy Efficiency in Buildings. American Council for an Energy Efficient Economy, Washington DC (2006)

Becker, S.: Generation and application of rules for quality dependent facade reconstruction. ISPRS Journal of Photogrammetry and Remote Sensing 64(6), 640–653 (2009)

Bénitez, S., Denis, E., Baillard, C.: Automatic Production of Occlusion-Free Rectified Façade Textures using Vehicle-Based Imagery. In: Proceedings of PCV 2010 - Photogrammetric Computer Vision and Image Analysis. International Archives of Photogrammetry, Remote Sensing and Spatial Geoinformation Sciences, vol. 38(3A), pp. 275–280 (2010)

Chandler, D.L.: The big picture on energy loss. MIT news, Massachusetts Institute of Technology, March 16 (2011), http://web.mit.edu/newsoffice/2011/ir-scanning-energy-0316.html (access on June 30, 2011)

Dick, A., Torr, P., Cipolla, R., Ribarsky, W.: Modelling and interpretation of architecture from several images. International Journal of Computer Vision 60(2), 111–134 (2004)

Eugster, H., Nebiker, S.: Real-time georegistration of video streams from mini or micro UAS using digital 3D city models. In: Proceedings of 6th International Symposium on Mobile Mapping Technology, Presidente Prudente, São Paulo, Brazil (2009)

Frueh, C., Sammon, R., Zakhor, A.: Automated Texture Mapping of 3D City Models With Oblique Aerial Imagery. In: Proceedings of the 2nd International Symposium on 3D Data Processing, Visualization, and Transmission (3DPVT 2004), Thessaloniki, Greece (2004)

Green, P.: Reversible Jump Markov Chain Monte Carlo Computation and Bayesian Model Determination. Biometrika 82, 711–732 (1995)

Hennigan, M.: Supply of heat accounts for 47% of energy consumption says IEA - - largely ignored in climate change debate. In: Finfacts Ireland's Business & Finance Portal, http://www.finfacts.ie/irishfinancenews/article_1022290.shtml (access on June 30, 2011)

Hoegner, L., Kumke, H., Meng, L., Stilla, U.: Automatic extraction of textures from infrared image sequences and database integration for 3D building models. PFG Photogrammetrie Fernerkundung Geoinformation (6), 459–468 (2007)

Hoegner, L., Stilla, U.: Thermal leakage detection on building façades using infrared textures generated by mobile mapping. In: Proceedings of Joint Urban Remote Sensing Event (JURSE 2009). IEEE, Shanghai (2009)

Leibe, B., Schiele, B.: Combined Object Categorization and Segmentation with an Implicit Shape Model. In: Proceedings of ECCV 2004 Workshop on Statistical Learning in Computer Vision, Prague, Czech Republic, pp. 1–15 (2004)

Li, R.: Mobile Mapping - An Emerging Technology for Spatial Data Acquisition. Journal of Photogrammetric Engineering and Remote Sensing 63(9), 1085–1092 (1997)

Reznik, S., Mayer, H.: Implicit Shape Models, Model Selection, and Plane Sweeping for 3D Facade Interpretation. The International Archives of the Photogrammetry, Remote Sensing and Spatial Information Sciences 36(3/W49A), 173–178 (2007)

Ripperda, N.: Grammar Based Facade Reconstruction using RjMCMC. PFG Photogrammetrie Fernerkundung Geoinformation (2), 83–92 (2008)

Sirmacek, B., Hoegner, L., Stilla, U.: Detection of windows and doors from thermal images by grouping geometrical features. In: Stilla, U., Gamba, P., Juergens, C., Maktav, D. (eds.) JURSE 2011 - Joint Urban Remote Sensing Event, pp. 133–136 (2011)

Stilla, U.: Verfahrensvergleich zur automatischen Erkennung in Metall geschlagener Zeichen. Universität, Fakultät für Elektrotechnik, Karlsruhe, Dissertation (1993)

Stilla, U., Kolecki, J., Hoegner, L.: Texture mapping of 3D building models with oblique direct geo-referenced airborne IR image sequences. In: Proceedings of ISPRS Hannover Workshop 2009: High-resolution Earth Imaging for Geospatial Information. International Archives of Photogrammetry, Remote Sensing and Spatial Geoinformation Sciences, vol. 38(1-4-7/W5) on CD (2009)

Tuttas, S., Stilla, U.: Window detection in sparse point clouds using indoor points. In: PIA11Photogrammetric Image Analysis. International Archives of Photogrammetry, Remote Sensing and Spatial Geoinformation Sciences, vol. 37(3/W22) on CD (2011)

Werner, T., Zisserman, A.: New Techniques for Automated Architectural Reconstruction from Photographs. In: Heyden, A., Sparr, G., Nielsen, M., Johansen, P. (eds.) ECCV 2002. LNCS, vol. 2351, pp. 541–555. Springer, Heidelberg (2002)

Yastikli, N., Jacobsen, K.: Direct sensor orientation for large scale mapping – potentials, problems, solutions. The Photogrammetric Record 20(111), 274–284 (2005)

Fast Marching for Robust Surface Segmentation

Falko Schindler and Wolfgang Förstner

Department of Photogrammetry, University of Bonn
Nussallee 15, 53115 Bonn, Germany
falko.schindler@uni-bonn.de, wf@ipb.uni-bonn.de
http://www.ipb.uni-bonn.de

Abstract. We propose a surface segmentation method based on Fast Marching Farthest Point Sampling designed for noisy, visually reconstructed point clouds or laser range data. Adjusting the distance metric between neighboring vertices we obtain robust, edge-preserving segmentations based on local curvature. We formulate a cost function given a segmentation in terms of a description length to be minimized. An incremental-decremental segmentation procedure approximates a global optimum of the cost function and prevents from under- as well as strong over-segmentation. We demonstrate the proposed method on various synthetic and real-world data sets.

1 Introduction

Multi-view stereo reconstruction and laser range acquisition is gaining importance in photogrammetry and computer vision. Not only is aerial photogrammetry and airborne laser scanning a well established source for dense 2.5D or 3D reconstructions of millions and billions points; upcoming technologies like small unmanned aerial vehicles, time-of-flight cameras and even low-cost sensors developed for entertainment industries are emerging, enabling to capture colored point clouds in very short time. Many algorithms tackling the task of semantic understanding, however, require a data reduction pre-process to reduce computational complexity by removing redundant information. Pre-segmentation of images and 2.5D or 3D surfaces is a promising strategy for data reduction that we will focus on throughout this paper.

Given a triangulated point cloud we want to find homogeneous segments w.r.t. pre-determined features, e.g., direction of normals, location of gravity centers or color. While an under-segmentation will lead to loss of important information, over-segmenting the given surface is acceptable. Consecutive algorithms can easily merge segments based on more complex model knowledge, e.g., graphical models or incremental merging strategies (Attene et al. 2006). The unknown level of detail to be preserved implies the demand for a reasonable stopping criterion, e.g., the final number of segments.

We propose a segmentation algorithm based on Fast Marching Farthest Point Sampling (FastFPS, Moenning and Dogson 2003). To address the problem of specifying a stopping criterion we derive a theoretically founded cost function, enabling to evaluate given segmentations. Our contribution is to introduce

U. Stilla et al. (Eds.): PIA 2011, LNCS 6952, pp. 147–158, 2011.

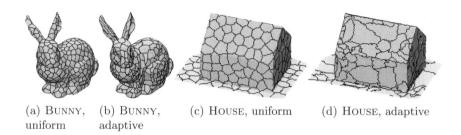

(a) BUNNY,   (b) BUNNY,   (c) HOUSE, uniform   (d) HOUSE, adaptive
uniform   adaptive

Fig. 1. FastFPS for uniform (a, c) or adaptive (b, d) surface segmentation on the free-form object BUNNY (a, b) and the polyhedral HOUSE (c, d). Note how the adaptive segmentation is sensitive to local curvature, thus yields more details at legs and ears and generalizes more strongly at the back (b). Especially when reconstructing polyhedral objects like buildings we prefer an adaptive, edge-preserving segmentation (d).

FastFPS for surface segmentation, to formulate a cost function, enabling to regulate an incremental and decremental segmentation strategy, and to introduce and to analyze distance metrics suited for surface segmentation.

The BUNNY[1] in Fig. 1(a) is an example for a uniformly over-segmented, curved surface. We will propose distance metrics to obtain an adaptive segmentation as in Fig. 1(b) that is particularly practical for piecewise planar, polyhedral objects like buildings (Fig. 1(c) and 1(d)).

2   Related Work

Our segmentation approach is based on FastFPS (Moenning and Dogson 2003). It iteratively applies farthest point sampling (Eldar et al. 1997) to cover the sampling domain as uniformly as possible. To determine the farthest point a Voronoi diagram is constantly updated via fast marching (Sethian 1996).

The idea of farthest point sampling is to repeatedly place a new seed point in an area of the sampling domain that is farthest from the current seeds (Eldar et al. 1997). In terms of Voronoi diagrams such a farthest point is usually found on the boundary between two or more Voronoi cells. At the beginning there are no seeds and all points are infinitely far away from the – currently empty – set of seeds. A first seed point is chosen randomly and its distance to all remaining points is to be determined. More seeds are found by iteratively picking the farthest point and updating all distances. One way to efficiently compute the distances is to apply fast marching.

Fast marching was introduced for planar domains (Sethian 1996) and extended for triangulated domains (Kimmel and Sethian 1998). It allows to approximate distance maps $d(\boldsymbol{x})$ from given seed points $\boldsymbol{x}_0$ for the whole sampling domain by propagating a wave front following the Eikonal equation

$$|\nabla d(\boldsymbol{x})| = F(\boldsymbol{x}) \ , \tag{1}$$

---

[1] http://graphics.stanford.edu/data/3Dscanrep/

with the boundary condition $d(\boldsymbol{x}_0) = 0$, i.e. the distance at the seed point is 0. Usually one is interested in geodesic distances, i.e. the friction $F(\boldsymbol{x})$ or speed $F^{-1}(\boldsymbol{x})$ is constant for all $\boldsymbol{x}$. An assignment of each sample point to its closest seed point is obtained implicitly. Alternatively we can formulate the propagation time dependent on local features, as it has been done for fast marching (Peyré and Cohen 2006) and for level sets (Xu et al. 2004).

The combination of fast marching and farthest point sampling was proposed for sampling point clouds and implicit surfaces (Moenning and Dogson 2003). Sampling seed points and updating a Voronoi diagram is equivalent to segmenting the sampling domain, i.e. determining a labeling l_n for each input point $n \in \{1 \ldots N\}$, as summarized in Algorithm 1.

A similar segmentation approach is based on geodesic centroidal tesselation (Peyré and Cohen 2004). It addresses reconstruction tasks in computer aided-design and thus solely focuses on laser scans or synthetic data with a very small amount of noise and rare outliers compared to visual reconstructions.

In the context of segmentation FastFPS is distantly related to Watershed (Beucher and Lantu 1979) being applied to mesh segmentation using fast marching (Page et al. 2003). Instead of heights locally defined for each pixel or surface point (Mangan and Whitaker 1999) FastFPS is based on pairwise distances between points that depend on the current seed distribution and vary permanently. FastFPS can locally adapt to the underlying image content or surface shape evaluating the pre-defined distance metric F. As proposed for point sampling (Moenning and Dogson 2003) a favoured number of samples is required. We will demonstrate how to determine the stopping criterion automatically.

Another related concept for surface segmentation starts bottom-up by labeling each triangle of a triangulated surface differently and iteratively merges similar neighbors w.r.t. to planarity (Garland et al. 2001). Like FastFPS this approach needs a user-defined number of favoured segments.

The remainder of the paper is organized as follows: We first will describe the concept of surface segmentation, thereby specify our objective in terms of an optimal segmentation result and provide the incremental/decremental sampling strategy. Section 4 gives details of the algorithm, especially the distance metric F, how to involve color and the incremental/decremental choice of seed points. Experiments on synthetic data demonstrate the sensitivity w.r.t. noise and small surface patches. Real data shows the versatility of the method.

3 Theory

3.1 Task Specification

We assume to be given a set of N points $\{\boldsymbol{x}_n\}$ in 3D space, observed with equal and independent uncertainty $\sigma = \sigma_x = \sigma_y = \sigma_z$. Introducing full covariance matrices Σ_n is possible as well. We assume a triangulation of the points to be available. The task is to assign labels $l_n \in \{1 \ldots L\}$ to each point n, such that equally labeled points are topologically connected via triangle edges. Connected components build the desired *segments*. Neighboring points living on one segment

initialize distances $\boldsymbol{d} = \infty$ and labels $\boldsymbol{l}$ as undefined;
for $l \leftarrow 1$ **to** L **do**
    set new seed $s \leftarrow \mathrm{argmax}_n\, d_n$, $d_s \leftarrow 0$, $l_s \leftarrow l$;
    initialize new front $\mathcal{Q} \leftarrow \{s\}$;
    while *front is not empty* $\mathcal{Q} \neq \{\}$ **do**
        remove front vertex $u \leftarrow \mathrm{argmin}_{q \in \mathcal{Q}}\, d_q$, $\mathcal{Q} \leftarrow \mathcal{Q} \setminus u$;
        foreach *neighbor* $v \in \mathcal{N}_u$ **do**
            compute new distance $d'_v = d_u + F(v)$;
            if *new distance is smaller* $d'_v < d_v$ **then**
                update neighbor $d_v \leftarrow d'_v$, $l_v \leftarrow l_u$;
                add vertex to front $\mathcal{Q} \leftarrow \mathcal{Q} \cup v$;
            end
        end
    end
end

Algorithm 1. Fast Marching Farthest Point Sampling. New seeds s are added iteratively by choosing the farthest point w.r.t. a distance map $\boldsymbol{d}$ that is constantly updated using fast marching and a metric F, yielding a labeling $\boldsymbol{l}$.

are supposed to share similar features like normals, curvature or color, while points on different segments are assumed to be different in normal, curvature or color. Normals and curvature can be derived from small neighborhoods.

A segmentation based on FastFPS would proceed as follows (Algorithm 1). Chose a random seed point s from where to compute geodesic distances d_n to all other points n using fast marching. I.e. initialize a set of front points $\mathcal{Q}$ with the neighbors of seed s and incrementally remove the front point u with smallest distance d_u and add its neighbors $\{v\}$ to front $\mathcal{Q}$. Update distances d_v and labeling $l_v \leftarrow l_u$ if $d_v + F(u, v)$ is smaller than a previously computed d_v. Fast marching stops, as soon as front $\mathcal{Q}$ is empty. Farthest point sampling continues with new seeds s always being the currently farthest point, until the required number of segments L is reached. Note that the first iteration is by far most expensive. Varying the number of segments can lead to under- or over-segmenting the surface.

To find a trade-off between under- and over-segmentation we formulate a cost function in terms of the description length for encoding all given points using a segmentation and the surface parameters of each segment. Our cost function

$$\Phi(\boldsymbol{l} \mid L) = \underbrace{N \operatorname{lb} L}_{\text{labeling}} + \underbrace{3L \operatorname{lb} \frac{R}{\varepsilon}}_{\text{parameters}} + \underbrace{2N \operatorname{lb} \frac{R}{\varepsilon}}_{\text{2D locations}} + \underbrace{\sum_n \left\{ \frac{\hat{v}_n(l_n)^2}{2\sigma^2 \ln 2} + \operatorname{lb} \frac{\sqrt{2\pi}\sigma}{\varepsilon} \right\}}_{\text{residuals}} \quad (2)$$

incorporates three terms, with R being the maximum range of one coordinate and the resolution $\varepsilon = \sigma/10$:

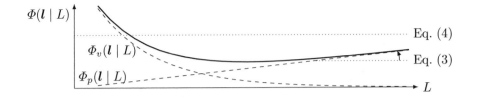

Fig. 2. Schematic diagram of $\Phi(l \mid L)$. It is the sum $\Phi_v(l \mid L) = \Omega(l \mid L)$ of the squared residuals, principally decreasing with the number l of segments, and the bits $\Phi_p(l \mid L)$ for coding the segments and the labeling of the points, which principally is slowly increasing with the number of segments. In reality, due to noise, the real optimization function is a noisy version of the smooth curve.

- *labeling*: For each point we to encode the segment it belongs to. Assuming the segments to be of approximately the same size the number of bits for each of the N points therefore is $\operatorname{lb} L$.
- *parameters*: We need to code surface parameters for each segment, e.g., the three parameters of a plane. Based on a resolution ε and a range R to be covered we need approximately $\operatorname{lb} R/\varepsilon$ bits to code each parameter.
- *2D locations* and *residuals*: We restrict all points n to live on their segment's surface. Therefore only the residuals $\widehat{v}_n(l_n)$ w.r.t. a best fitting surface for segment l_n and the 2D locations within the surface need to be coded (Leclerc 1989, Förstner 1989).

We expect Φ to rapidly decrease during the first iterations and to reach a local minimum, before gradually increasing again (Fig. 2). This is due to the exponentially decreasing sum of squared residuals Ω in combination with almost linearly increasing costs w.r.t. the growing number of segments L. The cost function Φ, however, is a noisy version of the ideal function shown in Fig. 2. This is due to the suboptimal criterion. The function Φ is N-dimensional, with N being the number of points, and highly non-convex. Nevertheless we will demonstrate an optimization strategy to approximate a global optimum using FastFPS.

3.2 Incremental/Decremental Search

The local minimum is characterized by an increase in Φ being smaller than the differential costs for encoding the L segments only

$$0 < \Phi(l \mid L) - \Phi(l \mid L - 1) < N(\operatorname{lb}(L) - \operatorname{lb}(L - 1)) + 3\frac{\operatorname{lb} R}{\varepsilon} \ . \tag{3}$$

In order to prevent from being prone to noisy data and outliers, leading to a wobbly behaviour of Φ, we only apply the first criterion in case

$$\widehat{\Omega} = \sum_n \widehat{v}_n^2 < T_\Omega \cdot N \cdot \sigma^2 \ . \tag{4}$$

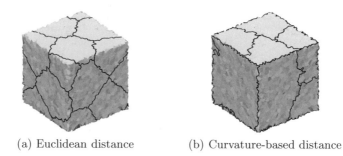

(a) Euclidean distance   (b) Curvature-based distance

Fig. 3. Segmentation results for Euclidean and curvature-based distance measure on the data set CUBE with 6000 vertices and $\sigma = 5$ mm noise at 1 m edge length

It requires the estimated sum of squared residuals $\widehat{\Omega}$ to be below a pre-defined threshold mainly depending on the expected variance of the data. The factor $T_\Omega \approx 10$ allows for larger residuals caused by violations of the expected Gaussian error distribution, e.g., few outliers not relevant for the overall segmentation.

4   Implementation

We apply the very same procedure (Algorithm 1) to surface segmentation with pre-defined number of segments and investigate several metrics F aiming at adaptive, robust, edge-preserving segmentations of polyhedral surfaces. Further we adjust the sampling strategy to better approximate an optimal segmentation.

4.1   Distance Metrics

Geodesics, i.e. pairwise Euclidean distances, are widely used for surface segmentation, possibly combined with shape-adaptive metrics, e.g., local curvature (Moenning and Dogson 2003). We will focus on the latter metric, compare it to Euclidean distances, propose a robustification and add radiometric features.

Euclidean distance vs. curvature. As shown in Fig. 3 and previously in Fig. 1, using a distance metric based on local curvature is crucial for segmenting planar patches without destroying straight edges. In Fig. 3(b) we compute normals for all points, by averaging the normals of all neighboring triangles. The distance F between two points is defined as the Euclidean distance of their normals. The effect of curvature-dependent segmentations is also visible with the ELLIPSOID in Fig. 4. At areas with low curvature the density is low.

Robust curvature. We improve the segmentation by computing the point's normals robustly. Rather than averaging the normals of neighboring triangles we take the median normals of the neighbors of second order, i.e. the neighbors of neighbors, or third order. Thereby the median of multiple normals is the

Fig. 4. Segmentation results for data set ELLIPSOID with 6000 vertices and $\sigma = 1$ mm noise at 4 m × 3 m × 2 m bounding box. The average segment size is clearly larger near the flat poles than at the relatively sharp equator.

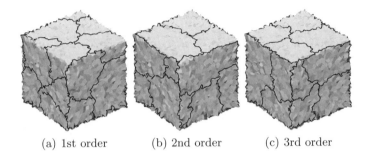

(a) 1st order   (b) 2nd order   (c) 3rd order

Fig. 5. Influence of the neighborhood size for robust curvature determination on the data set CUBE, here with 10 mm noise. Normals are obtained from directly neighboring triangles (a), neighbors of second order (b) or third order (c).

coordinate-wise median, normalized to unit length (Croux et al. 2002). As previously defined for first order normals, the distance F is the Euclidean distance between the normals of two neighboring points. Even when increasing the noise of the CUBE data set the segmentation successfully preserves all edges, when using robust normals of second or third order (Fig. 5).

Seed points at low curvature only. One effect to be considered when sampling based on curvature is to prevent seed points from being sampled at noisy edges and other highly non-planar regions. Points with large curvature tend to have large distances to all neighbors. They are likely chosen as seed point, but due to the large distance the front will not propagate to any neighbors and a tiny segment is generated, not improving the segmentation much. Many seeds are needed until all points of this type have been sampled. Instead of sampling the farthest point out of all available ones, we sort them by local curvature and restrict to the more planar half of them. Points close to edges are ignored when sampling seeds, leading to faster and more reasonable segmentations.

Color. We can easily extend the feature space or replace normals with different features, e.g., color. In case of photogrammetric reconstructions or laser range data combined with radiometric observations we may want to support the segmentation process using this information. The segmentation of a COLORED CUBE solely relying on color (Fig. 6(a)) or in combination with robust normals (Fig. 6(b)) yields intuitive segmentations.

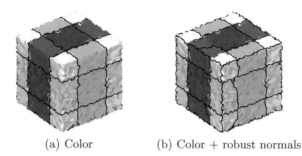

(a) Color   (b) Color + robust normals

Fig. 6. Segmentation of the data set COLORED CUBE with $\sigma = 5$ mm noise. Using color only, the surface is correctly segmented into 26 segments (a). When adding robust normals, the geometric edges of the cube are preserved as well (b).

4.2 Incremental/Decremental FastFPS

In Sect. 3 we formulated a cost function to be minimized. Applying Algorithm 1 yields promising results already, as shown in the previous section. Now we want to make use of the cost function (2) to determine the optimal number of segments automatically, while computing the segmentation. We search for the best segmentation in two steps: (1) increasing the number of segments sequentially until we likely find an over-segmentation and (2) decreasing the number of segments until a further reduction is likely to produce an under-segmentation.

When performing FastFPS, we evaluate the cost function in each iteration. The upper, orange line in Fig. 7(a) shows the decreasing costs for the iteratively increasing number of segments. At 6 segments, the expected number of segments, the labeling does not follow the edges well. The sum of squared residuals $\widehat{\Omega}$ is larger than expected and the costs Φ are still decreasing.

At 21 segments both criteria (3) and (4) are fulfilled. We do not stop increasing the number of segments immediately, but continue sampling two times more the current number of segments for even more robust results.

While the segmentation after the expected number of 6 iterations is rather poor (Fig. 7(b)), all edges are preserved when generating 63 segments (Fig. 7(d)). To avoid oversampling we start to decrease the number of segments decrementally. In each iteration we reset all points n' within the smallest region l': We remove the labels $l_{n'} = l'$, set the distances $d_{n'}$ back to infinity and set the current front $\mathcal{Q}$ to all labeled neighbors of points n'. We continue fast marching and obtain a complete labeling l and distance map d without label l'.

We proceed decrementally at almost constant costs Φ, as illustrated with the lower, blue line in Fig. 7(a). Suddenly, when removing one of the last 6 segments, the cost function rapidly increases by more than 10 %, alerting us to stop removing segments. We keep the labeling l at 6 segments, showing a significantly improved segmentation, while completely avoiding over-segmenting the surface.

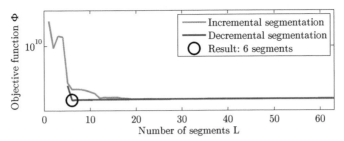

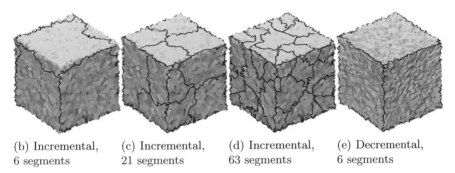

(a) Value of cost function $\Phi(l \mid L)$ during incremental (upper, orange line) and decremental (lower, blue line) segmentation process

| (b) Incremental, 6 segments | (c) Incremental, 21 segments | (d) Incremental, 63 segments | (e) Decremental, 6 segments |

Fig. 7. Influence of the incremental-decremental sampling strategy on the data set CUBE with $\sigma = 10$ mm noise. The surface is correctly segmented into 6 segments, approximating a minimum of the objective function $\Phi(l \mid L)$ defined in Sect. 3.

Note that we remove the smallest segment in each iteration of the decremental part. Thus larger planar areas might not be merged, when smaller, important segments are present, causing the algorithm to stop before being removed.

5 Experiments

After evaluating the sensitivity of our proposed segmentation procedure w.r.t. small structures and noisy data, we demonstrate its performance on multiple data sets generated by structure-from-motion or laser range acquisition methods.

5.1 Sensitivity Analysis

We demonstrate the sensitivity of our method using a synthetically generated STAIR of 1 m × 1 m size with varying height h from 10 cm down to 1 cm and Gaussian noise from 1 mm up to 10 mm. Table 1 lists the qualitative results of all 16 combinations, ranging from successfully segmented ($\checkmark$) to not recognized as edge at all ($\times$). Figure 8 shows the segmentation result for 4 combinations.

At 5 cm height and 2 mm noise the vertical segment is perfectly preserved. When further decreasing the signal-to-noise ratio, the segmentation becomes

Table 1. Visual evaluation of the segmentation for data set STAIR with 5000 vertices, average sampling distance of $\Delta x = 1.3$ cm, variable height h and noise σ. For some scenarios the algorithm successfully segmented the vertical part preserving straight edges ($\checkmark$). At increasing noise and decreasing height the vertical segment was segmented partly only ($\circ$) and finally not at all ($\times$). Circled combinations are depicted in Fig. 8.

$\Delta x = 1.4$ cm	$\sigma = 1$ mm	2 mm	5 mm	10 mm
$h = 10$ cm	⊘	$\checkmark$	$\checkmark$	$\checkmark$
$h = 5$ cm	$\checkmark$	⊘	$\circ$	$\circ$
$h = 2$ cm	$\checkmark$	$\circ$	⊙	$\circ$
$h = 1$ cm	$\circ$	$\circ$	$\times$	⊗

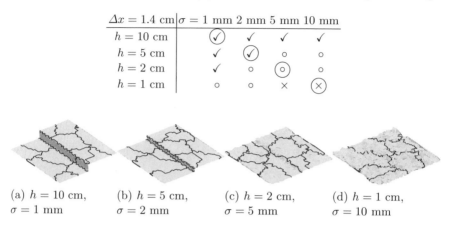

(a) $h = 10$ cm, $\sigma = 1$ mm

(b) $h = 5$ cm, $\sigma = 2$ mm

(c) $h = 2$ cm, $\sigma = 5$ mm

(d) $h = 1$ cm, $\sigma = 10$ mm

Fig. 8. Segmentation results for data set STAIR, sampled with 5000 vertices, increasing noise and decreasing height of the vertical segment.

incomplete ($\circ$), e.g., only preserving one of two edges, until the stair is not recognized at all ($\times$), e.g., at $h = \sigma = 1$ cm.

5.2   Real-World Data

We have applied our segmentation to multiple real data sets.

HOUSE is a triangulated high-resolution point-cloud of a small building model captured using a Perceptron ScanWorks V5 laser scanner mounted on a Romer measuring arm. This data set is characterized by very small noise in the order of tens of micrometers. Figure 9(a) shows the generated segmentation result. Planar areas are slightly over-segmented, while all edges are accurately preserved.

CITY and HILL are triangulations obtained from a historic city model using structured-light 3D scanning. Even smooth edges are preserved due to our robust, curvature-adaptive distance metric, as shown in Fig. 9(b) and 9(c).

COTTAGE is a meshed 3D point cloud, captured with terrestrial laser scanning. Seven scans from different viewpoints have been registered into one common coordinate frame. The segmentation in Fig. 9(d) is mostly reasonable. Large edges are completely preserved, while minor structures like doors, windows and some dormers are not prominent enough to be perfectly segmented.

BUILDING is a reconstruction from 18 images using the structure-from-motion software Bundler (Snavely et al. 2006) and the Patch-based Multi-view Stereo software (PMVS, Furukawa and Ponce 2007). The segmentation based on robust normals is shown in Fig. 9(e). Note the different segmentation density due to

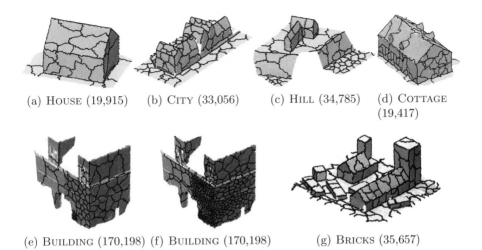

(a) HOUSE (19,915)   (b) CITY (33,056)   (c) HILL (34,785)   (d) COTTAGE (19,417)

(e) BUILDING (170,198) (f) BUILDING (170,198)   (g) BRICKS (35,657)

Fig. 9. Segmentation results for various real-world data sets. Robust normals have been used for all examples (a – g), while (f) was segmented using RGB color as well. The number of vertices is indicated in brackets.

higher point density near the corner that is covered by most of the images. In case of visual reconstructions we can use normals in combination with color, as shown in Fig. 9(f), preserving radiometric edges as well.

BRICKS is a visual reconstruction of multiple wooden bricks, captured with 48 images on a rotating turntable and processed with Bundler and PMVS.

Note that for real data our assumptions, e.g. Gaussian noise, are violated in some areas, leading to the visible over-segmentation, but still preserving edges.

All experiments were performed on a dual core machine using a Matlab implementation. Feature extraction takes a few minutes for point clouds of some ten thousands of points. The segmentation itself is computed within seconds.

6 Conclusion

We proposed a surface segmentation algorithm making use of the fast sampling approach FastFPS. We formulated the segmentation task as minimizing a cost function and presented an incremental-decremental algorithm to approximate a global optimum. Thereby our objective is to avoid loss of important information due to under-segmentation, since similar segments can be easily merged in a post-processing step, possibly using model knowledge. The cost function also allows to automatically stop the segmentation at statistically reasonable level-of-detail. Our robust distance metric is suitable for adaptive, edge-preserving segmentations of triangulated meshes with strong noise and outliers present, as shown in various experiments on both synthetic and real-world data.

The proposed cost function currently evaluates geometric features only and is designed for planar segments. It can be adapted to second-order or free-form surfaces, encoding both geometry and radiometry.

Acknowledgements. We are grateful to Friedrich Keller and Jérome Sänger for providing us with structured-light data from the historic city model of Hamburg, Germany, being result of their master thesis (Keller and Sänger 2010), supervised by Prof. Thomas Kersten and Prof. Jochen Schiewe.

References

Attene, M., Falcidieno, B., Spagnuolo, M.: Hierarchical Mesh Segmentation Based on Fitting Primitives. Visual Comput. 22(3), 181–193 (2006)

Beucher, S., Lantuéjoul, C.: Use of Watersheds in Contour Detection. In: Int. Workshop on Image Processing, Real-time Edge and Motion Detection/Estimation, pp. 17–21 (1979)

Croux, C., Haesbroeck, G., Rousseeuw, P.J.: Location Adjustment for the Minimum Volume Ellipsoid Estimator. Stat. Comput. 12(3), 191–200 (2002)

Eldar, Y., Lindenbaum, M., Porat, M., Zeevi, Y.Y.: The Farthest Point Strategy for Progressive Image Sampling. IEEE T. Image Process. 6(9), 1305–1315 (1997)

Förstner, W.: Image Analysis Techniques for Digital Photogrammetry. Photogrammetrische Woche, 205–221 (1989)

Furukawa, Y., Ponce, J.: Accurate, Dense, and Robust Multi-view Stereopsis. In: CVPR, pp. 1362–1376 (2007)

Garland, M., Willmott, A., Heckbert, P.S.: Hierarchical Face Clustering on Polygonal Surfaces. In: SIGGRAPH, pp. 49–58 (2001)

Keller, F., Sänger, J.: Automatisierte Generierung von historischen 4D-Stadtmodellen für die Darstellung innerhalb der Google Earth Engine am Beispiel der Freien und Hansestadt Hamburg. Master thesis, HafenCity University Hamburg (2010)

Kimmel, R., Sethian, J.A.: Computing Geodesic Paths on Manifolds. P. Natl. Acad. Sci. USA 95(15), 8431–8435 (1998)

Leclerc, Y.G.: Constructing Simple Stable Descriptions for Image Partitioning. Int. J. Comput. Vision 3(1), 73–102 (1989)

Mangan, A.P., Whitaker, R.T.: Partitioning 3D Surface Meshes using Watershed Segmentation. IEEE T. Vis. Comput. Gr. 5(4), 308–321 (1999)

Moenning, C., Dodgson, N.A.: Fast Marching Farthest Point Sampling. In: Eurographics (2003)

Page, D.L., Koschan, A.F., Abidi, M.A.: Perception-based 3D Triangle Mesh Segmentation Using Fast Marching Watersheds. In: CVPR, pp. 27–32 (2003)

Peyré, G., Cohen, L.: Surface Segmentation Using Geodesic Centroidal Tesselation. In: 3DPVT, pp. 995–1002 (2004)

Peyré, G., Cohen, L.: Geodesic Remeshing Using Front Propagation. Int. J. Comput. Vision 69(1), 145–156 (2006)

Sethian, J.A.: A Fast Marching Level Set Method for Monotonically Advancing Fronts. P. Natl. Acad. Sci. USA 93(4), 1591–1595 (1996)

Snavely, N., Seitz, S.M., Szeliski, R.: Photo Tourism: Exploring Photo Collections in 3D. ACM T. Graphic, 835–846 (2006)

Xu, M., Thompson, P.M., Toga, A.W.: An Adaptive Level Set Segmentation on a Triangulated Mesh. IEEE T. Med. Imaging 23(2), 191–201 (2004)

A Performance Study on Different Stereo Matching Costs Using Airborne Image Sequences and Satellite Images

Ke Zhu[1], Pablo d'Angelo[2], and Matthias Butenuth[1]

[1] Technische Universität München, Remote Sensing Technology
{ke.zhu,matthias.butenuth}@bv.tum.de
[2] German Aerospace Center, The Remote Sensing Technology Institute
pablo.angelo@dlr.de

Abstract. Most recent stereo algorithms are designed to perform well on close range stereo datasets with relatively small baselines and good radiometric conditions. In this paper, different matching costs on the Semi-Global Matching algorithm are evaluated and compared using aerial image sequences and satellite images with ground truth. The influence of various cost functions on the stereo matching performance using datasets with different baseline lengths and natural radiometric changes is evaluated. A novel matching cost merging Mutual Information and Census is introduced and shows the highest robustness and accuracy. Our study indicates that using an adaptively weighted combination of Mutual Information and Census as matching cost can improve the peformance of stereo matching for airborne image sequences and satellite images.

Keywords: Dense stereo matching, cost function, performance, observation constraints.

1 Introduction

Stereo matching has been a long lasting research topic in the computer vision community. The performance of a dense stereo matching method depends on all components including preprocessing, matching costs, aggregation, disparity optimization and postprocessing. Most work on dense stereo uses well known costs such as Absolute Differences or Birchfied-Tomasi (Birchfield and Tomasi, 1998), as these perform well on the Middlebury dataset (Scharstein and Szeliski, 2002, 2011) . The most intuitive cost assumes the consistency between intensities of two corresponding pixels. However, using different matching costs, like Absolute Differences (AD), Mutual Information (MI)(Viola and Wells, 1997) or Census (Zabih and Woodfill,1994) on the same stereo matching method can generate very different results (Hirschmüller and Scharstein, 2009); (Neilso and Yang, 2008).

Dense stereo algorithms are typically evaluated with a small baseline configuration, artificial and often ambient light sources. Radiometric changes due to vignetting, gamma changes etc. are often simulated by modifying small baseline

U. Stilla et al. (Eds.): PIA 2011, LNCS 6952, pp. 159–170, 2011.

images (Hirschmüller and Scharstein, 2009); (Neilso and Yang, 2008). But, these simulations do not capture all effects such as non-lambertian reflectance, while the inference at different lighting has been evaluated. In the evaluation of stereo matching costs using the Middlebury data (Hirschmüller and Scharstein, 2009), Census shows the best and the most robust overall performance. Mutual Information performs very well with global methods. On radiometrically distorted Middlebury datasets and datasets with varying illumination, Census and Mutual Information outperform AD clearly. However, the evaluation of matching cost performance for images with larger baselines and radiometric changes of remotely sensed images is so far not considered. The relationship between matching performance, cost functions and observation constrains is not discussed.

In this study, the Semi-Global Matching (SGM) method is selected as the stereo algorithm for evaluating different matching costs because of its robustness, speed and accuracy (Hirschmüller, 2008); (Zhu et al,2010). Three matching costs are evaluated: a non-parametric matching cost (Census), a matching cost based on Mutual Information (MI) and in addition, a new combined matching cost MI-Census (MIC). In contrast to previous studies (Hirschmüller and Scharstein, 2009); (Neilso and Yang, 2008), we use a high frame rate aerial image sequence with large baselines and stronger radiometric difference and a satellite datasets with large stereo angles.

We focus on a fundamental question: which relationship do the performance of stereo matching, cost functions and observation constrains have? We found that various matching costs perform differently under varying observation constrains. A novel matching cost, linearly merged of MI and Census (MIC), shows the most robust performance during increasing length of the baseline on real data.

The remainder of this paper is organized as follows: Section 2 describes the evaluated matching costs and the basics of SGM. The experiments on airborne optical image sequences and satellite datasets are evaluated and compared in Section 3. Conclusions and future work are presented in the last section.

2   Cost Functions and Semi-Global Matching

2.1   Cost Functions

Generally, the matching costs in this work are defined on intensity, instead of color. Color channels are averaged, if they are available. Two typical matching costs are selected: a non-parametric cost (Census) and a cost based on Mutual Information (MI). In addition, we combine linearly MI and Census with different weights to build a new matching cost (MIC).

Census is a non-parametric cost. It is invariant to monotonic gray value changes, and thus, can tolerate a large class of global and local radiometric changes. It encodes the local image structure within a transform window and defines a bit string where each bit describes the relative ordering between the computing pixel and its local neighbor. A bit is set if a pixel inside the window has a lower intensity than the center pixel. The distance between two bit strings is computed using the Hamming distance. In our work, a 9×7 window is used and supports the matching costs in the range of 0 to 63. ξ denotes a Census transform within a window, W. $\bigotimes$ computes the Hamming distance:

$$C_{Census}(p, d) = \bigotimes_W (\underset{W}{\xi}(p), \underset{W}{\xi}(p - d)). \tag{1}$$

$$\psi(u) = \int_o^T \left[\frac{1}{2}\left(\Lambda_o^{-1}u, u\right) + N^*(-u)\right] dt . \tag{2}$$

For easier combination with other costs, we rescale the matching costs into a range from 0 to 1023.

MI combines individual entropies H_l, H_r and the joint entropy $H_{l,r}$ of a stereo pair. This enables registering of images with complex radiometric relationships (Viola and Wells 1997). In this paper, we use the Hierarchical MI (HMI) for an efficient iterative learning (Hirschmüller, 2008):

$$MI(p, d) = H(p) + H(p - d) - H(p, p - d). \tag{3}$$

The mutual information cost is also rescaled to a range from 0 to 1023.

Due to the fixed local support, the disparity images generated by Census have object blurring (Brockers, 2009). Hence, a new matching cost in this paper is introduced merging MI and Census. This combination uses the advantages of both costs: the intuitive consistency and the local structure, linearly summated with different weights:

$$C_{MIC}(p, d) = w_{MI} \times C_{MI}(p, d) + (1 - w_{MI}) \times C_{Census}(p, d). \tag{4}$$

2.2 Semi-Global Matching

The Semi-Global Matching (SGM) method approximates a global, 2D smoothness constraint by combining many 1D constraints from different aggregation directions for pixelwise matching. The global energy for the disparity image is defined as $E(D)$:

$$E(D) = \sum_P (C(p, D_p) + \sum_{q \in N_p} P_1 [|D_p - D_q| = 1]$$
$$+ \sum_{q \in N_p} P_2 [|D_p - D_q| > 1] . \tag{5}$$

The first term sums the costs of all pixels in the image with their particular disparities D_p. The next two terms penalize the discontinuities with penalty factors P_1 and P_2, which differ in small or large disparity difference within a neighbourhood q of the pixel p. This minimization approximation is realized by aggregating $S(p, d)$ of path wise costs into a cost volume:

$$S(p, d) = \sum_r L_r(p, d). \tag{6}$$

$L_r(p, d)$ in 6 Eq. represents the cost of pixel p with disparity d along one direction r. It is described as following:

$$
\begin{aligned}
L_r(p, d) &= C(p, d) + min(L_r(p - r, d), \\
&\quad L_r(p - r, d - 1) + P_1, L_r(p - r, d + 1) + P_1, \\
&\quad \min_i L_r(p - r, i) + P_2) - \min_i L_r(p - r, i).
\end{aligned}
\tag{7}
$$

This regularisation term function favors planar and sloped surfaces, but still allows larger height jumps in the direction of cost aggregation. The disparity at each pixel is selected as index of the minimum cost from the cost cube.

In addition, P_2 is adapted to the local intensity gradient:

$$
P_2' = \frac{P_2}{1 + |I(p) - I(p - 1)|/W_{P_2}}.
\tag{8}
$$

In 8 Eq., $I_L(p)$ and $I_R(p, d)$ denote the intensity of pixel p in the left image and the intensity of its matched pixel at disparity d in the right image separately. Here, W_{P_2} is a parameter that controls the reduction of the penalty.

3   Evaluation

In this section, we test the three matching costs with SGM on an aerial image sequence with increasing length of the baseline and on satellite images representing different typical object areas. In addition, we tuned the smoothness parameters of SGM for all three costs in order to get the best performance. This tuning allows concentrating on the performance of the matching costs rather than the stereo method.

3.1   Evaluation Procedure and Reference Data

A continually recorded airborne optical image sequence is used to follow the impacts of matching costs on the performance during a changing baseline and stereo angles. The images are provided by the 3K camera system, consisting of three Canon EOS 1D Mark II cameras with a 50 mm lens (Kurz et al.,2007). The flight altitude is approximately 1500 meters above ground. Only the nadir views are used in this evaluation. The distance between each recorded observation is about 35 meters, the largest baseline we present in this work is about 250 meters. The original images are downsampled to reduce the inaccuracy of camera calibration. An 1.7 meter resolution LIDAR 3D point cloud is used as the ground truth. Additionally, we evaluate the matching costs on a Worldview-1 stereo image pair with a ground sampling distance of 50 cm, and a relatively large stereo angle of 35°. A 3D point cloud acquired by the Institut Cartogràfic de Catalunya (ICC) with airborne laser scanning is used as reference data. The density of the point cloud is approximately 0.5 points per square meter. The data is part of the ISPRS matching benchmark (Reinartz et al,2010). After stereo matching, the points are projected into UTM Zone 32 North for the aerial images and UTM Zone 31 North for the satellite images respectively to generate Digital Surface Models (DSM). Holes in the generated DSMs are filled with inverse distance weighted interpolation. We compute the Euclidean distance d between points in ground truth and the triangulated DSM. As the DSMs generated by stereo matching and to a lesser extend the points cloud might contain outliers which violate the assumption of a normal distribution, we follow (Höhle and Höhle,2009) and compute measures based on robust statistics, in addition to the classical mean and standard deviation values. This includes bad pixels, the normalized median deviation (NMAD)

$$NMAD = 1.4826 median_j(|d_j - median_i(d_i)|) \tag{9}$$

as a robust estimate of the standard deviation.

3.2   Results on Aerial Image Sequence

We evaluate our results in three specific areas shown in Figure 1: a city area, a church area and, lastly, a boundary area. The first area covers the whole area and allows the holistic evaluation. The second test area consist of a large and high church, in order to study the matching behaviours in complicated situation like large homogenous surface and occlusions. The last area includes all building edges for the discontinuity analysis. The evaluations on city and church area indicate the different properties of MI and Census by stereo matching. The penalty factors $P_1 = 750$, $P_2 = 1200$ and the adaptive parameter $W_{P_2} = 60$ are kept constant at 0.8 for all stereo pairs.

Figure 3 (a) illustrates the NMAD errors of MI, Census and MIC on the church area during increasing length of the baseline. MI fails mostly in the roof area since it is derived by gray value analysis. Census performs very robust in this area due to the local structural support. MIC is between Census and MI.

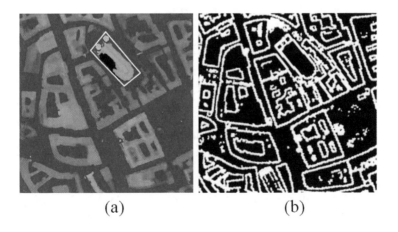

(a)   (b)

Fig. 1. Evaluation masks on city and church area (a) and mask on boundary area (b)

On the city area, Figure 3 (b), Hierarchical MI (HMI) does perform slightly better than Census for small baselines, but it decreases quickly with increasing baseline length, possibly due to the non-lambertian reflectance. In contrast, the fixed local support of Census causes some blurred edges on small baselines stereo pairs. It produces a noise disparity map, but shows the most robust behaviour for larger baselines, as visible on the church roof in Figure 6. Because of the accuracy of MI and the robustness of Census, we combine MI with Census to generate the matching cost MIC. It performs similar to MI on stereo pairs with small baselines, but keeps the robustness of Census for larger baselines.

We observe that the results using MI have sharper edges at discontinuities. In contrast, the fixed local support of Census causes slightly blurred edges. We apply the evaluation using the third mask generated by the gradient image of ground truth. Figure 3 (c) presents the bad pixel percents of Census, MI and MIC respectively. Generally, MI performs better than Census, but the errors of MI rise observably with large baselines. MIC is similar as MI using small baselines, besides robust like Census after fail of MI . The weight of MI w_{MI} for this evaluation is kept constant at 0.8 for all stereo pairs.

Since the different behaviours of MI and Census depend on the baselines, we tuned the weight w_{MI} during a changing baseline length, in order to reveal the relationship between the stereo baseline and the weight. Figure 4 demonstrates the error analysis on different weight combinations for MIC. This experimental result shows the larger the baseline of the stereo pair has, the smaller w_{MI} performs better. In other words, Census performs better as MI on data with larger baseline. The weight should be adapted on the observation constrains, like stereo baseline. The results of the statistical evaluation using the boundary area are shown in Table 1.

In addition, P_2 adapted to the local intensity gradient improves the performances for MI clearly. In Figure 2, the comparison of details between disparity images using and not using adaptive P_2 are shown. Both disparity images are generated by MI on the same stereo pair. The reconstruction with adaptive P_2 shows less errors particularly at inner courtyards.

Finally, we analyse and visualise the continuous performance changes using different matching costs during an increasing baseline lenght in Figure 6.

3.3   Results on Satellite Data

A small cutout of the stereo data and the reconstruction results for an urban area (Terrassa in Spain, Barcelona) are shown in Fig. 5. The full dataset covers mountainous, agricultural, forest, industrial and residential areas. The figure indicates that these images cannot be matched successfully using MI, while Census and the MIC perform reasonably well on this challenging dataset. The large black background in the MI image was incorrectly filled using this data. Table 2 shows the euclidean distance statistics between the LIDAR point cloud and the generated digital surface model for the city area shown in Fig. 5 and two other test areas (hilly forest and industrial area) against the LIDAR reference data. It is clearly visible that MIC performs slightly better than Census and that MI

NON adaptive P₂

adaptive P₂

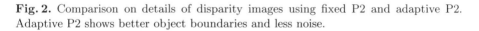

Fig. 2. Comparison on details of disparity images using fixed P2 and adaptive P2. Adaptive P2 shows better object boundaries and less noise.

does produce the largest errors. Experiments with various values for P_1, P_2 and W_{P_2} indicated that performance depends mostly on the cost function and not on the exact parametrisation of the stereo algorithm.

4   Conclusion and Future Work

In this work, two typical matching costs (MI and Census) and a novel matching cost (MIC) are evaluated using SGM on an aerial image sequence and satellite images with ground truth. In summary we found that the performance of different matching costs depends on the observation constrains like the length of the baseline and radiometric changes. More specifically, MI performs slightly better than Census in case of low radiometric changes and stereo pairs with small baselines, but fails in areas with local radiometric changes. MI keeps sharp edges at discontinuities and results in less noisy disparity maps when compared to Census. Census performs well for larger baselines, but results in slightly blurred object boundaries. For large baseline satellite stereo imagery Census performs

Table 1. Evaluation of matching results in the boundary area using different w_{MI} against ground truth LIDAR data. Bad pixels are the percentage of LIDAR points with an error > 5 m.

				Length of Baseline (m)				
w	35	70	105	140	175	210	245	280
0.0	20.4	14.6	13.2	13.0	12.7	12.9	12.8	12.8
0.1	19.9	14.4	13.1	12.9	12.7	12.6	12.7	12.7
0.2	19.5	14.2	12.9	12.7	12.6	12.4	12.6	13.0
0.3	19.0	13.9	12.7	12.5	12.4	12.5	12.5	12.5
0.4	18.3	13.5	12.5	12.3	12.2	12.2	**12.2**	**12.3**
0.5	17.9	13.2	12.3	12.2	12.0	**12.1**	12.2	12.3
0.6	17.4	13.1	12.2	**12.0**	**11.9**	12.1	12.2	12.5
0.7	17.9	13.0	**12.1**	12.1	12.0	12.2	12.3	12.5
0.8	16.5	13.0	12.2	12.2	12.1	12.4	12.6	13.0
0.9	16.2	**13.0**	12.5	12.4	12.6	13.0	13.0	12.9
1.0	**16.0**	13.4	13.0	12.9	13.0	13.3	13.5	13.7

Table 2. Evaluation of Matching results in three test areas against ground truth LIDAR Data. NMAD is the normalized median deviation and Bad pixels is the percentage of pixels with an absolute height error > 2 m.

Cost	P_1	P_2	W_{P_2}	w_{MI}	NMAD	Bad pixels
MIC	700	1400	200	0.3	0.72	15.8 %
Census	600	1300	200	-	0.74	16.8 %
MI	700	1400	200	-	1.10	25.8 %

significantly better than MI. In addition, Census works more suited in homogeneous areas as MI due to the fac that the local structure is transformed in the cost. The weighted sum of MI and Census (MIC) unifies the advantages of MI and Census and outperforms MI and Census on remotely sensed datasets.

Topics for future work include developing a methodology for evaluation of remotely sensed images against LIDAR ground truth. The main challenges for this task are changes due to multi-temporal data acquisition and a different resolution and acquisition properties of the sensors. In addition, the influence of different stereo algorithms on the performance of the matching cost functions will be evaluated in future work. The relationship between matching performance and observation constrains will be evaluated with other datasets and test regions with landcovers.

Acknowledgements. Special thanks are given to the data providers for the provision of the stereo data namely: Digital Globe for the Worldview-1 data and ICC Catalunya for the reference data.

References

Birchfield, S., Tomasi, C.: A pixel dissimilarity measure that is insensitive to image sampling. IEEE Transactions on Pattern Analysis and Machine Intelligence 20(4), 401–406 (1998)

Brockers, R.: Cooperative stereo matching with colorbased adaptive local support. Computer Analysis of Images and Patterns (2009)

Höhle, J., Höhle, M.: Accuracy assessment of digital elevation models by means of robust statistical methods. ISPRS Journal of Photogrammetry and Remote Sensing 64(4), 398–406 (2009)

Hirschmüller, H.: Stereo processing by semi-global matching and mutual information. IEEE Transactions on Pattern Analysis and Machine Intelligence 30(2), 328–341 (2008)

Hirschmüller, H., Scharstein, D.: Evaluation of stereo matching costs on image with radiometric differences. IEEE Transactions on Pattern Analysis and Machine Intelligence 31(9), 1582–1599 (2009)

Kurz, F., Müller, R., Stephani, M., Reinartz, P., Schroeder, M.: Calibration of a wide-angle digital camera system for near real time scenarios. In: ISPRS Workshop High Resolution Earth Imaging for Geospatial Information (2007)

Neilso, D., Yang, Y.: Evaluation of constructable match cost measures for stereo correspondence using cluster ranking. In: IEEE Conference on Computer Vision and Pattern Recognition (2008)

Reinartz, P., d'Angelo, P., Krauß, T., Poli, D., Jacobsen, K., Buyuksalih, G.: Benchmarking and quality analysis of dem generated from high and very high resolution optical stereo satellite data. In: ISPRS Symposium Commission I (2010)

Scharstein, D., Szeliski, R.: A taxonomy and evaluation of dense two-frame stereo correspondence algorithms. International Journal of Computer Vision 47(1), 7–42 (2002)

Scharstein, D., Szeliski, R.: Middlebury stereo vision research page, http://vision.middlebury.edu/stereo/ (visited on May 5, 2011)

Viola, P., Wells, W.M.: Alignment by maximization of mutual information. International Journal of Computer Vision 24(2), 137–154 (1997)

Zabih, R., Woodfill, J.: Non-parametric local transforms for computing visual correspondancen. In: Proc. European Conference of Computer Vision (1994)

Zhu, K., d'Angelo, P., Butenuth, M.: Comparison of Dense Stereo using CUDA. In: European Conference on Computer Vision, ECCV Workshop, Computer Vision on GPUs (2010)

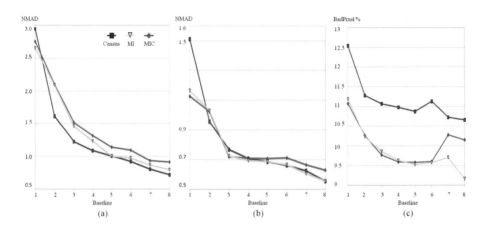

Fig. 3. Evaluation on church (a) and city area (b): indexes 1 to 8 denote the different matching pairs with increasing baseline. The Y-axis denotes the percentage of NMAD errors. On the church area, Census performs better than MI and MIC generally. On the city area, MIC is robust both with small baselines and large baselines.Evaluation on boundary area (c): MIC performs well such as MI with small baselines and steady like Census with large baselines.

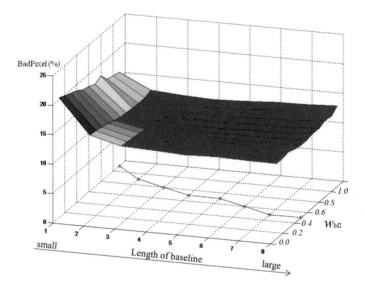

Fig. 4. Weight tuning for w_{MI} during increasing of baseline length. The positions getting minimal error are projected at the Baseline-Weight surface and show the weight trend.

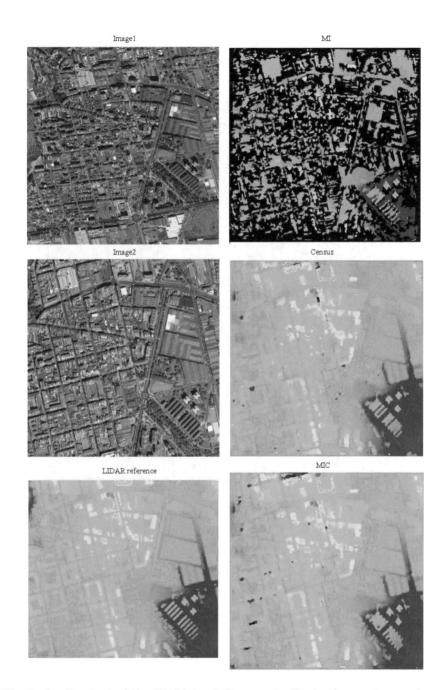

Fig. 5. Small cutout of the Worldview-1 Stereo pair. First column: stereo pair and LIDAR reference data. Second column: Results after stereo matching with different cost functions, orthographic reprojection and discontinuity preserving interpolation.

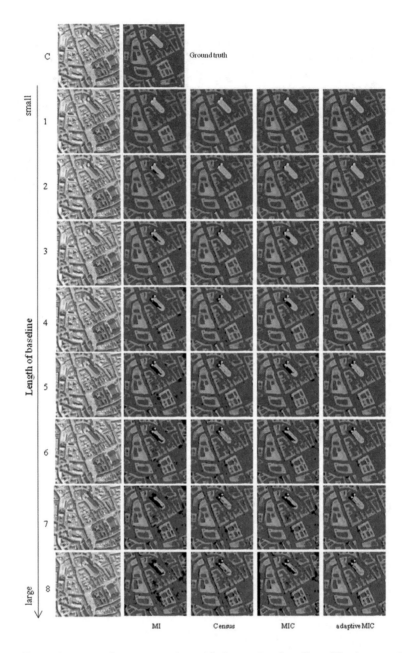

Fig. 6. Disparity maps for stereo pairs with increasing baseline. The images 1 to 8 are matched with the centre image C. The results for MI, Census, MIC and adaptive weighted MIC are shown in columns 2-5. The black areas indicate failures of the left-right check. The ground truth DSM (Digital surface model) from laser scanning is shown next to the centre image.

Fusion of Digital Elevation Models Using Sparse Representations

Haris Papasaika[1], Effrosyni Kokiopoulou[2], Emmanuel Baltsavias[1],
Konrad Schindler[1], and Daniel Kressner[3]

[1] Institute of Geodesy and Photogrammetry, ETH Zurich, Switzerland
[2] Seminar for Applied Mathematics, ETH Zurich, Switzerland
[3] Mathematics Institute of Computational Science and Engineering, EPFL,
Switzerland

Abstract. Nowadays, different sensors and processing techniques provide Digital Elevation Models (DEMs) for the same site, which differ significantly with regard to their geometric characteristics and accuracy. Each DEM contains intrinsic errors due to the primary data acquisition technology, the processing chain, and the characteristics of the terrain. DEM fusion aims at overcoming the limitations of different DEMs by merging them in an intelligent way. In this paper we present a generic algorithmic approach for fusing two arbitrary DEMs, using the framework of sparse representations. We conduct extensive experiments with real DEMs from different earth observation satellites to validate the proposed approach. Our evaluation shows that, together with adequately chosen fusion weights, the proposed algorithm yields consistently better DEMs.

Keywords: DEMs, fusion, quality evaluation, learning.

1 Introduction

1.1 Motivation and Aims

Digital Elevations Models (DEMs) are one of the most important types of geodata. They are needed in a large number of applications, ranging from virtual globes and visualization to engineering and environmental planning. DEMs of larger areas are usually generated either by photogrammetric processing of aerial and satellite images, SAR (Synthetic Aperture Radar) interferometry, or laser scanning (mainly from airborne platforms). Each sensing technology has its own strengths and weaknesses, and even within one technology the variations in DEM quality are large (as an example, consider the characteristics of image matching algorithms). DEMs are available at different scales from tailor-made local models to national and even global coverage. We are primarily interested in large-scale national and global products, whose resolution, accuracy, error characteristics, and homogeneity vary a lot. In most cases, the DEM producers provide users

U. Stilla et al. (Eds.): PIA 2011, LNCS 6952, pp. 171–184, 2011.
© Springer-Verlag Berlin Heidelberg 2011

with information only on production technology, date of acquisition, and resolution, but only with coarse accuracy measures that fail to capture the local variations in data quality – sometimes only a single global number.

In an ideal world, one would of course obtain the raw measurements and sensor models from all sensors, and merge them by fitting a single DEM to the entire set of heterogeneous observations, along the way computing quality measures for every single height value. Unfortunately, this is usually not feasible in practice. Thus, one resorts to the next best solution, namely to fuse DEMs from different providers into a higher-quality product, and estimate its quality in the process from the available redundancy.

DEM fusion – and its necessary prerequisite, fine-grained quality characterization of the inputs – has several benefits: improved accuracy, homogeneity and completeness, as well as fine-grained quality information for the final product. We deal only with $2\frac{1}{2}$-D surfaces in regular grid format, which constitute the vast majority of large-scale DEMs (although our framwork could in principle be extended to TINs).

In this work we make two contributions:

- we develop a computationally efficient and flexible mathematical method for robust fusion of $2\frac{1}{2}$-D surface models. The formulation is *generic* and can be applied with any two input DEMs, independent of the sensor technology and processing with which they were created, making it useful for practical applications; it takes into account both prior information about plausible terrain shapes (in the form of a dictionary), and the local accuracy of the inputs, controled by interpretable weights; and it poses the complete fusion as a clean, convex mathematical optimisation problem that can be solved to global optimality, and in which the influence of the input DEMs is controlled by an interpretable set of local fusion weights.
- we propose a data-driven method, which allows one to derive local measures of DEM quality (and thus also fusion weights) for each point or segment of a DEM, if no such information is available. To this end we use as input geomorphological characteristics of the terrain (slope, roughness), which are derived directly from the DEMs, as well as optionally semantic information such as land-cover maps. Using existing high-quality ground-truth DEMs as reference, we learn regression functions relating the available geomorphological characteristics to the DEM quality, which then allow one to estimate the local quality of a new DEM.

The proposed method is evaluated in detail with three different satellite datasets and shows a significant improvement in DEM quality, consistently over all combinations of inputs.

1.2   Related Work

Surprisingly, there is a relatively small body of work about data fusion for combining DEMs. Schultz et al. (1999) develop a methodology to fuse two stereo-optical DEMs. The techniques discussed in that paper are based on the concept of using self-consistency to identify potentially unreliable points. Honikel (1999) applies two techniques which take advantage of the complementary properties of InSAR and stereo-optical DEMs. First, the cross-correlation of phases, respectively the gray values, are determined for each DEM point and used as fusion weights. The second technique takes advantage of the fact that errors of the DEMs are of different nature, and attempts to find regions where each DEM is less correct than the other, and to replace the data with the one from the more correct counterpart. In Damon (2002) and Gamba et al. (2003) the specific combination of InSAR and LIDAR data is considered. Roth et al. (2002) describe a technique to combine multi-source DEMs, based on the concept of height error maps. This requires the availability of a height error description and the fusion is done by a weighted averaging. Slatton et al. (2002) combine space-borne In-SAR data from the ERS-1/2 platforms with multiple sets of airborne C-band InSAR data using a multi-scale Kalman smoothing approach. Rao et al. (2003) fill holes in an InSAR DEM with height data derived with stereo optical matching. Kääb (2005) combined SRTM and ASTER DEMs to fill the gaps of SRTM, and then used the resulting DEM to derive glacier flow in the mountains of Bhutan. Podobnikar (2005) introduces a fusion technique based on the weighted sum of data sources with geomorphological enhancement. A DEM is modelled through the averaging of individual datasets but considering their quality. The main step of geomorphological enhancement is the generation of trend surfaces as low frequency functions.

2   Mathematical Formulation of Fusion

In the following, we describe the problem statement. Consider two noisy measurements y_l and y_h of a height field x, possibly at different resolutions, e.g., low and high respectively. We assume that the measurements have been produced from the original DEM x by the following model:

$$y_h = x + \epsilon_h \quad \text{and} \quad y_l = Lx + \epsilon_l, \tag{1}$$

where ϵ_h, ϵ_l are noise vectors and L is an unknown downsampling operator. In the case when the two measurements y_l and y_h are at the same resolution, the operator L equals to 1. The problem addressed in this paper is to fuse the noisy measurements y_l and y_h in order to recover the original DEM x. The hope is that the redundancy of the measurements will offer robustness against noise and result in an accurate estimation of x. The problem, as stated above, can be seen as a denoising problem – in the case of different resolutions, with simultaneous super-resolution for the coarser signal.

Problem formulation. In order to achieve robustness without oversmoothing, we pose the fusion problem in the framework of sparse representations. Sparse representations have been shown to result in state-of-the-art performance in image denoising Elad and Aharon (2006) and super-resolution problems Yang et al. (2008). To our knowledge, their potential has not been fully exploited in remote sensing problems. We work with local DEM patches to achieve computational efficiency and to ensure a moderately sized dictionary able to capture the variations in terrain shape. In what follows, y_h, y_l, and x thus denote local patches in the corresponding terrain models in (1).

We assume that x can be represented as a sparse linear combination of elements from a dictionary D (i.e., local terrain shapes). The dictionary is a basis set spanning the signal space and is typically overcomplete, that is, it contains more elements than the dimension of the signal space. The elements of the dictionary are called atoms. We say that x is sparsely represented over D if $x = D\alpha_0$, where $\alpha_0 \in \mathbb{R}^N$ is a sparse coefficient vector with most entries zero and very few non-zero entries (Figure 1). N denotes the size of the dictionary whose atoms are organized as columns of D. The sparsity of α_0 implies that already a few atoms are sufficient for obtaining a good approximation of x owing to the overcompleteness of the dictionary. Under this representation, the generative model (1) can be re-written as

$$y_h = \underbrace{D}_{:=D_h} \alpha_0 + \epsilon_h \quad \text{and} \quad y_l = \underbrace{LD}_{:=D_l} \alpha_0 + \epsilon_l, \tag{2}$$

where we have defined a high-resolution dictionary D_h and a low-resolution dictionary D_l. Both dictionaries are coupled via the relation $D_l := LD_h$. The key observation in (2) is that the *same* sparse coefficient vector α_0 is involved in both measured DEMs y_h and y_l. This leads to the following optimization problem in order to recover x from the measured y_l, y_h.

Optimization problem. Assume for a moment that D_h and D_l are available. We postpone the discussion of how to determine these two dictionaries until the end of this section. Given the two dictionaries D_h and D_l and the measurements y_l and y_h, we would like to recover the sparse coefficient vector α_0. Once α_0 has been computed, one can simply recover x by computing $D_h\alpha_0$.

$$\min_{\alpha \in \mathbb{R}^N} \underbrace{\|D_l\alpha - y_l\|_2^2}_{\text{low resolution}} + \underbrace{\|D_h\alpha - y_h\|_2^2}_{\text{high resolution}} + \underbrace{\tau\|\alpha\|_1}_{\text{sparsity term}} \tag{3}$$

The first two (data) terms correspond to the reconstruction error with respect to the observed DEMs y_l and y_h. The third (regularisation) term is associated with the ℓ^1 norm of the candidate solution vector α. It is well known that the minimization of the ℓ^1 norm encourages a sparse solution(see, e.g., Tibshirani (1996)). Since the true coefficient vector α_0 that we seek to recover is sparse, we would like our estimated solution α to be sparse as well. The parameter $\tau > 0$ controls the trade-off between data fitting and sparsity; its choice is discussed in Sec. 3.2. Finally, note that our approach naturally extends to more than two DEMs by including additional data fitting terms in (3).

The current formulation (3) implicitly assumes that both data terms have the same importance. However, this is not typically the case with DEMs, since the two inputs have, at each point, different accuracy, depending on the sensing technology and processing. It is therefore beneficial to include weights in the

problem formulation that will reflect such prior knowledge. We therefore modify
the optimization to include positive weight vectors w_l, w_h:

$$\min_{\alpha \in \mathbb{R}^N} \|\sqrt{w_l} \odot (D_l\alpha - y_l)\|_2^2 + \|\sqrt{w_h} \odot (D_h\alpha - y_h)\|_2^2 + \tau\|\alpha\|_1. \qquad (4)$$

Here, $\odot$ denotes component-wise multiplication, which offers flexibility in allowing for individual weights at each location. Section 3.1 discusses the choice of
these weights, which are crucial for a good fusion.

Consistency among neighbouring patches. Solving (4) for each patch independently would result in blocking artifacts along the patch borders. To remedy this
problem, we introduce overlap between patches and impose consistency between
neighbouring patches. More specifically, let P denote an operator that extracts
the overlap region between the current working patch and the patches that have
been computed before. Furthermore let y_p denote a vector that collects the values of the estimated DEM in the overlap region. Minimizing the discrepancy
$\|PD_h\alpha - y_p\|_2^2$ between overlapping patches will impose consistency and ensure
smooth transitions. Introducing this term into (4), we reach the final formulation
of our optimization problem:

$$\min_{\alpha \in \mathbb{R}^N} \|\sqrt{w_l} \odot (D_l\alpha - y_l)\|_2^2 + \|\sqrt{w_h} \odot (D_h\alpha - y_h)\|_2^2$$
$$+\beta\|PD_h\alpha - y_p\|_2^2 + \tau\|\alpha\|_1, \qquad (5)$$

where we have introduced the parameter $\beta > 0$ to control the influence of the
patch overlap factor. The choice of this parameter is discussed in Sec. 3.2.

Equation (5) can be written in compact form:

$$\min_{\alpha \in \mathbb{R}^N} \|\tilde{D}\alpha - \tilde{y}\|_2^2 \;+\; \tau\|\alpha\|_1, \qquad \text{where}$$

$$\tilde{D} = \begin{bmatrix} \sqrt{w_l} \odot D_l \\ \sqrt{w_h} \odot D_h \\ \sqrt{\beta}PD_h \end{bmatrix} \quad \text{and} \quad \tilde{y} = \begin{bmatrix} \sqrt{w_l} \odot y_l \\ \sqrt{w_h} \odot y_h \\ \sqrt{\beta}y_p \end{bmatrix}. \qquad (6)$$

Problem (6) is a convex ℓ^1-regularized least-squares problem that can be solved
to global optimality. Since optimization problems of this form constitute the
main computational kernel of compressed sensing applications, there exists a
wide selection of algorithms for their solution. Here, we use *Orthogonal Matching Pursuit* (OMP) Mallat (1998), because of its simplicity and computational
efficiency. Problem (6) is solved for each patch with OMP. Due to lack of space
we omit details on OMP and refer the interested reader to the original publication. The OMP code reproducing the results in this paper is available for
download at Elad (2011). Details concerning the processing time are discussed
in Sec. 4.

Dictionary construction. The proposed framework requires dictionaries
D_h, D_l, which must be acquired from training data. Different learning techniques
could be used to obtain a set of atoms from available high-quality DEMs. We

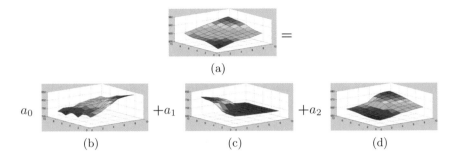

Fig. 1. Reconstruction of a 9×9 patch (a) from three non-zero atoms (b)-(d), where $[a_0, a_1, a_2]$ is the sparse non-zero coefficient vector.

have experimented with different methods and found that the best results are obtained by simple random sampling of patches from high resolution DEMs, followed by clustering to remove very similar samples. This is similar to the approach used in Yang et al. (2008). Hence, for the construction of D_h, we use a training set of high resolution DEMs of high quality (which are of course different from the test DEMs used in the evaluation). If D_l is of lower resolution, its atoms are obtained by downsampling the corresponding atoms in D_h with bicubic interpolation. The preparation of the dictionaries is off-line and needs to be performed only once. Our empirical results in Sec. 4 demonstrate that the dictionaries constructed with the above procedure are well suited for successfully representing real terrain patches using very few (less than ten) atoms.

3   Dem Quality and Weights

The DEM fusion method used in this research consists primarily of two steps: quality evaluation and fusion. It is assumed that the input DEMs are co-registered into the same coordinate system. The co-registration operates by minimizing 3D separations between a template (master) DEM and a second search (slave) DEM, see Gruen and Akca (2005). After co-registration, the low resolution DEM is re-sampled at the nodes of the high resolution DEM by bicubic interpolation.

3.1   Fusion Weights

The fusion is accomplished with the support of weight maps that reflect the estimated relative accuracy of the two DEMs at every single grid point. In some cases, DEM providers deliver such error maps, which can then be directly used for fusion. In most, cases, however, these maps are either not available or not reliable, and the weights need to be estimated from the data.

We have explored a data-driven strategy to find the weights based on geomorphological characteristics. Geometric properties of the terrain can be derived directly from a given DEM with local characteristics such as slope, aspect, roughness, curvature, etc. We calculate two such parameters, *slope* and *roughness*, and analyze their relation to the co-registration residuals.

The slope is extracted using Horn's formula Horn (1981) to find the first order derivatives in x and y direction. Roughness refers to the height variation within a local neighborhood and can be measured in different ways using, e.g., the standard deviation or fractal dimension. We have experimented with several methods and found the entropy to perform best for our purposes. The entropy $E(x, y)$ is defined as $E(x, y) = \sum(p \times \log p)$, where p are the probability densities of the heights, approximated by histogram counts. Each output grid cell contains the entropy value of the surrounding $n \times n$ neighborhood. We point out that the residuals vary (increase or decrease) in a non-random pattern with the two extracted geomorphological parameters. We learn the mapping from a parameter to the expected residual (accuracy) with Gaussian process regression. An example is shown in Figure 2(b). After the mapping, we adjust the expected residuals by linearly scaling the values between 0 and 100, eventually yielding an accuracy map. In the last step, we normalize the resulting accuracy maps of both input DEMs at each overlapping point. The reciprocal values are the weights used for the fusion.

3.2   Fusion of DEMs

The fused DEM covers the common area available in all given DEMs. After merging, a single DEM exists with the same grid spacing as the DEM with the smallest grid spacing.

According to the mathematical formulation of the fusion algorithm described in Sec. 2, we have to set the overlapping parameter β, the number of the non-zero atoms used in OMP, the patch size and the number of patches in the dictionary. In order to fine tune these parameters we performed numerous tests using artificial and real world datasets and we compared for each test the produced results with available high quality reference data. Best results have been achieved with the following set of parameters. The overlap parameter β is set within the interval $[0.5, 1.5]$. The number of non-zero atoms used in OMP is set between 7 and 15. Below 7 the results are not reliable and above 15 the processing time increases while the results do not improve any further. The minimum patch size should not be smaller than 3×3 and it should not be bigger than 9×9 because then the processing window becomes too complicated and it is more difficult to find a suitable combination of non-zero sparse atoms to reconstruct it. A "good" dictionary should contain atoms that describe every possible geomorphological structure, e.g., urban, forest, flat, mountainous areas. This ensures that OMP can find a well fitting combination of atoms for every patch.

4   Results and Discussion

In this section, we present the results of an experimental validation of the fusion methodology in three realistic DEM fusion examples. The test site is located at Thun, Switzerland, and characterized by areas with different morphology and land cover. We used three DEMs produced with image matching and SAR interferometry. Figure 2(a) shows the area of overlap. The validation was performed by comparing the input and the obtained DEMs after the fusion with a high quality reference lidar DEM provided by Swisstopo.

SPOT[1] Reference 3D DEM (S): 30m grid spacing. Image acquisition date: 30.09.2002. It is produced using image matching by SpotImage. The given absolute elevation accuracy for flat or rolling terrain (slope≤20%) is 10m, for hilly terrain (20 % ≤ slope ≤ 40%) is 18 m and for the mountainous terrain (slope> 40%) is 30m. The Reference 3D DEM is delivered with a High Resolution orthoimage (SPOT 5 sensor) with 5m ground pixel size.

ALOS/PALSAR[2] DEM (A): 15m grid spacing. Image acquisition date: master 19.06.2006 and slave 04.08.2006. L-Band (ca. 23 cm wavelength). It is produced by Sarmap SA. The overall accuracy is 20m and it has been estimated using the Lidar DEM.

ERS[3] DEM (E): 25m grid spacing. Image acquisition date: late autumn to early spring time, obtained from 1995 to 1998. C-Band (ca. 6cm wavelength). It is produced by Sarmap SA. The overall accuracy is 10.7m and it has been estimated using the Lidar DEM.

Lidar DEM (L): 2m grid spacing. The airborne lidar data were acquired for the Swisstopo in 2000 with a mean density of 1-2 points per m^2, depending on the terrain, and with first and last pulse recorded. The accuracy (1 σ) of the derived DEMs is 0.5m and 1.5m for vegetated areas.

The ALOS and the ERS DEMs are delivered with an accuracy map. The values on the accuracy map are derived according to the formula: $\sigma = \text{AF} \cdot (1 - \text{coherence}^2)/(2 - \text{coherence}^2)$, where $\text{AF} = R \cdot (\sin(\theta)/(B_n \cdot 4\pi/\lambda))$, R is the range, θ is the local incidence angle, B_n is the baseline normal component and λ is the wavelength. According to our experience these accuracy maps do not always depict the real quality of the DEMs.

We tested the fusion method by fusing (a) the ALOS with the SPOT DEM which results to a final F1 DEM, and (b) the ERS with the SPOT DEM which results to a final F2 DEM and (c) the ALOS with the ERS DEM which results to a final F3 DEM.

The three DEMs (S, A, and E) were co-registered to the reference DEM (L). Table 1(a) shows the results of the co-registration. A dictionary of 800 patches of size 9×9 was generated with elements drawn randomly from the lidar DEM. The dictionary was filtered using a K-means clustering algorithm with an eulidean distance measure of 10 m. The clustering reduced the dictionary to 720 patches. In all the fusion examples that we describe below we set the overlap parameter β to 1, the number of the non-zeros atoms used in OMP was set to 10 and we used a 9×9 patch size processing window.

---

[1] Système Pour l'Observation de la Terre.

[2] Advanced Land Observing Satellite/Phased Array type L-band Synthetic Aperture Radar.

[3] European Remote-sensing Satellite.

Table 1. (a) Co-registration results. σ_0 is the σ a posteriori, and T_x, T_y, and T_z are the three translations. (b-d) Statistical results of the ALOS-SPOT, ERS-SPOT and ALOS-ERS fusion for the complete area. All units are in meters.

(a)

Master	Slave	σ_0	T_x	T_y	T_z
L	A	13.4	18.6	6.4	1.0
L	E	8.9	-16.9	13.8	1.2
L	S	8.9	16.6	3.2	2.9

(b)

	ALOS-SPOT			
	MEAN	RMSE	MAD	σ(MAD)
L-A	-1.0	19.4	6.6	9.8
L-S	-0.8	15.5	4.4	6.6
L-F1	-0.7	11.0	4.2	6.2

(c)

	ERS-SPOT			
	MEAN	RMSE	MAD	σ(MAD)
L-E	-1.2	10.7	3.1	4.6
L-S	-0.8	15.5	4.4	6.6
L-F2	-1.2	9.7	2.7	4.0

(d)

	ALOS-ERS			
	MEAN	RMSE	MAD	σ(MAD)
L-A	-1.0	19.4	6.6	9.8
L-E	-1.2	10.7	3.1	4.6
L-F3	-0.7	10.9	3.1	4.6

After the fusion, error maps were computed by subtracting the individual DEMs (input and output) from the reference DEM (L) and several statistics measures were computed. For this reason, a grid was generated for all the DEMs at 2 m intervals according to the spatial resolution of the reference DEM. The statistics included in all the tables that follow are (a) the mean value (MEAN), (b) the root mean square error (RMSE), (c) the mean absolute deviation of the median value (MAD), and (d) the σ of the MAD. All units are in meters. At the end, we performed a more detailed analysis of the results in relation to the slope, and roughness. The slope and the roughness classes were obtained by processing the lidar DEM. For the calculations we used a 5×5 pixel window. The three slope classes are: Slope$\leq$15°, 15°<Slope$\leq$45°, Slope>45°. The three roughness classes are: Roughness$\leq$10, 10<Roughness$\leq$30, Roughness>30. The roughness is scaled in the interval $[0, 100]$.

All the tests are done using a computer with Intel Core i7, Q720, 1.6 GHz CPU and 8 GB RAM using only one core, and unoptimized Matlab code.

4.1 Fusion ALOS-SPOT

A grid was generated for the input DEMs at 15m intervals according to the spatial resolution of the ALOS DEM. After resampling, the input DEMs have a grid size of 800×1167. The processing time required for the fusion was 3.8 minutes. The weights for the ALOS DEM are calculated using the given accuracy map. For the calculation of the weights of the SPOT DEM a fairly good relationship was found between the height differences map of the two input DEMs and the slope. In Figure 2(b) the used weighting function is shown. It is a sum of 6th degree Gaussian sum that we fit to the original values using peak fitting.

In Table 1(b), we can see that compared to the ALOS DEM, the fusion achieved up to 43% improvement in RMSE while maintaining the resolution of 15m. Similarly, as compared to the SPOT DEM, the fusion improved the resolution to 15m from 30m while improving the RMSE by 29%. Figure 3 shows

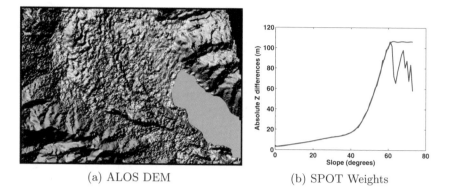

(a) ALOS DEM   (b) SPOT Weights

Fig. 2. (a) Overlap area. (b) Absolute Z differences between the Lidar and the SPOT DEM versus slope (mean every degree). The blue line are the original values. The red line is the Gaussians sum that we fit to the original values.

a detail of the Z difference images of the three DEMs. The error of the ALOS DEM is not introduced into the final DEM F1 which supports the choice of the weights.

The results of the slope and roughness assessment are presented in the Table 2. We notice that the fusion leads to an improvement especially for medium and high slopes and less for low slopes. The same behavior applies to the three roughness classes but to a lesser degree than for the slope.

Table 2. ALOS-SPOT fusion. Slope and roughness classes analysis.

Slope	$S{\leq}15°$, 56.2%			$15°{<}S{\leq}45°$, 37.8%			$S{>}45°$, 6.0%		
	mean	rmse	mad	mean	rmse	mad	mean	rmse	mad
L-A	-0.6	11.1	4.1	-0.8	23.6	11	-4.8	39.6	19.4
L-S	-0.2	6.3	3.1	-1.8	17.9	6.6	-13.3	39.9	14.1
L-F1	-0.1	5.4	3	-1.3	12.8	6.1	-7.4	26.2	12.9
Rough.	$R{\leq}10$, 17.2%			$10{<}R{\leq}30$, 25.9%			$R{>}30$, 56.9%		
	mean	rmse	mad	mean	rmse	mad	mean	rmse	mad
L-A	-1.6	9	0.2	0.3	8.5	4.2	-1.3	24.5	10.7
L-S	1.5	3.6	0.9	-0.8	4.4	2.2	-2.9	20.2	6.1
L-F1	1.4	3.4	0.9	-0.5	4.2	2.1	-1.9	14.1	5.7

4.2 Fusion ERS-SPOT

A grid was generated for the input DEMs at 25m intervals according to the spatial resolution of ERS. After resampling, the input DEMs have a grid size of 480 × 700. The processing time required for the fusion was 1.3 minutes. The weights for the ERS DEM are calculated using the given accuracy map. The weights for the SPOT DEM are calculated as described above.

In Table 1(c), we can see that as compared to the ERS DEM, the technique achieved up to 10% improvement in RMSE while maintaining the resolution of 25m. Similarly, as compared to the SPOT DEM, the technique improved the

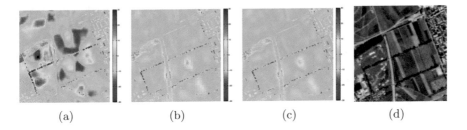

(a)   (b)   (c)   (d)

Fig. 3. ALOS-SPOT fusion example. (a) Residuals between the L and A DEM, (b) Residuals between the L and S DEM, (c) Residuals between the L and F1 DEM. (d) SPOT orthoimage. The colored Z residuals are mapped in the interval [-30,30]. The bar unit is meters.

resolution to 25m from 30m while improving the RMSE by 37%. Figure 4 shows a detail of the Z difference images of the three DEMs. The errors of the ERS DEM are not introduced into the final DEM F2.

The results of the slope and roughness assessment are presented in the Table 3. The analysis of these results conforms to the analysis for ALOS-SPOT fusion. Here the improvement by fusion is larger for medium and high slopes and roughness than for low ones.

Table 3. ERS-SPOT fusion. Slope and roughness classes analysis.

Slope	$S \leq 15°$, 56.2%			$15° < S \leq 45°$, 37.8%			$S > 45°$, 6.0%		
	mean	rmse	mad	mean	rmse	mad	mean	rmse	mad
L-E	-0.9	5.6	1.6	1.1	12.7	6.7	3	24.7	12.1
L-S	-0.2	6.3	3.1	-1.8	17.9	6.6	-13.3	39.9	14.1
L-F2	-0.6	5.2	1.5	-1.4	12.4	6.2	-7.2	24.8	17.2

Rough.	$R \leq 10$, 17.2%			$10 < R \leq 30$, 25.9%			$R > 30$, 56.9%		
	mean	rmse	mad	mean	rmse	mad	mean	rmse	mad
L-E	-1.4	2.4	0.3	-0.8	4.5	1.9	0.9	13.8	6.4
L-S	1.5	3.6	0.9	-0.8	4.4	2.2	-2.9	20.2	6.1
L-F2	-0.7	1.8	0	-0.5	3.8	1.5	-1.5	11.8	4.6

4.3   Fusion ALOS-ERS

A grid was generated for the input DEMs at 15m intervals according to the spatial resolution of the ALOS DEM. After resampling, the input DEMs have a grid size of 800×1167. The processing time required for the fusion was 3.8 minutes. The weights are calculated using the given accuracy maps, given the fact that the weights are inversely proportional to the standard deviation values. The values of the accuracy maps are rescaled to the interval $[0, 1]$. In Table 1(d), we can see that as compared to the ALOS DEM, the technique achieved up to 45% improvement in RMSE while maintaining the resolution of 15m. Similarly, as compared to the ERS DEM, the technique improved the resolution to 15m from 25m while not improving at all the RMSE. Figure 5 shows a detail of the Z difference images of the three DEMs. In the ALOS DEM a large blunder exists

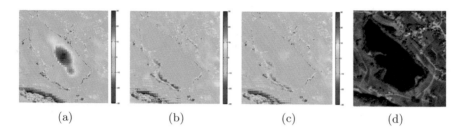

(a)   (b)   (c)   (d)

Fig. 4. ERS-SPOT fusion example. (a) Residuals between the L and E DEM, (b) Residuals between the L and S DEM, (c) Residuals between the L and F2 DEM. (d) SPOT Orthoimage. The colored Z residuals are mapped in the interval [-30,30]. The bar unit is meters.

Table 4. ALOS-ERS fusion. Slope and roughness and land cover classes analysis.

Slope	$S \leq 15°$, 56.2%			$15° < S \leq 45°$, 37.8%			$S > 45°$, 6.0%		
	mean	rmse	mad	mean	rmse	mad	mean	rmse	mad
L-A	-0.6	11.1	4.1	-0.8	23.6	11	-4.8	39.6	19.4
L-E	-0.9	5.6	1.6	1.1	12.7	6.7	3	24.7	12.1
L-F3	-0.9	5.5	1.6	1	12.7	6.6	2.9	24.7	12.1
Rough.	$R \leq 10$, 17.2%			$10 < R \leq 30$, 25.9%			$R > 30$, 56.9%		
	mean	rmse	mad	mean	rmse	mad	mean	rmse	mad
L-A	-1.6	9	0.2	0.3	8.5	4.2	-1.3	24.5	10.7
L-E	-1.4	2.4	0.3	-0.8	4.5	1.9	0.9	13.8	6.4
L-F3	-1.4	2.4	0.3	-0.8	4.5	1.9	0.9	13.8	6.4

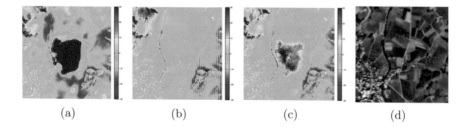

(a)   (b)   (c)   (d)

Fig. 5. ALOS-ERS fusion example. (a) Residuals between the L and A DEM, (b) Residuals between the L and E DEM, (c) Residuals between the L and F3 DEM. (d) SPOT orthoimage. The colored Z residuals are mapped in the interval [-30,30]. The bar unit is meters.

which does not appear in the ALOS accuracy map, so this blunder is introduced into the final result F3.

The results of the slope and roughness assessment are presented in the Table 4. Here for medium and large slopes / roughness there is no impovement by fusion while for low values the improvement is significant.

5   Conclusions and Future Work

We have proposed a methodology for DEM fusion based on sparse representations. First, we have introduced a mathematical framework for the fusion. Next, we have proposed a way to calculate the weight maps for the input DEMs when no prior information is available. We provide experimental evidence using real DEMs that indicates the advantages of the proposed approach after the examination of the post-fusion DEMs. Strategies that take advantage of some complementary factors like the edginess, the land cover or the special attributes of the DEMs production technology are likeley to be realized in the near future for the calculation of the weight maps.

Acknowledgements. We acknowledge support of this research by the Commission for Technology and Innvovation (CTI), Switzerland within the framework of the project Synergos, in cooperation with the company Sarmap SA, Switzerland, by the Swiss Federal Office of Topography, Bern who provided the lidar DEM and by Sarmap SA, Switzerland who provided the ALOS/PALSAR and the ERS DEMs.

References

Damon, J.: Fusing Lidar and IfSAR DEMs: a seven-step methodology. In: 22nd ESRI International Conference (2002)

Elad, M., Aharon, M.: Image denoising via sparse and redundant representations over learned dictionaries. IEEE Trans. on Image Processing 15(12), 3736–3745 (2006)

Elad, M.: Michael Elad personal webpage, software (2011),
http://www.cs.technion.ac.il/~elad/software/

Gamba, P., Dell'acqua, F., Houshmand, B.: Comparison and fusion of Lidar and In-SAR digital elevation models over urban areas. International Journal of Remote Sensing 24(22), 4289–4300 (2003)

Gruen, A., Akca, D.: Least squares 3D surface and curve matching. ISPRS Journal of Photogrammetry & Remote Sensing 59(3), 151–174 (2005)

Honikel, M.: Strategies and methods for the fusion of digital elevation models from optical and SAR data. International Archives of Photogrammetry and Remote Sensing 32(7-4-3W6), 83–89 (1999)

Horn, B.: Hill shading and the reflectance map. Proceedings of the IEEE 69(1), 14–47 (1981)

Kääb, A.: Combination of SRTM3 and repeat ASTER data for deriving alpine glacier flow velocities in the Bhutan Himalaya. Remote Sensing of Environment 94(4), 463–474 (2005)

Mallat, S.: A Wavelet Tour of Signal Processing, 2nd edn. Academic Press, London (1998)

Podobnikar, T.: Production of integrated digital terrain model from multiple datasets of different quality. International Journal of Geographical Information Science 19(1), 69–89 (2005)

Rao, Y.S., Rao, K.S., Venkataraman, G., Khare, M., Reddy, C.: Comparison and fusion of DEMs derived from InSAR and optical stereo techniques. In: Third ESA International Workshop on ERS SAR Interferometry (2003)

Roth, A., Knöpfle, W., Strunz, G., Lehner, M., Reinartz, P.: Towards a global elevation product: combination of multi-source digital elevation models. In: Joint International Symposium on Geospatial Theory, Processing and Applications (2002)

Schultz, H., Riseman, E.M., Stolle, F.R., Woo, D.-M.: Error detection and DEM fusion using self-consistency. In: International Conference on Computer Vision (1999)

Slatton, K., Teng, S., Crawford, M.: Multiscale fusion of InSAR data for hydrological applications. In: Symposium on Terrain Analysis for Water Resources Applications (2002)

Tibshirani, R.: Regression shrinkage and selection via the lasso. J. Royal. Statist. Soc B. 58(1), 267–288 (1996)

Yang, J., Wright, J., Huang, T.S., Ma, Y.: Image super-resolution as sparse representation of raw image patches. In: IEEE Conf. on Computer Vision and Pattern Recognition (2008)

Change Detection in Urban Areas
by Direct Comparison
of Multi-view and Multi-temporal ALS Data

Marcus Hebel[1], Michael Arens[1], and Uwe Stilla[2]

[1] Fraunhofer Institute of Optronics, System Technologies and Image Exploitation
IOSB, Gutleuthausstr. 1, 76275 Ettlingen, Germany
{marcus.hebel,michael.arens}@iosb.fraunhofer.de
[2] Department of Photogrammetry and Remote Sensing,
Technische Universität München, 80290 München, Germany
stilla@tum.de

Abstract. Change detection in urban areas requires the comparison of multi-temporal remote sensing data. ALS (airborne laser scanning) is one of the established techniques to deliver these data. A novelty of our approach is the consideration of multiple views that are acquired with an oblique forward-looking laser scanner. In addition to advantages in terms of data coverage, this configuration is ideally suited to support helicopter pilots during their mission, e.g., with an obstacle warning system, terrain-referenced navigation, or online change detection. In this paper, we present a framework for direct comparison of current ALS data to given reference data of an urban area. Our approach extends the concept of occupancy grids known from robot mapping, and the proposed change detection method is based on the Dempster-Shafer theory. Results are shown for an urban test site at which multi-view ALS data were acquired at an interval of one year.

Keywords: Airborne laser scanning, LiDAR, change detection, multi-temporal data analysis, urban areas.

1 Introduction

1.1 Problem Description

Identification and analysis of changes in urban areas are common approaches to tasks like damage inspection, traffic monitoring, or documentation of urban development. Typically, changes of urban objects can be explained by human influences (e.g., construction, extension, or demolition of buildings). Moreover, seasonal effects (e.g., the foliation state of trees) and disasters (e.g., earthquakes) can cause considerable changes that occur on different time scales. Several types of changes are of interest when multi-temporal remote sensing data are compared. Typical categories include objects that have appeared, disappeared, moved (e.g., cars), transformed, or changed their spectral characteristics. Airborne laser scanning (ALS) is well suited to provide 3D measurements which

U. Stilla et al. (Eds.): PIA 2011, LNCS 6952, pp. 185–196, 2011.
© Springer-Verlag Berlin Heidelberg 2011

allow direct comparison of geometric features. In this context, a basic requirement for detecting differences between multiple ALS point clouds is an accurate
registration and alignment of the multi-temporal data.

Furthermore, additional requirements must be met by the data acquisition
and data analysis if the laser scanner is used to support short-term operations
such as the surveillance of urban areas, terrain-referenced navigation, or detection of rapid changes. Examples can be found in assistance systems for helicopter
pilots, obstacle avoidance, landing operations in urban terrain, search and res-
cue missions, emergency services, or disaster management. These applications
require methods for immediate processing of range measurements instead of the
classical offline treatment of preprocessed ALS data.

1.2   Overview

Airborne laser scanning usually combines a LiDAR (light detection and ranging)
device with highly accurate navigational sensors mounted on an aircraft. Typically, an IMU (inertial measurement unit) and a GNSS receiver (global navigation satellite system, e.g., GPS, the Global Positioning System) are operated
synchronously with a LiDAR scanning mechanism.

The intention to use this sensor system for change detection implies that 3D
data of the urban area in question had been acquired at an earlier date, so that
currently measured ALS data can be compared to these. In this paper, we address change detection in the case that both the reference data and the current
3D data were acquired by an ALS system. In addition, we require this ALS system to allow access to the component's raw measurements, i.e., the range data,
the scanning geometry, and the IMU/GNSS trajectory. In contrast to classical
nadir data acquisition, we capture the scene with an oblique forward-looking
laser scanner. This configuration is indispensable for some of the applications
mentioned in Section 1.1. During acquisition of the reference data, multiple criss-
crossing flight lines are used. Therefore, this setup has the additional advantage
of full terrain coverage (e.g., facades of buildings etc.). Overall, we distinguish
two different stages of ALS data acquisition and processing:

1. The creation of the database is not time-critical, i.e., the urban area can be
   scanned several times from multiple aspects with a calibrated sensor, while
   the data are processed and optimized offline. In (Hebel and Stilla 2007), we
   describe a method for the preclassification and the automatic registration of
   such ALS data.
2. During the mission, new ALS measurements are to be aligned and compared
   to the reference data. Regarding this task, we described a fast segmentation
   method in (Hebel and Stilla 2008) that is based on scanline analysis of ALS
   data. Matching of planar objects, which are identified in both the current
   data and the reference data, can be used to correct absolute errors of the
   sensor position (Hebel and Stilla 2010).

In this paper, we focus on the comparison step, and we start from the premise
that the system calibration and data alignment issues are solved. Classical

methods of change detection in ALS data typically compare the point clouds themselves. In contrast, we include knowledge on empty space that we observe during the data acquisition. With the assumption of a straight-lined propagation of laser pulses, we state that the space between the laser source and the reflecting 3D point must be empty (or transparent). Additionally, we allow for the occupancy of space behind the reflecting spot to be unknown, as long as it is not affected by other laser measurements. This consideration handles occlusions and changes implicitly, such that the latter are identifiable by conflicts of empty space and occupied space along the direction of the laser pulse (which we call henceforth "laser beam"). In robot mapping, such information is often managed in so-called occupancy grids. In this paper, we adapt some of these concepts for the use with 3D laser data. Instead of evaluating occupancy conflicts on raster cells, we identify these conflicts at the exact position of the 3D points. In the next section, we give an overview of related work on change detection and occupancy grids. Our own methodology is explained in Section 3. A description of our ALS setup and experimental results can be found in Section 4. Finally, Section 5 presents a brief discussion and our conclusions.

2   Related Work

In the last decades, change detection in urban areas has been explored by various groups. Most of them approach this task with different intentions and with different sensors. A typical example is the automatic update of building databases. In (Champion et al. 2009) some contexts and an evaluation of different approaches are described. In an overall analysis, it is concluded that LiDAR offers high economical effectiveness and represents a viable basis for future operative systems. The use of ALS for change detection with regard to buildings has been proposed, for instance, in (Murakami et al. 1999). Typically, a digital surface model (DSM) is generated by interpolating the 3D points onto a 2D grid, and changes are detected by computing the difference of these DSM data. To increase reliability of the change detection results, Vögtle and Steinle (2004) classify the laser points into the classes bare-earth, building, and vegetation. We have described a similar classification approach in (Hebel and Stilla 2007) which is used to optimize the automatic registration of overlapping point clouds. The analysis of multi-temporal ALS data is sometimes proposed to assess damage to buildings, e.g., after earthquakes. Hommel (2009) puts strong emphasis on the elimination of vegetation in the ALS data, as this class of points could be misinterpreted, depending on the foliation state of the vegetation in the different data sets. A similar argumentation can be found in (Rutzinger et al. 2010), and it was confirmed in our experiments. However, other applications are conceivable wherein the detection and analysis of urban vegetation are of prime importance. A recent study on DSM-based change detection methods for urban areas and a detailed survey of related work can be found in (Matikainen et al. 2010).

Unlike the comparison of DSMs, the applications mentioned in Section 1.1 require a different strategy for data processing. There are two reasons for this: (*i*) we consider oblique views that lead to varying occlusions and point density depending on the aspect angle, (*ii*) the comparison of current ALS data to given reference data should be executable in line with the data acquisition.

Similar boundary conditions are given if ranging sensors are used on mobile robots (whose position and movement are known) in order to generate global maps from local and uncertain sensor data. Most commonly, 2D maps that are horizontal slices of 3D space, are taken as a basis. Moravec and Elfes (1985) were the first to represent these maps by an array of cells labeled *unknown*, *empty*, and *occupied*, with values ranging from 0 to 1 to define the "degree of certainty". Puente et al. (1991) distinguish two different approaches to fuse information within such occupancy grids. These approaches are: (*i*) probabilistic estimation based on Bayes' theorem, and (*ii*) the combination rule of the Dempster-Shafer theory of evidence (Shafer 1976).

Detailed work on autonomous navigation of mobile robots by a combination of probabilistic occupancy grids with neural networks was done by Thrun (1998). The evidence theory of Dempster-Shafer is commonly used for data fusion. In the context of occupancy models, it can substitute the probabilistic approach, and it has the additional advantage of evaluating conflicting information implicitly (Moras et al. 2011). In this paper, we evaluate such conflicts in multi-aspect and multi-temporal ALS data, which we organize in 3D raster cells. Similarly, Himmelsbach et al. (2008) proposed to use a $2\frac{1}{2}$D occupancy grid that acts like a hash table for the retrieval of 3D points. A description of the strengths and weaknesses of a 3D-based approach is given in the next paragraph.

3   Strategy for Data Processing

Two different operating modes of ALS data acquisition were explained in Section 1.2. In stage (1), a 3D voxel grid that covers the complete urban area is filled with information. During stage (2), we decide whether current ALS measurements confirm or contradict this information in the database. Fig. 1 illustrates such a 3D voxel grid and the process of ALS data acquisition. Within occupancy grids, the data are typically downsampled or interpolated to match the raster cells. Consequently, the details and positioning accuracy of detectable changes would be bounded by the resolution of the occupancy grid. On the other hand, a fine-grained 3D grid would lead to a huge amount of data.

Instead of evaluating the occupancy of space for the voxels themselves, we use the grid structure only to store information on the proximity of laser beams (and points). Once established, this data structure enables us to identify all candidates of old laser range measurements that may interfere with a new one. Furthermore, the cell size can be chosen comparatively wide (e.g., five times the average point-to-point distance), resulting in a moderate amount of data. Since the grid is only used as a search structure, the selection of the cell size has only minor impact on the results.

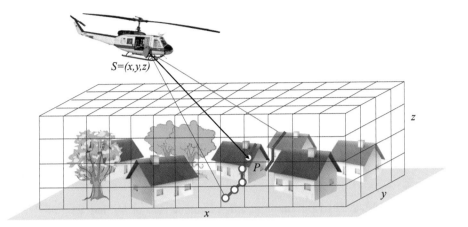

Fig. 1. ALS data acquisition and 3D voxel grid

3.1   Generation of the Database

In stage (1), each laser pulse's origin s is stored in an indexed list $\mathbf{L}$, together with the measured range r, such that $p = s + r$ are the coordinates of the respective laser point. The sensor position s and the direction of r are interpolated from the synchronously recorded GNSS/IMU information which is typically captured with a frequency lower than the pulse repetition rate of the laser scanner. If multiple returns are received for a single laser pulse, these simply lead to multiple entries in $\mathbf{L}$. Furthermore, let r_0 denote the respective unit vector $r/\|r\|$. Two cell arrays $\mathbf{V_P}$ and $\mathbf{V_R}$, both representing voxel grids as depicted in Fig. 2, are filled with indices of $\mathbf{L}$ in the following way: Each index $i \in \mathbf{L}$ is included in a single cell of $\mathbf{V_P}$ according to the 3D position of the laser point p_i that corresponds to this index. Therefore, $\mathbf{V_P}$ simply represents a rasterization of the point cloud. Beyond that, $\mathbf{V_R}$ is used to store all indices of laser beams that traverse the voxels. To cope with this task, we implemented a 3D variant of Bresenham's algorithm, that is well-known in computer graphics for efficient raster line drawing. For a single laser range measurement (s_i, r_i), Fig. 2 illustrates how its index i is distributed among cells of $\mathbf{V_P}$ and $\mathbf{V_R}$. Each cell in $\mathbf{V_P}$ or $\mathbf{V_R}$ can receive either none, one or multiple indices, depending on the number of laser points contained in this voxel, or depending on the number of laser beams that run through this voxel, respectively.

3.2   Modeling the Occupancy of Space

Following the terminology of the Dempster-Shafer theory, let U denote the universal set that contains all possible states of the observed system. In our case, we observe the occupancy of space at a given 3D position, so $U = \{emp, occ\}$ is the universal set, where emp and occ are abbreviations for "empty" and "occupied". The power set 2^U of U is given as the set $\{\emptyset, \{emp\}, \{occ\}, U\}$. A so-called belief

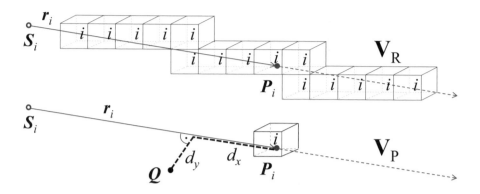

Fig. 2. Distribution of an index i among cells of $\mathbf{V_P}$ and $\mathbf{V_R}$

mass in the interval $[0,1]$ is assigned to each element of this power set, with the additional properties that the empty set $\emptyset$ has zero mass, and the sum of all other masses is one:

$$m : 2^U \to [0,1] , \quad m\left(\emptyset\right) = 0, \quad \sum_{A \in 2^U} m\left(A\right) = 1 . \tag{1}$$

An assignment that fulfills these criteria is called "basic belief assignment". The Dempster-Shafer theory makes use of the mass assignments to define upper and lower bounds of an interval that contains the classical probability. These bounds are called "plausibility" and "belief". Except for equation (1), the value of $m\left(U\right)$ does not concern $\{emp\}$ or $\{occ\}$ itself, as each of these has its own mass. Instead, the mass $m\left(U\right)$ of the universal set U is interpreted as the degree of ignorance. If $m\left(U\right)$ equals one, this means that the occupancy of space at the given position is totally unknown. We model the impact of a laser range measurement $p = s + r$ on the assignment of masses to a position q in 3D space in the following way: First, let d_x denote the longitudinal distance of q to p (cf. Fig. 2):

$$d_x = (q - p) \cdot r_0 . \tag{2}$$

Similarly, let d_y denote the transverse distance of q to p:

$$d_y = \|(q - p) \times r_0\| . \tag{3}$$

On the basis of the distances d_x and d_y, we define the following belief masses (at position q caused by p):

$$m_{q,p}\left(\emptyset\right) = 0 ,$$

$$m_{q,p}\left(\{emp\}\right) = \left(1 - \frac{1}{1 + e^{-\lambda d_x - c}}\right) \cdot e^{-\kappa d_y^2} , \tag{4}$$

$$m_{q,p}\left(\{occ\}\right) = \left(\frac{1}{1 + e^{-\lambda d_x - c}} - \frac{1}{1 + e^{-\lambda d_x + c}}\right) \cdot e^{-\kappa d_y^2} ,$$

$$m_{q,p}\left(U\right) = 1 - m_{q,p}\left(\{emp\}\right) - m_{q,p}\left(\{occ\}\right) .$$

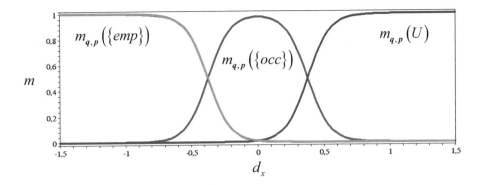

Fig. 3. Belief assignment to points on the laser beam $(d_y = 0)$

By definition, (4) fulfills the conditions (1), so these equations represent a basic belief assignment. The respective first factor in $m_{q,p}(\{emp\})$ and $m_{q,p}(\{occ\})$ is composed of sigmoid functions. One of these is used to describe free space in front of p, the other characterizes the lack of knowledge behind the laser point. In between, the inverse sum of the sigmoid functions reflects the actual occupancy at the position of p. Fig. 3 shows the interaction of the sigmoid functions and the ratio of the belief masses along the laser beam, with the parameters in equations (4) set to $\lambda=12$ and $c=5$. Outside of the beam axis, the second factor in $m_{q,p}(\{emp\})$ and $m_{q,p}(\{occ\})$ describes a Gaussian profile that fades to ignorance (transverse distribution). The parameters (λ, c, κ) describe the fuzziness of the laser points. They should be chosen to conform (at least) to the physical characteristics of the laser range measurements. This means that $m_{q,p}(\{occ\})$ should reflect the point positioning accuracy, which is influenced, for example, by the scanning precision and the range resolution of the specific laser scanning device. If $m_{q,p}(\{occ\})$ is too narrow, most range measurements would not interfere with another. Otherwise, if $m_{q,p}(\{occ\})$ is too broad, this would lead to false detections.

3.3   Combination of Evidence from Different Measurements

In the previous section we considered a single range measurement $p = s + r$ and its influence on the mass assignment to a position q. In case we observe two or more laser beams in the neighborhood of q, we need to combine the respective mass assignments. Let $p_1 = s_1 + r_1$ and $p_2 = s_2 + r_2$ be two independent laser range measurements. Equations (4) define different sets of mass assignments to the position of q, which are given by m_{q,p_1} and m_{q,p_2}, respectively. For better readability, we abbreviate $m_{q,p_1}(\{emp\})$ to $m_1(e)$ and $m_{q,p_1}(\{occ\})$ to $m_1(o)$ etc.

Using these notations, we apply Dempster's rule of combination to calculate the joint mass m from the sets m_1 and m_2. The amount of conflict C between the two mass sets is measured as follows ("empty in m_1 and occupied in m_2, or vice versa"):

$$C = m_1(e)\,m_2(o) + m_1(o)\,m_2(e) \quad . \tag{5}$$

Within Dempster's rule of combination, conflicting evidence is ignored, which is achieved by the normalization factor $(1 - C)$ as follows:

$$m(e) = \frac{m_1(e)\,m_2(e) + m_1(e)\,m_2(U) + m_1(U)\,m_2(e)}{1 - C} \quad ,$$

$$m(o) = \frac{m_1(o)\,m_2(o) + m_1(o)\,m_2(U) + m_1(U)\,m_2(o)}{1 - C} \quad , \tag{6}$$

$$m(U) = \frac{m_1(U)\cdot m_2(U)}{1 - C} \quad ,$$

$$m(\emptyset) = 0$$

The operations (6) are commonly written as $m = m_1 \oplus m_2$ and result in a new set m of belief masses that is a combination of m_1 and m_2. It should be noted that $\oplus$ is commutative and associative. Therefore, even an arbitrary number of belief assignments can be combined by $\oplus$ in a unique way.

3.4   Change Detection

In stage (2), we decide whether a new ALS measurement $q = s_Q + r_Q$ confirms or contradicts the mass assignments which we obtain from old measurements that we recorded in $\mathbf{L}$. Conflicts occur if the laser beam (s_Q, r_Q) traverses *occupied* space in front of q, or if q comes to lie in a region that is marked *empty*.

We address the latter case first. Let $v_q \subset \mathbf{V_R}$ denote the cells of $\mathbf{V_R}$ which correspond to the position of q. This subset v_q may comprise only the voxel that includes q, or an additional neighborhood. It is expected that v_q contains the indices of laser beams in $\mathbf{L}$ which may affect the mass assignment to the position of q. Let I_q be the set of indices which are associated with v_q. On the one hand, we consider the joint mass m_q resulting from all measurements p_i in $\mathbf{L}$ where $i \in I_q$:

$$m_q = \bigoplus_{i \in I_q} m_{q,p_i} \quad . \tag{7}$$

On the other hand, the mass assignment m_q^* that we obtain from $q = s_Q + r_Q$ itself is given as:

$$m_q^*(\{emp\}) = m_q^*(U) = m_q^*(\emptyset) = 0, \quad m_q^*(\{occ\}) = 1 \quad . \tag{8}$$

Based on these assignments, we can identify conflicts between m_q and m_q^* in the same way as it is done in equation (5), resulting in a measure of conflict $C_q = m_q(\{emp\})$.

The other type of conflict is caused by occupied space that is encountered while the laser pulse propagates from s_Q to q. To find these conflicts, we extend the list $\mathbf{L}$ to include mass assignments to every point p in $\mathbf{L}$. We initialize these masses to an *unknown* occupancy:

$$m_p(\{emp\}) = m_p(\{occ\}) = m_p(\emptyset) = 0, \quad m_p(U) = 1 \quad . \tag{9}$$

We use Bresenham's line drawing algorithm in 3D to identify grid cells in $\mathbf{V_P}$ that are affected by the laser beam $(\mathbf{s}_Q, \mathbf{r}_Q)$. Let $v_{\mathbf{p}}$ denote this subset of $\mathbf{V_P}$, and let $I_{\mathbf{p}}$ be the set of indices associated with $v_{\mathbf{p}}$. For every position $\mathbf{p}_i$ with $i \in I_{\mathbf{p}}$, we update the mass set $m_{\mathbf{p}_i}$ to the joint mass of $m_{\mathbf{p}_i}$ and $m_{\mathbf{p}_i,\mathbf{q}}$:

$$m_{\mathbf{p}_i} \leftarrow m_{\mathbf{p}_i} \oplus m_{\mathbf{p}_i,\mathbf{q}} \;\; \forall i \in I_{\mathbf{p}} \; . \tag{10}$$

After the laser scanning process has left the reach of a point $\mathbf{p}$ in the database, we evaluate the accumulated mass assignment $m_{\mathbf{p}}$ and its conflict to $m_{\mathbf{p}}^*$, which is given analogous to equation (8). We obtain $C_{\mathbf{p}} = m_{\mathbf{p}}(\{emp\})$ as a measure of conflict.

3.5   Including Additional Attributes

If the proposed methods are applied to typical ALS data, vegetation is likely to cause conflicting belief masses. This is to be expected, since vegetation typically leads to laser points that are blurred and delocalized due to a large echo width. Some laser pulses penetrate the vegetation and mark this space *empty*. Others are reflected by the foliage, indicating the same space is partially *occupied*. Furthermore, vegetation is subject to seasonal changes. If the detection of such changes is of minor importance, it is advisable to treat vegetation in a different way than ground level, buildings, or other man-made objects. Besides full waveform analysis, local principal component analysis (PCA) and region growing are common approaches to ALS point classification. Since the generation of the database in Section 3.1 is not time critical, we derive an additional weighting factor from local PCA that increases the amount of $m(U)$ for all measurements which relate to vegetation.

4   Experiments

The data that we analyzed for this study were acquired during field campaigns in 2008 and 2009, using a RIEGL LMS-Q560 laser scanner (version 2006) in combination with an Applanix POS AV 410 inertial navigation system. All sensors were attached to a helicopter of type Bell UH-1D. Our current experimental setup lacks online data access, so the experiments described in this section were conducted in a post-processing mode based on the stream of recorded raw data. With our configuration and settings, each scan line of the laser scanner covered a field of view of 60° subdivided into 1000 angular steps. The inclination angle of the laser scanner was set to 45° while flying with the helicopter's nose pitched down (Fig. 1). Due to aviation security reasons, the minimum flight level had to be restricted to 1000 ft. These boundary conditions led to laser strips with a width of 500 m and an average point-to-point distance of 0.5 m. In April 2008, a test site was approached in a cross pattern, resulting in an accumulated point cloud which includes 5,400,000 points with an average point density of 16 pts/m². Fig. 4a shows a rendered visualization of these reference data, where each point is gray-value coded according to the echo amplitude, which is derived from full waveform analysis. The cell size of $\mathbf{V_R}$ and $\mathbf{V_P}$ was chosen to be $2\times2\times2$ m^3, resulting in two cell arrays of the dimensions $300\times300\times50$ (which corresponds to $600\times600\times100$ m^3) to cover the area in question. After the distribution of $\mathbf{L}$-indices among these cells, the memory requirements of $\mathbf{V_P}$ and $\mathbf{V_R}$ amount to 1.1 GB in total. The test site was scanned again in August 2009, using the same sensors and a similar setting.

Based on the recorded data stream of a single strip (south-to-north), we successively applied the methods described in Section 3. The parameters (λ, c, κ) in equations (4) were set to $\lambda=12$, $c=5$, $\kappa=8$ as shown in Fig. 3. First results of this experiment are depicted in Fig. 4b. Conflicts $C_p \geq 0.5$ are shown in red (objects that have disappeared), whereas conflicts $C_q \geq 0.5$ are colored yellow (objects that have appeared). In this example, vegetation obviously causes a lot of conflicts C_q, which can be ascribed to seasonal influences (April vs. August). As described in Section 3.5, we may derive additional attributes in an independent manner (e.g., local PCA, region growing) and classify the reference data in $\mathbf{L}$ to the classes ground, vegetation, and building. In case we want to focus on man-made changes, this classification allows us to decrease the influence of data points in the vegetation class. The result is shown in Fig. 4c and Fig. 4d. In addition to the previous color-coding, green points now indicate that these are (most likely) part of an unchanged building. The remaining conflicts are mainly caused by moved cars, demolition, and newly constructed buildings.

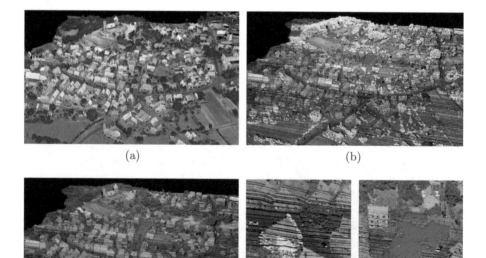

(a)   (b)

(c)   (d)

Fig. 4. (a) View of the reference data (April 2008), (b) conflicts of mass assignments (August 2009), (c) result of change detection, (d) close-up view

5 Discussion and Conclusion

In this paper, we have presented a framework for ALS-based change detection in urban areas. Our methodology is inspired by the concept of occupancy grids, and we implemented Dempster's rule of combination to fuse multiple measurements. During this process, conflicts between different belief assignments are evaluated with regard to change detection. The proposed methods are inherently realtime capable, as opposed to classical methods of point cloud analysis that start after the complete data set was obtained. Modern ALS instruments show a trend toward increasing performance and realtime processing. A typical example is online waveform analysis (e.g., RIEGL VQ-580). Furthermore, the presented techniques have high potential for parallelization, and the time-consuming evaluation of exponential functions can be replaced by look-up tables. We expect that an efficient implementation of the proposed methods can work in realtime on an operational system.

The main conceptual advantage of the proposed methods is the handling of occlusions as unknown space, which would otherwise require a more complex case-by-case analysis. In contrast to probabilistic approaches, the Dempster-Shafer theory allows an explicit representation of ignorance. Therefore, even partially non-overlapping ALS data can be combined and compared without causing erroneously detections of changes. Different from the well-known concept of (2D) occupancy grids, we evaluate the occupancy of space at the discrete 3D positions of the laser points, without declining the given resolution of the laser scanner.

The experiments described in Section 4 demonstrated that spatial changes can be reliably detected, provided that the data are properly aligned. Seasonal changes in vegetation, changes of buildings (e.g., extensions, demolition), and moved cars are found by our automatic method. However, a few unresolved problems remain: For now, we ignored changes that occurred within the time slot in which the reference data were captured. The minimum size of detectable changes is limited by the point density and the respective point positioning accuracy, which need to be modeled correctly by means of the parameters (λ, c, κ). A more quantitative evaluation is still missing, for which we would require the ground truth or simulated data. These issues will be part of our future work.

References

Champion, N., Rottensteiner, F., Matikainen, L., Liang, X., Hyyppä, J., Olsen, B.P.: A Test of Automatic Building Change Detection Approaches. In: CMRT 2009, International Archives of Photogrammetry, Remote Sensing and Spatial Information Sciences, Paris, vol. 38(3/W4), pp. 145–150 (2009)

Hebel, M., Stilla, U.: Automatic Registration of Laser Point Clouds of Urban Areas. In: PIA 2007, International Archives of Photogrammetry, Remote Sensing and Spatial Information Sciences, München, vol. 36 (3/W49A), pp. 13–18 (2007)

Hebel, M., Stilla, U.: Pre-classification of Points and Segmentation of Urban Objects by Scan Line Analysis of Airborne LiDAR Data. In: Proceedings of Commission III, XXI ISPRS Congress 2008. The International Archives of Photogrammetry, Remote Sensing and Spatial Information Sciences, Beijing, vol. 37(Part B3a), pp. 105–110 (2008)

Hebel, M., Stilla, U.: LiDAR-supported Navigation of UAVs Over Urban Areas. Surveying and Land Information Science, Journal of the American Congress on Surveying and Mapping 70(3), 139–149 (2010); ISSN (printed) 1538-1242, ISSN (electronic) 1559-7202

Himmelsbach, M., Müller, A., Lüttel, T., Wünsche, H.-J.: LIDAR-based 3D Object Perception. In: Proceedings of 1st International Workshop on Cognition for Technical Systems, München, p. 7 (2008)

Hommel, M.: Verification of a Building Damage Analysis and Extension to Surroundings of Reference Buildings. In: Laserscanning 2009, International Archives of the Photogrammetry, Remote Sensing and Spatial Information Sciences, Paris, vol. 38(3/W8), pp. 18–23 (2009)

Matikainen, L., Hyyppä, J., Ahokas, E., Markelin, L., Kaartinen, H.: Automatic Detection of Buildings and Changes in Buildings for Updating of Maps. Remote Sensing 2(5), 1217–1248 (2010)

Moras, J., Cherfaoui, V., Bonnifait, P.: Moving Objects Detection by Conflict Analysis in Evidential Grids. In: Proceedings of the IEEE Intelligent Vehicles Symposium IV 2011, Baden-Baden (2011)

Moravec, H.P., Elfes, A.: High Resolution Maps from Wide Angle Sonar. In: Proceedings of the IEEE International Conference on Robotics and Automation, St. Louis, pp. 116–121 (1985)

Murakami, H., Nakagawa, K., Hasegawa, H., Shibata, T., Iwanami, E.: Change Detection of Buildings Using an Airborne Laser Scanner. ISPRS Journal of Photogrammetry and Remote Sensing 54(2-3), 148–152 (1999)

Puente, E.A., Moreno, L., Salichs, M.A., Gachet, D.: Analysis of Data Fusion Methods in Certainty Grids - Application to Collision Danger Monitoring. In: Proceedings of the IEEE International Conference on Industrial Electronics, Control and Instrumentation, Kobe, pp. 1133–1137 (1991)

Rutzinger, M., Rüf, B., Höfle, B., Vetter, M.: Change Detection of Building Footprints from Airborne Laser Scanning Acquired in Short Time Intervals. In: ISPRS TC VII Symposium 100 Years ISPRS, International Archives of Photogrammetry, Remote Sensing and Spatial Information Sciences, Vienna, vol. 38(7b), pp. 475–480 (2010)

Shafer, G.: A Mathematical Theory of Evidence. Princeton University Press, Princeton (1976)

Thrun, S.: Learning Metric-Topological Maps for Indoor Mobile Robot Navigation. Artificial Intelligence 99(1), 21–71 (1998)

Vögtle, T., Steinle, E.: Detection and Recognition of Changes in Building Geometry Derived from Multitemporal Laserscanning Data. In: XX ISPRS Congress 2004, International Archives of the Photogrammetry, Remote Sensing and Spatial Information Sciences, Istanbul, vol. 35(B2), pp. 428–433 (2004)

Towards Airborne Single Pass Decimeter Resolution SAR Interferometry over Urban Areas

Michael Schmitt[1], Christophe Magnard[2], Thorsten Brehm[3], and Uwe Stilla[1]

[1] Photogrammetry & Remote Sensing, Technische Universitaet Muenchen,
Munich, Germany
`michael.schmitt@bv.tum.de, stilla@tum.de`
[2] Remote Sensing Laboratories, University of Zurich, Zurich, Switzerland
`christophe.magnard@geo.uzh.ch`
[3] Fraunhofer Institute for High-Frequency Physics and Radar Techniques,
Wachtberg, Germany
`thorsten.brehm@fhr.fraunhofer.de`

Abstract. Airborne cross-track Synthetic Aperture Radar interferometers have the capability of deriving three-dimensional topographic information with just a single pass over the area of interest. In order to get a highly accurate height estimation, either a large interferometric baseline or a high radar frequency has to be used. The utilization of a millimeter wave SAR allows precise height estimation even for short baselines. Combined with a spatial resolution in the decimeter range, this enables the mapping of urban areas from airborne platforms. The side-looking SAR imaging geometry, however, leads to disturbing effects like layover and shadowing, which is even intensified by the shallow looking angle caused by the relatively low altitudes of airborne SAR systems. To solve this deficiency, enhanced InSAR processing strategies relying on multi-aspect and multi-baseline data, respectively, are shown to be necessary.

Keywords: InSAR, urban areas, very high resolution, DSM.

1 Introduction

Airborne single pass SAR interferometry (InSAR) allows deriving the topography of extended areas by combining two simultaneously acquired complex SAR images to an interferogram and then exploiting the phase of this interferogram. With the advent of very high resolution SARs that are capable of resolutions in the decimeter range, the analysis of urban areas by methods based on interferometric SAR data have become an increasingly important research topic. Several papers for instance have been published dealing with the challenge of building extraction from InSAR datasets based on image analysis (Stilla et al., 2003; Thiele et al., 2007). Concurrently, more and more papers are published on the use of tomographic approaches exploiting multiple baselines to

U. Stilla et al. (Eds.): PIA 2011, LNCS 6952, pp. 197–208, 2011.

overcome the problems arising from the layover effect that has become more important since resolutions have reached sub-meter qualities (Baselice et al., 2009; Reale et al., 2011). Last but not least, the use of InSAR images recorded from different aspect angles has been investigated to fill in the missing information in the shadow areas caused by the side-looking SAR imaging geometry (Thiele et al., 2010; Soergel et al., 2003).

This paper deals with the possibilities and challenges of utilizing airborne decimeter resolution InSAR data for the analysis of densely built-up urban areas and is organized as follows: In Section 2, the MEMPHIS sensor is introduced, before in Section 3 forward and backward geocoding procedures are described. In Section 4 the test dataset considered in this paper is shown. Section 5 discusses some experimental results and proposes solutions to the occurring challenges. Section 6 finally draws a conclusion and gives an outlook.

2   MEMPHIS SAR System

MEMPHIS is an acronym for **M**illimeterwave **E**xperimental **M**ultifrequency **P**olarimetric **H**igh Resolution **I**nterferometric **S**ystem and was developed by the Research Institute for High- Frequency Physics and Radar Techniques of the FGAN, now Fraunhofer FHR (Schimpf et al., 2002). In the airborne side-looking configuration, it can be operated at 35 GHz (Ka band) as well as 94 GHz (W band) with a bandwidth of either 200 MHz in low resolution mode or 800 MHz in high resolution mode. With these modes, slant range resolutions of 75 cm and 19 cm, respectively, can be realized. Interferometric single pass measurements, even in a multi-baseline configuration, are possible by installing four receiving antennas with different baselines. The smallest and the largest available baselines in 35 GHz mode are 5.5 cm and 27.5 cm and lead to height ambiguities of about 275 m and 55 m, respectively. The processing of the interferometric raw data is carried out by the Remote Sensing Laboratories of the University of Zurich and is described in (Magnard et al., 2007) and (Magnard et al., 2010). Since MEMPHIS is still an experimental system, it is commonly mounted on a C-160 Transall (see Fig. 1) and flown at low altitudes of about 300 to 1000 m above ground level. In combination with a mean viewing angle of about 60°, this leads to a typical swath size of 600 m in range direction and up to 3000 m in azimuth direction.

3   Interferometric Geocoding Concepts

3.1   Interferometric Pre-processing

Before the interferometric data can be geocoded, i.e. three-dimensional information in a geodetically defined reference frame or map projection can be retrieved, the single look complex (SLC) SAR images have to be pre-processed. This conventionally includes the following steps:

Fig. 1. MEMPHIS mounted on a C-160 Transall

– *Image coregistration:*
Two SLC images have to be aligned to sub-pixel accuracy, e.g. by cross-correlation of their amplitude values. For MEMPHIS data, the misalignment already falls below one pixel due to the small distance between the receiving horns and their inclination.

– *Interferogram generation:*
The actual interferogram is created by calculating the product between the complex value of each pixel of one image by the complex conjugate of the corresponding pixel of the second image.

– *Multilooking and coherence estimation:*
To mitigate phase noise, a number of neighboring pixels have to be averaged, which is called complex multilooking for complex pixels. For decimeter resolution data of densely built-up urban areas only adaptive algorithms for complex multilooking and simultaneous coherence estimation in the vein of (Vasile et al., 2004) or (Deledalle et al., 2011) are suitable.

– *Interferogram flattening:*
In order to work with just the topographically induced phase, the phase contribution caused by the imaging geometry has to be removed. Therefor, the simulated phase of the ideally flat earth is subtracted from the interferogram.

– *Phase unwrapping:*
Since interferograms are complex images, calculating the phase gives an angle modulo 2π. Thus, the interferometric phase has to be unwrapped if the height ambiguity is smaller than the overall height variations within the scene. For smaller baselines or relatively flat urban scenes without skyscrapers, this crucial step in SAR interferometry can be avoided.

– *Absolute phase retrieval:*
From the filtered and unwrapped topographic phase, finally the absolute interferometric phase has to be retrieved. First, the phase image is unflattened,

i.e. the flat-earth phase contribution is re-added. Afterwards, at least a single ground control point has to be used to determine the so-called phase constant refining the interferometric calibration.

3.2   Interferometric Geocoding

From the absolute interferometric phase, topographic height information can be reconstructed. Conventionally, this is done in slant range geometry by different phase-to-height conversion methods (Small et al., 1996) before transforming the resulting height grid to a geodetic reference frame.

Forward Geocoding. Since the work of our group focuses on the utilization of multi-aspect InSAR data, we have decided to use the straight-forward geometry of the interferometric range-Doppler equations (IRDE) that directly relate RADAR measurements and three-dimensional object points. For MEMPHIS a linear flight track as well as zero-Doppler processed data are assumed so we can simply write:

$$R = \|\boldsymbol{P} - \boldsymbol{S}_M\| \tag{1}$$

$$\boldsymbol{V}_M \left(\boldsymbol{P} - \boldsymbol{S}_M\right) = 0 \tag{2}$$

$$\phi = -\frac{2\pi}{\lambda} \left(\|\boldsymbol{P} - \boldsymbol{S}_M\| - \|\boldsymbol{P} - \boldsymbol{S}_{Sl}\|\right) \tag{3}$$

R is the slant range distance between the object point $\boldsymbol{P}$ and the master sensor position $\boldsymbol{S}_M$. $\boldsymbol{V}_M$ denotes the master sensor velocity, while $\boldsymbol{S}_{Sl}$ symbolizes the slave sensor position. Finally, ϕ denotes the absolute interferometric phase and λ the RADAR wavelength.

Equations (1)-(3) form a non-linear equation system that has to be solved for the unknown object coordinates $\boldsymbol{P} = [X, Y, Z]^T$ for each interferogram pixel. The result is an irregular point cloud that can be fused with point clouds from other aspects, before the data is resampled to the final surface grid.

Backward Geocoding. As proposed in (Schmitt & Stilla, 2011), the Doppler equation (2) can easily be inverted to

$$t = \frac{(\boldsymbol{P} - \boldsymbol{S}_{0,M}) \boldsymbol{V}_M}{\|\boldsymbol{V}_M\|^2}, \tag{4}$$

so that starting from a known object point $\boldsymbol{P}$ the azimuth time t and with (1) and (3) also the slant range distance R and the ideal absolute interferometric phase ϕ can be calculated straight-forwardly. $\boldsymbol{S}_{0,M}$ here denotes the master sensor position for the first azimuth bin.

Then the observed interferometric phase corresponding to the (t, R) SAR image coordinates is measured, so one can calculate the difference of ideal (i.e. simulated) phase and measured phase using

$$\Delta\phi = \|\phi_{measured} - \phi_{simulated}\| . \tag{5}$$

If this is carried out for all hypotheses of a height search interval positioned in a pre-defined surface grid, the geocoded height can be determined by searching for the minimal difference between simulated and measured phase for all height hypotheses. The main advantage of backward geocoding compared to conventional forward geocoding is that the result is not an irregular point cloud, but a 2.5D height model in already gridded form.

4   The Test Dataset

Our study area is the main campus of Technische Universitaet Muenchen (TUM) located in the Maxvorstadt neighborhood of Munich, Germany (target coordinates: $48°08'56''N, 011°34'02''E$). The scene mainly contains dense building blocks, but also some larger buildings surrounded by patches of concrete or lawn, respectively, as well as many urban trees. An optical image of the test area is shown in Fig. 2.

Fig. 2. Optical image of the test scene ©Google Earth

The test dataset originally comprised of four data takes in multi-aspect configuration with non-orthogonally crossing flight trajectories (see Table 1). Due to the fact that only low-precision navigation data was available, problems during SAR focussing occurred so that the fourth aspect had to be discarded.

Table 1. Test Dataset (Munich)

Radar band	Ka band (35 GHz)
Wavelength	8.55 mm
Pixel spacing (slant range)	5 cm (azimuth) / 19 cm (range)
Effective baseline used	27.5 cm
Heading angles	$11°/70°/169°/(250°)$
Off-nadir angle	$60°$
Aircraft altitude	2460 ft AGL

Although for each aspect 4 SAR images were acquired simultaneously, only the two acquisitions with the longest baseline were used for this preliminary study. Since no phase unwrapping was required for the test scene, a utilization of multi-baseline techniques is at the moment investigated for the solution of the layover problem. The magnitude image and the phase image of aspect 3 as derived by the filter proposed in (Deledalle et al., 2011) is shown in Fig. 3.

Fig. 3. Left: MEMPHIS magnitude image of the test scene. Flight direction (heading angle: $169°$) is from top to bottom, range direction from left to right. Right: Flat earth corrected interferometric phase of the same aspect.

5   Interferometry Results for the Munich Test Scene

In order to assess the potential of airborne millimeter wave SAR interferometry over urban areas, conventional interferometric processing utilizing both forward as well as backward geocoding have been carried out for the test dataset introduced in section 4. Note that all heights are given above the WGS84 ellipsoid.

5.1   Forward Geocoding Results

Fig. 4 exemplarily shows the height reconstruction achieved by classic forward geocoding for aspect 1 (heading angle $11°$). The point cloud was rasterized by

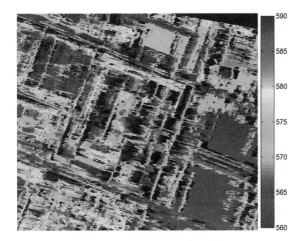

Fig. 4. Height image generated by forward geocoding of aspect 1. Note the black image parts containing no information. The heading angle of the flight was $11°$.

simply tiling the dataset with respect to a grid resolution of 0.2 m, which corresponds to the range resolution of the MEMPHIS data and is thus also considered for the backward geocoding procedure. If multiple points fell into one tile, the average height was chosen for this tile. Additionally, the resulting height image was filtered with a maximum homogeneity neighbor filter (Garnica et al., 2000).

It has to be emphasized that the black parts of the height image are not caused by RADAR shadow. Since the shadowing effect does appear in SAR images, there is seemingly an interferometric phase also in shadow parts of the data - although these phase observations just contain noise and no topographic information. However, the parts of the surface grid that dont contain any height values simply were not imaged by the sensor.

In comparison, the consequence of shadowing is shown in Fig. 6, depicting image details of the results for aspect 3 (heading angle $169°$). It can be noticed, how phase noise caused by RADAR shadow results in height noise.

5.2   Backward Geocoding Results

In order to show the applicability of backward geocoding for interferometric data of urban scenes, the method mentioned in section 3.2 was also applied to the data of aspect 1. As can be seen in Fig. 5, now every part of the scene is covered with height values, although a daubing effect appears where actually no information was available (cf. Fig. 4).

5.3   Comparison of Forward and Backward Geocoding

According to section 5.1 and 5.2 it is obvious that both geocoding methods basically lead to the same result. The main difference is that the forward created data seems noisier, which can especially be seen in Fig. 6.

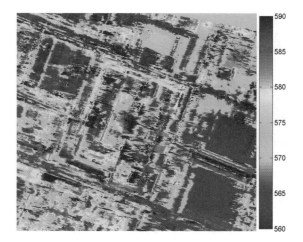

Fig. 5. Height image generated by backward geocoding of aspect 1. Not that the height search interval was centred on a mean terrain height of 570 m.

Recalling section 5.1, Fig. 6 also enables a comparison of the effects of shadowing and surface parts that were not mapped by the sensor: To the northern side of the "Alte Pinakothek" building, artificial height noise appears, corresponding to a patch of low coherence caused by RADAR shadow, while in the forward geocoding data several smaller areas don't contain any height information at all.

It has also to be noted that many obvious errors appear in both height maps. This can be caused by several phenomena:

- For this study, we have considered every interferogram pixel during geocoding. A masking of low-coherent phase observations was not applied.
- Although a first sidelobe reduction has been carried out using a Kaiser Window (Thomas et al., 2000), some strong sidelobes have not yet been removed from the data. They can easily be perceived in the magnitude and phase images shown in Fig. 3.
- Additional errors may have been induced due to the fact that no high-precision inertial navigation data was available for SAR focussing.

New data has been acquired during a campaign in June 2011 making use of a high-end inertial navigation system. It is therefore expected that the overall quality of the data can be notably improved in the future.

5.4   Benefit of Multi-aspect Data

The benefit of a multi-aspect InSAR configuration can be assessed by combining the point clouds resulting from the aspects 1, 2, and 3 (see Fig. 7).

For Fig. 7, all surface points which are based on a low-coherent phase ($\gamma <$ 0.5), mainly indicating shadow areas in single pass InSAR data, were masked

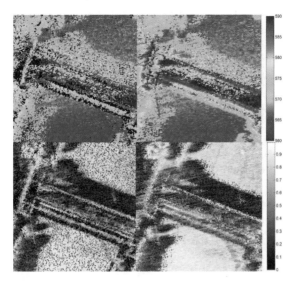

Fig. 6. Height grid detail for the "Alte Pinakothek" generated from aspect 3 (heading angle: 169°). Left: Forward geocoding results. Right: Backward geocoding results. Top: Reconstructed heights. Bottom: Geocoded coherence values.

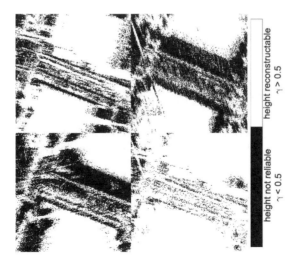

Fig. 7. Binary maps of reliable surface points. From top left to bottom right right: Aspect 1 (heading angle: 11°), aspect 2 (heading angle: 70°), aspect 3 (heading angle: 169°); combination of all three aspects.

in the backward reconstruction grids of all three available aspects. The combination, however, shows that the overall coverage can be significantly enhanced by utilizing multi-aspect InSAR acquisitions. This is especially noticeable in the large shadow area located to the northern side of the "Alte Pinakothek" building, where now almost all parts of the scene are covered by interferometric phase observations with appropriate coherence.

5.5   Additional Remarks

It has to be stated, however, that, although the overall structure of the scene can be perceived from the interferometric reconstruction, there are quite some problematic parts, especially, where the building blocks stand very close to each other (cf. the upper left corners of Figs. 4 and 5, respectively).

This is caused by an intermixture of layover and shadowing as sketched in Fig. 8.

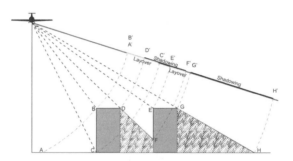

Fig. 8. Layover and shadowing for densely built-up inner city areas. Note that most parts of the scene are affected by at least one of both effects.

As can be seen in Fig. 8, most parts of a dense urban scene are affected by at least one of the two important SAR imaging effects, while even mixtures of layover and shadowing can occur (e.g. [D'C'] or [E'F'] in Fig. 8). Thus, not only "front porches" appear in the resulting height data, but also even more serious disturbances, since the noise phase caused by RADAR shadow and the phase ramps (Thiele et al., 2007) caused by layover mix.

In order to give a coarse approximation, the ground area affected by layover and shadowing can be given by

$$l_{Layover} = \cot\left(\theta\right) \cdot h \tag{6}$$

and

$$l_{Shadow} = \tan\left(\theta\right) \cdot h, \tag{7}$$

respectively. With an average off-nadir angle $\theta = 60°$ and a typical building height $h = 15m$, layover spans about 8.7 m in front of the building, while shadowing affects theoretically about 26 m of ground. If you now consider a typical road width of also 15 m, roads are not visible at all, while a large fraction is affected by both shadowing and layover. Furthermore, as can also be seen in Fig. 8, the bottom part of the second building's front facade is not imaged either. Summarized this means: With the typical low-altitude configuration of MEMPHIS, shadowing prevents a full 3D reconstruction of buildings for densely built-up inner-city areas. The reconstruction of street heights then again can only be solved by utilizing an orthogonal aspect with a sensor looking direction parallel to the road. Still, problems will occur in the courtyards of building blocks where the ground is shadowed from all directions. Thinking about future processing strategies, ideally the shadow pixels are masked and not considered for further processing, while the layover pixels have to be further analyzed in order to find the top height contribution of the respective resolution cell.

6 Conclusion and Outlook

From the experimental results shown in this paper, two main conclusions are obvious:

1. The problem of RADAR shadowing can partly be tackled by utilizing InSAR data from multiple aspects. This way, completing height reconstruction by filling in the missing heights of one aspect by data from different aspects becomes possible.
2. Nevertheless, the layover effect still causes artificial heights (so-called "front porches") which need to be coped with separately. Ongoing research focuses on the exploitation of MEMPHIS' multi-baseline capabilities.

However, the most severe problems of urban mapping by means of (interferometric) SAR remote sensing occur in high-density areas, where frequently layover and shadowing mix. Additionally, due to low flying heights and relatively flat looking angles, some parts of the city scene will not be imaged at all.

It is, however, expected that by combining multi-aspect and multi-baseline data, both effects will be mitigated in a way such that digital surface model (DSM) generation of urban areas by airborne single pass SAR interferometry in the decimeter range will become feasible.

References

Baselice, F., Budillon, A., Ferraioli, G., Pascazio, V.: Layover Solution in SAR Imaging: A Statistical Approach. IEEE Geoscience and Remote Sensing Letters 6, 577–581 (2009)

Deledalle, C.-A., Denis, L., Tupin, F.: NL-InSAR: Nonlocal Interferogram Estimation. IEEE Transactions of Geoscience and Remote Sensing 49, 1441–1452 (2011)

Garnica, C., Boochs, F., Twardochlib, M.: A New Approach to Edge-Preserving Smoothing for Edge Extraction and Image Segmentation. International Archives of Photogrammetry, Remote Sensing and Spatial Information Sciences 33(B3), 320–325 (2000)

Magnard, C., Meier, E., Ruegg, M., Brehm, T., Essen, H.: High Resolution Millimeter Wave SAR Interferometry. In: Proceedings of IEEE International Geoscience and Remote Sensing Symposium 2007, pp. 5061–5064 (2007)

Magnard, C., Meier, E., Small, D., Essen, H., Brehm, T.: Processing of MEMPHIS Millimeter Wave Multi-Baseline InSAR Data. In: Proceedings of IEEE International Geoscience and Remote Sensing Symposium 2010, pp. 4302–4305 (2010)

Reale, D., Fornaro, G., Pauciullo, A., Zhu, X., Bamler, R.: Tomographic Imaging and Monitoring of Buildings with Very High Resolution SAR Data. IEEE Geoscience and Remote Sensing Letters 8, 661–665 (2011)

Schimpf, H., Essen, H., Boehmsdorff, S., Brehm, T.: MEMPHIS A Fully Polarimetric Experimental Radar. In: Proceedings of IEEE International Geoscience and Remote Sensing Symposium 2002, pp. 1714–1716 (2002)

Schmitt, M., Stilla, U.: Fusion of Airborne Multi-Aspect InSAR Data by Simultaneous Backward Geocoding. In: Proceedings of Joint Urban Remote Sensing Event 2011, pp. 53–56 (2011)

Small, D., Pasquali, P., Fuglistaler, S.: A Comparison of Phase to Height Conversion Methods for SAR Interferometry. In: Proceedings of IEEE International Geoscience and Remote Sensing Symposium 1996, pp. 342–344 (1996)

Soergel, U., Thoennessen, U., Stilla, U.: Iterative Building Reconstruction in Multi-Aspect InSAR Data. International Archives of Photogrammetry, Remote Sensing and Spatial Information Sciences 34 (3/W13), 186–192 (2003)

Stilla, U., Soergel, U., Thoennessen, U.: Potential and Limits of InSAR Data for Building Reconstruction in Built-Up Areas. ISPRS Journal of Photogrammetry and Remote Sensing 58, 113–123 (2003)

Thiele, A., Cadario, E., Schulz, K., Thoennessen, U., Soergel, U.: InSAR Phase Profiles at Building Locations. International Archives of Photogrammetry, Remote Sensing and Spatial Information Sciences 36 (3/W49A), 203–208 (2007)

Thiele, A., Wegner, J.D., Soergel, U.: Building Reconstruction from Multi-Aspect InSAR Data. In: Soergel, U. (ed.) Radar Remote Sensing of Urban Areas, pp. 187–214. Springer Science+Business and Media B.V., Heidelberg (2010)

Thomas, G., Flores, B.C., Sok-Son, J.: SAR Sidelobe Apodization Using the Kaiser Window. In: Proceedings of IEEE International Conference on Image Processing 2000, pp. 709–712 (2000)

Vasile, G., Trouve, E., Ciuc, M., Buzuloiu, V.: General Adaptive-Neighborhood Technique for Improving Synthetic Aperture Radar Interferometric Coherence Estimation. Journal of the Optical Society of America A: Optics, Image Science, and Vision 21, 1455–1464 (2004)

Regionwise Classification of Building Facade Images

Michael Ying Yang and Wolfgang Förstner

Department of Photogrammetry,
Institute of Geodesy and Geoinformation,
University of Bonn,
Nussallee 15, 53115 Bonn, Germany
michaelyangying@uni-bonn.de,
wf@ipb.uni-bonn.de
http://www.ipb.uni-bonn.de

Abstract. In recent years, the classification task of building facade images receives a great deal of attention in the photogrammetry community. In this paper, we present an approach for regionwise classification using an efficient randomized decision forest classifier and local features. A conditional random field is then introduced to enforce spatial consistency between neighboring regions. Experimental results are provided to illustrate the performance of the proposed methods using image from eTRIMS database, where our focus is the object classes *building*, *car*, *door*, *pavement*, *road*, *sky*, *vegetation*, and *window*.

Keywords: Classification, conditional random field, random decision forest, segmentation, facade image.

1 Introduction

This paper presents an investigation into the semantic scene interpretation in the context of terrestrial man-made scenes. Our goal is the interpretation of the scene contained in an image as a collection of meaningful regions. The result of such an interpretation could be a rich image description useful for 3D city models of high level of detail, which are mainly used for visualization purposes, by thematic attributes to eventually obtain truly 3D geoinformation systems for complete cities. In this paper we focus on the problem of multi-class classification of building facade image regions.

Facade classification is the task of estimating the position and size of various structural (e.g. window, door) and non-structural elements (e.g. sky, road, building) in a given image (Fröhlich et al., 2010). Despite the substantial improvements during the past decade, the classification task remains a challenging problem, which receives a great deal of attention in the photogrammetry community (Rottensteiner et al., 2007; Korč and Förstner, 2008; Fröhlich et al., 2010; Kluckner and Bischof, 2010; Teboul et al., 2010).

Recently, an increasingly popular way to solve various image interpretation problems like object segmentation, stereo and single view reconstruction is to formulate them using image regions obtained from unsupervised segmentation algorithms. These methods are inspired from the observation that pixels constituting a particular region

U. Stilla et al. (Eds.): PIA 2011, LNCS 6952, pp. 209–220, 2011.

often have the similar property. For instance, they may belong to the same object. This approach has the benefit that higher order features based on all the pixels constituting the region can be computed and used for classification. Further, it is also much faster as inference now only needs to be performed over a small number of regions rather than all the pixels in the image.

An image dataset showing urban buildings in their environment has been made public by Korč and Förstner (2009), which is called eTRIMS dataset. It allows benchmarking of facade image classification. Most of the images of this data set show facades in Switzerland and Germany. Regarding terrestrial facade images in this dataset, the most dominant objects are building, window, vegetation, and sky.

In this work, randomized decision forest (RDF) (Breiman, 2001) is adopted as the classifier, which gives good classification results on building facade images. Because of its rather local nature, a conditional random field (CRF) (Lafferty et al., 2001) is often introduced to enforce spatial consistency. We show that CRF classification results give average performance of 65.8% accurarcy on eTRIMS 8-class dataset (Korč and Förstner, 2009). The remainder of the paper is organized as follow. Sec. 2 reviews some existing methods for building facade image classification. RDF classifier for performing image classification, and refinement with a CRF are described in Sec. 3. In Sec. 4, we show our results of RDF and CRF with respect to the classification of facade images. We finally conclude with a brief summary in Sec. 5.

2   Related Works

Previous works on building facade classification mostly regard the facade classification problem as multiple object detection tasks. Building facade detection is a very active research area in photogrammtery and computer vision. Drauschke and Förstner (2008) present a feature selection scheme with Adaboost for detecting buildings and building parts, where some of these features are used for classification in this paper. Graphical models are often used for integrating further information about the content of the whole scene in recent approaches (Kumar and Hebert, 2003; Verbeek and Triggs, 2007). In another paradigm, the bag of words, objects are detected by the evaluation of histograms of basic image features from a dictionary (Sivic et al., 2005). However, both approaches have not been tested with high resolution building images. Furthermore, the bag of words approaches have not applied to multifarious categories as building, and it is rather slow and the most time consuming part of the whole system.

Support vector machines are widely considered as a good classifier. Schnitzspan et al. (2008) propose hierarchical support vector random fields that SVM is used as a classifier for unary potentials in conditional random field framework. While the training and cross-validation steps in support vector machines are time consuming, randomized decision forest (RDF) (Breiman, 2001) is introduced to significantly speed up the learning and prediction process. Existing work has shown the power of a RDF as a useful classifier (Bosch et al., 2007; Lepetit et al., 2005; Maree et al., 2005). The use of a RDF for semantic segmentation is investigated in Shotton et al. (2008); Dumont et al. (2009); Fröhlich et al. (2010). These approaches utilize simple color histogram features or pixel differences. Multi-class facade segmentation by combining a machine learning approach with procedural modeling as a shape prior is presented by Teboul et al.

(2010). Generic shape grammars are constrained so as to express buildings only. Randomized forests are used to determine a relationship between the semantic elements of the grammar and the observed image support. Drauschke and Mayer (2010) also use random forest as one of the classifiers to evaluate the potential of texture filter banks for the pixelwise classification of facade images in eTRIMS dataset. Fröhlich et al. (2010) combine an RDF and local features for pixelwise labeling of facade images. Compared to Fröhlich et al. (2010), we derive the RDF classification on the image region level, rather than pixel level, and use a CRF to refine the classification results, where we incorporate location potentials and pairwise potentials in the CRF model. Other related works using the eTRIMS dataset concentrate on reconstructing the facade with grammar (Ripperda and Brenner, 2009) or detection of structural elements (e.g. windows and balconies (Wenzel and Förstner, 2008)), while we focus on multi-class image classification.

3   Classification

3.1   Randomized Decision Forest

We take randomized decision forest (RDF) (Breiman, 2001) as the classifier which operates on the regions defined by some unsupervised segmentation methods. In order to train the classifier, each region is assigned the most frequent class label it contains. Then a RDF is trained on the labeled data for each of the object classes. As illustrated in Fig. 1, a RDF is an ensemble classifier that consists of T decision trees (Shotton et al. (2008)). According to a decision tree learning algorithm, a decision tree recursively splits left or right down the tree to a leaf node. We use the extremely randomized trees (Geurts et al. (2006)) as learning algorithm. A feature vector d_i of image region i is classified by going down each tree. This process gives a class distribution at the leaf nodes and also a path for each tree. The class distributions $P(x_i \mid d_i)$ is obtained by averaging the class distribution over the leaf nodes for all T trees.

We now describe how the features are constructed from low-level descriptors. For each region, we compute an 178-dimensional feature vector, first incorporating region area and perimeter, its compactness and its aspect ratio. For representing spectral information of the region, we use 9 color features as Barnard et al. (2003): the mean and the standard deviation of the RGB and the HSV color spaces. Texture features derived from the Walsh transform (Petrou and Bosdogianni, 1999; Lazaridis and Petrou, 2006) are also used. Additionally we use mean SIFT descriptors (Lowe, 2004) of the image region. SIFT descriptors are extracted for each pixel of the region at a fixed scale and orientation, which is practically the same as the HOG descriptor (Dalal and Triggs, 2005), using the fast SIFT framework in Vedaldi and Fulkerson (2008). The extracted descriptors are then averaged into one l_1-normalized descriptor vector for each region. Other features are derived from generalization of the region's border and represent parallelity or orthogonality of the border segments.

3.2   Refinement with a CRF

In order to enforce spatial consistency between neighboring regions, we must introduce constraints that allow us to reduce misclassification that occurs near the boundaries of

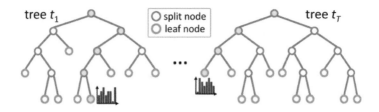

Fig. 1. Decision forest. A forest consists of T decision trees. A feature vector is classified by descending each tree. This gives, for each tree, a path from root to leaf, and a class distribution at the leaf. As an illustration, we highlight the root to leaf paths (yellow) and class distributions (red) for one input feature vector. (Figure courtesy by Jamie Shotton (Shotton et al., 2008).)

image regions. Conditional random fields provide a natural way to incorporate such constraints by including them in the pairwise potentials of the model.

Given a random field $\boldsymbol{X}$ defined over a graph $\mathcal{H} = (\mathcal{V}, \mathcal{E})$, the complete model for determining the optimal labeling $\boldsymbol{x} = \{x_i\}$ has a distribution of the Gibbs form

$$P(\boldsymbol{x} \mid \boldsymbol{d}) = \frac{1}{Z} \exp\left(-E(\boldsymbol{x} \mid \boldsymbol{d})\right) \qquad (1)$$

with the energy function defined as

$$E(\boldsymbol{x} \mid \boldsymbol{d}) = \sum_{i \in \mathcal{V}} E_1(x_i) + \alpha \sum_{\{i,j\} \in N} E_2(x_i, x_j) \qquad (2)$$

where α is the weighting coefficient in the model, and Z is the normalization factor. The set $\mathcal{V}$ is the set of nodes in the complete graph. The set N is the set of pairs collecting neighboring. E_1 is the unary potential, which represents relationships between variables and local observed data. E_2 is the pairwise potential, which represents relationships between variables of neighboring nodes.

The graphical model is illustrated in Fig. 2. Nodes connection and numbers correspond to segmentation of a building facade image. The blue edges between the nodes represent the neighborhoods.

The local unary potentials E_1 independently predict the label x_i based on the image $\boldsymbol{d}$:

$$E_1(x_i) = -\log P(x_i \mid \boldsymbol{d}) \qquad (3)$$

The label distribution $P(x_i \mid \boldsymbol{d})$ is usually calculated by using a classifier. The label distribution defined directly by the probability outputs provided by RDF for each region. The classifier which results from this is very specific. It finds regions which resemble regions that were seen in the training samples without considering the neighboring regions.

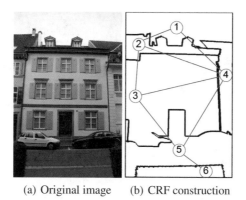

(a) Original image   (b) CRF construction

Fig. 2. Illustration of the CRF model architecture. Nodes connection and numbers correspond to segmented regions of a building facade image.

Based on the fact that RDF classifier does not take class label location information explicitly, we incorporate location potentials (similar to (Shotton et al., 2006)) in unary potentials. The location potential $-\log Q(x_i \mid \boldsymbol{d})$ takes the form of a look-up table with an entry for each class and region center location, where

$$Q(x_i \mid \boldsymbol{d}) = \left(\frac{N_{x_i,\hat{i}} + 1}{N_{\hat{i}} + 1}\right)^2$$

The index $\hat{i}$ is the normalized version of the region index i. $N_{x_i,\hat{i}}$ is the number of regions of class x_i at normalized location within certain neighborhood in $\hat{i}$, and $N_{\hat{i}}$ is the total number of regions at location in $\hat{i}$. The location potentials capture the dependence of the class label on the rough location of the region in the image. Here, we use part of annotation images in 8-class eTRIMS Database (Korč and Förstner, 2009) to learn the location potentials, but ensure no overlap between these images and testing images in the experimental part. Some learned location potentials are illustrated in Fig. 3. Therefore, the unary potentials E_1 is written as

$$E_1(x_i) = -\log P(x_i \mid \boldsymbol{d}) - \log Q(x_i \mid \boldsymbol{d}) \tag{4}$$

The pairwise potentials E_2 describe category compatibility between neighboring labels x_i and x_j given the image $\boldsymbol{d}$, which take the form

$$E_2(x_i, x_j) = \frac{1 + 4\exp(-2c_{ij})}{0.5(N_i + N_j)} \delta(x_i \neq x_j) \tag{5}$$

where c_{ij} is the norm of the color difference between regions in the LUV color space. N_i is the number of regions neighbored to region i, and N_j is the number of regions neighbored to j. The potentials E_2 are scaled by N_i and N_j to compensate for the irregularity of the graph $\mathcal{H}$. We refer the reader to Shotton et al. (2006); Gould et al. (2008) for more details about designing pairwise potentials.

(a) building   (b) road

(c) sky   (d) vegetation

Fig. 3. Example location potentials. *Sky* tends to occur at the top part of images, while *road* tends to occur at the bottom part of images, and *building* tends to occur in the middle part of images. Here, the dark blue area indicates the most likely locations of one class, while the dark red area indicates the most unlikely locations.

3.3   Learning and Inference

The weighting parameter α, represents the tradeoff between pairwise regularization and the confidence in unary potentials, is the model parameter that should be learned. We estimate α by cross validation on the training data. Once the model has been learned, inference is carried out with the multi-label graph optimization library of (Boykov et al., 2001;   Kolmogorov and Zabih,   2004;   Boykov and Kolmogorov,   2004)   using α-expansion. Since the CRF is defined on the graph of regions, inference is very efficient, taking less than half a second per image.

4   Experimental Results

We conduct experiments to evaluate the performance of the proposed model on the the 8-class eTRIMS Database (Korč and Förstner, 2009). In the experiments, we take the ground-truth label of a region to be the majority vote of the ground-truth pixel labels. We randomly divide the images into training and test data sets.

4.1   eTRIMS Database

We start with the eTRIMS 8-class Database which consists of 60 annotated building facade images, labeled with 8 classes: *building, car, door, pavement, road, sky, vegetation, window*. The ground-truth labeling is approximate (with foreground labels often overlapping background objects).

We segment the facade images using mean shift algorithm (Comaniciu and Meer, 2002), tuned to give approximately 480 regions per image. In all 60 images, we extract around 29 600 regions. We have following statistics. Compared to the ground-truth labeling, almost 33% of all the segmented regions get the classlabel *building*. 25% of all regions get the classlabel *window*. These statistics are very comprehensive, because facade images typically show buildings typically contain many windows. Furthermore, 19% of the regions get the classlabel *vegetation*, and 2% belong to *sky*, and the last 21% of the regions are spread over most of other classes. We randomly divide the images into a training set with 40 images and a testing set with 20 images.

4.2   RDF Classification Results

We take the RDF classifier, run experiments 5 times, and obtain overall averaging classification accuracy 58.8%. The number of decision trees is chosen as $T = 250$. Random chance would give $1/8 = 12.5\%$, and thus RDF results are about 5 times better than chance. In the whole paper, accuracy values are computed as the percentage of image pixels assigned to the correct class label, ignoring pixels labeled as void in the ground truth. Fig. 4 *Left* shows the classification results over all 8 classes. The classification accuracy with respect to numbers of decision trees T for training are shown in Fig. 4 *Right*. While increasing the number of decision trees, the classification accuracy also increases. After 250 iteration, the accuracy converges. So we choose $T = 250$ for performing experiments above.

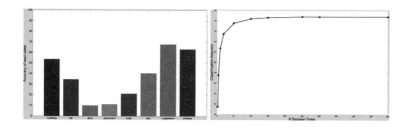

Fig. 4. *Left*: accuracy of each class of RDF classifier. The horizontal-axis reads *building, car, door, pavement, road, sky, vegetation, window*, while the vertical-axis reads $[0, 100]$. *Right*: classification accuracy with respect to numbers of decision trees for training. The horizontal-axis reads $[0, 500]$, while the vertical-axis reads $[40, 60]$.

Fig. 5 presents some result images of RDF method. The black regions in all the result images and ground truth images correspond to background. The quality inspection of the results in Fig. 5 shows that RDF classifier yields fair results. However, there exists some misclassification for each class. For example, the incorrect results at windows are often due to the reflectance of vegetation and sky in the window panes. Most sky regions are classified correctly. However, sky region is assigned label *car* in one image (last image in Fig. 5).

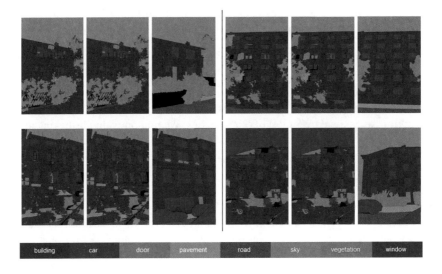

Fig. 5. Example images of eTRIMS database and classification results based on a randomized decision forest. (For each image triplet, *left*: test image, *middle*: result, *right*: ground truth.)

4.3   CRF Refinement Results

We run experiments 5 times, and obtain overall averaging classification accuracy 65.8% by applying CRF to the whole test set. For comparison, the RDF classifier alone gives an overall accuracy of 58.8%.Therefore, the location, and pairwise potentials increase the accuracy by 7%. For correct recovery of most *sky* regions, the location potentials increase the accuracy by 3%. This seemingly small numerical improvement corresponds to a large perceptual improvement (cf. Fig. 6). The weighting parameter, learned by cross validation on the training data, is $\alpha = 0.8$. Table 1 shows the confusion matrix.

Qualitative results of CRF on the eTRIMS dataset are presented in Fig. 6. The quality inspection of the results in these images shows that CRF yields good results. The greatest accuracies are for classes which have low visual variability and many training examples (such as window, vegetation, building, and sky) whilst the lowest accuracies are for classes with high visual variability or few training examples (for example door, car, and pavement). We expect more training data and the use of features with better lighting invariance properties will improve the classification accuracy. Objects such as car, door, pavement, and window are sometimes incorrectly classified as *building*, due to the dominant presence of building in the image. This kind of problem may be resolved by some detection schemes. For example, detecting windows, cars, and doors should resolve some of such ambiguities. Furthermore, 36% of pavement is misclassified as road, and 44% of road is misclassified as pavement. Objects, such as pavement and road, can be confused with each other. This effect is partially attributable to inaccuracies in the manual ground truth labeling, where pixels are often mislabeled near object boundaries.

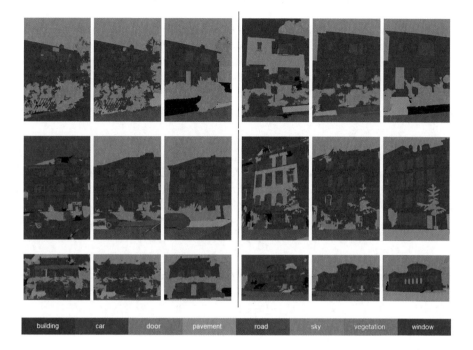

Fig. 6. Qualitative classification results of CRF on the eTRIMS database. (For each image triplet, *left*: RDF classification result, *middle*: CRF refinement result, *right*: ground truth.)

Table 1. Pixelwise accuracy of image classification using CRF on the eTRIMS 8-class database. The confusion matrix shows the classification accuracy for each class (rows) and is row-normalized to sum to 100%. Row labels indicate the true class (Tr), and column labels the predicted class (Pr). (b = *building*,c = *car*,d = *door*, p = *pavement*,r = *road*,s = *sky*,v = *vegetation*,w = *window*.)

Pr \ Tr	b	c	d	p	r	s	v	w
b	**71**	2	1	1	1	2	10	12
c	12	**35**	0	12	11	0	30	0
d	42	0	**16**	1	6	0	8	27
p	11	15	0	**22**	36	0	14	2
r	4	8	0	44	**35**	0	9	0
s	13	0	0	0	0	**78**	8	1
v	18	5	2	1	1	0	**66**	7
w	19	1	1	0	0	1	3	**75**

5   Conclusions and Future Work

In this paper, we demonstrate an approach to regionwise classification of building facade images based on a randomized decision forest (RDF) and local features. In our
experiments on eTRIMS dataset (Korč and Förstner, 2009), we have shown that this
approach produces fair classification results. When we refine the classification with a
conditional random field (CRF), which penalizes pairs of regions that are very different
in color, we consistently improve both our quantitative and especially our qualitative
results.

Since neighboring regions in facade images are not independent from each other,
CRF models these dependencies directly by introducing pairwise potentials. However,
standard CRF works on a local level and long range dependencies are not addressed
explicitly in the CRF. Our future work will try to set up a hierarchical model to integrate
neighborhood and partonomy relations in a unified CRF model. A similar concept has
been raised in Yang et al. (2010), where the model is denoted as hierarchical conditional
random field (HCRF).

Acknowledgements. The work is funded by Deutsche Forschungsgemeinschaft (German Research Foundation) FO 180/16-1. The authors gratefully acknowledge the
support.

References

Barnard, K., Duygulu, P., Freitas, N.D., Forsyth, D., Blei, D., Jordan, M.: Matching words and
    pictures. Journal of Machine Learning Research 3, 1107–1135 (2003)
Bosch, A., Zisserman, A., Muñoz, X.: Image classification using random forests and ferns. In:
    IEEE International Conference on Computer Vision, pp. 1–8 (2007)
Boykov, Y., Kolmogorov, V.: An experimental comparison of min-cut/max-flow algorithms for
    energy minimization in vision. IEEE Transactions on Pattern Analysis and Machine Intelli-
    gence 26, 1124–1137 (2004)
Boykov, Y., Veksler, O., Zabih, R.: Fast approximate energy minimization via graph cuts. IEEE
    Transactions on Pattern Analysis and Machine Intelligence 23, 1222–1239 (2001)
Breiman, L.: Random forests. Machine Learning 45(1), 5–32 (2001)
Comaniciu, D., Meer, P.: Mean shift: A robust approach toward feature space analysis. IEEE
    Transactions on Pattern Analysis and Machine Intelligence 24(5), 603–619 (2002)
Dalal, N., Triggs, B.: Histograms of oriented gradients for human detection. In: IEEE Conference
    on Computer Vision and Pattern Recognition, pp. 886–893 (2005)
Drauschke, M., Förstner, W.: Selecting appropriate features for detecting buildings and building
    parts. In: Proceeding of the 21st Congress of the International Society for Photogrammetry
    and Remote Sensing (ISPRS), vol. (B3b), pp. 447–452 (2008)
Drauschke, M., Mayer, H.: Evaluation of texture energies for classification of facade images.
    In: ISPRS Technical Commission III Symposium on Photogrammetry Computer Vision and
    Image Analysis, pp. 257–262 (2010)
Dumont, M., Marée, R., Wehenkel, L., Geurts, P.: Fast multi-class image annota-
    tion with random subwindows and multiple output randomized trees. In: Interna-
    tional Conference on Computer Vision Theory and Applications (VISAPP), vol. 2,
    pp. 196–203 (2009)

Fröhlich, B., Rodner, E., Denzler, J.: A fast approach for pixelwise labeling of facade images. In: International Conference on Pattern Recognition, pp. 3029–3032 (2010)

Geurts, P., Ernst, D., Wehenkel, L.: Extremely randomized trees. Machine Learning 63(1), 3–42 (2006)

Gould, S., Rodgers, J., Cohen, D., Elidan, G., Koller, D.: Multi-class segmentation with relative location prior. International Journal of Computer Vision 80(3), 300–316 (2008)

Kluckner, S., Bischof, H.: Image-based building classification and 3d modeling with super-pixels. In: ISPRS Technical Commission III Symposium on Photogrammetry Computer Vision and Image Analysis, pp. 233–238 (2010)

Kolmogorov, V., Zabih, R.: What energy functions can be minimized via graph cuts? IEEE Transactions on Pattern Analysis and Machine Intelligence 26(2), 147–159 (2004)

Korč, F., Förstner, W.: Interpreting terrestrial images of urban scenes using discriminative random fields. In: Proceeding of the 21st Congress of the International Society for Photogrammetry and Remote Sensing (ISPRS), pp. 291–296 (2008)

Korč, F., Förstner, W.: eTRIMS image database for interpreting images of man-made scenes. Technical Report TR-IGG-P-2009-01 (2009),
http://www.ipb.uni-bonn.de/projects/etrims_db

Kumar, S., Hebert, M.: Discriminative random fields: a discriminative framework for contextual interaction in classification. In: IEEE International Conference on Computer Vision, pp. 1150–1157 (2003)

Lafferty, J., McCallum, A., Pereira, F.: Conditional Random Fields: Probabilistic Models for Segmenting and Labeling Sequence Data. In: International Conference on Machine Learning, pp. 282–289 (2001)

Lazaridis, G., Petrou, M.: Image registration using the Walsh transform. IEEE Transactions on Image Processing 15(8), 2343–2357 (2006)

Lepetit, V., Lagger, P., Fua, P.: Randomized trees for real-time keypoint recognition. In: IEEE Conference on Computer Vision and Pattern Recognition, pp. 775–781 (2005)

Lowe, D.: Distinctive image features from scale-invariant keypoints. International Journal of Computer Vision 60(2), 91–110 (2004)

Maree, R., Geurts, P., Piater, J., Wehenkel, L.: Random subwindows for robust image classification. In: IEEE Conference on Computer Vision and Pattern Recognition, pp. 34–40 (2005)

Petrou, M., Bosdogianni, P.: Image Processing: The Fundamentals. Wiley, Chichester (1999)

Ripperda, N., Brenner, C.: Evaluation of structure recognition using labelled facade images. In: Denzler, J., Notni, G., Süße, H. (eds.) Pattern Recognition. LNCS, vol. 5748, pp. 532–541. Springer, Heidelberg (2009)

Rottensteiner, F., Trinder, J., Clode, S., Kubik, K.: Building detection by fusion of airborne laser scanner data and multi-spectral images: Performance evaluation and sensitivity analysis. ISPRS Journal of Photogrammetry and Remote Sensing 62(2), 135–149 (2007)

Schnitzspan, P., Fritz, M., Schiele, B.: Hierarchical support vector random fields: joint training to combine local and global features. In: Forsyth, D., Torr, P., Zisserman, A. (eds.) ECCV 2008, Part II. LNCS, vol. 5303, pp. 527–540. Springer, Heidelberg (2008)

Shotton, J., Johnson, M., Cipolla, R.: Semantic texton forests for image categorization and segmentation. In: IEEE Conference on Computer Vision and Pattern Recognition, pp. 1–8 (2008)

Shotton, J., Winnand, J., Rother, C., Criminisi, A.: Textonboost: joint appearance, shape and context modeling for multi-class object recognition and segmentation. In: Leonardis, A., Bischof, H., Pinz, A. (eds.) ECCV 2006. LNCS, vol. 3951, pp. 1–15. Springer, Heidelberg (2006)

Sivic, J., Russell, B.C., Efros, A.A., Zisserman, A., Freeman, W.T.: Discovering objects and their locations in images. In: IEEE International Conference on Computer Vision, pp. 1–8 (2005)

Teboul, O., Simon, L., Koutsourakis, P., Paragios, N.: Segmentation of building facades using procedural shape priors. In: IEEE Conference on Computer Vision and Pattern Recognition, pp. 3105–3112 (2010)

Vedaldi, A., Fulkerson, B.: Vlfeat: An open and portable library of computer vision algorithms (2008), http://www.vlfeat.org/

Verbeek, J., Triggs, B.: Region classification with markov field aspect models. In: IEEE Conference on Computer Vision and Pattern Recognition, pp. 1–8 (2007)

Wenzel, S., Förstner, W.: Semi-supervised incremental learning of hierarchical appearance models. In: Proceeding of the 21st Congress of the International Society for Photogrammetry and Remote Sensing (ISPRS), vol. (B3b), pp. 399–405 (2008)

Yang, M.Y., Förstner, W., Drauschke, M.: Hierarchical conditional random field for multi-class image classification. In: Proceedings of the Fifth International Conference on Computer Vision Theory and Applications, vol. 2, pp. 464–469 (2010)

Supervised Classification of Multiple View Images in Object Space for Seismic Damage Assessment

Markus Gerke

University of Twente, Faculty of Geo-Information Science and Earth Observation –
ITC, Department of Earth Observation Science, Hengelosestraat 99, P.O. Box 217,
7500AE Enschede, The Netherlands
http://www.itc.nl

Abstract. Classification of remote sensing image and range data is normally done in 2D space, because anyhow most sensors capture the surface of the earth from a close-to vertical direction and thus vertical structures, e.g. at building façades are not visible anyways. However, when the objects of interest are photographed from off-nadir directions, like in oblique airborne images, the question on how to efficiently classify those scenes arises. In this paper a study on classification in 3D object space is presented: image features from individual oblique airborne images, and 3D geometric features derived from matching in those images are projected onto voxels. Those are segmented and classified. The study area is Port-Au-Prince (Haiti), where images have been acquired after the earthquakes in January 2010. Results show that through the combination of image evidence as realized by the projection into object space the classification becomes more accurate compared to single image classification.

Keywords: AdaBoost, Classification, Feature, Fusion, Learning, Performance, Point Cloud, Random Trees.

1 Introduction and Related Work

Supervised image classification of airborne or satellite data is normally applied directly to (2D) image observations. From a classical remote sensing point this is quite reasonable since anyhow most sensors capture the surface of the earth from a close-to vertical direction; displacement of 3D objects when projected onto a reference plane are mostly neglectable and vertical structures are not visible anyways. When height data from an airborne lidar scanner or from matching in nadir images is involved, only so called 2.5D information, i.e. one height value per planar location is available and no 3D structures. The height information is then normally used as an additional feature in the 2D classification framework.

However, when the objects of interest are photographed from multiple off-nadir directions, like in oblique airborne images, the question on how to efficiently classify those scenes arises.

U. Stilla et al. (Eds.): PIA 2011, LNCS 6952, pp. 221–232, 2011.
© Springer-Verlag Berlin Heidelberg 2011

One possibility to approach this problem is to perform classification in the individual images and then combine the results in object space. In this case the classifier can only use features as observable in one 2D-projection of the object of interest, see for instance (Gerke and Kerle, 2011).

An alternative is to classify directly in 3D space. Entities to be classified are then defined in 3D, for instance using volume elements (voxels). One advantage of such a procedure is that voxels which are observable in multiple images can be classified exploiting all available information at once.

In computer vision literature quite some papers on the problem of 3D scene classification is available. Johnson and Hebert (1999) generate so-called spin images: those are 2D projections of 3D surfaces and spin images generated from a 3D model-library are matched against spin images from observed 3D surfaces. The observation can be from a laser scanner or image matching techniques. In (Huber et al., 2004) the technique has been extended to object recognition through learning of relationships between object parts. Through this approach, however, only geometric properties of objects are exploited, so spectral information from images is not directly involved. If the object surface is not smooth or if it is noisy, the spin image quality may bias the classification performance significantly. This restriction probably also applies for a method relying on so called depth gradient images (Adán et al., 2011) or surface descriptors, like for instance presented in (Wahl et al., 2003). Another geometry-based classification approach is presented in (Csákány and Wallace, 2003). Surface features are learned and classified, the presented test data is from a laser scanner. The good classification performance is also possible because the approach is limited to a number of shape primitives.

Another approach to object classification is pursued in content based image retrieval systems. Those techniques are being applied also to remote sensing data imaging man-made structures, see homepage of the *eTRIMS* project (eTRIMS, 2011) as an example. However, one has to keep in mind that the classification is again done in 2D image space, so the same problem as mentioned above will occur when multiple-view images are being used.

Interestingly Brostow et al. (2008) take the other direction: they compute features directly in 3D space from a sparse point cloud as derived from a moving camera on a car applying structure from motion techniques. Those features are then projected into 2D images in order to apply classification in 2D space. So, finally the authors are able to classify the scene as visible from a particular camera location, but they exploit depth information.

In this paper a study on 3D supervised image classification in object space is presented; the images for the experiment are oblique airborne images which have been acquired by the Pictometry system (Pictometry, 2011; Petrie, 2009). Features from individual oblique images and from a point cloud computed from the images are projected onto voxels in object space, and the voxels are classified applying a state-of-the-art machine learning technique; actually AdaBoost and Random Trees are compared in this paper.

This technique is applied in a case study to images captured over Haiti, after the earthquake in January 2010. The aim is to classify building damage, and oblique airborne images are well suited for this task: opposed to vertical images, building façade are visible in oblique images and information on the (health) status of façades is crucial for an effective damage assessment (Gerke and Kerle, 2011).

The remainder of this paper is organised as follows: in the next section the dataset being used in this study is introduced, in section 3 the approach to 3D supervised classification is presented, and in section 4 classification results are presented and discussed, while the last section gives an outlook to future work.

2   Study Area and Data

The oblique airborne images being used in this study have been acquired by Pictometry Inc. over the capital of Haiti in so-called Neighborhood mode, resulting in a GSD (ground sampling distance) ranging between 10cm in the fore- and 16cm in the background. For every point on the ground at least one image per viewing direction is available; however, stereo overlap from a single direction is not guaranteed since the along-track overlap is smaller than 50%. The consequence is that the number of oblique images observing a particular area may vary from 4 (no stereo from any direction) to 8 (stereo from all 4 directions). Pictometry also captures vertical images, but releases them only after they have been orthorectified. Since no further (quality) information on the employed DTM is available, those images are not considered here. Figure 1 shows parts of the study areas. Area 1 is covered by North, East and West looking images. The South-facing images are not used, since they were captured after a series of aftershocks a few days later. The aim is to map building damage and thus it is important that the scene did not change in between the image takes. Area 2 is covered by East, West and South looking images; the North facing images are missing for the same reason just mentioned for area 1. The first area shows a densely built-up area in the centre of Port-Au-Prince, while the second area is characterised by a less dense building pattern.

3   Approach

A number of processing steps are necessary prior to performing the actual classification. Those processing steps are:

1. Geometric (pre) processing: given the raw images from the data provider they first need to be oriented and calibrated. Dense image matching followed by ray forward intersection provides a 3D point cloud which needs to be outlier filtered and put into a voxel structure.
2. Reference labeling: since a supervised classification scheme is applied some reference data for training is needed, but also an independent validation set.
3. Segmentation and feature extraction: clusters of voxels and image segments are defined and features are extracted from individual images and from the 3D point cloud

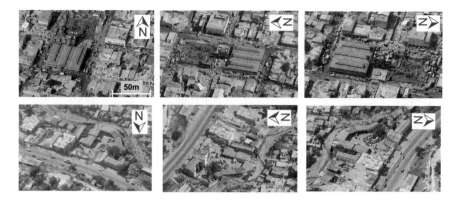

Fig. 1. Part of study areas. Top area 1: oblique images facing North, East, West direction. Bottom area 2: oblique images facing South, East, West direction. Images: ©Pictometry, Inc.

4. Voxel augmentation: the voxels obtain a final unique segment id and image features are projected onto individual voxels. Features from multiple images are merged.

Some of the processing steps are detailed in the following.

3.1   Geometric (pre)Processing

Image orientation The Pictometry images were downloaded via Pictometry online[1]. Since no camera calibration and exterior orientation information is obtainable through that service a semi-automatic aerial triangulation has been performed, including camera self-calibration, using the approach presented in (Gerke, 2011). Some ground information from post disaster GeoEye-1 images and LiDAR data provided by the Worldbank (Haugerud, 2010) was only used to fix the unknown datum parameters, i.e. translation, rotation and scale, with respect to the used map projection. The relative orientation within the block was supported through horizontal lines defined at buildings that were considered stable, i.e. not affected by the earthquake. Gerke (2011) showed that the use of scene constraints significantly enhances the accuracy in indirect sensor orientation.

Dense image matching, filtering and voxel computation. The dense matching approach from Furukawa and Ponce (2010) was applied to compute a dense 3D point cloud. Depth information at façades is required, and those are very often only visible in two overlapping oblique images. This has to be considered, and thus also 2 ray points were allowed for the forward intersection. The 3D points were put into a voxel structure and at the same time outliers were removed:

---

[1] http://pol.pictometry.com. The support by Pictometry is gratefully acknowledged.

Fig. 2. Point clouds, area 1. From left to right voxels overview: original colour, grey values coding height, zoom-in to original point cloud.

The 3D space is partitioned into equally spaced voxel cubes (here a spacing of 1m was used). The requirement is that a minimum of original 3D points are located in a particular voxel cube and that a voxel is adjacent to a minimum of valid voxels in order to be accepted. At this stage, only the original points are used, this means no quantification is done. Through the requirement of minimum original points in a voxel and minimum number of neighbours, most outliers are removed, since very often those are isolated points. For the classification the voxel centres were computed; the colour assigned to a voxel centre is the median value of the colours from all original points located in that voxel cube. Figure 2 shows an overview of test area 1 voxel centres: original colour left, height, coded in grey values and a zoom-in to the original point cloud.

3.2   Segmentation of Images and Voxels

A further preparation step concerns the segmentation. In classification methods it is common not to classify individual entities, but groups of them. The reason is to overcome problems related to noise and mixed information assigned to a single entities. In the raster domain either regular clusters of $n \times n$ pixels are chosen or a pre-segmentation is performed, e.g. based on homogeneity.

In this study a mixed strategy is pursued. In order to obtain segments representing smooth objects, a segmentation of the voxel centres was performed. The surface growing approach as described in (Vosselman and Maas, 2010, chapter 2.3.3) was applied to cluster those voxels which probably belong to the same plane. Such a procedure leaves quite a lot voxels un-segmented when located on a destroyed building, vegetation or rubble piles. For this reason, individual images were segmented as well, using the graph-based technique from Felzenszwalb and Huttenlocher (2004), which efficiently groups pixels similar to the perceptual appearance within a local neighbourhood. The segmentation algorithm is attractive because it balances intra-segment and inter-segment heterogeneity differences. How the final segmentation of the voxel is derived will be explained below in section 3.4.

3.3   Feature Computation Per Image and in 3D Point Cloud

Features for the classification were derived from the images directly, but also from the 3D point cloud in order to account for additional geometric properties of the objects. In the images the following features were computed per image segment:

- *Hue and Saturation*: per segment the median value of those colour channels was captured. In contrast to original RGB values at least the Hue is more insensitive against illumination changes.
- *Texture*: per segment the median standard deviation from a running $n \times n$ window inside the segment was computed. In order to account for differently sized structures, this filter was applied 3 times, with n=3,9,27.
- *Straight lines direction*: in images showing man-made structures a number of straight lines can be observed, e.g. on roofs or at façades. Therefore, per image segment the dominant direction of straight lines, extracted with the line growing operator according to Burns et al. (1986) was used as a feature.

From the 3D point cloud some features were computed per segment as well: Planes were fitted through all 3D points corresponding to a particular segment. The *residual error of plane normals* was used as a feature to encode geometrical homogeneity: on a planar face, such as an intact roof, the residual error is supposed to be much smaller compared to a rubble pile. In addition, the *Z-component of the plane normal* was encoded as a feature to distinguish vertical from other planes.

Since points in inhomogeneous areas are not assigned to a segment as derived from the voxels, the described features are computed in segments as obtained from projecting individual image segments to the point cloud. The projection method is described in the next paragraph.

3.4   Projection of Features and Labels onto Voxels and Definition of Final Voxel Segments

Most features, reference label information, and also segmentation information are obtained from individual images, so an important task now is to assign that information to the voxels as defined in 3D space. Two main problems need to be solved. First, it must be ensured that a particular voxel cube is really *visible* in a particular image, so the first task is to perform a visibility analysis. Second, since normally a voxel is visible from multiple images, a *unique segment, feature value and reference label* must be computed from all available information.

Whether a voxel of interest is visible in a particular image is checked by analysing the viewing ray from the camera centre to the voxel centre: if this one is not destructed by other voxels, the voxel is assumed being visible. This method can only be an approximation since voxels are assumed to be entirely solid, and it is assumed that each object in the scene is represented. In experiments, however, quite reasonable results have been obtained. An additional problem is that several image pixels will be projected onto a voxel, because the GSD is normally smaller than the edge size of a voxel. Depending on the type of information (segment, feature, label) either the majority (segment id, label) or the median feature value is chosen for that voxel.

For every voxel only a single segment, feature value per feature type and reference label can be assigned. Therefore, in case information from multiple images is projected onto a voxel, a unique value needs to be found.

For the segments the following strategy is implemented: if a voxel is already part of a segment from 3D point segmentation, that segmentation is kept. If no segmentation information is retrieved from that step, all segmentation information from the pixel as projected from individual images is analysed. The segment id being part of the largest individual segment is taken as the final segment id of that voxel. The disadvantage of this procedure is that it does not consider neighbourhood relations.

For final values per feature type again the median value is considered, and for the label, again the majority is selected. Since finally, the classification will be based on segments, and not on individual voxels, the feature values and label information is summarized per voxel segment, using the same computation rule as just described.

3.5   Supervised Classification of Voxels

Upon completion of the data processing described above, each voxel is assigned to a unique segment, and each segment has assigned a number of feature values and a reference label. The data is now split into a training and a validation set in order to perform and assess supervised classification. In this study two different approaches to supervised classification are applied and compared: a) AdaBoost and b) RandomTrees. The idea behind the meta-learning algorithm AdaBoost (adaptive boosting, (Freund and Schapire, 1996)) is to train so-called weak learners from observations. A weak learner is in general very simple, in our case decision stumps (Iba and Langley, 1992). In a number of rounds individual weak hypotheses are generated by the learner, where after each round a weighting scheme is applied to focus on wrongly classified samples in the next round. The assumption is that the combination of all those weighted hypotheses finally leads to a strong classifier.

Random Trees (RTrees, (Breiman, 2001)) are similar to decision trees. The training is done by only selecting randomized subsets of features. Since this is done several times, it leads to independent trees, and the collection of those is also referred to as Random Forest. One important difference between AdaBoost and RTrees is that the first one generalises through a flat decision structure, since only decision stumps are used, while the latter generalises through random samples. RTrees are known to be faster than AdaBoost which makes them more attractive for real-time applications.

In this study an empirical comparison of the classification accuracy from those two methods is performed, but the focus is on the actual application in the 3D case rather than on analysing the deeper differences between AdaBoost and RTrees. For the same reason other classification methods like Support Vector Machines are not further considered here.

4   Results

The data processing has been done for both test areas separately. Some experiments shall answer the following questions:

1. Per test area, using a part of the reference for training the classifiers, and the remaining part for validation:
   (a) How does the classification of voxel segments per viewing direction compare to the case when all information is merged?
   (b) Do AdaBoost and RTrees perform differently?
2. How well are the classifiers transferable, from one area to the next?

Question 1a) is to test whether the assumption made in the begin can be verified in this case study: If features from image information and computations in 3D space are merged from all viewing directions the classification result is better compared to the case when only features from single directions are used. For this purpose in every test area approximately a third of all reference voxel segments was defined as training set, the remaining ones were used for validation.

4.1   Per Test Area

Because of space restrictions in this paper not the entire confusion matrices, but only the accuracy per object class are shown, i.e. how many voxel segments of a particular class have correctly been classified. In Figure 3 results for both test areas are shown. From top to bottom one chart per class is given. In each chart the number of segments available in the verification set is encoded at the y-axis through the height of the bars. For each available viewing direction the classification accuracy in absolute number of segments is shown, for both methods, AdaBoost and RTrees. The right hand group gives the result for the merged case, i.e. where the segments have been defined and features have been computed from all 3 directions.

In the merged case for all classes and in both areas the maximum number of segments is available, which is quite reasonable. Compared to the number of segments available in single images, for the two classes *Façade* and *Tree/Vegetation* the merge of all viewing directions brings most increase.

The absolute number of segments varies considerably: from less than 20 (*Tree/Vegetation* in area 1, *Roof destroyed/rubble* in area 2) to around 500 (*Roof intact* in area 1). This observation can be explained by the nature of the two test areas: area 1 does not show much vegetation, and in test area 2 only one some buildings are heavily damaged, while in general the majority of roofs is still intact.

Looking at the absolute number of correctly classified segments, some more interesting observations can be made. For the class *Façade* in both areas and *Tree/Vegetation* in area 2 the gain of the chosen strategy to merge features from all directions is most significant. For both areas the number of correctly classified *Façade* segments in the merged case is much higher than the sum from the single directions. In area 1 in the individual directions 42 segments

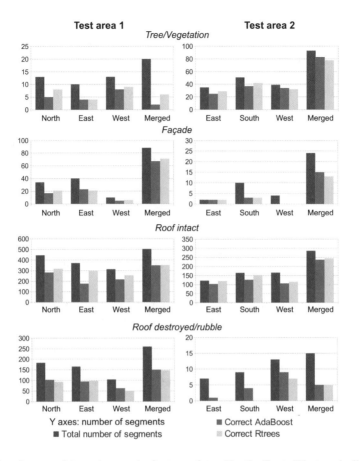

Fig. 3. Results per object class, only features from North, East, West and all merged (test area 1) and South, East, West, merged from test area 2. The number of segments available and absolute number of correct classified segments from AdaBoost and Random Trees is shown through the bars. Note the differing scales on y-axes.

are classified correctly by RTrees, while from the merged case it is 70. In area 2 the proportions are similar, although the total number of segments is smaller. The class *Roof intact* also profits in both areas from the merging, while for the classes with low absolute number of segments (*Tree/Vegetation* in area 1, *Roof destroyed/rubble* in area 2) the merge has a negative effect on the correctly classified segments.

In most cases Random Tree classification outperforms AdaBoost. The largest differences occur in the *Roof intact* class in area 1, but in most other cases discrepancies are marginal. Interestingly, for the merged cases the differences are no more significant, except or *Tree/Vegetation* in area 1, where only a few training samples are available.

4.2 Transferability

In order to assess the transferability of trained classifiers the following experiment has been undertaken: The whole test area 1 was used to train AdaBoost and RTrees, and the trained classifiers where then validated in test area 2, using the entire reference set. In Table 1 the results are presented for the merged case.

Table 1. Classification correctness per class, merged voxel information for test area 2. The upper part shows results from training in that particular area, while the lower part shows results when training was done in area 1.

Train in area	Method	Tree/Veg.	Façade	Roof intact	Roof destroyed
2 (here)	AdaBoost	89.2	62.5	82.9	33.3
	RTrees	83.9	54.2	85.7	33.3
1 (other)	AdaBoost	40.3	53.8	74.0	29.0
	RTrees	70.2	**64.1**	**87.4**	22.6

The upper two rows show the result from training in area 2 directly, i.e. the percentages are the same as displayed in Figure 3, right hand side, merged case. The lower two rows show the percentage of correctly classified segments for all four classes, but the classifiers have been trained in entire area 1. In that scenario Random Trees outperform AdaBoost; even the transferred trained classifier from test area 1 classifies *Façade* and *Roof intact* more accurate compared to a training in the particular area 2.

4.3 Analysis and Conclusions

The observations made above allow to state that the combination of image evidence from different viewing angles enhances the supervised classification result. Here, this was demonstrated for façades and vegetation, and to a lesser degree for roofs. The latter ones are mostly anyhow visible in all viewing angles from oblique airborne images, since they are not subject to (self-) occlusion to the same extent as façades or vegetation. This means, the merge of information just brings redundant information for roof classes, which only marginally enhances the classification accuracy.

For classification in independent viewing directions it can be argued that the Random Tree classifier performs mostly slightly better than AdaBoost. As can be expected the overall classification performance is also correlated with the number of available training samples. This was also shown here: If only a few samples were available, both classifiers did not perform well in general, and with increasing number of samples, i.e. in the merged cases, both classifiers performed similar.

The transferability of Random Trees works quite well; for the classes *Façade* and *Roof intact* the validation result with transferred classifier was even better than with the classifier trained in the actual area. For *Tree/Vegetation* and *Roof destroyed/rubble* the results were worse. For the trees and vegetation this might have got to do with the large dependency on colour features (Gerke and Kerle, 2011). The number of vegetation objects in the dense built-up area 1 is small and the species of trees there is probably different compared to the sparse building compounds in area 2. Therefore, it is likely that the colour feature footprints are different and that the other features cannot compensate for that entirely.

5 Future Work

The results obtained through merging features in object space are quite promising. Future work concerning classification can go towards an exploitation of neighbourhood relations in 3D, so to extend for instance the idea behing CRF models (Lafferty et al., 2001; Kumar and Hebert, 2006) to the third dimension. Another idea is to become independent from training data at all, e.g. to implement a rule-based classification.

Further it will be interesting to move from (voxel) segments to objects, i.e. to perform a comprehensive scene analysis, including object recognition. For the application of disaster mapping after an earthquake this would mean to infer individual building damage levels (Gerke and Kerle, 2011). In particular the structure-graph-technique presented by Hartz (2009) seems to be promising.

Concerning the applications a whole bunch of interesting studies can be performed, e.g. to fuse quite different sensor data, like from airborne and terrestrial platforms.

References

Adán, A., Merchán, P., Salamanca, S.: 3D scene retrieval and recognition with depth gradient images. Pattern Recognition Letters 32(9), 1337–1353 (2011)

Breiman, L.: Random forests. Machine Learning 45(1), 5–32 (2001)

Brostow, G., Shotton, J., Fauqueur, J., Cipolla, R.: Segmentation and recognition using structure from motion point clouds. In: Forsyth, D., Torr, P., Zisserman, A. (eds.) ECCV 2008, Part I. LNCS, vol. 5302, pp. 44–57. Springer, Heidelberg (2008)

Burns, J., Hanson, A., Riseman, E.: Extracting straight lines. IEEE Transactions on Pattern Analysis and Machine Intelligence 8(4), 425–455 (1986)

Csákány, P., Wallace, A.: Representation and classification of 3-d objects. IEEE Transactions on Systems, Man, and Cybernetics, Part B: Cybernetics 33(4), 638–647 (2003)

eTRIMS: Homepage eTRIMS – E-Training for Interpreting Images of Man-Made Scenes (2011), http://www.ipb.uni-bonn.de/projects/etrims/index.html (accessed April 30, 2011)

Felzenszwalb, P., Huttenlocher, D.: Efficient graph-based image segmentation. International Journal of Computer Vision 59(2), 167–181 (2004)

Freund, Y., Schapire, R.E.: Experiments with a new boosting algorithm. In: Machine Learning: Proceedings of the Thirteenth International Conference, pp. 148–156. Morgan Kaufmann, San Francisco (1996)

Furukawa, Y., Ponce, J.: Accurate, dense, and robust multi-view stereopsis. IEEE Transactions on Pattern Analysis and Machine Intelligence 32(8), 1362–1376 (2010)

Gerke, M., Kerle, N.: Automatic structural seismic damage assessment with airborn e oblique pictometry imagery. Photogrammetric Engineering & Remote Sensing 77(9) (in press, 2011)

Gerke, M.: Using horizontal and vertical building structure to constrain indirect sensor orientation. ISPRS Journal of Photogrammetry and Remote Sensing 66, 307–316 (2011)

Hartz, J.: Learning probabilistic structure graphs for classification and detection of object structure. In: IEEE Proceedings of the International Conference on Machine Learning and Applications (2009)

Haugerud, R.: Consistency analysis of world bank - imagecat - rit/kucera haiti earthquake lidar data (2010)

Huber, D., Kapuria, A., Donamukkala, R., Hebert, M.: Parts-based 3d object classification. In: Proceedings of the 2004 IEEE Computer Society Conference on Computer Vision and Pattern Recognition, CVPR 2004, vol. 2, pp. II-82–II-89 (2004)

Iba, W., Langley, P.: Induction of one-level decision trees. In: Ninth International Conference on Machine Learning, pp. 233–240 (1992)

Johnson, A., Hebert, M.: Using spin images for efficient object recognition in cluttered 3d scenes. IEEE Transactions on Pattern Analysis and Machine Intelligence 21(5), 433–449 (1999)

Kumar, S., Hebert, M.: Discriminative random fields. International Journal of Computer Vision 68(2), 179–201 (2006)

Lafferty, J., McCallum, A., Pereira, F.: Conditional random fields: Probabilistic models for segmenting and labeling sequence data. In: Int. Conf. on Machine Learning, pp. 282–289 (2001)

Petrie, G.: Systematic oblique aerial photography using multi frame cameras. Photogrammetric Engineering & Remote Sensing 75(2), 102–108 (2009)

Pictometry: Homepage Pictometry International Corporation (2011), http://www.pictometry.com (accessed April 30, 2011)

Vosselman, G., Maas, H.G. (eds.): Airborne and Terrestrial Laser Scanning. Whittles, Caithness (2010)

Wahl, E., Hillenbrand, G., Hirzinger, G.: Surflet-pair-relation histograms: a statistical 3d-shape representation for rapid classification. In: Proceedings of Fourth International Conference on 3-D Digital Imaging and Modeling, 3DIM 2003, pp. 474–481 (2003)

Conditional Random Fields for Urban Scene Classification with Full Waveform LiDAR Data

Joachim Niemeyer[1], Jan Dirk Wegner[1], Clément Mallet[2],
Franz Rottensteiner[1], and Uwe Soergel[1]

[1] Institute of Photogrammetry and GeoInformation, Leibniz University Hannover,
Nienburger Str. 1, 30167 Hannover, Germany
{niemeyer,wegner,rottensteiner,soergel}@ipi.uni-hannover.de
[2] Laboratoire MATIS, Institut Géographique National, Université Paris Est,
73 avenue de Paris, 94165 Saint-Mandé, France
clement.mallet@ign.fr

Abstract. We propose a context-based classification method for point clouds acquired by full waveform airborne laser scanners. As these devices provide a higher point density and additional information like echo width or type of return, an accurate distinction of several object classes is possible. However, especially in dense urban areas correct labelling is a challenging task. Therefore, we incorporate context knowledge by using Conditional Random Fields. Typical object structures are learned in a training step and improve the results of the point-based classification process. We validate our approach with two real-world datasets and by a comparison to Support Vector Machines and Markov Random Fields.

Keywords: Conditional Random Fields, 3D Point Cloud, Full Waveform LiDAR, Urban, Classification.

1 Introduction

Airborne LiDAR (Light Detection And Ranging) has become a standard technology for the acquisition of elevation data in remote sensing. A new generation of laser scanners captures the full waveform (FW) of the backscattered pulse and provides additional valuable hints for classification purposes, which is mainly used in forestry today. However, object detection in other types of complex scenes can also benefit from FW data. In urban areas the classification of a point cloud is an essential but challenging task, required to generate products such as three-dimensional (3D) city models. Urban scenes include many different objects like buildings of various shapes, hedges, single trees, grouped vegetation, fences, and ground in complex spatial arrangements (Fig. 1). Here, FW data can support the separation of objects that are close to each other. Further improvements can be achieved by considering spatial structures. Thus, the adjacency of some object classes can be modelled to be more likely than other combinations. For example, it is not likely that points labelled as buildings are surrounded by water. In this paper we present a powerful approach for contextual classification of a point cloud obtained with FW laser scanners.

U. Stilla et al. (Eds.): PIA 2011, LNCS 6952, pp. 233–244, 2011.

Fig. 1. 3D point cloud of an urban scene. Ground truth (left) and classified points (right). Classes *ground* (grey), *building* (red), and *vegetation* (green).

1.1 Related Work

Many approaches for object extraction from LiDAR data have been developed. Most of them focus on a certain object class like buildings or vegetation. In this case the classification task is reduced to a binary decision process. The classification of an entire point cloud into several object classes is more challenging. In some cases, non-probabilistic approaches like Support Vector Machines (SVM) are used. For instance, in our previous work (Mallet, 2010) a point-based multi-class SVM-classification was applied to FW data. Although SVM are known to work well even with high dimensional feature spaces, this type of approach labels each point without considering its neighbourhood. It may thus lead to inhomogeneous results in complex scenes such as urban areas. Other classifiers such as Random Forests exhibit similar characteristics (Chehata et al., 2009). An improvement can be achieved by incorporating contextual information. Common probabilistic approaches are based on graphical models such as Markov Random Fields (MRF) and Conditional Random Fields (CRF) (cf. Section 2). MRFs have become a standard technique for considering context in classification processes. As the application of graphical models to large LiDAR datasets leads to high computational costs, those context-based approaches became feasible only recently. First research on contextual point cloud labelling was carried out in the fields of robotics and mobile terrestrial laser scanning. Anguelov et al. (2005) proposed a classification of a terrestrial point cloud into four object classes with Associated Markov Networks (AMN), a subclass of MRF. This approach is based on a segmentation, assigning all points within a segment to the same class. Neighbouring points are assumed to belong to the same object with high probability. Thus, an adaptive smoothing of classification results is performed. In order to reduce the number of graph nodes, ground points are eliminated based on thresholds before the actual classification. Munoz et al. (2008) also used point-based AMNs, but they extended the original isotropic model to an anisotropic one, in order to emphasize certain orientations of edges. This directional information enables a more accurate classification of objects like power lines. Rusu et al. (2009) were interested in labelling an indoor robot environment described by point clouds. For object detection points are classified using CRFs according to the geometric surface they belong to, such as cylinders or planes. They applied a point-wise classification method, representing every point as a node of the graphical model. Compared to our application they deal with very few points (≈ 80000), and they even reduce this dataset by about 70% before the classification based on some restrictions concerning the objects' positions. CRF were also used by Lim and Suter (2007) for point-wise classification of terrestrial LiDAR data. They limit the computational complexity by adaptive point reduction. The same authors improved their approach (2009) by segmenting the points in a previous step and classifying these 'super-pixels' afterwards. They also considered both a local and a regional neighbourhood. An approach utilizing CRFs for remotely sensed LiDAR point clouds is presented in (Shapovalov et al., 2010). They classify a point cloud obtained from airborne laser scanning. Similar to the work mentioned previously, a segmentation is carried out in a preliminary step by k-means clustering. This step helps to cope with noise. However, small objects are not represented in the segmentation because they are merged with larger ones. As a consequence, important object details might be lost. A second restriction of the approach is feature selection. The authors solely use geometric features such as angles, spin images, height distributions, and shape parameters. On the one hand, this method is flexible because these features can be calculated for every point of a cloud, but on the other hand, usually additional point attributes such as intensity values are available and can be incorporated to improve the classification. Today, more features can be derived by the FW laser scanning technique. A combination of geometrical features and those obtained by FW analysis is expected to result in a more robust classification.

1.2 Contribution

We propose a new probabilistic approach for classification of LiDAR data by applying CRFs to point clouds. It combines three main advantages to improve the classification accuracy. Firstly, we utilize point clouds acquired by FW sensors. The point attributes like the echo width provide additional features and enable a more reliable separation of object classes. Secondly, we do not perform a segmentation, which usually leads to smoothing effects and loss of information, but we apply a point-based classification to preserve even small objects. Thirdly, CRFs provide a flexible classification framework that is also capable to model the spatial structure of the data. The proposed supervised classifier is able to learn context to find the most likely label configurations. Due to these three characteristics, our framework yields good results even in urban areas, which will be shown by an evaluation of the method.

2 Conditional Random Fields

Conditional Random Fields (CRF) have originally been proposed by Lafferty et al. (2001) to label sequential data. They are probabilistic models and thus provide probabilities instead of crisp decisions, which is a major benefit in terms of post-processing. CRFs belong to the family of graphical models as, for example, Markov Random Fields (MRF), and represent data as a graph $G(\boldsymbol{n}, \boldsymbol{e})$ consisting of nodes $\boldsymbol{n}$ and edges $\boldsymbol{e}$. The nodes $\boldsymbol{n}$ can represent spatial units such as pixels in images or points of point clouds. In our case, each node n_i corresponds to a single point i of the LiDAR point cloud. The edges $\boldsymbol{e}$ link pairs of adjacent nodes n_i and n_j in the graph; they can be used to represent contextual knowledge. The goal of our classification is to assign class labels $\boldsymbol{y}$ to all nodes $\boldsymbol{n}$ in $G(\boldsymbol{n}, \boldsymbol{e})$ based on data $\boldsymbol{x}$. Here, $\boldsymbol{y}$ is a vector whose element y_i corresponds to the class label of the node n_i. In the multi-class case, the labels can take more than two values, each corresponding to a single object class. Thus, the class labels of all nodes are determined simultaneously in this process, and multiple object classes are discerned.

In order to highlight the theoretical differences between MRFs and CRFs we will first give a short review of MRFs. A MRF is a *generative* approach that models the joint probabilities $P(\boldsymbol{x}, \boldsymbol{y})$ of the data and the labels, in a way similar to the Bayesian Theorem:

$$P(\boldsymbol{y}|\boldsymbol{x}) = \frac{1}{Z(\boldsymbol{x})} \exp\left(\sum_{n_i \in \boldsymbol{n}} \log P_i(x_i|y_i) + \sum_{n_i \in \boldsymbol{n}} \sum_{n_i \in N_i} \beta \cdot \delta(y_i = y_j) \right) . \quad (1)$$

In (1), the joint distribution $P(\boldsymbol{x}, \boldsymbol{y})$ is decomposed into a product of factors $P(\boldsymbol{x}|\boldsymbol{y}) \cdot P(\boldsymbol{y})$, whereas the probability of the data is represented by the partition function $Z(\boldsymbol{x})$, which acts as normalisation constant turning potentials into probabilities. The difference to the Bayes Theorem is that the prior $P(\boldsymbol{y})$ is replaced by a random field over the labels. The data observed at node n_i are represented by x_i, and P_i is the likelihood function for node n_i. N_i is the set of all nodes n_j linked to a particular node n_i by an edge. The function $\delta(y_i = y_j)$ yields $+1$ if $y_i = y_j$ and -1 otherwise. Hence, the prior term $\beta \cdot \delta(y_i = y_j)$ will increase the posterior probability if neighbouring labels are identical by a weight $\beta > 0$, whereas it will penalize the inequality of neighbouring labels. Both will lead to a smoothed classification (Kumar and Hebert, 2006).

CRFs, unlike MRFs, are *discriminative* models that model the posterior distribution $P(\boldsymbol{y}|\boldsymbol{x})$ directly, leading to a reduced model complexity compared to MRFs (Kumar and Hebert, 2006):

$$P(\boldsymbol{y}|\boldsymbol{x}) = \frac{1}{Z(\boldsymbol{x})} \exp\left(\sum_{n_i \in \boldsymbol{n}} A_i(\boldsymbol{x}, y_i) + \sum_{n_i \in \boldsymbol{n}} \sum_{n_j \in N_i} I_{ij}(\boldsymbol{x}, y_i, y_j) \right) . \quad (2)$$

In (2), the same symbols are used as in (1). $A_i(\boldsymbol{x}, y_i)$ is called the association potential. It links the data to the class labels and can be interpreted in a similar way as the data term in the MRF model. The difference is that the association potential of a single node n_i may depend on all the data $\boldsymbol{x}$ rather than only on the data observed at the node n_i. The assumption of conditionally independent features of different nodes inherent in the model described by (1) is relaxed for CRFs. $I_{ij}(\boldsymbol{x}, y_i, y_j)$ is called the pairwise interaction potential. Unlike the prior term in (1), it is not only dependent on the class labels at the two nodes linked by an edge, but also on potentially all the observed data $\boldsymbol{x}$. For instance, this property can be used to compensate for the smoothing effect of MRFs, if the observed data indicate that the class labels of two nodes are different. This along with the possibility to integrate the entire data $\boldsymbol{x}$ makes CRF a very flexible technique for contextual classification. The model in (2) only provides a framework that can be filled by various probabilistic classifiers for the potentials. We use generalized linear models (GLM) for both the association potential A_i and the interaction potential I_{ij}:

$$A_i(\boldsymbol{x}, y_i) = \log P'(y_i|\boldsymbol{x}) \text{ where } P'(y_i = l|\boldsymbol{x}) \propto \exp\left(\boldsymbol{w}_l^T \cdot \boldsymbol{h}_i(\boldsymbol{x})\right) \qquad (3)$$

$$I_{ij}(\boldsymbol{x}, y_i, y_j) = \begin{cases} \boldsymbol{v}_l^T \cdot \boldsymbol{\mu}_{ij}(\boldsymbol{x}) & \text{if } y_i = y_j = l \\ 0 & \text{if } y_i \neq y_j \end{cases} . \qquad (4)$$

In (3), $\boldsymbol{h}_i(\boldsymbol{x})$ is a feature vector of node n_i computed from data $\boldsymbol{x}$. As stated above, we are not restricted to data only of that node (as in the MRF case) but may also include data of other nodes. $P'(y_i = l|\boldsymbol{x})$ is the probability for the label of node n_i taking the value l given the data. $\boldsymbol{w}_l$ is a vector of feature weights for class l. There is one such vector per class, which has to be determined by training. In (4), $\boldsymbol{\mu}_{ij}(\boldsymbol{x})$ is an edge feature vector, determined for each edge in the graph and potentially depending on all observations, and $\boldsymbol{v}_l$ is an associated vector of feature weights that has to be learned from training data. Note that the weights are only required if the two labels are identical, so that there is again one such weight vector per class. As the MRF model in (1), the model for the interaction potentials (4) will have a smoothing effect, but the degree of smoothing is dependent on features $\boldsymbol{\mu}_{ij}(\boldsymbol{x})$: if the difference of the node features $\boldsymbol{h}_i(\boldsymbol{x})$ and $\boldsymbol{h}_j(\boldsymbol{x})$ is used to define $\boldsymbol{\mu}_{ij}(\boldsymbol{x})$, a high difference could suppress smoothing. This leads to small objects changes being better preserved if there is sufficient evidence in the data, which is a major advantage in complex urban areas.

3   CRFs Applied to 3D-FW Point Clouds

The classification is performed on point clouds acquired by airborne FW laser scanners. We are interested in the object classes *ground*, *building* and *vegetation*. In Section 3.1 we discuss the advantages of FW data for classification. Due to the irregular distribution of the LiDAR points, an adaptive graph structure is required for the CRF, which is presented in Section 3.2. The features are described in Section 3.3. Finally, training and inference are discussed in Section 3.4.

3.1   Full Waveform LiDAR

Classical laser scanners only provide the coordinates of first and last echoes. A new generation of LiDAR sensors is able to record the entire signal of the backscattered energy. Thus, information about any illuminated objects in the path of the pulse is contained in this waveform. We operate on pre-processed data in terms of a point cloud derived from Gaussian decomposition of raw wave-forms (Wagner et al., 2006). Apart from the position of the echoes (correspond-ing to peaks in the waveforms), additional indicators related to the geometry and the radiometric properties of the illuminated objects can be the amplitude A and the width σ of the Gaussians (Fig. 2). In particular, applications dealing with vegetation extraction benefit from this technology: the echo width and the fact that there are frequently multiple echoes have turned out to be discrimi-native features for vegetation (Chehata et al., 2009) and even enable single tree detection and tree species classification. Thus, most of the research in FW laser scanning has dealt with forestry applications. However, classifications of complex urban scenes can benefit from this additional information as well (Mallet, 2010). The echo width, for instance, is related to the slope of the illuminated object and to the local surface roughness because it is broadened on slanted or rough sur-faces. Consequently it can help to separate oblique roofs and flat ground points or smooth objects from vegetation. For classification tasks, multiple echoes as well as the local distribution of points also provide hints for points belonging to a certain object type. For example, a volumetric distribution indicates trees, whereas points distributed on a plane may be associated to ground or roofs.

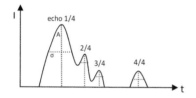

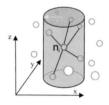

Fig. 2. Backscattered energy recorded by full waveform laser scanner. Gaus-sians are fitted to the sampled signal. Features amplitude A and width σ can be used to characterise echoes.

Fig. 3. Generation of graph structure. All points within a vertical cylinder with radius r are linked by edges to the currently investigated point n_i in the centre.

3.2   Graph Architecture

Compared to images a point cloud is more complex, because points are irreg-ularly distributed in 3D space. There is no straightforward definition of the neighbourhood that can be used to define the edges of the graph. In contrast, images are arranged in a lattice, and each pixel has a defined number of neigh-bours (usually four or eight). Thus, a graph structure with an adaptive number of edges per node is required for point clouds in order to capture locally vary-ing point densities. In our application, each point (node) n_i is linked to the points located within a vertical cylinder of radius r whose axis passes through n_i (Fig. 3). This radius, which has to be specified by the user, and the point density determine the number of neighbours of each node and thus the number of edges emanating from a node. The impact of varying radii r is analysed in

Section 4.4. We chose a cylinder for defining the local neighbourhood in order to make sure that points on tree canopies and points near the roof edges will have links to ground points. This will be very helpful in classification because, for instance, the local height differences can be used as edge features, which can give valuable hints for the local configuration of classes. An alternative definition of the local neighbourhood, e.g. a spherical neighbourhood or k nearest neighbours, could not ensure this important information to be preserved. In any case, based on the cylindrical neighbourhood, we construct a graphical model with a varying number of edges per node according to the local point density. This results in a fairly complex graph structure.

3.3   Features

For each 3D point, a set of geometrical and FW features can be determined. In our previous work (Chehata et al., 2009), the contribution of these features to urban point cloud classification using Random Forests was analysed. Based on the experience gained in that work, we selected ten features for classification in our CRF-based method: amplitude, echo width, normalized echo number, height difference between first and last echo, distance to ground, variances of normal vectors and elevations, residuals of an estimated plane as well as the features omnivariance and planarity based on the eigenvalues of the local scatter matrix. A detailed description of the features can be found in (Chehata et al., 2009). In addition, a bias parameter of value one is added to each feature vector (Kumar and Hebert, 2006). These features are determined for each node n_i and represent the node feature vectors $h_i(x)$ in the association potentials (3). The edge features $\mu_{ij}(x)$ in the interaction potentials (4) are defined as the differences of the two adjacent node feature vectors, thus $\mu_{ij}(x) = h_i(x) - h_j(x)$.

3.4   Training and Inference

Due to the fact that our graph $G(n, e)$ contains cycles, exact training and inference is computationally intractable, so that approximative methods have to be applied in both cases.

The weight vectors w_l and v_l for the node and edge features in the association (3) and interaction potentials (4) are derived by training. For that purpose, a fully labelled point cloud is required. The training task is a non-linear numerical optimisation problem, in which a cost function is minimized. Following Vishwanathan et al. (2006), we use the limited memory Broyden-Fletcher-Goldfarb-Shanno (L-BFGS) method for optimisation of the objective function $f = -\log(P(\theta|x, y))$, where θ is a parameter vector containing the weight vectors w_l and v_l for all classes l. The L-BFGS method requires the computation of the objective function and its gradient as well as an estimation of the partition function $Z(x)$ (2) in each iteration; we use the method described in (Vishwanathan et al., 2006) in the variant with Loopy Belief Propagation (LBP) (Frey and MacKay, 1998) for that purpose.

LBP, a standard iterative message passing algorithm for graphs with cycles, is also used for inference, i.e., for determining the optimum configuration of labels based on maximising $P(\boldsymbol{y}|\boldsymbol{x})$ (2). Although this technique does not ensure convergence to the global optimum, it has been shown to provide good results.

The result of inference is a probability value per class for each 3D point. Maximum a posteriori (MAP) selects the highest probability and assigns the corresponding object class label to the point.

4   Experiments

In this section we present experiments in order to evaluate the classification performance of our proposed method. First, we describe the datasets. Then, the point-wise CRF classification results are assessed on two datasets. For performance validation a comparison to state-of-the-art classifiers SVM and MRF is done. An analysis of the impact of varying neighbourhood size keeping in mind the computational costs is given afterwards. This section finishes with a discussion of our approach.

4.1   Datasets

We evaluate our algorithm on two airborne LiDAR datasets, acquired by a RIEGL LMS-Q560 FW laser scanner (under leaf-on conditions), depicted in Fig. 4. The first one, Bonnland, is a rural scene in Germany of about 2.02 ha, and consists of scattered buildings, streets, single trees, forested areas, and grassland. 759,790 points were recorded. The other dataset (553,033 points, 1.93 ha), was acquired in Kiel, also situated in Germany, and has a suburban character with regularly arranged buildings, streets, and lots of vegetation. The point density is about $3.7 \frac{points}{m^2}$ and $2.9 \frac{points}{m^2}$, respectively. We fixed the cylinder radius according to (5) (Section 4.4) to 0.75 m (Bonnland) and 1 m (Kiel).

Ground truth was generated by labelling both point clouds manually. This fully classified 3D data can be considered to be almost accurate and is used for training and validation.

4.2   Results of CRF-Classification

For evaluation purposes we divided each dataset into three parts of nearly the same sizes of about 250,000 points (Bonnland) and 184,330 points (Kiel). We performed three-fold cross-validation for both datasets. Parameters are trained on two parts of the data and tested on the third. This is done three times (i.e., folds), each time with another combination of the data subsets. Finally, we report the mean performance parameters of all three trials. Experiments show that our approach leads to good results. Two subsets of the classification results are illustrated in Fig. 4. In particular the overall accuracy for dataset Bonnland is 94.3 % (Table 1) with a standard deviation of 0.2 % for the three trials. For all three classes completeness and correctness rates are above 88 %. The overall accuracy in Kiel amounts to 89.3 % (standard deviation 0.6 %).

Fig. 4. Classification results of datasets Bonnland (*left*) and Kiel (*right*)

Table 1. Classification performance with completeness and correctness rates [%]

Bonnland		SVM	MRF	CRF
ground	corr.	97.4	94.5	95.5
	comp.	85.5	95.6	95.5
building	corr.	28.9	94.3	88.1
	comp.	82.0	81.7	88.2
vegetation	corr.	90.9	92.5	94.0
	comp.	71.6	93.4	93.9
overall accuracy		**80.3**	**93.8**	**94.3**

Kiel		SVM	MRF	CRF
ground	corr.	78.2	86.6	91.1
	comp.	93.1	94.4	93.5
building	corr.	52.5	93.1	85.7
	comp.	67.8	75.2	86.6
vegetation	corr.	81.6	85.2	88.2
	comp.	26.0	81.4	83.4
overall accuracy		**74.3**	**87.1**	**89.3**

4.3   Comparison to SVM and MRF

In order to evaluate the effectiveness of our CRF model, we compared the results of our method to those obtained by two state-of-the-art classifiers: SVM and MRF. SVM are a common approach for a large variety of classification tasks. This non-probabilistic method yields good performance, but a drawback is the very local functional principle. MRF overcome this disadvantage by incorporating contextual information into the classification process. We used GLM and Potts model as prior terms for MRF. Table 1 depicts the results of the comparison. As expected, the non-probabilistic classification based on SVM (with Gaussian kernel) leads to the worst results. Note that there are many class assignment errors because a considerable number of vegetation points are labelled as *buildings*. Thus, the correctness rate for building points is only 28 % in Bonnland. In addition, several errors occur on roofs. Due to the point-based classification, no context is incorporated (despite of feature calculation within a small local neighbourhood) and it is not possible to separate flat objects into roof or ground. An improved classification performance is obtained with MRFs. In case of Bonnland, the overall accuracy increases by 13.5 percentage (93.8 % vs. 80.3 %). Although this rate is obviously better, especially the completeness rate of object class *building* is relatively low (81 % Bonnland and 75 % Kiel). CRFs further improve the results. Fig. 5 gives an example for the different performances. It shows a building with oblique and flat roof parts (highlighted with arrows). Especially the flat-roofed part is difficult to classify due to features

Fig. 5. Comparison of results obtained from SVM, MRF and CRF classification. Yellow arrows show a flat roof, whereas blue arrows mark an oblique roof.

similar to ground. SVM and MRF cannot detect it, whereas CRF extracts the roofs nearly without errors. It benefits from the more general model and enables a correct classification.

4.4   Optimal Neighbourhood Size

A critical parameter is the radius r of the cylinder used for graph construction. It is the only one that has to be specified manually. As the number of neighbours within this radius is strongly correlated to the point density of the scene, we analysed this number directly. Fig. 6 depicts the relation of overall accuracy and the number of linked edges, which corresponds to the number of neighbours. We performed tests for 1-10, 15 and 20 neighbours per node. It can be seen, that increasing the number of edges leads to slightly increased overall accuracy. The best result is achieved for 20 edges. However, since the computational complexity increases considerably with higher number of edges, we decided to use the local maximum at 7 neighbours for the experiments. The relation between point density, number of edges and cylinder radius r is given by

$$r = \sqrt{\frac{\text{number of edges}}{\text{point density} \cdot \pi}} \; . \tag{5}$$

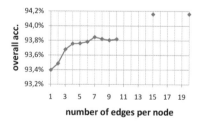

Fig. 6. Overall accuracy related to the number of edges per node

4.5   Computational Costs

The high degree of obtained details with the CRF-classification is related to a higher computational burden. Consisting of many nodes and edges, CRF applied to point clouds are computationally expensive. Especially the training is time intensive due to the iterative optimisation steps, whereas the final classification time is negligible. For a training area of Kiel consisting of 403,221 nodes and 1,775,582 edges with 11 features each, 253 min were required. The classification of the unlabelled point cloud with 177,343 nodes and 770,735 edges took 0.9 min. In contrast, parameter training for MRF of the same area with the same number of nodes and edges took 202 min. We processed the tests on a machine with a 2.8 GHz Quad-Core CPU and 16 GB RAM.

4.6   Discussion

Our experiments revealed that CRFs show the best performance for point cloud labelling. In contrast to non-probabilistic local classifiers like SVM the accuracy can be improved using graphical models that take into account context information. Building roofs, for example, are classified correctly (Fig. 5, yellow arrows). Compared to a standard MRF our approach further improved the overall accuracy slightly, in case of Kiel by 2.2 percentage. In particular, completeness rates of classes *building* and *vegetation* benefit from using CRFs (Table 1). Complex objects like the flat roof in Fig. 5 (yellow arrows) can be classified correctly. Although it is computationally costly in terms of time and memory, this approach provides a FW point cloud classification with high accuracies and preserves details due to the point based method. Thus it is suitable for advanced requirements in remote sensing. An additional advantage of CRFs are the directly resulting probabilities, which allow the introduction of a separate class for points with low posteriors $P(y|x)$.

5   Conclusions and Outlook

In this paper we have addressed the task of 3D point cloud classification. We applied the probabilistic machine learning approach Conditional Random Fields (CRF) to label several object classes, namely *ground*, *buildings*, and *vegetation*. By incorporating local context and full waveform features classification performance is improved. Our method shows good results for our two datasets of Bonnland and Kiel. Overall accuracy rates yield 94.3 % and 89.3 %, respectively. It is demonstrated that the results are more accurate compared to state-of-the-art classifiers Support Vector Machines (SVM) and Markov Random Fields (MRF). Future work will comprise a more sophisticated formulation of contextual knowledge. In urban areas, for instance, parcels are often bounded by hedges or fences. These typical arrangements can be used to improve classification results further. Moreover, we are going to validate other training and inference methods.

Acknowledgment. We used the 'Matlab toolbox UGM', developed by Mark Schmidt, www.cs.ubc.ca/~schmidtm/Software/UGM.html. This work is funded by the German Research Foundation (Deutsche Forschungsgemeinschaft, DFG).

References

Anguelov, D., Taskar, B., Chatalbashev, V., Koller, D., Gupta, D., Heitz, G., Ng, A.: Discriminative learning of markov random fields for segmentation of 3d scan data. In: Proc. of IEEE CVPR, vol. 2, pp. 169–176 (2005)

Chehata, N., Guo, L., Mallet, C.: Airborne lidar feature selection for urban classification using random forests. IntArchPhRS 38(3), 207–212 (2009)

Frey, B., MacKay, D.: A revolution: Belief propagation in graphs with cycles. In: Advances in Neural Information Processing Systems, vol. 10, pp. 479–485 (1998)

Kumar, S., Hebert, M.: Discriminative random fields. International Journal of Computer Vision 68(2), 179–201 (2006)

Lafferty, J., McCallum, A., Pereira, F.: Conditional random fields: Probabilistic models for segmenting and labeling sequence data. In: Proc. 18th Int. Conference on Machine Learning, pp. 282–289 (2001)

Lim, E., Suter, D.: Conditional random field for 3d point clouds with adaptive data reduction. In: Int. Conference on Cyberworlds, pp. 404–408 (2007)

Lim, E., Suter, D.: 3d terrestrial lidar classifications with super-voxels and multi-scale conditional random fields. Comp. Aided Design 41(10), 701–710 (2009)

Mallet, C.: Analysis of Full-Waveform Lidar Data for Urban Area Mapping. Ph.D. thesis, Télécom ParisTech (2010)

Munoz, D., Vandapel, N., Hebert, M.: Directional associative markov network for 3-d point cloud classification. In: Int. Symposium 3DPVT (2008)

Rusu, R., Holzbach, A., Blodow, N., Beetz, M.: Fast geometric point labeling using conditional random fields. In: IEEE IROS, pp. 7–12 (2009)

Shapovalov, R., Velizhev, A., Barinova, O.: Non-associative markov networks for 3d point cloud classification. In: PCV 2010. IntArchPhRS, vol. 38(A), pp. 103–108 (2010)

Vishwanathan, S., Schraudolph, N., Schmidt, M., Murphy, K.: Accelerated training of conditional random fields with stochastic gradient methods. In: 23rd Int. Conference on Machine Learning, pp. 969–976 (2006)

Wagner, W., Ullrich, A., Ducic, V., Melzer, T., Studnicka, N.: Gaussian decomposition and calibration of a novel small-footprint full-waveform digitising airborne laser scanner. ISPRS Journal of Photogrammetry and Remote Sensing 60(2), 100–112 (2006)

Statistical Unbiased Background Modeling for Moving Platforms

Michael Kirchhof[1] and Uwe Stilla[2]

[1] Herborn, Germany
michael.kirchhof@gmx.de
[2] Photogrammetry and Remote Sensing, Technische Universitaet Muenchen
stilla@tum.de

Abstract. Statistical background modeling is a standard technique for the detection of moving objects in a static scene. Nevertheless, the state-of-the-art approaches have several lacks for short sequences or quasi-stationary scenes. Quasi-static means that the ego-motion of the sensor is compensated by image processing. Our focus of attention goes back to the modeling of the pixel process, as it was introduced by Stauffer and Grimson. For quasi-stationary scenes the assignment of a pixel to an origin is uncertain. This assignment is an independent random process that contributes to the gray value. Since the typical update schemes are biased we introduce a novel update scheme based on the join mean and join variance of two independent distributions. The presented method can be seen as an update for the initial guess for more sophisticated algorithms that optimize the spatial distribution.

1 Introduction

Detection of foreground objects and moving objects is an important task in traffic monitoring and security surveillance applications and is still of growing interest in computer vision and remote sensing. A lot of work has been done in analyzing the spectral, spatial, and temporal domain isolated from each other. There are already some approaches that are able to combine the spectral and the temporal domain. Depending on the application the contributions rely on different assumptions. In these approaches all pixels are treated independently from each other. The spatial connectivity is ignored in the modeling but addressed in the post-processing. While our application is based on a stabilization of a non-stationary camera which results in an spatial bias over time, we have to consider the spatial connections in the modeling as well. These scenes are called quasi-stationary. Many contributions address the stabilization of sequences or even homography estimation which can be used for this task. Some representative contributions are (Kirchhof and Stilla 2006), (Strehl and Aggarwal 2000) and (Davis 1998). Typically, the registration in terms of homographies or affine mappings are computed with Random-Sample-Consensus (RANSAC) (Fischler and Bolles 1981) from a set of corresponding features (Shi and Tomasi 1994) between consecutive frames. This registration can be stitched together to perform mosaicking which is equivalent to a complete stabilization of the sequence.

U. Stilla et al. (Eds.): PIA 2011, LNCS 6952, pp. 245–256, 2011.

1.1 Motivation

Background subtraction is a well known robust method to detect moving objects. While the state-of-the-art methods work well for stationary scenes, it is a challenging task to adapt them for non-stationary scenes. The time to observe an image region can be very short. Therefore the time to initialize the local distributions is limited. The more adaptive algorithms work generally with a Gaussian single model (GSM). But they have the disadvantage that the background distribution has to be learned from images of the empty scene. This can not be ensured for non-stationary scenes. In addition, the registration error for consecutive frames can not be modeled yet. The requirement of spatial information in the modeling process changes the focus of attention to the update process. The goal is to treat this information correctly. While various contributions focus on optimizing the detection map due to spatial soundness, our focus was the pixel process in order to compute a better initial guess for the detection map. There are two problems that require an optimization: First, in the traditional formulation of the update scheme the estimator for the variance is biased. Second, as mentioned before, we address the problem of a quasi-stationary camera. Therefore the spatial bias has to be modeled. In addition, the weights within the update where optimized with respect to the short observation time. The goal was to reduce initialization time while keeping the robustness of the background model. Since our application is a quasi-stationary scene we assume that the background can be modeled by one single Gaussian distribution. But in contrast to the common approaches we store the statistics for the "foreground" as well. This enables us to revise our initial decision if the observed pixel is foreground or not. Additionally this distribution can be used to decide if a foreground object has recently stopped its motion.

1.2 Related Work

For a stationary camera Stauffer and Grimson modeled the measuring process of each individual pixel as a statistical process defined by a sum of Gaussian distributions (Stauffer and Grimson 1999). This process is called pixel process in the following. Having such a distribution one can statistically decide between stationary and moving scene regions resulting in a detection map. Recent developments focus on the optimization of the detection map taking the spatial information into account. In general this leads to a formulation of Markov-Random-Field (Zhou et al. 2005), (Seki et al. 1997). The optimization of this random field is known to be np-hard, but various methods are already proposed to solve this problem. In this contribution we disregard this spatial information and focus on the statistical modeling.

For quasi-stationary scenes background pixel can often be observed in less than 50 frames. This 50 frames are often the lower bound for initialization of the statistics for a Gaussian-multi-model (GMM) as it was introduced by Stauffer and Grimson (1999). In contrast to the Gaussian-single-model can be initialized quite fast but the statistic has to be learned from an empty scene (Wren 1997).

2   Methodology

In this section we introduce our improvements for the statistical modeling and for the update of the distributions. The proposed method has two parameters: 1. The period of time an object has to be observed at the same location until it is labeled as recently stopped and 2. the period of time an object has to be observed at the same location until it is treated as background. In addition to this at least a lower bound for the variance of the individual pixels has to be given since a zero variance can be computed from the image but is not valid for further processing. This lower bound can be interpreted as the sensors white noise.

2.1   Modeling of the Pixel Process

In analogy to the approach of Stauffer and Grimson (1999) we assume that the gray value $F(x_0, y_0, t)$ at the pixel position (x_0, y_0) and the time instance t is a random process depending on the origin of the projection. This pixel process $\{X_1, \ldots, X_t\} = \{F(x_0, y_0, t) : 1 \leq t \leq T\}$ is represented by a sequence of random variables X_i. Assuming further that the projection origin is constant and equally illuminated over time the sequence $\{X_1, \ldots, X_t\} = \{F(x_0, y_0, t) : 1 \leq t \leq T\}$ is a normal distributed measure of the true gray value at the origin. Its estimate is given by the mean μ_{x_0, y_0} and the corresponding standard deviation σ_{x_0, y_0}. The assumption of a constant illumination is no hard restriction since a slide change is addressed by a limited weight of the resulting distribution.

To reduce the complexity and for better readability we skip the pixel position for the rest of the paper. For an ideal sensor we can assume that the standard deviation σ_{0t} of the sensors noise in gray values is about 1–2 gray values. The same assumption still holds if the origin of the pixel is at the foreground. Because of this a mixture of two Gaussian distributions is used to model the pixel process. In addition to this in many approaches (e.g. Stauffer and Grimson 1999) the background is modeled as a mixture of some Gaussians as well (GMM). This is because repetitive motions for example leaves in the wind should not be treated as foreground. Our approach can easily be adapted to this models, but in this contribution we keep it as simple as posible.

In practice one has to consider that almost all outdoor scenes are instationary. This is because the camera is affected by wind, vibrations of the platform or even motion of the platform. After image-based stabilization (or registration) of these scenes we call them quasi-stationary. Taken this into account, we assume that the registration has an uncertainty of one pixel. Because of this we treat the gray value measured in an individual pixel as normal distributed measurement as well. While we take the gray value of the individual pixel as estimate for its mean μ_t we estimate the variance σ_t^2 in the frame t from the local gray value variance $\sigma_{x_0, y_0, t}^2$ in a 3 by 3 neighborhood. The superposition of the sensors noise σ_{0t} and the registration error results in the local variance

$$\sigma_t^2 = \sigma_{0t}^2 + \sigma_{x_0,y_0,t}^2. \tag{1}$$

To build up a recursive formulation for the weighted mean μ_{t+1} of the random variables $X_1, \ldots, X_t$ and the random variable X_{t+1} the age of the distribution a_t, namely the number of contributing measurements has to be taken into account. To ensure that the background estimate adapts the current illumination condition the age of the distribution is limited by a threshold $a_{\max}$ which we determine by

$$a_{\max} = \text{frame rate} * ti. \tag{2}$$

The time ti defines the memory length of the distribution. Experiments have proved that a time of one minute is applicable for all natural scenes. At the same time the weight of a distribution should be reduced, if it is not observed. The resulting update scheme for the age is given by

$$a_{t+1} = \left\{ \begin{array}{l} \min\left(\{a_t + 1, a_{\max}\}\right), \text{ if match} \\ \max\left(a_t - \Delta_a a_{\max}, 0\right), \text{ otherwise.} \end{array} \right\} \tag{3}$$

This is equivalent to continuously losing information that is older than $a_{\max}$. The oblivion can be modeled as well by computing the mean value from the last t measurements. But in contrast to the introduced update scene this would require to store the last t measurements and much more operations have to be done to compute the distribution. But the method would be much slower and need much more memory space. A comparable approach can be found in (Wren 1997).

Let us summarize the model of the pixel process before we introduce the update scheme:

The sequence of gray values of an individual pixel after stabilization is treated as a sequence of random variables $\{X_1, \ldots, X_t\} = \{F(x_0, y_0, t) : 1 \leq t \leq T\}$. Their distribution is modeled as sum of two Gaussian distributions: One for the background and one for the foreground. Each of them is modeled with the three parameters: (limited) age, mean and standard deviation. Because of the registration error the random variables X_i are biased as well. This bias is modeled as Gaussian distribution as well with mean X_i. The corresponding standard deviation is estimated from the 3 by 3 neighborhood of the individual pixel.

2.2   Updating the Distributions

Before we can define how to update the distributions we have to define what to update. Assuming we want to ensure that 99% of the visible background is correctly detected, we get a matching distance of $3\sigma_t$ for the background statistic. Therefore a grey value g is defined to match the distribution $N(\mu_t, \sigma_t)$ if $\|g - \mu_t\| <= 3\sigma_t$. An update of the distribution of the weighted mean $\hat{X}_t \sim N(\mu_t, \sigma_t)$ is only done if the normal distributed grey value $X_{t+1} \sim N(X_{t+1}, \sigma_{t+1})$ matches the distribution.

Let $w_{\hat{t}}$ and w_{t+1} be the weights of the distributions $N(\mu_t, \sigma_t)$ respectively $N(X_{t+1}, \sigma_{t+1})$. Than the mean of the mixed distribution $\widehat{X}_{t+1} \sim \frac{w_{\hat{t}}}{w_{\hat{t}}+w_{t+1}} N(\mu_t, \widehat{\sigma}_t) + \frac{w_{t+1}}{w_{\hat{t}}+w_{t+1}} N(X_{t+1}, \sigma_{t+1})$ is given by

$$\mu_{t+1} = E\left(\frac{w_{\hat{t}}\widehat{X}_t + w_{t+1}X_{t+1}}{w_{\hat{t}} + w_{t+1}}\right) \tag{4}$$

$$= \frac{w_{\hat{t}}}{w_{\hat{t}} + w_{t+1}} E\left(\widehat{X}_t\right) + \frac{w_{t+1}}{w_{\hat{t}} + w_{t+1}} E(X_{t+1}) \tag{5}$$

$$= \frac{\mu_t w_{\hat{t}} + X_{t+1}w_{t+1}}{w_{\hat{t}} + w_{t+1}}. \tag{6}$$

The weights w can be computed directly from the corresponding age a of the distributions

$$w_{\hat{t}} = a_t \tag{7}$$
$$w_{t+1} = 1 \tag{8}$$

or in combination with the standard deviation σ

$$w_{\hat{t}} = \frac{a_t}{\sigma_t^2} \tag{9}$$
$$w_{t+1} = \frac{1}{\sigma_{t+1}^2}. \tag{10}$$

In the first case the data is only weighted by its age. Therefore the weight of each measurement only depends on the size of the contributing dataset. In this case no assumptions on the underlying distribution are made. Therefore the resulting mean and variance are simply the first two moments of the underlying distribution.

In the second case one assumes that both 'measurement sets' are representatives of the same normal distributed random variable. One can prove with Chauchy-Schwarz-inequality that the weighting with the variances gives the smallest variance for the resulting normal distribution.

The state-of-the-art update for the variance is given by

$$\widehat{\sigma}_{t+1}^2 = \frac{w_{\hat{t}}}{N} var\left(\widehat{X}_t\right) + \frac{w_{t+1}}{N} var(X_{t+1}), \tag{11}$$

where $N = w_{\hat{t}} + w_{t+1}$.

The computation of the unbiased update for the variance is more complex. Computing the expectation value for the variance of the joint probability density function finally results in

$$\widehat{\sigma}_{t+1}^2 = \frac{w_{\hat{t}}}{N}\left(\widehat{\sigma}_t^2 + \mu_t^2\right) + \frac{w_{t+1}}{N}\left(\sigma_{t+1}^2 + X_{t+1}^2\right) - \mu_{t+1}^2. \tag{12}$$

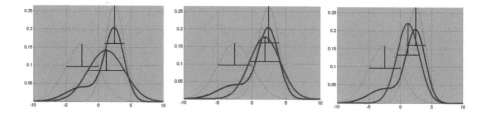

Fig. 1. Example of a mixture of normal distributions with weights 0.4 and 0.6. The red curve is the resulting normal distribution. Left: Mean and variance are computed by weighted mean. Middle: Mean and variance are computed by weighted mean including the Mahalanobis-distance. This is equivalent to the assumtion that the distributions belong to the same normal distribution. Right: mean and variance are computed with the unbiased estimator excluding the Mahalanobis-distance.

In the paper of Stauffer and Grimson (1999) the weights in the update scheme are multiplied by the Mahalanobis-distance ρ between the observation X_{t+1} and the matching distribution $N\left(\mu_{i,t}, \sigma_{i,t}\right)$ with density function

$$\eta\left(x, \mu_{i,t}, \sigma_{i,t}\right) = \frac{1}{\sqrt{2\pi}\sigma_{i,t}} e^{-\frac{\left(x - \mu_{i,t}\right)^2}{\sigma_{i,t}^2}} \tag{13}$$

which is given by

$$\rho = \eta\left(X_{t+1}, \mu_{i,t}, \sigma_{i,t}\right). \tag{14}$$

This represents the assumption that all the contributing data belong to the same normal distribution and results in the smallest variance Fig. 1 middle. In our case we assume that the observations X_t belong to individual distributions and the resulting mean and variance are simply the first two moments of an unknown mixture of distributions. The resulting distribution in the biased case is shown in Fig. 1 left. The very large variance is due to the biased variance estimation. In comparison Fig. 1 right shows the same mixture of Gaussians but combined with the proposed unbiased estimator.

3   Experiments

In this section we compare the performance of the proposed algorithm with a implementation of Stauffer and Grimson 1999, a modification with local variance of the observations and a second modification with local variance and the unbiased update scheme. The output of the algorithms were all smoothed with the same morphological opening and a simple bounding box over the connected components. These bounding boxes where evaluated in terms of completeness

Fig. 2. Left: One image of the benchmark scene provided by the OTCBVS workshop. Right:

and correctness. Correctness is measured by the correct positives divided by the sum of correct positives and false positives; completeness by dividing the correct positives by the sum of correct positives and false negatives. As benchmark scene we used stationary thermal video from the OTCBVS workshop (see Fig. 2). Since we are interested in the performance of the algorithm due to matching noise of a previous stabilization approach, the scene was virtually shaken in both image directions by an independent normal distributed registration error of 0, 0.1, 0.3, 0.5 and 0.7 pixels. To make the results comparable the shaken scenes were stored, so that all algorithms use exact identical input data. All algorithms used the same parameter (learning rate 0.002 and matching distance 3σ). Figure 3 shows the resulting completeness and correctness for all four algorithms. About five percent of the resulting detection maps were analyzed to achieve the results. Figure 2 right gives an impression of the evaluated results.

Coming back to the focus, the proposed algorithm was performed on a thermal scene taken by a helicopter showing two persons walking (see figure 4). The registration between consecutive frames given by a homography is computed by RANSAC from a set of correspondences tracked with KLT (Lucas and Kanade 1981). This procedure is very robust and not effected by moving image region due to foreground objects. Nevertheless the registration error after RANSAC will be much more than one or two pixel. An initial weak detection map is computed by simply threshold the gray value difference between consecutive frames. All pixels in the weak background (inversion of the detection map) are used to minimize the gray value difference between consecutive frames. The resulting registration error is within one pixel which is sufficient for the proposed background modeling approach presented in section 2.

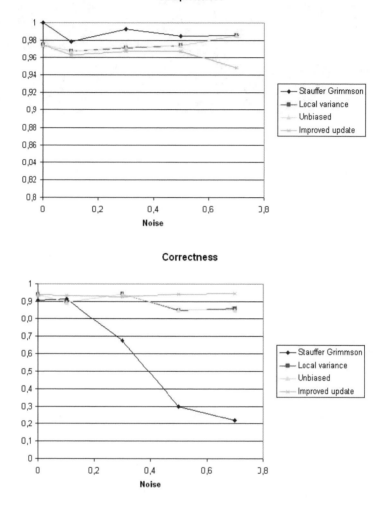

Fig. 3. Top: Correctness of the algorithms plotted over the registration noise. Increasing the noise has a heavy impact to the correctness of the state of the art approach. While adding the local variance reduces the impact the optimization of the update scene results in almost no correlation between noise and correctness. Bottom: Completeness of the algorithms plotted over the registration noise. Increasing the noise does rarely affect the resulting completeness for all algorithms. The deviation in the performance of the algorithms is smaller than 1.0%.

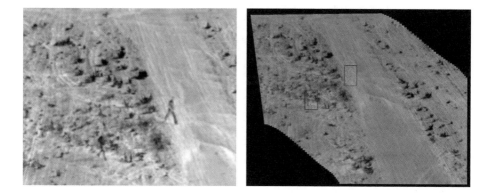

Fig. 4. Left: One frame of the thermal scene taken by a helicopter. Right: Exemplary result of the proposed method. The figure shows the computed background with the detection result.

To show the underlying motion the resulting background model (mean of the first distribution) was superimposed by the detection map (Fig. 4). The detection map belongs to the frame of Fig. 4.

In a third experiment the long term behavior of the algorithm was tested. For this task the parking lot in front of a supermarket was observed 25 hours from a roof in the neighborhood (see Fig. 5). The goal here was to show that the algorithm was able to capture the continuous changes in illumination without affecting the detection results. Figure 5 shows an exemplary detection map for a frame in the middle of the sequence.

Fig. 5. Left: One frame of the long term thermal scene taken from a roof. Right: The same frame overlaid with the detection map (blue) of the proposed method.

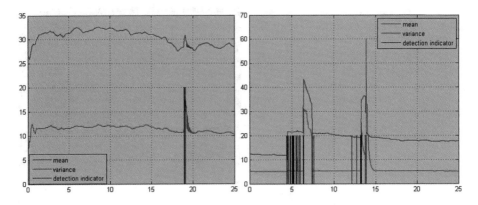

Fig. 6. Mean and variance of the background evaluated for an isolated pixel on a 25 hours measurement. Black indicates detections. Left: The pixel corresponds to an origin at the park. The distribution adapts to the illumination without any false detections. Right: Origin of the pixel is located at a parked lot.

Figure 6 shows the parameters of the distribution and the detection result over time. Figure 6 right belongs to a parking lot where a car parked from about 6:00 am to 7:00 am. The motion of the car is indicated by the detection indicator. After a short time the car is defined as background. Because the car is hot the mean jumps up. While standing there the car cools down to the background temperature.

4   Discussion and Conclusion

We introduced various adoption to the statistical background modeling approach introduced by Stauffer and Grimson 1999. This adoption makes the algorithm able to cope with scenes from a moving observer. The sequences are stabilized with a homography. The tested state-of-the-art version of the approache is not able to cope with the resulting registration error. Figure 3 shows a comparison of the performance under various noise conditions. The noise has almost no effect to the completeness which means that almost all objects are detected. This was expected because foreground objects result in a large gray value difference and the variance is only hardly affected by the registration noise. In regions with a large gradient the registration error leads to larger gray value differences than usual for a stationary sequence. Therefore the noise has a heavy impact to the correctness. Without modeling the registration error the correctness decreases to 0.2. The modeling of the registration error in terms of local variance estimation reduces the false alarm rate increasing the correctness in the noisiest case to 0.85. Obviously the improvement with the unbiased estimator has almost no impact on the result. The reason seems that the variation between matching distributions are quite small so that the reduction of the variance is very low. The novel introduced update scheme in combination with the local variance and the unbiased estimator is not affected by the noise. The correctness is almost stable with 0.95 which is much better than expected. Coming to the conclusion of the first experiment the introduced methodology is almost invariant under noise of less than one pixel. Analyzing isolated the unbiased variance estimator brings almost no improvement unless mathematical soundness.

In the second experiment figure 2 and 4 we switched from simulated registration noise to a real 'quasi-stationary scene'. The scene captured by a helicopter shows two people walking through the desert. As can be seen in Figure 2 without the motion information it would be hardly possible to distinguish the pedestrians from the ground. Even though the background could not be learned from an empty scene there are no false detections in the regions which were initialized with the pedestrians. The experiment proves that the algorithm captures the requirements for a stabilized scene.

The third experiment (Fig. 5 and 6) focuses on the long term stability of the algorithm and its adaptiveness to changes in illumination. The algorithm is able to change between background and foreground definition within the defined time. Therefore hot vehicles become background and one can observe their cooling down. This adoption is very important when scene regions are observed for a short time only while the background can not be learned from an empty scene as it's usual for sequences from a moving observer.

4.1   Future Work

The results of all experiments can be highly improved by optimizing the spacial connectivity of the detection maps. Since all statistics are known one can apply EM optimization to the data (Vasconceles, and Lippman 1997) or Markov-Random-Field (Zhou et al. 2005) (Seki et al. 1997).

The integration of more complex stabilization approaches without planarity assumption have to be done. One interesting class of approaches for this task deal with multiple-homography assuming only a rigid scene geometry. Some investigation have already be done by Zelnik-Manor and Irani (2002), Kirchhof (2008) and Shashua and Avidan (1996). A lot of optimization has to be done do make the estimation of this unknown set robust and reproducible. Therefore the rigidity of the background is already used to decrease the degree of freedom. Using the already known detection map from the previous frame might further increase the robustness of this algorithms while 'non-rigid' foreground obejects are present. A similar feedback loop was used in (Kirchhof and Stilla 2006) to make homography estimation more robust.

References

Davis, J.: Mosaics of Scenes with Moving Objects. In: Computer Vision and Pattern Recognition, pp. 354–360 (1998)

Fischler, M.A., Bolles, R.C.: Random Sample Consensus: A Paradigm for Model Fitting with Applications to Image Analysis and Automated Cartography. Communications of the Association for Computing Machinery 24(6), 381–395 (1981)

Kirchhof, M., Stilla, U.: Detection of moving objects in airborne thermal videos. ISPRS Journal of Photogrammetry and Remote Sensing 61(3-4), 187–197 (2006)

Kirchhof, M.: Linear Two View Multiple Plane Geometry. Pattern Recognition and Image Analysis 3 (2008)

Lucas, B.T., Kanade, T.: An Iterative Image Registration Technique with an Application to Stereo Vision. In: Image Understanding Workshop, pp. 130–212 (1981)

Seki, M., Wada, T., Fujiwara, H., Sumi, K.: Background detection based on the cooccurrence of image variations. In: IEEE Conference on Computer Vision and Pattern Recognition, pp. 65–72 (2003)

Shashua, A., Avidan, S.: The Rank 4 Constraint in Multiple View Geometry. In: Buxton, B.F., Cipolla, R. (eds.) ECCV 1996. LNCS, vol. 1065, pp. 196–206. Springer, Heidelberg (1996)

Shi, J., Tomasi, C.: Good Features to Track. In: IEEE Conference on Computer Vision and Pattern Recognition, pp. 593–600 (1994)

Stauffer, C., Grimson, W.E.L.: Adaptive background mixture models for real-time tracking. In: International Conference on Computer Vision and Pattern Recognition, vol. 2, pp. 246–252 (1999)

Strehl, A., Aggarwal, J.K.: MODEEP: A motion-based object detection and pose estimation method for airborne FLIR sequences. Machine Vision and Applications 11(6), 267–276 (2000)

Vasconceles, N., Lippman, A.: Empirical Bayesian EM based Motion Segmentation. In: IEEE Conference on Computer Vision and Pattern Recognition, pp. 532–572 (1997)

Wren, C., Azarbayejani, A., Darrell, T., Pentland, A.: Pfinder: Real-time Tracking of the Human Body. IEEE Transactions on Pattern Recognition and Machine Intelligence 7, 780–785 (1997)

Zelnik-Manor, L., Irani, M.: Multiview Constraints on Homographies. IEEE Transactions on Pattern Recognition and Machine Intelligence 24(2), 214–223 (2002)

Zhou, Y., Gong, Y., Taok, H.: Background modeling using time dependent markov random field with image pyramid. In: IEEE Conference on Motion (2005)

A Scheme for the Detection and Tracking of People Tuned for Aerial Image Sequences

Florian Schmidt and Stefan Hinz

Institute of Photogrammetry and Remote Sensing (IPF),
Karlsruhe Institute of Technology (KIT),
76128 Karlsruhe, Germany
{florian.schmidt,stefan.hinz}@kit.edu

Abstract. This paper addresses the problem of detecting and tracking a large number of individuals in aerial image sequences that have been taken from high altitude. We propose a method which can handle the numerous challenges that are associated with this task and demonstrate its quality on several test sequences. Moreover this paper contains several contributions to improve object detection and tracking in other domains, too. We show how to build an effective object detector in a flexible way which incorporates the shadow of an object and enhanced features for shape and color. Furthermore the performance of the detector is boosted by an improved way to collect background samples for the classifier training. At last we describe a tracking-by-detection method that can handle frequent misses and a very large number of similar objects.

Keywords: Aerial image sequences, object detection, classifier training, people tracking.

1 Introduction

Aerial images sequences taken from high altitude allow to quickly overview wide areas and to analyze temporal changes. Automatic methods are needed to extract useful information in an appropriate manner out of this huge amount of digital data. This paper addresses this demand and proposes a method to detect and track a large number of people in aerial image sequences (Fig. 1). The results generated by our approach are especially useful in applications in which wide areas have to be monitored simultaneously as e.g. during mass events or for the evaluation of infrastructure.

1.1 Challenges and Contribution

The task of tracking individuals in aerial image sequences is very challenging and differs considerably from other domains due to the following reasons. A single person consists only of a few pixels in size and its appearance is influenced by changing atmospheric conditions (Fig. 2). The number of individuals can vary from hundreds up to many thousands which all look very much alike. Aerial

U. Stilla et al. (Eds.): PIA 2011, LNCS 6952, pp. 257–270, 2011.

Fig. 1. Part of a typical aerial image which we use in our analysis

images include lots of person-like objects in particular in a complex urban environment. The sequences have a very low frame rate and are affected by the motion of the camera platform.

This paper explains how we handle these challenges. It contains the following key contributions:

1. We show how to build an effective detector for tiny objects by incorporating enhanced features in a flexible way which are tuned for certain characteristics as color, shape or shadow.
2. We present two methods to improve the way of collecting background samples for the classifier training.
3. A tracking-by-detection method is described which can handle frequent misses and which constructs reliable tracklets in a fast way for a very large number of similar objects.

1.2   Related Work

The use of image sequences taken from an airborne platform for surveillance tasks has been studied for many years. In most cases different methods for moving object detection are employed as in (Kumar et al., 2001), (Medioni et al., 2001), (Benedek et al., 2009) and (Reilly et al., 2010a). However these techniques are sensitive to the parallax effect and changing lighting conditions and do not work well for small or static objects. Appearance-based approaches overcome these problems since they work on single images. They have been successfully applied for car detection e.g. in (Yu et al., 2006), (Grabner et al., 2008) and (Leitloff et al., 2010).

Although there is an overwhelming amount of literature about the detection and tracking of people in terrestrial videos, only few publications exist which use data of airborne platforms for this task. Xiao et al. (2008) presented a system which is based on moving object detection. Though they achieved reasonable results for vehicles, the algorithm failed for small and slow moving persons. In (Miller et al., 2008) Harris corner features are used to detect individuals and to avoid the motion dependency. Yet the poor results did not confirm their approach. Reilly et al. (2010b) achieved a good detection rate with a two stage procedure. Assuming that persons are upright shadow casting objects, they filter the image for candidate regions which fulfill this constraint. Afterwards the candidates are classified as human or clutter by using wavelet features. Although we utilize the shadow of persons as well, we integrate this information directly in an appearance-based framework. In Burkert et al. (2010) persons are detected by applying a sequence of segmentation algorithms. The resulting regions are tracked by calculating optical flow between consecutive images. It is questionable if these simple methods will yield robust results in more complex situations.

2   Overview of the Proposed Approach

We employ a tracking-by-detection framework to solve the problem of localizing and tracking individuals through a sequence of aerial images. The following sections describe in detail how we cope with the numerous challenges which arise in the domain of wide area surveillance. First we explain how we have designed an optimal detector for our object class (section 2.1) and how we have trained it in an efficient way (section 2.2). Afterwards we illustrate the tracking algorithm which links the previously generated detections (section 2.3).

2.1   Detector Design

One has to face particular problems when trying to detect individuals in images that have been taken in vertical direction from an altitude of, e.g. 1500 m. The size of a single person decreases to about 4 by 4 pixel at a ground sampling distance of 0.15 cm. Clouds and other atmospheric conditions can lower the signal-to-noise ratio even more, so that in some cases the shadow of a person is the only visible cue (Fig. 2).

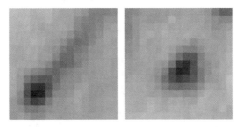

Fig. 2. Example of a person with and without shadow at a common pixel size of 15 cm

Most of the related work on object detection in aerial image sequences is based on algorithms for moving object detection. However these approaches do not work for static objects. They are furthermore unsuitable for very small and slow moving objects because of the moving camera and the improper alignment of the aerial images. For this reason we have decided to use an appearance-based approach instead in which features are extracted inside of a detection window and passed to a trained classifier to make a decision about the presence of an object. We use *Gentle AdaBoost* (Friedman et al., 2000) as classifier. This method has been successfully applied to detect very small objects e.g. by Leitloff et al. (2010) with cars in satellite images or by Smal et al. (2010) with spots in fluorescence microscopy images.

In general a sequence of complex preprocessing steps for geometric normalization and image alignment has to be applied to images taken from airborne platforms to perform further analysis. These tasks are not subject of this paper and have to be done in advance, c.f. (Kumar et al., 2001) or (Thomas et al., 2008). Our algorithm assumes orthorectified, georeferenced images of a fixed ground sampling distance as input data (Fig. 1). We execute nevertheless one object specific normalization which is explained in the following paragraph.

Incorporating the Shadow of a Person. An appearance-based detection approach works best if the feature values of one object class have a low variability in feature space. This can be achieved by choosing invariant features and by normalizing systematic influences. Since we use geometric normalized images from a nadir camera, single persons already have a similar dot-like shape (Fig. 2). The shadow casted by a person is an important additional cue for detection. Yet its appearance is highly variable and can only be modeled explicitly in the particular case when a single person stands isolated on a uniform ground like it has been done by Reilly et al. (2010b).

We propose to incorporate the potential object shadow directly in the appearance-based detection framework instead. This way we fuse information about a person and its potential shadow on the classifier level. The implicit model that is learned during the training of the classifier acts more flexible in ambiguous situation and shows better detection results.

Depending on the global position and the time of year and day the shadow of a person has different length and direction. Since we have georeferenced images, we use the available metadata to turn the images to correct for the different direction of the sun. Afterwards the shadows will always point in upward direction. This normalization step reduces the variance in object appearance. The benefit of geometric normalization exceeds clearly the minor information loss due to the necessary resampling.

We design the size of the detection window so that it covers the body of a single person and also a good part of its shadow (Tab. 1). In the training procedure we use samples of persons with shadow and without. The AdaBoost classifier has shown to be flexible enough to cope with this variation and combine all cues in the best way.

Object-specific Haar-like Features. Choosing the right features to describe the object of interest is a crucial step in appearance-based object detection. They should be invariant against noise and systematic variations and they should discriminate well between the object and background class. We have the additional requirement in our domain that the features have to be computable inside a very small detection window.

We use Haar-like features since they meet all stated requirements. They extract information about the shape of an object, they can be computed very fast at constant time in a window of at least 2 by 2 pixels and they are furthermore invariant to constant and linear changes in lighting (Viola and Jones, 2001).

The basic set of Haar-wavelet features introduced by Oren et al. (1997) has been extended to the more flexible Haar-like features (Viola and Jones, 2001), (Smal et al., 2010). This feature class can be generalized even more to better suit the shape of the object of interest (Fig. 3). Though these customized features can be assembled from the basic Haar-wavelet features, they lead to a faster detector since less features have to be extracted.

Fig. 3. A certain Haar-like feature is calculated by subtracting the sum of all pixel of the black from the white rectangle. The factor α is required to compensate for the differences in rectangle size. Five object-specific Haar-like features out of the 24 prototypes we have used to describe the specific shape of people in aerial images.

Rectangle Feature Class. Although shape provides the most dominating cues for object detection, we want to use color as complementary and supporting feature. Since our objects are very small, it is not feasible to extract a color histogram. Instead we could use the pixel values inside the detection window as feature values, however they would be very sensitive to noise.

For this reason we introduce the *rectangle feature class*. A single feature of this class is a value computed on a single channel in an arbitrarily shaped rectangle inside the detection window. We calculate mean and variance of all pixels inside a rectangle, as this can be done fast and analog to the Haar-like features. The mean value responds to color while the variance responds to homogeneity in object appearance. Since we want to utilize the rectangle features to represent the appearance of the object and not of its shadow, we use a smaller detection window as for the Haar-like features (Tab. 1).

Color Space and Window Size. The *rgb* color space is often not the best choice when processing color images because of the high correlation between its channels. Instead we use the *i1i2i3* color space (Ohta et al., 1980) since it separates color and intensity information and is easy to compute. Table 1 displays an overview of our detector design. For every feature class we choose the optimal window size and color channel. By doing so, we get a detector which is particularly suitable for our object class. Furthermore the initial number of possible features is smaller which reduces the time for feature selection and training.

Table 1. Overview of the designed detector

Feature class	Channel	Window size	Potential features
Haar-like	i1	9 x 15	9477
Rectangle	i1	9 x 9	3969
Rectangle	i2	9 x 9	3969
Rectangle	i3	9 x 9	3969

2.2   Training the Classifier

The training phase is essential in appearence-based object detection. Good samples for the object and background class are the base for good results. Object samples have to be collected manually by selecting individuals in training images. It is however far more difficult to gather appropriate background samples since this class is a priori boundless.

Usually the training samples should capture the entire distribution of feature values for both classes. However by using the binary AdaBoost classifier one just needs to find the right samples which define the boundary between object and background class in feature space. This can be done effectively by training the classifier in an iterative bootstrapping fashion (Sung and Poggio, 1998), (Grabner et al., 2008). We take all samples of the object class and a few manually marked background samples to start the training. We use a fixed number of stumps as weak learners. Afterwards we run the classifier on aerial images that do not contain any person. All detections in these images are therefor false positives and could be added to the set of background samples. Yet this would increase the number of negative samples very quickly to an unfeasible high number. So we add only very few randomly chosen false positives and repeat the training process until the number of false detections in images without persons decreases to a desired rate.

Confidence-aware Collection of Background Samples. One drawback of the described method is that other objects which look similar to the object of interest and which appear in the background images are added to the set of background samples. This general problem has a large effect in our application domain since aerial images contain lots of person-like objects. Although the *Gentle AdaBoost* classifier (Friedman et al., 2000) is less sensitive to outliers in the training data, the best results are achieved if background and object class are not mixed.

We solve this problem by calculating a confidence measure for each detection. In general the AdaBoost detection score is unbounded and the decision for object or background class is based solely on the sign of the weighted sum of the answers of all weak learners. Yet the detection score can be converted to a more useful normalized confidence measure by dividing it by the sum of the weights of all weak learners (Grabner et al., 2008):

$$conf(\mathbf{x}) = \frac{\sum \alpha_n \cdot h_n^{weak}(\mathbf{x})}{\sum \alpha_n} \tag{1}$$

The confidence measure of each false positive detection can now be exploited to prevent a mixing of the training samples of object and background class. Instead of choosing false detections randomly, we prefer those with lowest confidence above 0. This strategy concentrates on ambiguous samples close to the decision border and reduces considerably the chance of mixing both classes during the iterative semi-automatic recording of background training samples.

Background Samples in Object Proximity. The detector would generate a lot of false detection if the associated classifier would have been trained exclusively with background samples from images without any objects. These false positives would occur especially in the close surrounding of the objects of interest, mainly in their shadow.

The reason for this behavior is that the classifier has not seen this area during training. We solve this problem by using also aerial images where the position of all existing persons has been marked. We collect background samples as described previously but do only consider all false detections which have a minimum distance to any marked person.

2.3   Detection and Tracking

We run the trained detector over a predefined region of interest inside an aerial image. The result is a confidence map where pixel values close to -1 indicate background and values close to $+1$ object positions. The confidence score has been calculated independently for every pixel. So we estimate the continuous two-dimensional confidence distribution with a Gaussian kernel. Afterwards we apply a non-maxima suppression to get a finite set of potential object positions. Only those candidate positions whose confidence score exceeds a fixed detection threshold are finally passed on to the tracking algorithm.

Tracking-by-detection with Frequent Misses. In our application domain we have to deal with frequent misses due to the fact that changing atmospherical conditions can lower the signal-to-noise ratio to the point where single persons are hardly visible anymore. In addition, people often walk or stand in groups so that they merge visually to an undefined blob. Our detector does not work in these situations since it is trained to locate only isolated persons.

The tracking-by-detection method would fail if the percentage of misses is to high. Therefore we lower the detection threshold to reduce the miss rate to a minimum at the cost of more false alarms. The hard decision between background and object class is postponed in this way from the detection to the tracking stage where more information is available.

Tracking a Large Number of Objects in Clutter. Tracking in aerial images requires an algorithm that can handle lots of objects at the same time. This demand increases even more as we allow a lot of false detections during the detection stage. Further challenges arise because of a low frame rate of, e.g. 2 Hz and the fact the objects of interest have similar appearance. The true motion of individuals is furthermore affected by the inaccuracy in image alignment in a magnitude of few pixels.

We adapt an iterative Bayesian tracking approach similar to the one used by Betke et al. (2007) to track a large number of flying bats. A certain person is described using the following basic states:

1. position (x, y, confidence)
2. motion (direction, velocity)
3. color (r, g, b)

Information about position and color is provided by the detection algorithm. Additionally we calculate optical flow between consecutive images to extract motion information at the location of every observation. As most people move only a few pixels between two images, optical flow is well suited to get a good estimate for object motion.

A fast to compute near constant velocity motion model is used to predict object states for every new image. These predictions are linked afterwards with new observations on the base of state affinity. We apply the efficient gating strategy of Collins and Uhlmann (1992) to limit the number of possible associations and reduce the complexity of the data association problem. Objects with no assigned measurement are marked as *lost objects* and measurements without objects as *new objects*.

We analyze all connections and establish an affinity matrix for each cluster of connected components. The matrix elements represent affinity scores, which are calculated in a similar fashion as in (Wu and Nevatia, 2007). The affinity matrix serves as input for the the association module. We are looking only for one to one associations between objects and observations and prohibit split and merge situations.

There are several methods to solve this task. Some search for a global optimum by maximizing the overall association affinity while others make use of greedy, heuristic methods. We use the *direct link* method of Huang et al. (2008). It does not provide a global optimum for the assignment problem but it generates reliable associations in a simple and fast way. A measurement is assigned to an object only if the affinity exceeds a certain minimum and only if the affinity to all other objects and measurements is considerable lower.

If an object is assigned successfully to an observation, its states are updated with a fast α-β-filter. Lost objects with no association are not tracked any further. This restriction ensures the non-overlapping constraint and prevents wrong associations in our domain with high object density and low frame rate.

In the final step of each iteration we calculate a track confidence for each object by averaging over the detection confidence of every position. If this score is below a certain threshold, the entire track is marked as clutter and discarded from further processing.

3 Experiments and Results

We have several aerial image sequences available to evaluate the proposed approach. They have all been taken with a camera facing in vertical direction from an altitude of about 1500 m resulting in a ground sampling distance of about 20 cm up to 15 cm. They show different big events with lots of people in an urban environment (Fig. 1). All sequences have a frame rate of 2 Hz yet the number of frames covering a certain area varies from 4 up to 18. The atmospherical conditions differ between sunny, cloudy and foggy.

For the training of our detector we have collected about 1500 object samples and the same amount of background samples as described in section 2.2. We have used 70 % of them to train a *Gentle AdaBoost* classifier with stumps as weak learners. We achived a low test error of about 7 % on the remaining 30 % of the samples. The initial number of features could be reduced from above 21000 to just 16 resulting in a fast and accurate object detector. The number of selected Haar-like features and rectangle features is nearly even. Almost all of them are extracted on the intensity channel *i1* which reveals the minor role of color information for our application.

We have manually marked the tracks of all persons in four different sequences (Fig. 4) to generate a reference for the evaluation of the detection and tracking algorithm. Altogether we have 40 frames available, each one containing about 100 up to 300 individuals. There is a large number of different evaluation metrics for object detection and tracking (Baumann et al., 2008), however we chose correctness and completeness to be sufficient for our purpose. We define a correct match between detection and reference if the distance of centroids is below 50 cm. We allow merge situations but no split situations. Tracking is evaluated by comparing all automatically generated links between consecutive images with the reference. A link is defined as correct if both associated detections match the position of the same person in the reference data.

Fig. 4. The first image of each of our four test sequences in original quality with no visual enhancement. We use the following symbols for their representation in the evaluation charts: ♦,■,▲,◄.

Figure 5 displays the results of our detection algorithm as precision-recall curve. Our method is able to achieve high values for completeness and correctness yet not simultaneously. Only one test sequence stands out getting clearly better results. This is because it contains much less person-like clutter as the other three sequences. The results apparently show the limits of a pure detection-based approach in our domain. In many cases it is not possible to discriminate between persons and other objects solely on the base of appearance.

If we compare the detection results only with isolated persons in the reference (Fig. 5, dashed lines), the completeness increases up to 20 %. The reason for this is that our detector has been trained to find separated individuals. Groups of closely spaces persons merge to irregular shaped blobs and cannot be detected with our method.

The tracking algorithm usually fills in some missed detection and suppresses false alarms. Yet the improvement in detection is small in our case as can be seen in Fig. 6. This is because of our conservative tracking approach which allows tracks to be formed only in unambiguous situations and which prohibits multiple predictions. These restrictions could be eased to get better results. Yet at the same time a more precise motion model and a more complex data association method would be needed to account for the high object density in our domain.

The impact of the afore-mentioned problems is reflected in Fig. 6 and 8, too. Although high values are possbile for the correctness of retrieved links, the overall completeness is quiet low in all test sequences. The tracking fails especially in crowded situations when individuals are barely discriminable. Fig. 6 also shows the necessity to postpone the decision between objects and clutter from the detection to the tracking stage as it has been done in our approach. In doing so, the link completeness has been increased considerably.

The results illustrate that it is not yet feasible to use the generated tracks for a comprehensive individual behavior analysis. Yet it is possible to generate short but reliable tracklets which could be used to obtain statistics about the general motion of persons in a certain region of interest. If longer tracks are needed the presented approach needs to be extended to follow individuals even in crowded, complex situations.

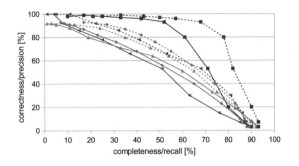

Fig. 5. Results of the detection algorithm with varying confidence threshold for four different test sequences. The evaluation is done twice, first time with the complete reference data (continuous) and second time only with isolated persons (dashed).

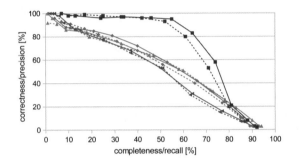

Fig. 6. Comparison of the detection results after frame-wise detection (dashed) and after tracking (continuous) for all four test sequences

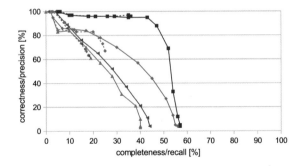

Fig. 7. Results of the tracking algorithm for four test sequences with varying confidence threshold for track confirmation. The evaluation is done twice using different detection results as input for the tracking. At first all detections with a confidence above the standard threshold have been used ($conf > 0$, dashed). Afterwards the threshold has been lowered considerably ($conf > -0.6$, continuous).

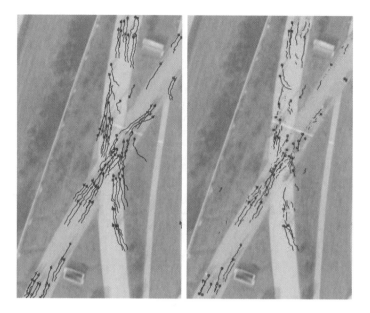

Fig. 8. Visual comparison of the reference tracks on the left and the automatically generated ones on the right for the entire sequence ■

4   Conclusion

In this paper we proposed an appearance-based approach to detect individuals in aerial images. It comprises enhanced Haar-like features for the object shape, rectangle features for color information and a detector which is especially designed for the small size of a single person and its potential shadow. We used AdaBoost as binary classifier and demonstrated a way to collect background samples for its training very efficiently.

Our detection method achieves good results on isolated persons and in scenarios with few person-like clutter. The performance drops however in situations when people merge into groups and when a lot of clutter is present.

Furthermore we presented a tracking-by-detection algorithm which can handle a very large number of individuals and clutter in a fast way. The negative effects of a decreased detection performance are alleviated by postponing the final decision between object and background from the detection to the tracking stage. The tracking method generates short but reliable tracks of individuals which could be used to extract statistics about the general motion in a certain region of interest.

In future work these short tracks will be the base of a hierarchical tracklet-based framework in which gaps are closed and tracks are extended by the use of high level post-processing steps as in Huang et al. (2008).

References

Baumann, A., Boltz, M., Ebling, J., Koenig, M., Loos, H.S., Merkel, M., Niem, W., Warzelhan, J.K., Yu, J.: A review and comparison of measures for automatic video surveillance systems. EURASIP Journal on Image and Video Processing, 30 (2008)

Benedek, C., Sziranyi, T., Kato, Z., Zerubia, J.: Detection of object motion regions in aerial image pairs with a multilayer markovian model. IEEE Transactions on Image Processing 18(10), 2303–2315 (2009)

Betke, M., Hirsh, D.E., Bagchi, A., Hristov, N.I., Makris, N.C., Kunz, T.H.: Tracking large variable numbers of objects in clutter. In: IEEE Conference on Computer Vision and Pattern Recognition, pp. 1–8 (2007)

Burkert, F., Schmidt, F., Butenuth, M., Hinz, S.: People tracking and trajectory interpretation in aerial image sequences. In: Photogrammetric Computer Vision and Image Analysis. IAPRS, vol. XXXVIII, Part 3A, pp. 209–214 (September 2010)

Collins, J., Uhlmann, J.: Efficient gating in data association with multivariate gaussian distributed states. IEEE Transactions on Aerospace and Electronic Systems 28(3), 909–916 (1992)

Friedman, J., Hastie, T., Tibshirani, R.: Additive logistic regression: A statistical view of boosting. The Annals of Statistics 28(2), 337–374 (2000)

Grabner, H., Nguyen, T.T., Gruber, B., Bischof, H.: On-line boosting-based car detection from aerial images. ISPRS Journal of Photogrammetry and Remote Sensing 63(3), 382–396 (2008)

Huang, C., Wu, B., Nevatia, R.: Robust object tracking by hierarchical association of detection responses. In: Forsyth, D., Torr, P., Zisserman, A. (eds.) ECCV 2008, Part II. LNCS, vol. 5303, pp. 788–801. Springer, Heidelberg (2008)

Kumar, R., Sawhney, H., Samarasekera, S., Hsu, S., Tao, H., Guo, Y., Hanna, K., Pope, A., Wildes, R., Hirvonen, D., Hansen, M., Burt, P.: Aerial video surveillance and exploitation. Proceedings of the IEEE 89(10), 1518–1539 (2001)

Leitloff, J., Hinz, S., Stilla, U.: Vehicle detection in very high resolution satellite images of city areas. IEEE Transactions on Geoscience and Remote Sensing 48(7), 2795–2806 (2010)

Medioni, G., Cohen, I., Bremond, F., Hongeng, S., Nevatia, R.: Event detection and analysis from video streams. IEEE Transactions on Pattern Analysis and Machine Intelligence 23(8), 873–889 (2001)

Smal, I., Loog, M., Niessen, W., Meijering, E.: Quantitative comparison of spot detection methods in fluorescence microscopy. IEEE Transactions on Medical Imaging 29(2), 282–301 (2010)

Ohta, Y.I., Kanade, T., Sakai, T.: Color information for region segmentation. Computer Graphics and Image Processing 13(3), 222–241 (1980)

Oren, M., Papageorgiou, C., Sinha, P., Osuna, E., Poggio, T.: Pedestrian detection using wavelet templates. In: IEEE Conference on Computer Vision and Pattern Recognition, pp. 193–199 (1997)

Reilly, V., Idrees, H., Shah, M.: Detection and tracking of large number of targets in wide area surveillance. In: Daniilidis, K. (ed.) ECCV 2010, Part III. LNCS, vol. 6313, pp. 186–199. Springer, Heidelberg (2010a)

Reilly, V., Solmaz, B., Shah, M.: Geometric constraints for human detection in aerial imagery. In: Daniilidis, K., Maragos, P., Paragios, N. (eds.) ECCV 2010. LNCS, vol. 6316, pp. 252–265. Springer, Heidelberg (2010)

Smal, I., Loog, M., Niessen, W., Meijering, E.: Quantitative comparison of spot detection methods in fluorescence microscopy. IEEE Transactions on Medical Imaging 29(2), 282–301 (2010)

Sung, K.K., Poggio, T.: Example-based learning for view-based human face detection. IEEE Transactions on Pattern Analysis and Machine Intelligence 20(1), 39–51 (1998)

Thomas, U., Rosenbaum, D., Kurz, F., Suri, S., Reinartz, P.: A new software/hardware architecture for real time image processing of wide area airborne camera images. Journal of Real-Time Image Processing 4(3), 229–244 (2008)

Viola, P., Jones, M.: Rapid object detection using a boosted cascade of simple features. In: IEEE Conference on Computer Vision and Pattern Recognition, vol. 1, pp. 511–518 (2001)

Wu, B., Nevatia, R.: Detection and tracking of multiple, partially occluded humans by bayesian combination of edgelet based part detectors. International Journal of Computer Vision 75, 247–266 (2007)

Xiao, J., Yang, C., Han, F., Cheng, H.: Vehicle and person tracking in aerial videos. In: Stiefelhagen, R., Bowers, R., Fiscus, J.G. (eds.) RT 2007 and CLEAR 2007. LNCS, vol. 4625, pp. 203–214. Springer, Heidelberg (2008)

Yu, Q., Cohen, I., Medioni, G., Wu, B.: Boosted markov chain monte carlo data association for multiple target detection and tracking. In: International Conference on Pattern Recognition, vol. 2, pp. 675–678 (2006)

Event Detection Based on a Pedestrian Interaction Graph Using Hidden Markov Models

Florian Burkert and Matthias Butenuth

Technische Universität München, Remote Sensing Technology,
Arcisstraße 21, 80333 München, Germany
{florian.burkert,matthias.butenuth}@bv.tum.de
http://www.lmf.bv.tum.de/

Abstract. In this paper, we present a new approach for event detection of pedestrian interaction in crowded and cluttered scenes. Existing work is focused on the detection of an abnormal event in general or on the detection of specific simple events incorporating only up to two trajectories. In our approach, event detection in large groups of pedestrians is performed by exploiting motion interaction between pairs of pedestrians in a graph-based framework. Event detection is done by analyzing the temporal behaviour of the motion interaction with Hidden Markov Models (HMM). In addition, temporarily unsteady edges in the graph can be compensated by a HMM buffer which internally continues the HMM analysis even if the representing pedestrians depart from each other awhile. Experimental results show the capability of our graph-based approach for event detection by means of an image sequence in which pedestrians approach a soccer stadium.

Keywords: Event detection, pedestrians, trajectory interpretation, Hidden Markov Model, aerial image sequences.

1 Introduction

Our goal is the detection of events in crowds by robustly analyzing a dynamic pedestrian graph using Hidden Markov Models in which the edges represent motion interaction between pedestrians.

In the last decades, research in the analysis of crowds of pedestrians has been intensified (Zhan et al., 2008). At big events like religious meetings, festivals or demonstrations, visual surveillance can help to prevent a crowd from disasters like mass panics or from casualties at more individual incidents like brawls. Image sequences and video data from airborne platforms provide an ideal overview over crowds and are mostly free of occlusions (Burkert et al., 2010). To this end, trajectories of detected and tracked pedestrians can be used to perform event detection based on the interaction between them. However, the trajectory of an individual does not necessarily provide exact information about the designated motion destination at each frame of an image sequence, because the motion of an individual is fluctuating to a certain degree. Even if a pedestrian intends to

U. Stilla et al. (Eds.): PIA 2011, LNCS 6952, pp. 271–283, 2011.

walk straight ahead or to stand still, slight deviations to the left or right will occur to some extent. Therefore, the event detection system has to be robust concerning slight fluctuations of motion direction when analyzing the sequential motion interaction between a pair of pedestrians. In a crowd, the sequential analysis of the motion interaction between each pair of pedestrians then allows for pointing out areas of potential dangerous motion patterns.

The importance of crowd analysis is visible by numerous publications concerning all important steps in the workflow, including object detection, tracking and event detection. Zhan et al. (2008) present a survey which is motivated by the immense growth of the world population since the 1960s. The main input data for event detection are either trajectories or optical flow. Event detection systems using optical flow are capable to detect abnormal events in crowds of high density (Adam et al., 2008; Andrade et al., 2006; Mehran et al., 2009). However, specific behaviour of individuals cannot be inferred by using a static optical flow field which is laid over an image. Also, systems using optical flow are not capable to deduce a semantic description of the type of the abnormal event. Besides optical flow analysis of crowds, more work has been done on the analysis of discrete trajectories. For the learning and analysis of trajectories, Hidden Markov Models (HMM) (Rabiner, 1989) have often been applied in the last years, which have been developed originally for speech recognition. Depending on the application, several extensions of HMM have been developed and utilized for event detection, such as coupled HMM (CHMM) (Oliver et al., 2000) or switched dynamical HMM (SD-HMM) (Nascimento et al., 2010). The classification of recurring human trajectories within busy surveillance scenes is achieved in the work of Nascimento et al. (2010), where low level models of a given set are concatenated using SD-HMM in order to recognize human trajectories. Human trajectory mining is performed in the work of Calderara and Cucchiara (2010) by clustering frequent behaviours of pedestrians using different similarity measures. A similar motivation leads to the work of Kuettel et al. (2010) who automatically learn spatio-temporal dependencies of moving agents and show experimental results from traffic scenes on intersections. However, by classifying or mining recurring trajectories, only a very stringent model containing some trajectory clusters can be built which is not flexible enough to cope with individual and spontaneous motion patterns that do not match the recurring paths. Learning of recurring trajectories can also be used for the detection of outliers from the expected typical motion patterns (Basharat et al., 2008; Hu et al., 2006; Porikli and Haga, 2004). The outliers, so called anomalies or unusual events, can only be detected if a certain amount of data about the usual events is available beforehand. To this end, the monitored scene has to provide specific conditions which can be followed by the majority of the observed objects, such as entrance doors for pedestrians or driving lanes for vehicles. The calculation of secondary output features of trajectories such as speed, direction or acceleration is very popular for event detection (Oliver et al., 2000; Hongeng et al., 2004; Porikli et al., 2004; Burkert et al., 2010). Nevertheless, the selection of such features has to be compatible with the chosen motion model and the application.

In our approach, we overcome limitations of the related work with regard to our goal of event detection in crowds, considering individual motion patterns as well as a semantic description of the scene. We use trajectories instead of optical flow because significant information can be drawn from discrete coordinates and the resulting specific interactions between neighbouring pedestrians. The modeling of pedestrians in a graph which is dynamic over the whole sequence allows for an analysis of the entire scene and not just one or two pedestrians. We use secondary output features of each defined pair of trajectories to deduce simple motion patterns which represent interaction between pedestrians. The sequential behaviour of the simple motion patterns is analyzed by HMM. The HMM is learned from synthetic data which represents the simple motion patterns in an ideal way. We focus on the detection of simple motion patterns and combine them afterwards in the dynamic pedestrian graph. This higher level analysis allows us to interpret resulting large scale clusters or individual events in the scene. At this level, prior knowledge from social and traffic sciences such as the social force model (SFM) (Helbing and Molnar, 1995) will be used.

The outline of this paper is as follows: In section 2 we show the basics of HMM. Section 3 describes our system for robust, graph-based event detection. In section 4 we show experimental results and in section 5 we conclude and discuss future work.

2   Hidden Markov Models

A Hidden Markov Model (HMM) is a probabilistic model which is represented by a directed acyclic graph and shows the simplest form of a Dynamic Bayesian Network. The system which is underlying the HMM is a Markov chain of hidden states. At each time step, an observable output of the model is generated which only depends on the current hidden state.

2.1   Parameters of a HMM

A HMM provides clear Bayesian semantics. It is defined by the following set of parameters (Rabiner, 1989):

- A set of N hidden states $\{s_1, s_2, ..., s_N\}$, the state at time t is denoted as q_t
- A set of M observations $\{v_1, v_2, ..., v_M\}$, the observation at time t is denoted as o_t
- The transition probability matrix A with the elements a_{ij} denoting the transition probabilities from s_i to s_j

$$a_{ij} = P\left(q_t = s_j | q_{t-1} = s_i\right). \tag{1}$$

$$\sum a_{ij} = 1 \forall i, a_{ij} \geq 0. \tag{2}$$

– The observation probabilities distribution $b_j\,(v_k)$ for an observation v_k

$$b_j\,(v_k) = P\,(o_t = v_k | q_t = s_j)\,. \tag{3}$$

$$\sum_k b_j\,(v_k) = 1 \forall i, b_j\,(k) \geq 0. \tag{4}$$

– The initial probabilities π_i that s_i is the initial state

$$\pi_i = P\,(q_1 = s_i)\,. \tag{5}$$

$$\sum \pi_i = 1, \pi_i \geq 0. \tag{6}$$

2.2   Inference in HMM

Several inference problems are associated with HMMs which can be chosen depending on the application. A common task is to find the complete sequence of hidden states $\{q_1, q_2, ..., q_T\}$ which is most likely having generated a given sequence of observations $\{o_1, o_2, ..., o_T\}$, where T is the length of the sequence. The problem of finding the maximum over all possible hidden states can be solved by the *Viterbi algorithm* (e.g. Rabiner, 1989). The Viterbi algorithm can be solved if a complete and terminated sequence of observations is available. For our problem of event detection in real-time, that is simultaneously with the image sequence, the Viterbi algorithm is not suitable. In contrast, filtering is the task to compute the probability distribution over the hidden states $\{s_1, s_2, ..., s_N\}$ at a certain time step t, given the sequence of observations up to this time step $\{o_1, o_2, ..., o_{t-1}, o_t\}$. Filtering can efficiently be performed by the *forward algorithm* (Rabiner, 1989). The forward algorithm is appropriate to solve our task because it is not depending on an already terminated sequence and, thus, can be iteratively applied at every new frame of the image sequence.

The forward algorithm employs so called forward variables $\alpha_t\,(s_i)\,, 1 \leq i \leq N$ which are calculated at each time step t for every hidden state s_i , given a HMM λ. λ consists of the transition probability matrix A, observation probabilities $b_j\,(k)$ and the initial probabilities π_i. The forward variable is defined as

$$\alpha_t\,(s_i) = P\,(o_1, o_2, ..., o_t, q_t = s_i | \lambda)\,. \tag{7}$$

$\alpha_t\,(s_i)$ describes the probability to produce the observation sequence until t and to reach state s_i at time t, given the HMM λ. At the first time step $t = 1$, the initialization of the forward algorithm is performed by

$$\alpha_1\,(s_i) = \pi_i b_i\,(o_1)\,. \tag{8}$$

The initialization of the forward variables is only depending on the initial probabilities π_i and the observation o_1. At further time steps $t, 2 \leq t \leq T$ the recursion of the forward algorithm is performed by

$$\alpha_t\,(s_j) = b_j\,(o_t) \sum_i \alpha_{t-1}\,(s_i)\,a_{ij}\,. \tag{9}$$

The recursion step is depending on the observation o_t and on all forward variables of the previous time step $\alpha_{t-1}(s_i)$, multiplied by their transition probabilities to state s_j. At each time step t, the state s_i for which $\alpha_t(s_i)$ becomes maximal is denoted as the current state of the system.

3   Graph-Based Event Detection

We evaluate a dynamic pedestrian graph for robust event detection in crowds which can change the topology dynamically at each frame of the image sequence. We analyze the interaction between pedestrians to perform HMM-based event detection which is robust to fluctuant and partially departing pedestrians.

3.1   Pedestrian Motion Model

The input data for event detection are trajectories of pedestrians. We analyze the interaction between pairs of pedestrians, our motion model consists of three motion features. The motion features are combined in simple motion patterns which we then use to interpret a crowds behaviour.

Motion Features. We use three motion features which are calculated from pairs of trajectories at every time step. A pair of trajectories is defined by two pedestrians which are sufficiently close to each other such that an interaction takes place. The motion features are, firstly, the sum of the velocities of both pedestrians $\sum v_{ij}$, secondly, the variation of the distance between both pedestrians $\triangle d$ and, thirdly, the average pedestrian density in a specified area around both pedestrians $\mu(n_{ij})$. The motion features serve as the observations in the HMM. Figure 1 depicts two trajectories illustrating the motion features. The velocity v_i of both pedestrians is calculated at each time step using the frame rate and the covered distance since the last time step. The variability of the distance is defined as $\triangle d = d_t/d_{t-1}$, with d_{t-1} being the distance at time step t-1 and d_t being the distance at time step t. Thus, $\triangle d > 1$ for an increasing distance and $\triangle d < 1$ for a decreasing distance. The density of pedestrians is calculated by counting the number of pedestrians within a specified radius r and relating it to the area. The feature we are using is the arithmetic average of the densities at both pedestrians $\mu(n_{ij})$, such that no imbalance occurs in the case that one pedestrian stands at the edge of a group and one pedestrian walks in an open area. Summarized, the feature vector is composed of $[\sum v_{ij}, \triangle d, \mu(n_{ij})]$.

Simple Motion Patterns. We define six simple motion patterns which occur when pedestrians are close to each other. These simple motion patterns are the basis for event detection and define the type of the motion interaction of neighboring pedestrians in combination. Table 1 shows the six motion patterns and their characteristics with regard to the motion features speed, variability of distance and density. For better understanding, Table 1 shows the speed of a single pedestrian and not the sum of both neighbours. The variability of distance

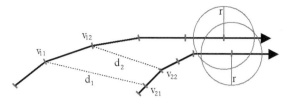

Fig. 1. Motion features derived from trajectories: v_{it} is the velocity of trajectory i at frame t, d_t is the distance at frame t and r is the radius in which the pedestrian density is computed

explicitly leads to a statement for the combined direction of the pair of pedestrians. The motion pattern standing has no defined direction, but at a speed closely to 0 the variability of distance is about 1. Furthermore, the straight motion patterns queueing, walking and running are parallel; hence the variability of distance is about 1. The motion patterns diverging with $\triangle d > 1$ and converging with $\triangle d < 1$ have self-explanatory direction characteristics.

HMM have to be learned offline, which is usually done by training data from real world scenarios. However, we do not use data from surveillance cameras to learn the HMM because we focus on cluttered scenes which occur at big events. Learning from real world data always relies on frequently recurring motion paths within the scene of interest, which we cannot assume to be available for any place where a big event may be held. Anyway, a system for semantic detection of a specific event like a brawl cannot be learned from real world data, because such an event does not happen iteratively. Instead, we use synthetic data which represent simple motion patterns to learn the HMM. The data is generated by moving agents which follow rules of motion depending on Table 1.

Table 1. Simple motion patterns and their characteristics concerning speed, variability of distance and density

Type	Speed(m/s)	$\triangle d$	Density
Standing	>0.15	≈ 1	variable
Queueing	>0.50	≈ 1	high
Walking	>2.00	≈ 1	medium
Running	>5.00	≈ 1	medium/low
Diverging	0.50-5.00	> 1	variable
Converging	0.50-5.00	< 1	variable

3.2   Evaluation of a Dynamic Pedestrian Graph for Event Detection

Graph-Based Approach. Event detection in a crowd is performed on the basis of a dynamic pedestrian graph. The graph is capable of robustly changing its topology because it is dynamically updated at every frame. Nodes in the graph represent pedestrians, edges in the graph represent motion patterns between pairs of pedestrians which are dynamically analyzed using HMM.

A problem arises when large groups of pedestrians are modeled in the graph. The number of edges and the computational cost is $N * (N - 1))/2$ for a number of N pedestrians. Therefore, we introduce edge weights based on a Gaussian function including the pedestrian density to significantly reduce the number of edges in the graph. To this end, only edges which are representing relevant interactions between adjacent pedestrians are considered in the graph.

Calculation of the Edge Weight. We introduce the weight function $w_{ij}(d, n)$ with $0 \leq w_{ij} \leq 1$ between two nodes i and j:

$$w_{ij} = \exp\left(-\frac{d_{ij}^2}{2 * \left(\frac{1}{\sqrt{n*2}}\right)^2}\right) \tag{10}$$

On the one hand, the weight w_{ij} depends on the distance d_{ij} between the pedestrians representing the nodes i and j. On the other hand, the weight w_{ij} depends on the density n, representing the number of pedestrians per square meter. The weight function is a Gaussian function with height 1, $\mu = 0$ and $\sigma = 1/(\sqrt{n} * 2)$. The width σ of the Gaussian is designed in such manner, that the weight w_{ij} receives high values for all neighboring pedestrians i and j that interact with each other. An interaction is supposed to take place between those pedestrians that are directly adjacent to each other. Therefore, at high densities the weight w_{ij} is only high between two pedestrians that have an offset of a few decimeters, where at low densities the weight w_{ij} can be high even if adjacent pedestrians have an offset of some meters. We introduce a threshold which is applied to the weight in order to determine which edges in the graph are constructed and which edges are omitted.

Graph Updating. Our graph based approach for event detection in crowds needs to represent dynamic behaviour of pedestrians. Therefore, the pedestrian graph is capable of dynamically changing its topology at every frame depending on the new configuration of pedestrians in the scene. Figure 2 a) shows an example of a small group of pedestrians, given by four trajectories. The dotted lines which are connecting the trajectories denote particular time steps. Figures 2 b), 2 c) and 2 d) show the corresponding graphs containing the four pedestrians. The topology changes by the insertion of a new edge between nodes 2 and 3. This is because the distance between the associated pedestrians 2 and 3 is decreasing during the sequence. The density is supposed to be constant. The width of the lines which represents the edge of interest in Figures 2 c) and 2 d) is increasing in consequence of the lower distance.

There are three potential preconditions of how our system can deal with the sequential interaction analysis, depending on the graph configuration in the previous step. The first case is that an edge already existed in the previous time step and will further exist, such that the corresponding interaction analysis can be continued. The second case is that two pedestrians are converging and the weight w_{ij} exceeds the threshold t_w. In this case, a new edge is generated and the analysis

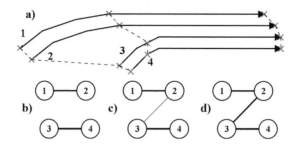

Fig. 2. (a) Dynamic graph updating exemplified by four synthetic trajectories. (b, c, d) Three representative graphs showing the pedestrian topology at particular frames (related to the dotted lines)

of this interaction is started. The third case is that two pedestrians diverge and the weight w_{ij} falls below the threshold t_w. In this case, the dynamic pedestrian graph no longer incorporates the corresponding edge due to the small weight.

Robust Event Detection. The analysis of the interaction between a pair of pedestrians is performed by HMM. In detail, the forward algorithm is used to derive the type of motion pattern as defined in Table 1 for each edge in the graph at each frame. Edges in the graph can arise or disappear during the sequence because of the dynamic behaviour of the crowd described in the previous section. If all pedestrians would move with linear velocity or direction, the corresponding HMM analysis of an interaction would be performed for a compact period of time. This ideal case is covered by the three cases described in the last section. However, pedestrians do not move in a linear way but tend to slightly deviate to the left or right while walking. Therefore, the interaction analysis bears the risk of being interrupted for some time steps, if pedestrians depart from each other awhile. To overcome this risk and to achieve a robust sequential analysis of the motion interaction, a HMM buffer is used when analyzing the dynamic pedestrian graph. The HMM buffer is internally activated for a definable number of frames when the weight of an edge decreases below the threshold. The HMM analysis can be resumed consistently if the weight increases again as long as the buffer is active. In this case, the temporarily omitted corresponding edge is retroactively constructed in the graph of the elapsed time steps. Thus, no fragments of the corresponding pedestrian interaction can arise. If the weight does not increase again, the corresponding interaction analysis is closed and the edge is finally deleted.

4   Experimental Results

We show experimental results for robust event detection in crowds based on a dynamic pedestrian graph. The dataset is described in the next section, afterwards results are shown which represent significant scenes and demonstrate the robustness of our approach.

4.1 Dataset

The dataset used for the experiments is an image sequence taken by an airborne camera platform of the German Aerospace Center (DLR). The area of interest is a soccer stadium, where thousands of people are approaching the gates. We use trajectories of pedestrians which have been generated manually from the image sequence to avoid at that time disturbing influences. The image sequence contains 16 frames taken at a frame rate of 0.5 Hz. The ground resolution is 0.15m at a flight height of 1000m. The area of interest is shown in Figure 3 on the left, the pedestrian trajectories are depicted in white. For the experiments we focus on two scenes. The trajectories from these two scenes are shown in Figure 3 on the right, denoted A and B in the image. In scene A, some pedestrians are passing a narrow area between a queue and a wall. In scene B, pedestrians are predominantly walking in one direction to approach the stadium gates and only some outliers are standing or crossing.

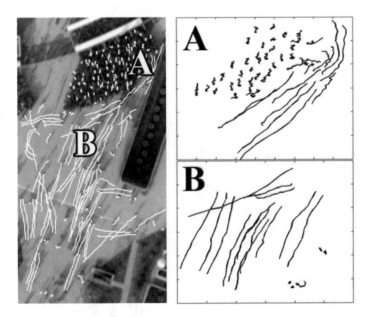

Fig. 3. Left: Last image of the sequence, trajectories in white. Right: trajectories from scene A (top) and scene B (bottom).

4.2 Event Detection Results

The event detection results of pedestrian interaction in scenes A and B are shown in Figure 4 and 5, respectively, represented by frames 2, 4, 7, 10, 13 and 16 each, respectively, the colorbar represents the six motion patterns. In Figure 4, the bulk of queueing pedestrians is successfully detected, which is displayed by the yellow edges in the pedestrian graph during the whole sequence. Pedestrians which are passing the queue are either connected by light or dark blue edges, representing the alternating converging and diverging interactions between them and the pedestrians at the border of the queue. Walking pairs of pedestrians which are passing the queue are correctly connected by an orange edge among each other. In Figure 5, most of the pedestrians are walking towards the stadium, which is correctly detected as shown by the orange edges in the pedestrian graph. Some standing pedestrians are detected for example in the lower area, where one of them leaves the others at the end of the sequence. The detection of this motion pattern is shown by the green edges (standing) at the beginning of the sequence and the dark blue edges (diverging) at the end of the sequence.

The presented results demonstrate the potential of our approach for graph based event detection by analyzing motion interaction in groups of pedestrians. Using HMM, the sequential behaviour of motion interaction between two pedestrians can reliably be analyzed. In some frames outliers of the predominant motion pattern between a pair of pedestrians arise, which are caused by the typical human fluctuating motion behaviour. The dynamic pedestrian graph can deal with changing topology during the sequence and, therefore, adapt required edges. By applying a HMM buffer our event detection system is robust in the case that interacting pedestrians depart from each other awhile or pedestrian densities change during a sequence. This robustness is exemplified in Figure 6: the top row contains three consecutive pedestrian graphs where the edges between node 7 and nodes 5 and 6 are not present in the middle frame, which were

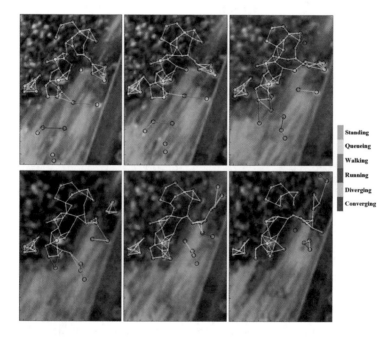

Fig. 4. Event detection results for scene A (frames 2, 4, 7, 10, 13 and 16) showing pedestrians passing a queue in a narrow area by a wall (colorbar on the right)

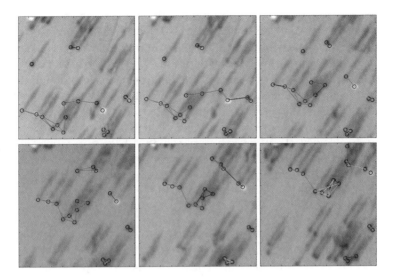

Fig. 5. Event detection results for scene B (frames 2, 4, 7, 10, 13 and 16) showing some pedestrians approaching the stadium and some standing

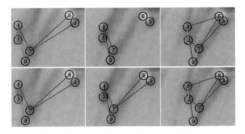

Fig. 6. Three frames of a pedestrian graph without HMM buffer (upper row) and with the HMM buffer (lower row)

produced by event detection without the HMM buffer. The second row contains the event detection result using the HMM buffer. Here, the corresponding edges exist such that a continuous and robust analysis of the interaction between the pedestrians represented by nodes 5, 6 and 7 can be performed. The six motion patterns we have defined represent human motion behaviour in a simple manner, such that areas of homogeneous behaviour as well as specific behaviour of only a few pedestrians can be inferred.

5   Conclusions

In this paper, we present a new approach for robust event detection in crowded scenes. We use a dynamic pedestrian graph to model all pedestrians in a scene simultaneously. Edges in the graph represent interaction between neighbouring pedestrians. A set of simple motion patterns is defined describing the type of interaction which is analyzed by HMM. The graph can change its topology during the sequence and is robust against fluctuating and partly departing pedestrians. Future work will deal with higher level analysis of the graph for automatic detection of complex events like dangerous situations and remarkable motion behaviour. To achieve this goal, expert knowledge from traffic and social sciences will be incorporated to design an improved graph analysis module. At this analysis, the rules for pedestrian motion from the SFM have to be considered. This module will form a higher hierarchical semantic level than the basic analysis in this paper. In addition, future work will focus on problems using automatically generated trajectories which may be incomplete.

Acknowledgments. We thank the German Aerospace Center (DLR) providing the image sequence and the International Graduate School of Science and Engineering (IGSSE) of Technische Universität München for supporting this study.

References

Adam, A., Rivlin, E., Shimshoni, I., Reinitz, D.: Robust Real-Time Unusual Event Detection using Multiple Fixed-Location Monitors. IEEE Transactions on Pattern Analysis and Machine Intelligence 30(3), 555–560 (2008)

Andrade, E.L., Blunsden, S., Fisher, R.B.: Hidden Markov Models for Optical Flow Analysis in Crowds. In: 18th International Conference of Pattern Recognition, ICPR 2006, pp. 460–463 (2006)

Basharat, A., Gritai, A., Shah, M.: Learning Object Motion Patterns for Anomaly Detection and Improved Object Detection. In: 21th IEEE Conference on Computer Vision and Pattern Recognition, CVPR 2008, pp. 1–8 (2008)

Burkert, F., Schmidt, F., Butenuth, M., Hinz, S.: People Tracking and Trajectory Interpretation in Aerial Image Sequences. In: International Archives of Photogrammetry, Remote Sensing and Spatial Information Sciences, Comm. III (Part A), pp. 209–214 (2010)

Calderara, S., Cucchiara, R.: People Trajectory Mining with Statistical Pattern Recognition. In: 23rd IEEE Conference on Computer Vision and Pattern Recognition Workshops, CVPR 2010 (2010)

Helbing, D., Molnar, P.: Social Force Model for Pedestrian Dynamics. Physical Review E 51(5), 4282–4286 (1995)

Hongeng, S., Nevatia, R., Bremond, F.: Video-Based Event Recognition: Activity Representation and Probabilistic Recognition Methods. Computer Vision and Image Understanding 96(2), 129–162 (2004)

Hu, W., Xiao, X., Fu, Z., Xie, D., Tan, T., Maybank, S.: A system for learning statistical motion patterns. IEEE Transactions on Pattern Analysis and Machine Intelligence 28(9), 1450–1464 (2006)

Kuettel, D., Breitenstein, M.D., Van Gool, L., Ferrari, V.: Learning Object Motion Patterns for Anomaly Detection and Improved Object Detection. In: 23rd IEEE Conference on Computer Vision and Pattern Recognition, CVPR 2010, pp. 1951–1958 (2010)

Mehran, R., Oyama, A., Shah, M.: Abnormal Crowd Behaviour using Social Force Model. In: 22nd IEEE Conference on Computer Vision and Pattern Recognition, CVPR 2009, pp. 935–942 (2009)

Nascimento, J.C., Figueiredo, M.A.T., Marques, J.S.: Trajectory Classification using Switched Dynamical Hidden Markov Models. IEEE Transactions on Image Processing 19(5), 1338–1348 (2010)

Oliver, N.M., Rosario, B., Pentland, A.P.: A Bayesian Computer Vision System for Modeling Human Interactions. IEEE Transactions on Pattern Analysis and Machine Intelligence 22(8), 831–843 (2000)

Porikli, F., Haga, T.: Event Detection by Eigenvector Decomposition using Object and Frame Features. In: 17th IEEE Conference on Computer Vision and Pattern Recognition Workshops, CVPR 2004 (2004)

Rabiner, L.R.: A Tutorial on Hidden Markov Models and Selected Applications in Speech Recognition. Proceedings of the IEEE 77(2), 257–286 (1989)

Zhan, B., Monekesso, D.N., Remagnino, P., Velastin, S.A., Xu, L.: Crowd Analysis: A Survey. Machine Vision and Applications 19(5-6), 345–357 (2008)

Trajectory Extraction and Density Analysis of Intersecting Pedestrian Flows from Video Recordings

Matthias Plaue, Minjie Chen, Günter Bärwolff, and Hartmut Schwandt

Institut für Mathematik,
Technische Universität Berlin,
Straße des 17. Juni 136,
10623 Berlin, Germany
{plaue,minjie.chen,baerwolf,schwandt}@math.tu-berlin.de
http://page.math.tu-berlin.de/~plaue/pedflows.html

Abstract. Empirical data of human crowd behaviors are indispensable for the further understanding of pedestrian dynamics. In this paper, we describe a technique for the semi-automatic extraction of pedestrian trajectories from video recordings of human crowds. This method works on data obtained from an arbitrary observation angle and does not require additional information like the heights of the pedestrians etc. It is thus suitable for the analysis of data that have not been specifically prepared for this purpose, such as surveillance videos. We employ this method to analyze video recordings from a series of experiments that we conducted last year to reproduce pedestrian flows under controlled conditions. From these data we also estimate the continuous density of these pedestrian flows via a nearest-neighbor kernel density method which we argue is particularly suited for particle densities in general and human crowds consisting of multiple populations in particular.

Keywords: density estimation, human crowd analysis, intersecting pedestrian flows, velocimetry, video analysis.

1 Introduction

1.1 Motivation and Aim

The study of pedestrian dynamics has important applications in crowd management such as devising strategies for the evacuation of buildings or public places. In order to evaluate the predictive power of mathematical models designed to emulate human crowd behavior, it is a common procedure to compare numerical simulations based on these models with empirical data. These empirical data are usually extracted from video recordings of either naturally occurring human crowds or pedestrian flows that have been produced under controlled conditions. In general, the latter are devised to demonstrate crowd behavior in special situations such as evacuation or passing through a bottleneck. In our work, we put a

U. Stilla et al. (Eds.): PIA 2011, LNCS 6952, pp. 285–296, 2011.

particular emphasis on analyzing intersecting pedestrian flows, and in Section 2 we describe experiments that were conducted with this task in mind.

In Section 3 we describe a technique to semi-automatically extract the spatio-temporal positions of a low density crowd at close range from an arbitrary observation angle but without prior knowledge of the pedestrians' heights.

Furthermore, different modeling approaches demand the extraction of different types of data: For example, the social force and cellular automaton model aim at predicting pedestrian trajectories, whereas continuum methods adopted from fluid mechanics describe the dynamics via the density and flow of the crowd. The estimation of the density of a crowd consisting of only a few pedestrians is a challenging task because of the low number of samples. In this context, we propose a variable width kernel density estimation described in Section 4.

Finally, a short discussion of the results and an overview of future work will be given in Sections 5 and 6.

1.2   Related Work

The modeling of pedestrian behaviors can be either microscopic or macroscopic (consult Daamen et al. (2002) for a condensed overview on the topic). Macroscopic models—considering the grouped pedestrians as flows—focus on the relationships of density, distribution and speed of the flow from a physics perspective (Helbing (1997)). In comparison to this, microscopic models are devised for agent-based simulations or the like. The social force model (Helbing et al. (2000)) and cellular automaton model (Burstedde et al. (2001), Schadschneider (2002)) are two important examples from this category. The social force model has been further deployed by Helbing (2001) to describe pedestrian groups with two different, intersecting flow directions. With an advanced tuning of the system parameters, the model renders diffusion-like patterns of the intersecting flows. In the cellular automaton model, dynamics (of pedestrians) are described by the state change of the physical environment which is first to be approximated into a structured grid. Chen et al. (2008) propose an extended cellular automaton model with consideration of the local density; this model still remains to be verified with solid empirical data.

In video analysis, Boltes et al. (2010) present an automatic procedure of pedestrian trajectory extraction, however, it requires that additional markers must be attached to the pedestrians, this condition is not always easy to meet. Alternatively, artificial neural networks have been investigated for the pattern recognition of pedestrian heads in the video for trajectory extraction (Johansson (2008)). Due to the fact that both pattern recognition and tracking are hard problems (with the aim to deliver a 100%-correct solution), we introduce here a semi-automatic system with additional user control.

Another difficulty that has been troubling us seems to be the different definitions of "density" used in various contexts: in continuous (i. e., macroscopic) models density has more or less a statistical taste, whereas in microscopic models it is rather meant to be associated with objects of a discrete nature. With the ongoing work (Huth et al. (2011)), a new hybrid method with combination of macro- and microscopic simulation of pedestrian dynamics is attempted. To this purpose, a unified definition of density, applicable in both contexts seems not to be surplus.

2   Experimental Setup

During the Lange Nacht der Wissenschaften (*Long Night of the Sciences*) 2010 in Berlin, we conducted a series of experiments in the entrance area of the Department of Mathematics building of Technische Universität Berlin to produce intersecting pedestrian flows under controlled conditions. To this end, four volunteer groups of event visitors (labeled green, red, white, and blue) were instructed to move from opposite sides of the observation area to create various scenarios: two groups and four groups intersecting from perpendicular directions, two groups meeting head-on, and two groups meeting head-on from an angle of slightly less than 180°. In this paper, we use the perpendicular intersecting of two groups, red (54 subjects) and green (46 subjects), for illustration.

The scene was recorded from a gallery at a height of about six meters with seven networked and temporally synchronized JVC VN-V25U surveillance video cameras. Here, we will analyze the data of the central camera only, which covered the area where the actual intersecting of the pedestrian flows took place.

Due to constructional limitations, as can be seen from Figure 1, it was not possible to install the cameras to provide a bird's eye view. Furthermore, the participants came from all age groups, including children, and it was thus necessary to devise a method to extract the pedestrians' floor positions without knowing their respective heights beforehand. We would like to mention that this situation is very different from the experimental setups found in the common literature, where a bird's eye view installation of the camera(s) in sufficient height provides an advantageous perspective that allows the experimenter to neglect the effect of the pedestrians' different heights within a reasonable tolerance range.

3   Trajectory Extraction

Assuming that lense distortion is negligible, the pinhole camera model computes the image coordinates (ξ, η) from the (Cartesian) world coordinates (X, Y, Z) of an object in the scene:

$$\xi = \frac{a_1 X + a_2 Y + a_3 Z + \alpha}{c_1 X + c_2 Y + c_3 Z + 1}, \quad \eta = \frac{b_1 X + b_2 Y + b_3 Z + \beta}{c_1 X + c_2 Y + c_3 Z + 1}. \tag{1}$$

Here, we also assume that the orthogonal projection of the focal point onto the image plane coincides with the center of the image, the origin of the image coordinate system (Kraus (2007)).

Fig. 1. Pedestrian head and floor positions, at time $t = t_1$

We determined the 11 camera parameters $(a_1, \ldots, c_3, \alpha, \beta)$ by measuring the world and image coordinates of 29 fixed reference points in the scene, and solving the resulting overdetermined linear system of equations via the least-squares method. Inaccuracies in measuring the parameters are controlled by using as many reference points as possible; note, however, that no fewer than six reference points would be sufficient. Also note that with respect to our world coordinates, the observation area's floor coincides with the plane $Z = 0$.

Our algorithm to determine the positions of each pedestrian above ground from the video data consists of four steps and will be described in the following.

Step 1: Head Tracking

The video is shown in frames sequentially. For each frame, the user marks the image regions of heads of new incoming pedestrians that enter the scene. This template is used to determine the position of the head in the next frame via the Lucas–Kanade tracking method (Shi and Tomasi (1994)). Based on the shift from frame to frame as well as the residual (i.e., difference between the found texture and the template), an error score is computed for each person. If this score is too high (or the user spots a possible tracking error regardless of the score), the head position/template will be manually corrected.

Note that we did not employ a fully automated method for people or head detection, in particular since we had to assign each pedestrian to one of the intersecting crowds manually anyway. Also, we argue that human supervision is nevertheless in any case necessary to provide reliable results.

Step 2: Heights of the Pedestrians

Once the image coordinates of the pedestrians' heads have been determined, the video is played back again from the beginning frame by frame. For each pedestrian in the frame, the head positions are shown together with the corresponding floor positions, initially under the assumption that every pedestrian has a standard height of $h = 1.70\,\mathrm{m}$: The world coordinates $(X, Y, 0)$ of the floor positions, and therefore also the image coordinates via Eq. (1), may be determined via the linear system of equations

$$
\begin{pmatrix} \xi_H c_1 - a_1\,\xi_H c_2 - a_2 \\ \eta_H c_1 - b_1\,\eta_H c_2 - b_2 \end{pmatrix} \cdot \begin{pmatrix} X \\ Y \end{pmatrix} = \begin{pmatrix} \alpha - \xi_H - h(\xi_H c_3 - a_3) \\ \beta - \eta_H - h(\eta_H c_3 - b_3) \end{pmatrix},
\tag{2}
$$

where (ξ_H, η_H) are the image coordinates of the head. In each frame the user may correct the floor position of a pedestrian by simply clicking into the frame, and the current height and floor position coordinates are updated by solving the linear system of equations

$$
\begin{pmatrix} \xi_H c_1 - a_1\,\xi_H c_2 - a_2\,\xi_H c_3 - a_3 \\ \eta_H c_1 - b_1\,\eta_H c_2 - b_2\,\eta_H c_3 - b_3 \\ \xi_F c_1 - a_1\,\xi_F c_2 - a_2 \qquad 0 \\ \eta_F c_1 - b_1\,\eta_F c_2 - b_2 \qquad 0 \end{pmatrix} \cdot \begin{pmatrix} X \\ Y \\ h \end{pmatrix} = \begin{pmatrix} \alpha - \xi_H \\ \beta - \eta_H \\ \alpha - \xi_F \\ \beta - \eta_F \end{pmatrix}
$$

via the least-squares method; (ξ_F, η_F) are the new image coordinates of the floor position.

Step 3: World Coordinates for the Pedestrians

Each pedestrian is assigned a final height value equal to either the arithmetic mean of the height values from the user's corrections in Step 2, or equal to the standard height $h = 1.70\,\mathrm{m}$ if no user input for this pedestrian ever occurred during this step. Based on this final height value and the image coordinates of the head, for each frame we compute the pedestrian's world coordinates $(X, Y, 0)$ via Eq. (2); a sample image is shown in Figure 1.

By evaluating the same sequence twice, we estimate a random measurement error of 10 cm in determining the pedestrians' positions. As for systematic errors, we would like to mention that in addition to technical sources like lens distortion there are also practical issues to be given thought. A typical example would be the bias in the user's perception of the exact floor position. Also, unusual behavior of a pedestrian like, for example, bending down may lead to an erroneous measurement of the floor position since its location relative to the pedestrian's head changes. Obviously, these errors are difficult if not impossible to control (in a fully automated way, at least).

Step 4: Smooth Trajectories

The resulting data points $(t_i, X(t_i), Y(t_i))$, extracted at the time-stamps t_i, were then used to fit cubic B-splines with three segments per second to yield smooth trajectories $\boldsymbol{x}_j(t)$ and walking velocities $\boldsymbol{v}_j(t) = \frac{\mathrm{d}\boldsymbol{x}_j}{\mathrm{d}t}(t)$ for each of the $N = 100$ pedestrians, $j = 1, \ldots, N$; see Figures 2, 3 and 4.

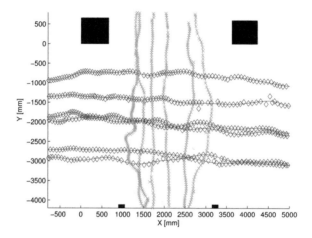

Fig. 2. Some examples of spline-smoothed trajectories and corresponding data points

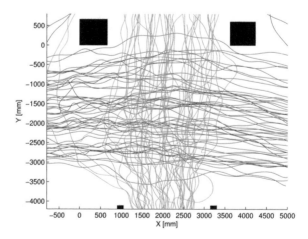

Fig. 3. Pedestrian paths $\boldsymbol{x}_j(t)$

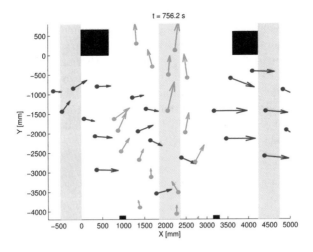

Fig. 4. Pedestrian positions $x_j(t)$ and velocity vectors $v_j(t)$ at fixed time $t = t_1$ (max. visible vector length corresponds to $1.4\,\mathrm{m/s}$)

4   Crowd Density Estimation

One major problem in human crowd analysis is the estimation of a continuous crowd density from sparse data. This is an important task for the validation of numerical simulations based on continuous models such as partial differential equations. For a large number N of particles in an observation area $\Omega \subset \mathbb{R}^n$ ($n = 2$ for a planar region, $n = 3$ for volumes) with positions $x_j \in \Omega$; $j = 1, \ldots, N$, the particle density $\rho(x)$ at a point $x \in \Omega$ may be understood as the number of particles N_0 contained in a sufficiently small neighborhood $\Omega_0 \subset \Omega$ of x, divided by the area or volume of this neighborhood:

$$\rho(x) \approx \frac{N_0}{|\Omega_0|}. \tag{3}$$

Naturally, this quantity depends on the choice of Ω_0, but if the number of particles is very large, this fact may be neglected for all practical purposes. For example, in fluid mechanics, global particle densities of the order of $N = 10^{26}$ particles per cubic meter are common, meaning that even in a tiny volume of $|\Omega_0| = 1\,\mu\mathrm{m}^3$ there are still $N_0 = 10^8$ particles on average to estimate the local density (in principle, at least), with a negligible relative measurement error of order $N_0^{-1/2} = 0.01\%$.

For human crowds, which contain much fewer "particles", Helbing et al. (2007) proposed the formula

$$\rho(t, x) = \frac{1}{\pi R^2} \sum_{i=1}^{N} \exp\left(-\frac{\|x_i(t) - x\|^2}{R^2} \right)$$

for computing the local density at some time t, where $R > 0$ is a suitable constant. This formula may in fact be interpreted as a Gaussian kernel estimator with fixed bandwidth. We argue that a pedestrian's "personal space" $A_j = \pi R^2$, i.e., the area exclusively claimed by this pedestrian, should be inferred from the data directly. In general, we also expect this value to vary with each pedestrian and depend on the current crowd configuration. Another approach which considers personal space for density estimation was discussed by Steffen and Seyfried (2010), evaluating the area of the Voronoi cells determined by the pedestrians' positions as Voronoi sites. Here, we propose the use of a nearest-neighbor Gaussian kernel estimator (Silverman (1986)) and assume that the observation area is the whole plane, $\Omega = \mathbb{R}^2$, for simplicity:

$$\hat{\rho}(t, \boldsymbol{x}) = \frac{1}{2\pi} \sum_{i=1}^{N} \frac{1}{(\lambda d_i)^2} \exp\left(-\frac{\|\boldsymbol{x}_i(t) - \boldsymbol{x}\|^2}{2(\lambda d_i)^2}\right),$$

where d_j is the Euclidean distance of $\boldsymbol{x}_j$ to the nearest other pedestrian or obstacle (such as the two columns seen in Figure 1), and $\lambda > 0$ is a smoothing parameter.

For a subset of pedestrians with indices $J \subset \{1, \ldots, N\}$, we simply restrict the above sum to these indices (while d_j is still understood as the minimal distance of $\boldsymbol{x}_j$ to *all* pedestrians and obstacles). This procedure yields an estimator $\hat{\rho}_J(t, \boldsymbol{x})$ that is compatible with the requirement that the densities of different populations simply add up to a total density: $\hat{\rho}_{J_1 \cup J_2}(t, \boldsymbol{x}) = \hat{\rho}_{J_1}(t, \boldsymbol{x}) + \hat{\rho}_{J_2}(t, \boldsymbol{x})$ with $J_1 \cap J_2 = \emptyset$. We will denote the estimated densities of the red and the green group in our experiments with $\hat{\rho}_R$ and $\hat{\rho}_G$, respectively.

Another argument in favor of our nearest-neighbor method is the fact that it yields the same average result as the "counting particles in a box" density for very dense crowds, as can be seen from estimating the expected value of particle numbers for a population with small particle distances d_j:

$$\frac{1}{|\Omega_0|} \int_{\Omega_0} \hat{\rho}(t, \boldsymbol{x}) \, \mathrm{d}^2 x = \frac{1}{|\Omega_0|} \sum_{i=1}^{N} \frac{1}{2\pi(\lambda d_i)^2} \int_{\Omega_0} \exp\left(-\frac{\|\boldsymbol{x}_i(t) - \boldsymbol{x}\|^2}{2(\lambda d_i)^2}\right) \mathrm{d}^2 x$$

$$\approx \frac{1}{|\Omega_0|} \sum_{i=1}^{N} \int_{\Omega_0} \delta\left(\boldsymbol{x}_i(t) - \boldsymbol{x}\right) \mathrm{d}^2 x = \frac{N_0}{|\Omega_0|},$$

where δ denotes the Dirac delta function.

Finally, for multiple populations, our estimator yields partial distributions that do not "mix" by design. Thus, the populations are effectively separated spatially, and structures such as lane formation are preserved which are likely to be smoothed out by other means of evaluation of the local density, see Figure 5.

5   Results and Discussion

In the following, we will give a brief discussion of the results so far. Note that Figures 1, 4 and 5(b) all refer to the same point in time when a lane formation event is present.

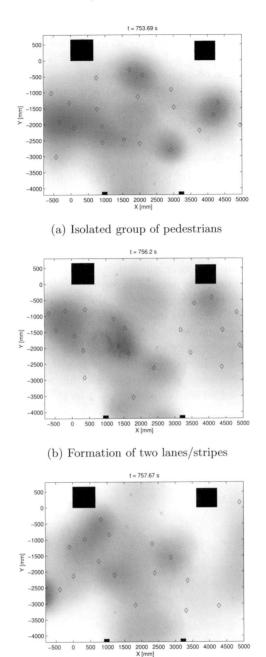

(a) Isolated group of pedestrians

(b) Formation of two lanes/stripes

(c) One flow spatially separates the other flow

Fig. 5. Color-coded estimated pedestrian densities for each population, $\hat{\rho}_R(t, \boldsymbol{x})$ and $\hat{\rho}_G(t, \boldsymbol{x})$ at fixed times $t = t_0, t_1, t_2$ (max. visible color saturation corresponds to ≥ 2.5 pedestrians per m^2)

In Figure 3, the pedestrian paths for both groups over the whole observation time are shown. This picture does not reveal much of the dynamics but gives an idea of the mean flow of the crowd.

Figure 4 illustrates the positions and velocities at a given point in time. As expected, the pedestrians seem to speed up upon exiting the intersection area. Figure 6 shows the average values of speed and density when passing the shaded regions in Figure 4. By average value of some function f along a pedestrian's trajectory $\boldsymbol{x}_j(t)$ when passing a region Ω_0 we mean

$$\langle f(\boldsymbol{x}_j(t)) \rangle = \frac{1}{|I|} \int_I f(\boldsymbol{x}_j(t)) \, \mathrm{d}t,$$

where $I = \{t \in \mathbb{R} | \boldsymbol{x}_j(t) \in \Omega_0\}$. Naturally, a pedestrian's speed is lower in high density areas; the black line represents a linear fit to all data points, with a mean squared error of $\sqrt{\mathrm{MSE}} = 0.24\,\mathrm{m/s}$. This finding is roughly consistent with the fundamental diagrams in the common literature which, however, manifest considerable differences among one another in various contexts of scenario, density and speed evaluation methodology and not the last, the pedestrians' cultural backgrounds (see Schadschneider and Seyfried (2009)) and references therein).

Figure 5 shows the estimated densities of both populations for three scenarios of particular interest. In order to avoid unrealistically high densities due to measurement inaccuracies that occasionally lead to erroneously close pedestrian positions, for practical reasons we imposed an additional requirement that d_j should always be at least 30 cm. We chose $\lambda = 1$ as the smoothing parameter.

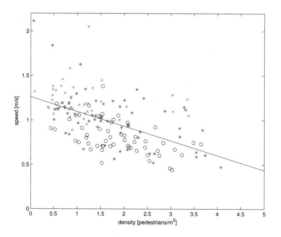

Fig. 6. Average speed $\langle \|\boldsymbol{v}_j(t)\| \rangle$ vs. average local density $\langle \rho(t, \boldsymbol{x}_j(t)) \rangle$ for each pedestrian of the red group, when passing the regions shaded in Figure 4 [circles: left region, asterisks: central region, crosses: right region]

6   Conclusions and Future Work

The main contributions of this paper include a technique to extract the pedestrian trajectories from video recordings that do not necessarily have to be prepared for this purpose. More precisely, with our algorithm it is possible to analyze video data recorded from a flat observation angle and without a priori knowledge of the pedestrians' heights. Furthermore, we propose a novel method to calculate continuous pedestrian densities from sparse data that is particularly suited for the analysis of human crowds consisting of multiple distinct populations such as intersecting pedestrian flows.

However, our work is still in progress, and there are a number of issues that we will address in the future:

- (non-parametrical) estimation of the smoothing parameter λ,
- merging trajectories from multiple cameras,
- quantitative methods to use the data in evaluating the results of numerical simulations designed to model intersecting pedestrian flows,
- flow vector field estimation.

Especially the first item is a pressing issue that we plan to resolve by finding an estimator that best fits the "counting pedestrians in a box" estimator in a multiscale approach. In other words, the optimal value of the smoothing parameter λ should produce local densities consistent with densities acquired from counting pedestrians in "medium sized" boxes about the points where they are evaluated. Alternatively, there are a number of established methods for bandwidth estimation available, see for example (Comaniciu et al. (2001); Comaniciu (2003)).

Acknowledgments. We would like to thank all university staff and students who helped with conducting the experiments, and we especially thank C. Neumann for carrying out the data analysis. We would also like to express our gratitude to all visitors of the Lange Nacht der Wissenschaften who participated.

The authors gratefully acknowledge the support of Deutsche Forschungsgemeinschaft (*German Research Foundation*) for the project SCHW548/5-1 + BA1189/4-1. The numerical calculations were made with the computing software Matlab by MathWorks.

Finally, we would like to thank the organizers of the conference PIA11, and we also thank the referees for their helpful comments and suggestions.

References

Boltes, M., Seyfried, A., Steffen, B., Schadschneider, A.: Automatic extraction of pedestrian trajectories from video recordings. In: Pedestrian and Evacuation Dynamics 2008, pp. 43–54 (2010)

Burstedde, C., Klauck, K., Schadschneider, A., Zittartz, J.: Simulation of pedestrian dynamics using a two-dimensional cellular automaton. Physica A 295, 507–525 (2001)

Chen, M.-J., Bärwolff, G., Schwandt, H.: Automaton model with variable cell size for the simulation of pedestrian flow (2008), An electronic version can be retrieved at: http://www.math.tu-berlin.de/~chenmin/pub/cbs080331.pdf (accessed June 17, 2011)

Comaniciu, D.: An algorithm for data-driven bandwidth selection. IEEE Pattern Analysis and Machine Intelligence 25(2), 281–288 (2003)

Comaniciu, D., Ramesh, V., Meer, P.: The variable bandwidth mean shift and data-driven scale selection. In: Proc. ICCV, pp. 438–445 (2001)

Daamen, W., Bovy, P.H.L., Hoogendoorn, S.P.: Modelling pedestrians in transfer stations. In: Pedestrian and Evacuation Dynamics, pp. 59–73 (2002)

Helbing, D.: Verkehrsdynamik: Neue physikalische Modellierungskonzepte. Springer, Heidelberg (1997)

Helbing, D.: Traffic and related self-driven many-particle systems. Rev. Mod. Phys. 73, 1067–1141 (2001)

Helbing, D., Farkas, I., Vicsek, T.: Simulating dynamical features of escape panic. Nature 407, 487–490 (2000)

Helbing, D., Johansson, A., Al-Abideen, H.Z.: Dynamics of crowd disasters: An empirical study. Phys. Rev. E 75, 046109 (2007)

Huth, F., Bärwolff, G., Schwandt, H.: An extended multi-phase transport model for pedestrian flow (in preparation, 2011)

Johansson, A.F.: Data-driven modeling of pedestrian crowds. PhD thesis, Technische Universität Dresden (2008)

Kraus, K.: Photogrammetry. In: Geometry from Images and Laser Scans. de Gruyter, Berlin (2007)

Schadschneider, A.: Cellular automaton approach to pedestrian dynamics - theory. In: Pedestrian and Evacuation Dynamics, pp. 75–85 (2002)

Schadschneider, A., Seyfried, A.: Empirical results for pedestrian dynamics and their implications for cellular automata models. In: Timmermans, H. (ed.) Pedestrian Behavior: Data Collection and Applications, pp. 27–43. Imprint Emerald Group Publishing Ltd. (2009)

Shi, J., Tomasi, C.: Good features to track. In: Proc. of the IEEE Comp. Soc. Conf. on Computer Vision and Pattern Recognition, pp. 593–600 (1994)

Silverman, B.W.: Density Estimation for Statistics and Data Analysis. Chapman and Hall, Boca Raton (1986)

Steffen, B., Seyfried, A.: Methods for measuring pedestrian density, flow, speed and direction with minimal scatter. Physica A 389, 1902–1910 (2010)

Measurement Accuracy of Center Location of a Circle by Centroid Method

Ryuji Matsuoka[1,2], Naoki Shirai[1], Kazuyoshi Asonuma[1],
Mitsuo Sone[2], Noboru Sudo[2], and Hideyo Yokotsuka[2]

[1] Kokusai Kogyo Co., Ltd.,
2-24-1 Harumi-cho, Fuchu,
Tokyo 183-0057, Japan
{ryuji_matsuoka,naoki_shirai,kazuyoshi_asonuma}@kkc.co.jp
[2] Tokai University Research & Information Center,
2-28-4 Tomigaya, Shibuya-ku,
Tokyo 151-0063, Japan
{ryuji,sone3}@yoyogi.ycc.u-tokai.ac.jp,
{sdo,yoko}@keyaki.cc.u-tokai.ac.jp

Abstract. This paper reports an investigation of the effect of digitization on the measurement accuracy of the center location of a circle by a centroid method. Although general expressions representing the measurement accuracy of the center location of a circle by the centroid method are unable to be obtained analytically, we have succeeded in obtaining the variances V of measurement errors for 39 quantization bits n ranging from one to infinity by numerical integration. We have succeeded in obtaining the effective approximation formulae of V as a function of the diameter d of the circle for any n as well. The results show that V would oscillate on an approximate one-pixel cycle in d for any n and decrease as n increases. The differences of V among the different n would be negligible when $n \geq 6$. Some behaviors of V with an increase in n are demonstrated.

Keywords: analysis, measurement, accuracy, circle, center, digitization.

1 Introduction

Circular targets are often utilized in photogrammetry, particularly in close range photogrammetry. Since a circle is radially symmetrical, circular targets are well suited for photogrammetric use such as camera calibration and 3D measurement. It is said that determination of the center of a circular target by digital image processing techniques is rotation-invariant and scale-invariant over a wide range of image resolutions. The center of a circular target can be estimated by centroid methods, by matching with a reference pattern, or by analytical determination of the circle center (Luhmann *et al.*, 2006).

We reported an experiment conducted in order to evaluate measurement methods of the center location of a circle by using simulated images of various

U. Stilla et al. (Eds.): PIA 2011, LNCS 6952, pp. 297–308, 2011.

sizes of circles (Matsuoka *et al.*, 2009). We investigated two centroid methods: intensity-weighted centroid method, which is called WCM for short from now on, and unweighted centroid method using a binary image created by thresholding, which is called BCM for short from now on, and least squares matching in the experiment. We made the experiment by the Monte Carlo simulation using 1024 simulated images of which the centers were randomly distributed in one pixel for each circle. The radius of a circle was examined at 0.1 pixel intervals from 2 to 40 pixels. The variances of measurement errors by both centroid methods in the experiment appeared to oscillate on a 0.5 pixel cycle in radius, even though the formula to estimate the center of a circle by each centroid method does not seem to produce such cyclic measurement errors. We wondered whether the oscillation of the measurement accuracy by the centroid methods might be caused by digitizing a circle.

In photogrammetry some papers on the precision and accuracy of measurement methods of the center location of a circle have been presented (Trinder, 1989, Trinder *et al.*, 1995, Shortis *et al.*, 1995). However, these papers reported experiments using limited sizes of the target and did not indicate that the measurement accuracy by centroid methods may oscillate on a one-pixel cycle in diameter.

On the other hand in computer vision Bose and Amir (1990) reported the investigation of the effect of the shape and size of a square, a diamond, and a circle on the measurement accuracy of its center location by the unweighted centroid method using a binarized image. They conducted the analysis of the measurement accuracy of the center location of a square and showed the standard deviations of the measurement errors of the center location of a square derived from the variances of the measurement errors of the center location of a line segment. However, we confirmed that their study would be incomplete and the measurement accuracy of the center location of a square from 2 to 22 pixels in side shown in their paper is that when the side of a square is infinite. Moreover, they executed the simulation on the measurement accuracy of the center location of a circle. In their simulation, 400 binarized circles were placed at 0.05 pixel intervals covering a range of one pixel in x and y direction, and the radius of a circle was examined at merely 0.25 pixel intervals. Consequently, there was no mention finding cyclic measurement errors of the center location of a circle in their paper.

Our previous paper (Matsuoka *et al.*, 2010) reported an analysis of the effect of sampling in creating a digital image on the measurement accuracy of the center location of a circle by WCM and BCM. We assumed that images were sampled but not quantized in digitization in the previous study. Although general expressions representing the measurement accuracy of the center location of a circle by WCM and BCM are unable to be obtained analytically, we succeeded in obtaining the variances of measurement errors by numerical integration and the effective approximation formulae of those. The results indicated that the variance of measurement errors by both WCM and BCM oscillate on a one-pixel cycle in diameter.

This paper reports an investigation of the effect of quantization in creating a digital image on the measurement accuracy of the center location of a circle by the centroid method. Since the effect of quantization cannot be analyzed individually, the analysis of the effect of digitization consisting of both sampling and quantization was carried out.

2   Outline of Analysis

2.1   Assumed Digital Image

When the quantization bit of a digital image is n bits, that is to say, the quantization level is $N = 2^n$ levels, we assumed that the gray value g_{ij} of the pixel (i, j) of the digital image is created by using the following equation (1):

$$g_{ij} = \text{int}\left(N \cdot a_{ij}\right) = \text{int}\left(2^n \cdot a_{ij}\right) \tag{1}$$

where a_{ij} $(0 \leq a_{ij} \leq 1)$ is the area of part of a circle inside the region $\{(x, y) \mid i \leq x \leq (i+1), \, j \leq y \leq (j+1)\}$, and $\text{int}(x)$ is the function to return the integer part of the value x. The image was assumed free of noise.

2.2   Investigated Centroid Method

Centroid methods are relatively simple and theoretically independent of the image resolution. Furthermore, centroid methods do not require a template dependent on the image resolution. Accordingly, centroid methods are often utilized in measurement of the target location in photogrammetry.

The centroid method in the study estimates the center location (x_C, y_C) of a circle by using the following equation (2):

$$\begin{cases} x_C = \dfrac{\sum_i \sum_j w_{ij} \cdot i}{\sum_i \sum_j w_{ij}} + \dfrac{1}{2} \\[2em] y_C = \dfrac{\sum_i \sum_j w_{ij} \cdot j}{\sum_i \sum_j w_{ij}} + \dfrac{1}{2} \end{cases} \tag{2}$$

where w_{ij} is the weight of the pixel (i, j) and we assumed that $w_{ij} = g_{ij}$ in the study.

We had investigated two popular centroid methods WCM and BCM in the previous study on the effects of sampling on the measurement accuracy of the center location of a circle (Matsuoka et al., 2010). When the effects of quantization are taken in account, WCM and BCM correspond to the centroid method in the study for infinite-bits $(n = \infty)$ quantization and that for one-bit $(n = 1)$ quantization respectively.

2.3   Evaluation of Measurement Accuracy

The measurement accuracy of the center location (x_C, y_C) of a circle was measured by the variances (V_x, V_y) and $V (= V_x + V_y)$ of errors $(\varepsilon_x, \varepsilon_y)$ in estimation of the center location. If it is assumed that a circle with the diameter d is placed as its center is located on $(s + d/2, t + d/2)$ $(0 \le s < 1, 0 \le t < 1)$, (x_C, y_C) and V are calculated by the following equation (3):

$$\begin{cases} V_x = \int_0^1 \int_0^1 \varepsilon_x^2 \, ds \, dt \\[2mm] V_y = \int_0^1 \int_0^1 \varepsilon_y^2 \, ds \, dt \\[2mm] V = \int_0^1 \int_0^1 \varepsilon^2 \, ds \, dt = \int_0^1 \int_0^1 \left(\varepsilon_x^2 + \varepsilon_y^2 \right) \, ds \, dt = V_x + V_y \end{cases} \tag{3}$$

The variances (V_x, V_y) and V were obtained by numerical integration, because those are unable to be obtained analytically.

We had demonstrated that V of the circle with the diameter d by BCM have irregularities in the one-pixel cycle of d and the irregularities would be caused by the discontinuity of $(\varepsilon_x, \varepsilon_y)$ versus the location (s, t) of a circle in the previous study (Matsuoka *et al.*, 2010). Accordingly, we obtained V by the midpoint rule.

Fig. 1 shows some distributions of $\varepsilon = \sqrt{\varepsilon_x^2 + \varepsilon_y^2}$ at $d = 3 + 75/128$ and $d = 3 + 88/128$ where V by BCM has large irregularities in the one-pixel cycle of $3 \le d \le 4$. The larger $\varepsilon(i, j)$ is, the brighter (i, j) is in Fig. 1. The discontinuity of ε decreases as n increases.

The diameter of a circle was examined at $1 / 32$ pixel intervals from 2 to 100 pixels in the numerical integration. $V_x = V_y$, $V = 2V_x$, because a circle is point symmetry. We show a root mean squares of errors (RMSE) $\sqrt{V}$ in the following figures.

3   Results and Discussion

3.1   Variance of Measurement Errors

The variances V of the measurement errors $(\varepsilon_x, \varepsilon_y)$ of the center location (x_C, y_C) of the circle were obtained by numerical integration. V were obtained as to 39 quantization levels where $N = 2^1$ (BCM), 3, 2^2, 5, 6, 7, 2^3, 10, 12, 14, 2^4, 20, 24, 28, 2^5, 40, 48, 56, 2^6, 80, 96, 112, 2^7, 160, 192, 224, 2^8, 320, 384, 448, 2^9, 2^{10}, 2^{11}, 2^{12}, 2^{13}, 2^{14}, 2^{15}, 2^{16}, ∞ (WCM). Fig. 2, Fig. 3 and Fig. 4 show the RMSE $\sqrt{V}$ of some quantization bits n against the diameter d of the circle.

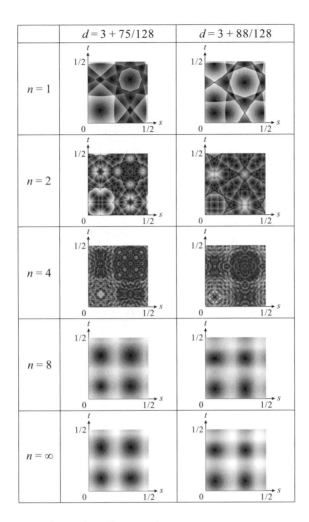

Fig. 1. Distribution of measurement errors ε

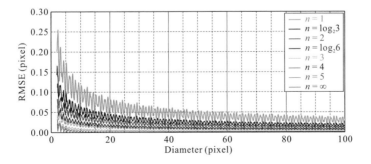

Fig. 2. RMSE $\sqrt{V}$ vs. diameter d from 2 to 100 pixels in d

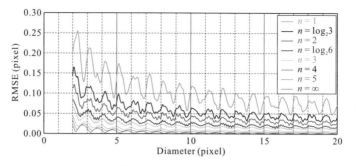

Fig. 3. RMSE $\sqrt{V}$ vs. diameter d from 2 to 20 pixels in d

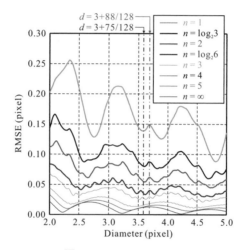

Fig. 4. RMSE $\sqrt{V}$ vs. diameter d from 2 to 5 pixels in d

The results of the numerical integration show the following:

- V would oscillate on an approximate one-pixel cycle in diameter for any n. V decreases as d increases. When d is small, V decreases rapidly with an increase in d.
- V decreases as n increases. When n is small, V decreases rapidly with an increase in n. The differences of V among the different n would be negligible when $n \geq 6$.
- When n is small, V has some irregularities in the approximate one-pixel cycle of d. The magnitude of the irregularities decreases as n increases. The irregularities would be caused by the discontinuity of ε as Fig. 1 shows.
- Our previous paper (Matsuoka *et al.*, 2010) reported that V by WCM has the local maxima and local minima where fra $(d) \approx 3/4$ and fra $(d) \approx 1/4$ in the one-pixel cycle respectively, while V by BCM has the local maxima and local minima where fra $(d) \approx 1/4$ and fra $(d) \approx 3/4$ in the one-pixel cycle

respectively. fra (x) is the function to return the fractional part of the value x. Fig. 2, Fig. 3 and Fig. 4 indicate that the local maxima and local minima of V in the approximate one-pixel cycle would move from fra $(d) \approx 3/4$ to fra $(d) \approx 1/4$ and from fra $(d) \approx 1/4$ to fra $(d) \approx 3/4$ as n increases respectively.

3.2   Approximation Formula of Measurement Accuracy

We decided to obtain an approximation formula of the variance V of the measurement errors $(\varepsilon_x, \varepsilon_y)$ of the center location (x_C, y_C) of the circle with the diameter d in order to estimate V easily and investigate features of the measurement accuracy. It was assumed that V can be expressed in the following formula (4) using the sine function for expressing the oscillation:

$$\sigma^2 = \left(\frac{a_A}{d^{p_A}} + b_A \right) \sin \left(2\pi \left(d - \delta \right) \right) + \left(\frac{a_B}{d^{p_B}} + b_B \right) \tag{4}$$

The initial phases δ of BCM $(n = 1)$ and WCM $(n = \infty)$ would be considered to be constant in the previous study (Matsuoka $et\ al.$, 2010). However, the results of the numerical integration indicate that δ may change as d increases as to any n except $n = 1$ and $n = \infty$. Accordingly, we assumed that δ can be expressed in the following formula (5):

$$\delta = s_\delta \cdot d + t_\delta \tag{5}$$

The unknown coefficients a_A, b_A, p_A, a_B, b_B, p_B, s_δ, t_δ in Equation (4) and Equation (5) were estimated by least-squares fitting using 3137 sets of (d, V) at 1 / 32 pixel intervals from 2 to 100 pixels in d. We adopted weights in inverse proportion to V in order to obtain an approximation formula that shows the oscillation clearly. The accuracy of the approximation formulae obtained by using (d, V) ranging from 2 to 100 pixels in d would be rather low when d is small such as $d \leq 20$. We obtained another approximation formulae obtained by using 577 sets of (d, V) from 2 to 20 pixels in d in order to estimate V when d is small. Table 1, Fig. 5, Fig. 6 and Fig. 7 show the estimated coefficients a_A, b_A, p_A, a_B, b_B, p_B, s_δ, t_δ. The connecting diameter d_C in Table 1 is the diameter where the difference of the moving averages of 0.5 pixel interval between two approximation formulae obtained by using (d, V) ranging from 2 to 100 pixels in d and (d, V) ranging from 2 to 20 pixels in d is the smallest. We utilized the approximation formula composed of two formulae obtained by using (d, V) ranging from 2 to 20 pixels in d and (d, V) ranging from 2 to 100 pixels in d. The formula obtained by using (d, V) ranging from 2 to 20 pixels in d was utilized when $d \leq d_C$, while the formula obtained by using (d, V) ranging from 2 to 100 pixels in d when $d > d_C$. Fig. 8 shows the estimated initial phase δ at $d = 2$, $d = 20$, and $d = 100$.

Table 1. Estimated coefficients in Equation (4) and Equation (5)

n	d_c	s_δ	t_δ (10^{-02})	a_A (10^{-02})	b_A (10^{-04})	p_A	a_B (10^{-02})	b_B (10^{-04})	p_B
1.0000 ($=\log_2 2$)	10 + 4 / 32	1.01452	-0.05221	3.93188	2.46955	0.94084	9.35997	1.21017	1.02499
		1.01066	-0.00117	4.10199	0.15434	0.98430	9.22346	0.25996	1.01307
1.5850 ($=\log_2 3$)	16 + 18 / 32	0.94642	0.30283	1.65881	2.49071	1.35579	3.87092	4.28582	1.19894
		0.98743	0.02622	1.07336	0.03604	1.01439	3.13467	0.15561	1.02600
2.0000 ($=\log_2 4$)	16 + 17 / 32	0.91177	0.46956	1.05791	1.44968	1.56439	2.11621	2.30178	1.25534
		0.97477	0.04194	0.52594	0.06357	1.05409	1.62651	0.15754	1.05306
2.3219 ($=\log_2 5$)	15 + 18 / 32	0.87589	0.66542	0.69038	0.72839	1.58332	1.38443	1.53033	1.30738
		0.96060	0.05588	0.32042	0.03929	1.07629	0.99057	0.10154	1.06189
2.5850 ($=\log_2 6$)	15 + 17 / 32	0.83968	0.86661	0.54909	0.48473	1.68249	0.98271	1.05812	1.33454
		0.94797	0.07233	0.21011	0.03078	1.08988	0.67532	0.07412	1.06971
2.8074 ($=\log_2 7$)	15 + 16 / 32	0.80840	1.02893	0.46932	0.36993	1.77997	0.75806	0.77279	1.36475
		0.93666	0.08361	0.15441	0.02844	1.11405	0.49941	0.05986	1.08139
3.0000 ($=\log_2 8$)	15 + 16 / 32	0.78041	1.15741	0.42142	0.28983	1.86835	0.62038	0.62849	1.41002
		0.92617	0.09602	0.11626	0.01963	1.11825	0.38279	0.05103	1.08992
3.3219 ($=\log_2 10$)	15 + 15 / 32	0.73678	1.33176	0.36253	0.18178	2.00297	0.47123	0.45676	1.50175
		0.90639	0.11943	0.07658	0.01189	1.14139	0.25406	0.03485	1.10540
3.5850 ($=\log_2 12$)	15 + 15 / 32	0.69673	1.50849	0.34433	0.12624	2.13065	0.39551	0.35459	1.59880
		0.88661	0.14377	0.05672	0.00831	1.17041	0.18411	0.02666	1.12195
3.8074 ($=\log_2 14$)	15 + 14 / 32	0.66595	1.63110	0.32775	0.08963	2.21326	0.35011	0.27957	1.68460
		0.86794	0.16464	0.04714	0.00751	1.21890	0.14305	0.02211	1.14145
4.0000 ($=\log_2 16$)	15 + 14 / 32	0.63989	1.71399	0.32434	0.06736	2.29867	0.32783	0.22704	1.78397
		0.84816	0.18820	0.04207	0.00681	1.27389	0.11508	0.01929	1.16287
5.0000	15 + 10 / 32	0.54145	1.76683	0.32752	0.01397	2.60790	0.30048	0.06689	2.28170
		0.71489	0.34603	0.05317	0.00284	1.77616	0.05762	0.00931	1.39523
6.0000	10 + 24 / 32	0.49731	1.33791	0.38768	0.00270	2.85130	0.37871	0.01611	2.73646
		0.61054	0.42575	0.07582	0.00065	2.16712	0.05931	0.00300	1.83992
7.0000	10 + 22 / 32	0.48515	0.80508	0.41525	0.00045	2.95318	0.41835	0.00408	2.91021
		0.53154	0.43415	0.14947	0.00011	2.52952	0.13209	0.00094	2.37528
8.0000	10 + 21 / 32	0.48212	0.45041	0.42177	0.00009	2.98889	0.43107	0.00099	2.97218
		0.49881	0.32390	0.26799	0.00002	2.80175	0.25647	0.00025	2.73644
9.0000	11 + 21 / 32	0.48150	0.25742	0.42143	0.00002	2.99927	0.43329	0.00022	2.99185
		0.49020	0.19243	0.35614	0.00000	2.93185	0.35367	0.00006	2.90276
∞	13 + 18 / 32	0.48043	0.06465	0.41697	0.00002	3.00307	0.42998	0.00001	3.00006
		0.48819	0.00544	0.41370	0.00000	2.99996	0.42760	0.00000	2.99857

Upper: Obtained by using (d, V) from 2 to 100 pixels in d
Lower: Obtained by using (d, V) from 2 to 20 pixels in d

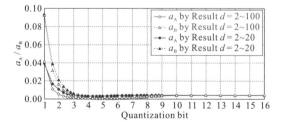

Fig. 5. Estimated coefficients a_A and a_B

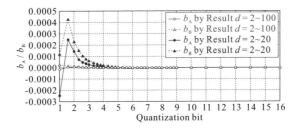

Fig. 6. Estimated coefficients b_A and b_B

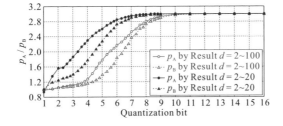

Fig. 7. Estimated coefficients p_A and p_B

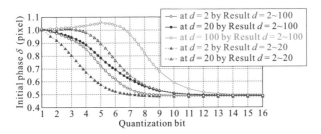

Fig. 8. Estimated initial phase δ

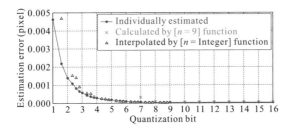

Fig. 9. Estimation error

Fig. 9 shows the RMS of the estimation error of V against the quantization bit n. The red solid circles, green crosses and blue triangles in Fig. 9 show the estimation errors by using the approximation formula obtained for each n

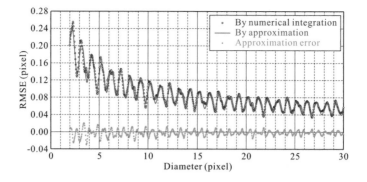

Fig. 10. RMSE $\sqrt{V}$ vs. diameter d when $n = 1$

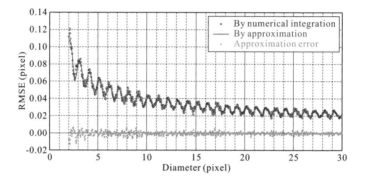

Fig. 11. RMSE $\sqrt{V}$ vs. diameter d when $n = 2$

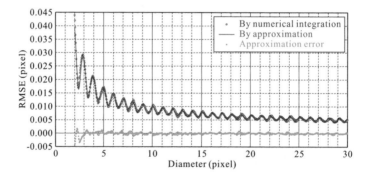

Fig. 12. RMSE $\sqrt{V}$ vs. diameter d when $n = 4$

individually, by using the approximation formula obtained for $n = 9$, and by linear interpolation by n using the approximation formulae obtained for the neighboring integers n respectively.

Fig. 10, Fig. 11 and Fig. 12 show the performance of the approximation formulae when $n = 1$, $n = 2$ and $n = 4$ respectively. The blue dots, red line and green dots in Fig. 10, Fig. 11 and Fig. 12 show $\sqrt{V}$ by the numerical integration, $\sqrt{V'}$ by the approximation, and the approximation errors $\sqrt{V'} - \sqrt{V}$ respectively.

The results of the approximation show the following:

- The differences of a_A, b_A, p_A, a_B, b_B, p_B, s_δ, t_δ between the different sets (d, V) from 2 to 20 pixels in d and from 2 to 100 pixels in d would not be negligible.
- a_A, b_A, p_A, a_B, b_B, p_B change gradually as n increases up to $n = 10$ except for b_A, b_B, when $n = 0$. The differences of a_A, b_A, p_A, a_B, b_B, p_B among the different n would be negligible when $n \geq 10$.
- Our previous study (Matsuoka $et\ al.$, 2010) indicated that the local maxima and local minima of V in the one-pixel cycle would be approximated to being inversely proportional to d^3 for WCM and d for BCM. Fig. 7 shows that p_A, p_B which are the exponents of the denominator of V, would move from 1.0 to 3.0 as n increases from 1 to ∞.
- δ increases as d increases as to any n except $n = 1$ and $n = \infty$. while δ decreases from 1.0 to 0.5 as n increases from 1 to ∞.
- The accuracy of the obtained approximation formula increases as n increases. The results would correspond to our recognition in the previous study (Matsuoka $et\ al.$, 2010) that the approximation formulae for WCM and BCM would be extremely effective and effective for ordinary use respectively.
- The approximation errors $\sqrt{V'} - \sqrt{V}$ shown in Fig. 10, Fig. 11 and Fig. 12 look periodic. The cause of the periodicity would be that the coefficient $(a_A/d^{p_A} + b_A)$ of $\sin\left(2\pi\left(d - \delta\right)\right)$ expressing the oscillation cannot approximate the local maxima and local minima of V in the one-pixel cycle accurately enough.
- As for the validity of the obtained approximation formulae, we concluded that the linear interpolation by n using the approximation formulae obtained for neighboring integers n would be effective when $n \geq 4$. Moreover when $n \geq 8$, the approximation formula obtained for $n = 9$ would be effective enough.
- Since general expressions representing the measurement accuracy are unable to be obtained analytically, we cannot find the cause of the above-mentioned behaviors of the measurement accuracy at this moment. The main remaining problems concerning the behaviors are as follows:
  - Why p_A and p_B would move from 1.0 to 3.0 as n increases from 1 to ∞?
  - Why δ increases as d increases as to any n except $n = 1$ and $n = \infty$?
  - Why δ decreases from 1.0 to 0.5 as n increases from 1 to ∞ as to any d?

4   Conclusion

Although general expressions representing the measurement accuracy of the center location of a circle by the centroid method are unable to be obtained analytically, we succeeded in obtaining the variances V of measurement errors for 39 quantization bits n ranging from one to infinity by numerical integration. We succeeded in obtaining the effective approximation formulae of V as a function of the diameter d of the circle for any n as well.

The results show that V would oscillate on an approximate one-pixel cycle in d for any n and decrease as n increases. When n is small, V decreases rapidly with an increase in n. The differences of V among the different n would be negligible when $n \geq 6$. Some behaviors of V with an increase in n were demonstrated. The exponent of d of the denominator of the local maxima and local minima of V in the one-pixel cycle would increase from 1.0 to 3.0 as n increases. The initial phase of the oscillation of V would decrease from 1.0 to 0.5 as n increases. Since general expressions representing the measurement accuracy are unable to be obtained analytically, we cannot find the cause of the behaviors at this moment.

We are planning to perform the following tasks:

- To obtain a general expression representing the measurement accuracy of the center location of a line segment against any n analytically in order to find the cause of the above-mentioned behaviors of the measurement accuracy of the center location of a circle.
- To find a more accurate formula representing the local maxima and local minima of V in the one-pixel cycle.
- To investigate the influence of image noises on the periodicity of the measurement accuracy.
- To investigate the effect of digitization on the measurement accuracy of the center location of a circle by another measurement methods such as least squares matching and structural measurement methods such as circle or ellipse fitting.

References

Bose, C.B., Amir, I.: Design of Fiducials for Accurate Registration Using Machine Vision. IEEE Transactions on Pattern Analysis and Machine Intelligence 12(12), 1196–1200 (1990)

Luhmann, T., Robson, S., Kyle, S., Harley, I.: Close Range Photogrammetry, pp. 183–190. Whittles Publishing, Caithness (2006)

Matsuoka, R., Sone, M., Sudo, N., Yokotsuka, H., Shirai, N.: Comparison of Measuring Methods of Circular Target Location. Journal of the Japan Society of Photogrammetry and Remote Sensing 48(3), 154–170 (2009)

Matsuoka, R., Sone, M., Sudo, N., Yokotsuka, H., Shirai, N.: Effect of Sampling in Creating a Digital Image on Measurement Accuracy of Center Location of A Circle. The International Archives of the Photogrammetry, Remote Sensing and Spatial Information Sciences XXXVIII, Part 3A, 31–36 (2010)

Shortis, M.R., Clarke, T.A., Robson, S.: Practical Testing of the Precision and Accuracy of Target Image Centring Algorithms. In: Videometrics IV, SPIE, vol. 2598, pp. 65–76 (1995)

Trinder, J.C.: Precision of Digital Target Location. Photogrammetric Engineering and Remote Sensing 55(6), 883–886 (1989)

Trinder, J.C., Jansa, J., Huang, Y.: An Assessment of the Precision and Accuracy of Methods of Digital Target Location. ISPRS Journal of Photogrammetry and Remote Sensing 50(2), 12–20 (1995)

Author Index